IRELAND'S OTHER POETRY
Anonymous to Zozimus

IRELAND'S OTHER POETRY
Anonymous to Zozimus

Edited by John Wyse Jackson
and Hector McDonnell

THE LILLIPUT PRESS
DUBLIN

First published 2007 by
THE LILLIPUT PRESS
62–63 Sitric Road, Arbour Hill
Dublin 7, Ireland
www.lilliputpress.ie

Copyright © John Wyse Jackson
and Hector McDonnell, 2007

ISBN 978 1 84351 122 9

A CIP record for this title is
available from The British Library.

10 9 8 7 6 5 4 3 2 1

Set in 10.5 pt on 12 pt Dante
Printed in England by MPG Books, Bodmin, Cornwall

Contents

(Verses are arranged alphabetically by author or, if anonymous, by title.
Inverted commas denote working titles have been supplied for this edition.)

Some Introductory Remarks   XV

Allen, Fergus, *The Fall*   I
    Après La Dance or George   3
Arthur McBride (Anon.)   4
The Athlone Landlady (Anon.)   5

The Bag of Nails (Anon.)   7
Ball O' Yarn (Anon.)   8
A Ballad of Master McGrath (Anon.)   9
Ballinamona (Anon.)   II
The Battle on the Stair (Anon.)   12
Behan, Brendan, *'Ireland's Struggle'* (attrib.)   14
    'Would You?' (attrib.)   15
Behan, Dominic, *The Sea Around Us*   15
    McAlpine's Fusiliers   16
Betjeman, John, *The Small Towns of Ireland*   17
    The Arrest of Oscar Wilde at the Cadogan Hotel   19
    'The Dingle Peninsula'   20
Biddy Mulligan (Anon.)   20
Blennerhassett, Hilda, *'He was an Irish Landlord'* (attrib.) 22
Boland, Charles J, *The Two Travellers*   23
The Boys from Ballysodare (Anon.)   25
The Boys of Fairhill (Anon.)   26

CONTENTS

Brian O'Linn (Anon.)	27
The British Army (Anon.)	28
Brother Bill and Jamima Brown (Anon.)	30
Browne, Harry T, The Giants' Causeway	31
Buckley, Ned, Our Army Jumping Team	32
Burke, Michael Courtenay, The Summons	33
Butler, Hubert, The Saints Leave Ireland – A Poem	34
The Buttermilk Lasses (Anon.)	40
Calvert, Raymond, The Ballad of William Bloat	42
Carrots from Clonown (Anon.)	43
The Chant of the Coal Quay (Anon.)	45
Chesterton, GK, 'Old King Cole'	45
Children's Rhymes (Anon.)	46
Coady, Michael, The Carrick Nine	48
The Cobbler (Anon.)	52
The Cod Liver Oil (Anon.)	53
Coffey, Brian, Kallikles	54
The College's Saturday Night (Anon.)	55
A Complete Account of the Various Colonizations of Ireland (Anon.)	57
Concanen, Matthew, 'A Tackle on Terence'	58
Connor, TW, She was one of the Early Birds	59
Costello, John, Bellewstown Hill	60
The Coughing Old Man (Anon.)	62
The Cow Ate the Piper (Anon.)	63
Craig, Maurice James, Ballad to a Traditional Refrain	65
Thoughts on Causality	66
Cronin, Anthony, 'Fairway's' Faraway	66
Crowley, Jimmy, Clonakilty Blackpudding	67
Dawson, William, The Lay of Oliver Gogarty	69
'De Valera had a Cat' (Anon.)	71
'The Delights of Dublin' (Anon.)	71
Description of Dublin (Anon.)	73
Ditty (Anon.)	74
Dockrell, Morgan, Prize Tips …	74
They have their Exits	75
Jacuzzi Fantasy	76
Donleavy, JP, 'Mary Maloney' and 'Did your Mother'	77
Donnelly, Charles, Mr Sheridan's Morning Prayer	77
Doran's Ass (Anon.)	78
Doyle, Arthur Conan, The Irish Colonel	79
Doyle, Martin, From 'Hints for the Small Farmers of Wexford'	80
Drury, Paddy, Kerry Places	82
The Dublin Fusiliers (Anon.)	83

Dunsany, Lord, *'There was a Young Thing on a Ship'*   84
Durcan, Paul, *Ashplant, New Year's Eve, 1996*   86

The Earthquake (Anon.)   87
The Enniskillen Horse (Anon.)   90

Fame (Anon.)   93
Farquhar, George, *'A Song of Trifles'*   94
Farren, Robert, *The Pets*   95
Finnegan's Wake (Anon.)   96
Fitzmaurice, Gabriel, *What's a Tourist?*   98
Flecknoe, Richard, *Of Drinking*   98
Fogarty, WP, *Private Judgment*   99
Forbes, Edward, *The Anatomy of the Oyster*   99
French, Percy, *Abdulla Bulbul Ameer*   101
    The Cycles Of Time   103
    Song of William, Inspector of Drains   104
    'Are Ye Right There, Michael?'   105
    Shlathery's Mounted Fut   107
    The Four Farrellys   109
French, RBD, *The Martyr*   111
    Sacrifice   113
    1940   115
    Green Little Island   116
'From Great Londonderry' (Anon.)   118

The Galbally Farmer (Anon.)   119
The Galway Races (Anon.)   120
Gavan, Mr, *Lanigan's Ball* (attrib.)   122
The Gay Old Hag (Anon.)   124
The Glendalough Saint (Anon.)   125
Godley, AD, *The Arrest*   126
    Phases Of The Celtic Revival   127
    The Paradise of Lecturers   129
    Switzerland   130
    Motor Bus   131
Gogarty, Oliver St John, *Molly*   132
    Suppose   133
    Sing a Song of Sexpence   133
    Brian O'Lynn   134
    On a Fallen Electrician   134
    Goosey Goosey Gander Censored   134
    Ringsend   134
Goldsmith, Oliver, *Description of an Author's Bed-Chamber*   135
    An Elegy on the Death of a Mad Dog   136

  Epitaph on Edward Purdon   137
  Song   137
  The March of Intellect (attrib.)   138
GPO Door (Anon.)   140
George Granville, Lord Lansdowne, *To Chloe*   141
Graves, AP, *The Rose of Kenmare*   141
Griffith, Arthur, *The Thirteenth Lock*   143
  Lucinda   146
  Valuable Recipe for the Emerald Isle   147
  The Song of the British 'Ero   149
Guinness and Company's Drayman (Anon.)   150

Halpine, Charles, *Sambo's Right to be Kilt*   152
  Truth in Parenthesis   153
Hamilton, Edwin, *To My First Love*   155
Hardebeck, Carl, *The Piper who Played before Moses*   156
Hargreaves, William, *Delaney's Donkey*   157
Harker, Mrs EAG, 'When Judas Iscariot'   159
Hartigan, Anne Le Marquand, *Heirloom*   159
Hartnett, Michael, *If I were King of England …*   160
The Hatchet: February 2nd, 1857 (Anon.)   161
Heaney, Seamus, *A Keen for the Coins*   163
Heaton, Mr, 'Bacon is Bacon'   163
Henry, James, 'On a Windy Day'   163
  Striking a Light at Night   164
Hodnett, George D, *Monto*   164
Hogan, Michael, 'Verses for the Unveiling of a Statue'   166
Holzapfel, Rudi, *Churchgate Collection*   166
Hot Asphalt (Anon.)   167
Howard, Crawford, *The Arab Orange Lodge*   169
The Humours of Donnybrook Fair (I) (Anon.)   171
Hyde, Douglas, 'Making Punch'   172

Ideal Poems: Y…s (Anon.)   174
In Praise of the City of Mullingar (Anon.)   175
'An Incident near Macroom' (Anon.)   177
Irish Castles in the Air (Anon.)   178
The Irish Jubilee (Anon.)   179
The Irish Rover (Anon.)   182

Jackson, Robert Wyse, *A Social Problem*   184
  Tra Oz Montes with *Very Blank Verse*   185
  A Fat Man's Tragedy   186
  Episode   188
Jackson, Seán, *Who wants to be a Milliner?*   188

Encounter with an Eileen 189
Johnny McEldoo (Anon.) 190
Jones, Paul, *Repentant Son* 191
    'Battle's a Cod' 192
    Ballade of Vanished Beauty 192

Katty Flannigan (Anon.) 194
Kavanagh, Patrick, *Who Killed James Joyce?* 195
    Justifiable Homicide 196
Kavanagh, Richie, *Chicken Talk* 196
Kearney, James, *The Ball of Dandyorum* 198
Kearney, Peadar, *Fish and Chips* 200
Kelly, James, *Down the Street where Jimmy Lives* 201
    The Ol' Black Can 202
'Kennedy's Bread' (Anon.) 203
Kennelly, Brendan, *To No One* 204
    Under the Table 204
    Your Wan's Answer 205
The Kerry Recruit (Anon.) 205
Kipling, Rudyard, *Shillin' a Day* 206
    The Irish Guards 1918 207
'The Knight of Glin' (Anon.) 209

La Femme Savante (Anon.) 210
Lancaster, Osbert, *Eireann Afternoon* 210
Lever, Charles, *Bad Luck to this Marching* 211
    It's Little for Glory I Care 212
    'Country Life' 213
    'What an Illigant Life' 213
    'Dublin City' 214
    'A Suitable Appointment' 214
    'Oh, Mary Brady' with 'Jimmie Joyce' 214
    Mickey Free's Ancestry 214
    'A Plea' 215
Lewis, CS, *March for Strings, Kettledrums, and Sixty-three Dwarfs* 215
Linehan, Fergus, *The Blackbird* 217
    The Shaving Ghost 218
Little Emily of Dee (Anon.) 220
The Lonely Man (Anon.) 221
A Longford Legend (Anon.) 223
Lord Tomnoddy (Anon.) 224
The Louse House of Kilkenny (Anon.) 225
Lover, Samuel, *The Birth of Saint Patrick* 227
    Paddy's Pastoral Rhapsody 228

Lowry, James M, *The Last of the Leprechauns*   228
    Tottie De Vere   230
Lysaght, Edward, *Love Versus the Bottle*   231

MacAlastair, Somhairle, *Battle Song of the Irish Christian Front*   232
McAllister, Alec, *The Breaking of Maggie*   233
Mac Donagh, Donagh, *Juvenile Delinquency*   235
McDonald, John, *The Orangeman's Hell*   236
MacDonogh, Patrick, *No Mean City*   239
MacGill, Patrick, *Fair Ladies*   239
McGonigall, William, *The Rattling Boy from Dublin*   240
McGovern, Iggy, *Pomes Indigest*   242
    Time Up   242
MacGowan, Shane, *The Sick Bed of Cuchulainn*   243
MacManus, M J, *The O'Flanagan-Brownes*   245
    A Ballade of Portadown   246
    The Author's Lament   247
    Pocket-Book Wisdom   248
MacNeice, Louis, *Night Club*   248
    Death of an Actress   249
    Bagpipe Music   250
Maginn, William, *Saint Patrick of Ireland, My Dear!*   251
Mahon, Derek, *Anglo-Irish Clerihews*   253
Mahony, Francis Sylvester, *The Bells of Shandon*   255
Makem, Tommy, *Lord Nelson*   257
Mangan, James Clarence, *Johnny Kenchinow*   258
    A Railway of Rhyme   260
    Stammering or Tipsy Ghazzel   260
Martin, Bob, *Killaloe*   261
'Martin Luther was a Friar' (Anon.)   262
Mathews, MJF, *Moryah*   262
Maxton, Hugh, *To a Dublin Host*   263
    Faxes to the Critic: III   264
Memory (Anon.)   264
Milligan, Spike, *You Must Never Bath in an Irish Stew*   264
    It would be Obscene   265
Milliken, Richard, *The Groves of Blarney* (attrib.)   265
    De Groves ov de Pool (attrib.)   268
Milne, Ewart, *Cockles and Mussels*   269
    When I Consider   271
    A Ballad of Christmas Days   271
    Long Live the King   274
Mitchell, Susan, *George Moore Eats a Grey Mullet*   274
    George Moore Becomes the Priest of Aphrodite   275
Monck, Mary, *A Tale*   276

Montgomery, James, *The Canal Boat*   277
Moore, Christy, *Joxer Goes To Stuttgart*   280
     Saint Brendan's Voyage   282
     The Rose of Tralee (Me and the Rose)   284
Moore, Thomas, *Moral Positions: A Dream*   288
     Epitaph on Robert Southey   289
     Nonsense   290
The Moore Statue (Anon.)   291
Mrs McGrath (Anon.)   291
Myler, Mary, *Putting my Foot in it*   293

Napoleon is the Boy for Kicking up a Row (Anon.)   294
The Native Irishman (Anon.)   295
Nell Flaherty's Drake (Anon.)   297
No Irish Need Apply (Anon.)   299

O'Brien, Con, *Bacon and Greens*   300
O'Brien, Flann, *Strange but True*   302
     We wouldn't Say it unless we Knew   302
     The Workman's Friend   302
     A Workin' Man   303
     'After Horace'   304
O'Brien, Jane Vere, *A Ballad*   306
O'Donovan, Harry, *The Charladies' Ball*   307
O'Flaherty, Charles, *The Humours of Donnybrook Fair (II)*   309
O'Higgins, Brian, *The Limb of the Law* (attrib.)   312
     The Grand International Show   313
     From the Trenches   314
     The Isle of Innisfree   315
     The Bonfire on the Border   316
O'Keeffe, John, *Jingle*   317
O'Kelly, Patrick, *The Curse of Doneraile*   317
The Old Alarm Clock (Anon.)   320
The Old Leather Breeches (Anon.)   321
The Old Woman from Wexford (Anon.)   323
On Deborah Perkins of the County of Wicklow (Anon.)   325
O'Riordan, Conal, *'Adam's First Poem'*   326
The Ould Orange Flute (Anon.)   327

Paddy MacShane's Seven Ages (Anon.)   329
Paddy's Burial (Anon.)   330
Paneful (Anon.)   332
The Pig (Anon.)   333
Pindaric Ode Written on a Winter Evening not Far from
     Sorrel Hill (Anon.)   333

CONTENTS

The Pope and the Sultan (Anon.)   334
Porter, Thomas Hamblin, *The Night-Cap*   335

Quin, Simon, *The Town of Passage* (attrib.)   336

The Ragman's Ball (Anon.)   339
The Rakes of Mallow (Anon.)   341
The Rearing of the Green (Anon.)   342
Retrospect (Anon.)   343
Rexfort, E R, *Wilde Oscar Wilde*   343
A Riddle (Anon.)   344
Rogers, Thorold, *The Bank of Ireland*   345
Ros, Amanda M, *On Visiting Westminster Abbey*   346
    Epitaph on Largebones – The Lawyer   347
Ryan, Darby, *The Peeler and the Goat*   347

'A Sailor Courted a Farmer's Daughter' (Anon.)   350
A Scattering of Limericks (Various authors)   351
Shalvey, Thomas, *Saint Kevin and King O'Toole*   361
'Shandon Steeple' (Anon.)   362
Shaw, George Bernard, 'Verse for Use while Petting a Dog'   362
    'Apples from Coole Park'   363
Sheehy, Eugene, *Bovril*   364
Sheridan, Niall, *Portrait of a Christian He-Man*   364
Sheridan, Richard Brinsley, *Song*   365
Simmons, James, *Cavalier Lyric*   366
A Skellig List, 1951 (Anon.)   366
Sparrow, Frank, *The Arts Club Circular*   370
Stapleton, Margery, *The Rock of Cashel*   372
    Lovely Jesus   372
Stevenson, John, *Ode to a Pratie*   372
    The Way we Tell a Story   373
Strong, LAG, *A Memory*   374
    The Brewer's Man   374
Stuart, Alexander, *Rival Deans: A Lay of Cashel*   375
Sullivan, TD, *Ladle it Well*   376
    Rigged Out   377
    A Letter   379
    A Glamorous Ballad   381
    Women's Ways   382
A Sup of Good Whiskey (Anon.)   382
Swift, Jonathan, *A Description of the Morning*   384
    An Elegy on Dicky and Dolly   384
    'The Dean as Landscape Gardener'   385
    On a Curate's Complaint of Hard Duty   386

'Castle Leslie' (attrib.) — 387
On Himself — 387
Synge, John Millington, *The Curse* — 387

A Tale of Horror (Anon.) — 388
Targin Tallyo (Anon.) — 389
The TCD Harriers (Anon.) — 390
Thackeray, William Makepeace, *The Crystal Palace* — 392
To George Moore on the Occasion of his Wedding (Anon.) — 395
The Town of Ballybay (Anon.) — 396
A Tragedy in Three Acts (Anon.) — 397
Trainor, John, *The Cruise of the Calabar* — 398
*'Twas an Irish Fight: How the English Fought the Dutch
    at the Battle of Dundee* (Anon.) — 400

Up the Pole (Anon.) — 402

Walsh, Edward, *Rapture!* — 404
Ward, Mrs, *A Song of the Ruins of Dunluce* — 405
Webb, DA, 'Mr JM Henry's Address ...' — 405
The Whig Missionary of 1835 (Anon.) — 406
Wilde, Oscar, 'On Cricket' (attrib.) — 407
Williams, Richard D'Alton, *Oh! For A Feed* — 408
    The Dream — 409
    The Jealous Stoneybatter Man — 412
Wilson, John Crawford, 'How Caesar was Driven from Ireland' — 413
Winstanley, John, *On Marriage* — 416
The Wonderful Grey Horse (Anon.) — 416

Yeats, Jack B, 'The Rabbits and the Hares' — 419
Yeats, WB, *For Anne Gregory* — 420

The Zoological Gardens (Anon.) — 421
Zozimus, *Saint Patrick was a Gentleman* — 422
    The Finding of Moses (2 versions) — 424
    The Song of Zozimus — 426

Acknowledgments — 429
Index of Titles and *First Lines* — 433

Some Introductory Remarks

Imagine the imaginary reader standing in an imaginary bookshop looking like a coffeeshop. 'Ireland's Other Poetry, eh?' the reader mutters, 'Anonymous to Zozimus? What's that title supposed to mean? And what does the lad on the cover have those bendy legs for?'

'That's a great book,' I interrupt. (An ex-bookseller of the old school, I cannot help making recommendations.) 'It's a big collection of poems that rhyme. Irish poems, mostly, but not in Irish, in English. A good few of them will make you laugh.'

Or perhaps I might say this:

'That is an anthology of the country's less academically respectable verses. The editors make the doubtful claim that they represent an under-appreciated aspect of the Hiberno-English poetic tradition.'

Well, let's settle for a position somewhere between the two. After all, the book does have two editors ...

For years, Hector McDonnell and I (JWJ) have been swapping bits of 'Ireland's Other Poetry' with each other. Hector would ring up with a comic ballad or a bit of Ulster folk poetry, and I might reply with some curiosity unearthed in the mucky foothills of the Joyce industry. Eventually it dawned on us that all this stuff deserved some sort of permanent resting place, and we set to work. Before long, a delectable mental picture had begun to form: on one side of the Irish literary fence a group of Famous Poets were preaching to their followers, while on the other side, peering at them curiously, was a ragged army of Anonymous Balladeers, Parodists, Stage Lyricists, Gifted Children, Rhymesters, Advertising Copywriters, Poetasters, Academics, Rock Singers,

Bards and Miscellaneous Versifiers. These neglected unfortunates would be our 'Other Poets'; we thought it was high time somebody offered them a home.

Legend has it that when Brendan Behan was asked the difference between prose and poetry, he replied:

> There was a young fellow named Rollocks,
> Who worked for Ferrier Pollocks,
>   As he walked on the strand,
>   With his girl by the hand,
> The water came up to his knees.

Now, that wasn't poetry, Behan explained, it was prose – though if the water had gone any higher up it would have been poetry all right. Of course he knew it was neither prose nor poetry, however high the water went. It was a limerick.

The split between 'serious' poetry and all other types of poetic composition – what we are calling 'Ireland's Other Poetry' – was complete by the end of the eighteenth century. After that, several different strands of verse in English were practised in Ireland, all at the same time. You could buy ballads in the streets of Dublin for a penny, but they rarely made it into books. Other brands of 'non-serious' verse appeared in popular magazines and newspapers, or were sung in the music-halls. As time passed, people who wrote the serious sort of poetry generally avoided publishing any of the other varieties, though they might produce them for private consumption. During the twentieth century, the old skills of verse-making became less important, and gradually most Irish poetry abandoned the trappings of regular metre and rhyme. The latest slim volumes in the bookshops of today are evidence that if your work favours traditional rhyme schemes, you will probably never see it in book form at all, unless you publish it yourself.

It is not that people in Ireland no longer write or enjoy this 'Other Poetry'. Far from it. Verses using rhyme and rhythm are everywhere around us still, good ones as well as bad. They are recited at company dinners and country weddings, and chanted in playgrounds, dressing-rooms and football coaches. They fill gaps in our regional papers and specialist magazines, and crop up in local histories and private memoirs. They are composed for competitions by schoolchildren, and for amatory purposes by teenagers. They are heard on radio phone-in programmes and comedy shows and television adverts, and appear on stage in pantomimes, revues and cabarets. And the songs and ballads of Christy Moore, Richie Kavanagh and Shane MacGowan, among many others, are an essential part of the country's current rich musical flowering.

For centuries on this island we have been very good at writing witty and quirky verses. The limerick claims dubious origin in abusive lines in eighteenth-century Irish about the cost of drink in the pubs of Croom, County Limerick. Irish also influenced the rhyme-schemes and rhythms of our other verse traditions, even the one that descended in a direct line from the satires and squibs of writers such as Jonathan Swift and Oliver Goldsmith (two poets whose best work ignores the divide between the serious and the comic). Largely for reasons of space, however, this book does not tackle poetry in Irish and, apart from Mangan's versions of the limericks from Croom (see page 352), all translations have also been left out of consideration.

At one point we thought that we might call the book 'Bigotry, Scorn and Wit'. We planned to reprint Mrs Cecil Frances Alexander's mid nineteenth-century hymn, 'All Things Bright and Beautiful', with its (now suppressed) verse:

> The rich man in his castle,
> The poor man at his gate;
> God made them, high or lowly,
> And ordered their estate.

But then we realized that the good lady's lines were in fact neither bigoted nor scornful, and they were certainly not very witty. They were simply the product of a particular social class at a particular time, a time when neither the rich nor even possibly the poor man would have much objected to them. Seen in this light, though several entries in this book now seem decidedly 'non-PC', very few would have greatly offended sensibilities in their own day. Arthur Griffith's acid-tongued verse satires, for example, are more shocking now than when they were written. Of course, the bounds of acceptability are constantly shifting – ten years ago, Richie Kavanagh's song 'Chicken Talk' would probably have been banned from mainstream radio. Now it's a children's favourite.

As the book took shape, we were keen to include a good many favourites. Room was found for a few well-turned couplets by Swift and his circle, for some of the best of Percy French, Oliver Gogarty and Flann O'Brien, and for glories like 'Monto' by George Hodnett. But we drew much more from the noble ranks of the almost forgotten. It was exciting to discover that poetry written for recitation or performance on stage or at private 'evenings' had generally been unnoticed by anthologists, and that there were also many surprises lurking in magazines published by institutions, clubs and religious orders, and in the universities. We were delighted to be given one of Kerry's elusive 'Skellig List' attacks on the unmarried. We found other wonderful local verses preserved in the obscurity of the county library system or in the Department of Irish Folklore at University College, Dublin (though many more, alas, must have died before they even got that length, as they were only lodged in the skulls of the people who first dreamed them up). 'Occasional' or 'light' verse, often thought to be a largely Anglo-Irish habit, has been almost invisible since the foundation of the state, but it has been made welcome in these pages, and so has the rich demotic verse tradition of County Antrim, still practically unknown to the rest of Ireland. For good measure we added a leavening of foreign contributors writing on Irish subjects, alongside some extraordinary verses written by the Irish in exile, particularly in the USA.

Soon enough we came to realize that our book could only scratch the surface of 'Ireland's Other Poetry': there was never going to be enough space or enough time to do the job as it deserved to be done. At least the nuggets we were finding would indicate where rich veins of ore still lay buried. Likely sources such as *Dublin Opinion* or the *Irish Times* or the Victorian comic rag, *Zozimus*, were consulted, but more remains to be found in them, as well as in countless other newspapers and magazines over three centuries. After reading 'Carrots from Clonown' in *The Second Album of Roscommon Verse*, I ought to have looked at *The First Album* too. But I didn't, and all too soon, the book was full to overflowing, and we found ourselves saying to would-be helpful friends – 'No, I don't care how good it is, don't tell me about it!' Fortunately, we had decided before we began that when we had gathered a healthy bookful of really good material, we would simply stop. There would be other days, other books.

Some of the verses here, perhaps most, do not aim for conventional 'artistic excellence'; but we hope any that fail *as poetry* may still remain effective and entertaining. A few virtually unforgettable examples even seem to derive their appeal from, to put it bluntly, the poet's inability to write verse at all. Readers may therefore be forgiven for wondering what prompted us to favour one poem or song over another. Such judgments are always a personal matter, but Hector and I agreed that not only should our choices normally use rhyme and rhythm, but each one had to display a certain spark, or sparkle, or surprise – something to make it memorable, and raise a smile or even a laugh. If both of us were enthusiastic about an entry, then, we reasoned, the chances were that there would be other readers who liked it too. Along the way, we found that the best way to appreciate the verses – and this may apply to poetry of all sorts – was to read them silently, and fairly slowly. Even so, we are quite aware that very few readers will approve of everything in these pages.

Most anthologies are organized as if people read them straight through from beginning to end. Since nobody ever actually does so, we have not arranged the book chronologically. Nor have we shoehorned the poems into those spurious sections favoured by Victorian poetry books – 'Songs of the Affections,' 'From Field and Fen', 'Moral, Sentimental and Satirical Odes,' etc. It would have been an impossible task in any case: among the almost 400 entries here, there are verses on food and philosophy, on Guinness and ghosts, on war, on murder, on love, on lighting a match. Masterpieces of wordplay and parody rub shoulders with sporting songs, advertising jingles and lyrics from the theatre or the hit parade. There is bawdy verse and malicious doggerel and stage Irish buffoonery, there is religious satire and political propaganda, and there is romantic whimsy and good honest abuse.

Instead, to make it as easy as possible for readers to locate what they are looking for, we have printed the entries alphabetically by author or, if we do not know the author, by title, with a contents page at the front of the book and an index at the back covering both titles and first lines. This arrangement allows the verses to retain a rewarding sense of surprise: as you finish reading one, you just do not know what strange specimen is going to come leaping at you around the corner.

We have tried to be sympathetic rather than pedantic in our approach to the editorial task, explaining obscure words and references in the headnotes only when it seemed essential for the appreciation of the poem. We have not agonised in too scholarly a fashion over textual variants and anomalies – where the punctuation or spelling of an anonymous source appeared to need amending, we have done so silently, and we have also generally removed any numbering of verses. Though our aim was to represent just about everyone of talent in this field that we could think of, every reader will find shocking omissions: you will search in vain for anything by James Joyce, for example. He might perhaps have enjoyed rubbing shoulders with so many miscellaneous Irish penmen and penwomen, but his works are both so familiar and evidently so valuable that we feel it is probably best humbly to beg his forgiveness and understanding, and omit him entirely.

Our alphabetical subtitle, 'Anonymous to Zozimus', deserves a short explanation. Zozimus was one of the many balladeers and poets who scraped a living in Ireland during the first half of the nineteenth century. He became an important figure for us as we prepared *Ireland's Other Poetry*, and we were mildly surprised not to find his name in either the late nineteenth-century *Cabinet of Irish Literature* or the 1991 *Field Day Anthology of Irish Writing*. After his death, this blind Dubliner (whose real name was Michael Moran) became almost a mythic figure, an urban Homer, heir to the Gaelic bards and a symbol of the island's ancient cultural wealth. His poems and songs, which do not seem to have been written down during his lifetime, began to travel from person to person, changing as they did so in a process of 'Chinese whispers'. Though the real voice of Zozimus may now be almost lost to folk-memory, the tradition of verse as entertainment which he passed on to his successors is a legacy that all of us in Ireland continue to enjoy. It is a privilege and a delight to be a part of that chain.

The illustrations that form an integral part of this book are the work of the Hector half of this editorial team. He is a professional artist who has enjoyed illustrating books of ballads and Flann O'Brien's wit over the years and, as he puts it, he has made drawings for this book not as a duty but simply as the spirit took him. His musings on his part in the compilation of the poetical side of this book now follow:

Hector McDonnell writes:
When John and I devised the idea for this book I knew that a major part of my own contribution would inevitably be the illustrations, but I promised to gather together as much poetry as I could muster. In the course of doing so, I began to feel that I represented the Other Ireland rather than the Other Poetry of this story, for the culture which raised me often feels about as far removed from that of Wexford or Dublin as that of Timbuctoo. But then, that is very much the point of properly rural Ireland – it is always so extremely local that the rest of the country does not seem to exist at all.

It was my fate to be brought up in an absurd Jacobethan castle in the Glens of Antrim, revelling in the surreal peculiarity of my family's ultra-English accents stranded in a linguistic Sargasso Sea of Ulster Scots which was so spectacularly broad and archaic that I can read the whole of Rabbie Burns without needing to look a word up in a dictionary. But then, round virtually every corner there seemed to lurk someone wanting to entertain us with his poetry, and that was the source I tried to explore.

About the best of these Glens poets was a man called James Kelly. He often spent his winter days working on local stretches of the coast road, a punishment imposed upon the unemployed by those who ran the Boroo, as our employment agency was usually called. Mostly, however, James was to be found helping out local farmers at times when extra hands were needed, or suchlike activities, but if he saw someone new approaching he would stop whatever he was doing and address them in verse. His happiest hours were spent at parties, waiting for his moment to take the floor, and I particularly fondly remember one Christmas when he appeared on the stage of the school hall, dressed in his usual old black suit, which he had transformed into a jester's outfit by tying many balloons round his ankles. He stood stock still, until the laughter subsided, and then launched into one of his very best works, a lament from his road mending days about the explosion of his Ol' Black Can (published below.)

There were many more of these wondrous entertainers, and some of their works have found a home in this anthology, though others had to be excluded, including, sadly, one that describes the consequences of a terrible wedding party, and in particular relates the following:

> Then there was wee Maggie's girl, and her but in her teens:
> She went and ate a full two pound tin of them John West Sardines.
> 'I've ate that mony fish,' says she, 'and them not even fried,
> My stomach's going in and oot in motion with the tide.'

Another local genius, Mat Meharg, ran a bicycle shop with his brother that had more of the air of a redundant witch's cavern than a commercial enterprise. His poems were every bit as funny as James Kelly's, and included an account of his journey through life, which in particular related how he had totally failed to settle down with a woman. Each verse described the delicious charms of some delightful lass or propertied older woman who seemed to be on the point of succeeding in tempting him away from bachelorhood, before he ended it with a dramatic pause followed by the refrain, 'But I thought I'd stay single awhile.'

I remember the agony of suspense this caused me when I first heard it, as I was constantly hoping that perhaps the next verse would finally reveal the lass who succeeded where the others had failed, but that never happened. I tried to track down his poetic legacy (he died some fifteen years ago), but then ran up against an insurmountable obstacle: his brother was still in the bicycle shop, and yes indeed he had the only extant copy of all the poems. Mat had written them out in his last years and then put them for safety in a cupboard. 'He locked them up in there before he died,' Mat's brother grimly related, 'and that's the way they're going to stay.'

I did however find other works for this anthology. Some were ones I had at one stage committed to memory, either in the hopes of amusing some friend, if he or she was prepared to listen to them, or else to contribute to the fun during the many sessions I have spent in a local pub that has musical evenings twice a week, the Skerry Inn. I did also try to broaden my catchment area and find other sources for this brand of poetry, though not, I am afraid, with much success, for wherever I went I suffered from the inevitable problem of not being a local My greatest failure came when I approached a man in Sligo who was said to have a great poetry repertoire. I explained what we were trying to do, but he only shook his head sadly, saying, 'I'm afraid there's precious little humour in this part of the country.'

Be that as it may, we have cobbled together a great store of Irish poetic fun, and I for one look at it all with much delight. I will be annoying my friends with newly acquired verse recitations for many years to come.

Fergus Allen

*Even before the poet Anonymous makes an appearance in
Ireland, the origins of mankind itself are explained by
Fergus Allen (b. 1921), who takes us on an excursion to the
Lord's great brewery at the beginning of the world.*

THE FALL

The Garden of Eden (described in the Bible)
Was Guinness's Brewery (mentioned by Joyce),
Where innocent Adam and Eve were created
And dwelt from necessity rather than choice;

For nothing existed but Guinness's Brewery,
Guinness's Brewery occupied all,
Guinness's Brewery everywhere, anywhere –
Woe that expulsion succeeded the Fall!

The ignorant pair were encouraged in drinking
Whatever they fancied whenever they could,
Except for the porter or stout which embodied
Delectable knowledge of Evil and Good.

In Guinness's Brewery, innocent, happy,
They tended the silos and coppers and vats,
They polished the engines and coopered the barrels
And even made pets of the Brewery rats.

One morning while Adam was brooding and brewing
It happened that Eve had gone off on her own,
When a serpent like ivy slid up to her softly
And murmured seductively, Are we alone?

O Eve, said the serpent, I beg you to sample
A bottle of Guinness's excellent stout,
Whose nutritive qualities no one can question
And stimulant properties no one can doubt;

It's tonic, enlivening, strengthening, heartening,
Loaded with vitamins, straight from the wood,
And further enriched with the not undesirable
Lucrative knowledge of Evil and Good.

So Eve was persuaded and Adam was tempted,
They fell and they drank and continued to drink,
(Their singing and dancing and shouting and prancing
Prevented the serpent from sleeping a wink).

Alas, when the couple had finished a barrel
And swallowed the final informative drops,
They looked at each other and knew they were naked
And covered their intimate bodies with hops.

The anger and rage of the Lord were appalling,
He wrathfully cursed them for taking to drink
And hounded them out of the Brewery, followed
By beetles (magenta) and elephants (pink).

The crapulous couple emerged to discover
A universe full of diseases and crimes,
Where porter could only be purchased for money
In specified places at specified times.

And now in this world of confusion and error
Our only salvation and hope is to try
To threaten and bargain our way into Heaven
By drinking the heavenly Brewery dry.

Drink and its effects are a recurring theme in Irish writing.
Though Fergus Allen published no poems in book form until
1993, there have been three collections since then. This tale of

a student encounter with a film-bore at the fag-end of a
night on the town appeared (under the pseudonym of 'Stylus
Pix') in May 1945, in TCD: A College Miscellany, *the*
leading undergraduate magazine of Trinity College, Dublin.

APRÈS LA DANCE
OR, GEORGE

At half-past three, distinctly haggard,
After the drums and drink we staggered
    Down to a café by the river
    To aggravate a queasy liver;
There Anne ate chips, dear Charles and Mabel
    Passed nearly if not wholly out,
    While I, consuming bottled stout,
Reclined upon the café table
    Sunk in an alcoholic coma.
    The gramophone played La Paloma.

Through gin-fogged eyes I looked and saw
A figure bowing to the floor,
    A figure sinewy and lean
    Whose skin and clothes were none too clean,
A figure fraught with gestures wild,
    Conducting with a grubby hand
    Some figmentary Russian band,
Who murmured as he bowed and smiled
    'Good morning, so you're drinking beer, –
    It's very nice to see you here.'

'Protruding yellow eye, Avaunt!
'Twill boot you nothing now to haunt
    The four of us; we wisely put
    The boot upon the other foot.'
But my intoxicated speech,
    Clogged with the vitamins in beer,
    Delivered with a drunken leer,
Could not deter this human leech.
    He sat. My self-control was strong,
    I said, 'How long, O Lord, how long?'

He spoke of Eisenstein and Lang,
Duvivier and Tobis Klang,
    Pudovkin, Pabst and Rene Clair,
    The faults of Metro-Goldwyn-Mayer;

3

He lauded men with Russian names,
    He spoke of cameramen and panning,
    Montage, dissolving, wipes and scanning,
Of close-ups, focal lengths and frames, –
    Of Grierson and the other gentry
    Who made the British Documentary.

At 6 a.m. I woke from sleep,
My tongue a furry coated heap,
    While by my side, like Acheron,
    That dreadful whisper whispered on.
I rose in rage, prepared to throttle
    That living libel on mankind,
    But suddenly I changed my mind, –
I killed him with a broken bottle.
    And now, I'm very much afraid,
    We're haunted by his restless shade.

Anonymous

*An anti-enlistment ballad from the time of the Napoleonic
Wars. Was it still being sung in the pubs of Liverpool in the
1950s? See line 6.*

ARTHUR McBRIDE

I had a first cousin called Arthur McBride,
He and I took a stroll down by the seaside,
A-seeking good fortune and what might betide,
It being on Christmas morning.
And then after resting we both took a tramp,
We met Sergeant Pepper and Corporal Cramp,
Besides the wee drummer who beat up for camp,
With hi rowdy dow-dow in the morning.

He says My good fellows, if you will enlist,
A Guinea you quickly shall have in your fist,
Besides a crown for to kick up the dust,
And drink the king's health in the morning.
Had we been such fools as to take the advance,
The wee bitter morning we had run to chance,
For you'd think it no scruple to send us to France,
Where we would be killed in the morning.

He says My young fellows, if I hear but one word,
I instantly now will out with my sword,
And into your bodies as strength will afford,
So now, my gay devils, take warning.
But Arthur and I we took in the odds,
We gave them no chance to lunge out their swords,
Our whacking shillelaghs came over their heads,
And paid them right smart in the morning.

As for the wee drummer, we rifled his pouch,
And we made a football of his rowdy dow-dow,
And into the ocean to rock and to row,
And bade him a tedious returning.
As for the old rapier that hung by his side,
We flung it as far as we could in the tide,
To the devil I bid you, says Arthur McBride,
To temper your steel in the morning.

Anonymous

*'The Athlone Landlady' is a comic song from the beginning
of the nineteenth century, whose verses read like expanded
limericks. It was shamelessly adapted by Charles Lever for
his 1841 novel, Charles O'Malley.*

THE ATHLONE LANDLADY

'Twas in the sweet town of Athlone
Liv'd the beautiful Widow Malone;
    She kept the Black Boy,
    Was an armful of joy,
And had plenty of lovers, och hone, och hone;
    O the world for you, Widow Malone.

There was Bolus the medical drone,
And Latitat all skin and bone;
　　But physic and law
　　Both stuck in her craw,
And she couldn't digest them, och hone, och hone,
　　O success to sweet Mistress Malone.

But Cupid, who's the devil's own,
Sent a lad who soon altered her tone;
　　'Twas brave Serjeant Mac Whack,
　　With long sword and broad back,
And his roguish black eyes at her thrown, och hone;
　　O they bothered poor Widow Malone.

The love-sick sweet Mistress Malone,
So fond of the soldier was grown,
　　That in secret she'd sigh,
　　'For the Serjeant I die,
Oh! I'm tired of lying alone, och hone.'
　　More of that to you, Mistress Malone.

Still the lawyer and doctor will groan,
And each tease the poor Widow, och hone!
　　Till one day Pat Mac Whack
　　Kick'd them out in a crack,
And a smack gave sweet Katty Malone, och hone;
　　'O you've won me,' cried Widow Malone.

Soon they wedded and bedded, och hone,
While with fun sure the stocking was thrown,
　　And he's the man of the house,
　　And his beautiful spouse
Is sweet Mistress Mac Whack, late Malone, Malone;
　　So more luck to you Mac Whack and Malone.

Anonymous

Of considerable, but uncertain, antiquity, both of the
following songs are driven by sly sexual innuendo ...

THE BAG OF NAILS

You very merry people all I pray you list a minute,
For though my song is not too long, there's something
 comic in it.
To sing of nails, if you permit, my sportive muse
 intends, sir,
A subject which I now have got just at my fingers'
 ends, sir.

This world is just a bag of nails, and they are very
 queer ones,
Some are flats, and some are sharps, and some are
 very dear ones;
We've sprigs and spikes and sparables, some both
 great and small, sir,
Some love nails with monstrous heads, and some love
 none at all, sir.

A bachelor's a hob nail, and he rusts for want of use,
 sir,
The misers have no nails at all, they're all a pack of
 screws, sir;

My enemies will get some clouts, where'er they
    chance to roam, sir,
For Irishmen, like hammers, will be sure to drive them
    home, sir.

The doctor nails you with his bill, that often proves a
    sore nail,
The coffinmaker wishes you as dead as any door nail;
You'll often find each agent to be nailing his employer;
The lawyer nails his client, but the Devil nails the
    lawyer.

Dame Fortune is a bradawl, and she often does con-
    trive it,
To make the nail go easy whereso'er she likes to drive
    it;
Then if I gain your kind applause for what I've sung
    or said, sirs,
You will admit that I have hit the right nail on the
    head, sirs.

Anonymous

BALL O' YARN

In the merry month of June
When the roses were in bloom
And the little birds were singing their sweet charms,
Sure I spied a pretty miss
And I kindly asked her this:
'May I wind up your little ball of yarn?'

'Yerra no, kind sir,' said she,
'You're a stranger unto me
And perhaps you have got some dearly other
    charmer.'
'Yerra no, my turtle dove
You're the only one I love
And won't meddle with your little ball of yarn.'

Now I took her to a grove
Beneath a shady green
With no intentions of doing her any harm,

And to my great surprise
When I looked into her eyes
I was winding up her little ball of yarn.

Now nine months have passed and gone
Since I met this fair young one
And now she's holding a baby in her arm.
I said, 'My pretty miss,
Sure I never dreamed of this
When I was winding up your little ball of yarn.'

Now come all ye young and old,
Take a warning when you're told:
Never rise too early in the morn.
Be like the blackbird and the thrush:
Keep one hand upon your bush
And the other on your little ball of yarn.

Anonymous

One of Ireland's most famous sporting ballads.

A BALLAD OF MASTER McGRATH

Eighteen sixty nine being the date of the year,
Those Waterloo sportsmen and more did appear
For to gain the great prizes and bear them awa',
Never counting on Ireland and Master McGrath.

On the twelfth of December, that day of renown,
McGrath and his keeper they left Lurgan town;
A gale in the Channel, it soon drove them o'er,
On the thirteenth they landed on fair England's shore.

And when they arrived there in big London
    Town,
Those great English sportsmen they all
    gathered round –
And some of the gentlemen gave a 'Ha!
    Ha!'
Saying: 'Is that the great dog you call Master
    McGrath?'

And one of those gentlemen standing around
Says: 'I don't care a damn for your Irish greyhound,'
And another he laughs with a scornful 'Ha! Ha!'
We'll soon humble the pride of your Master
    McGrath.'

Then Lord Lurgan came forward and said: 'Gen-
    tlemen,
If there's any amongst you has money to spend –
For you nobles of England I don't care a straw –
Here's five thousand to one upon Master McGrath.'

Then McGrath he looked up and he wagged his old
    tail,
Informing his lordship, 'I know what you mane,
Don't fear, noble Brownlow, don't fear them, agra,
For I'll tarnish their laurels,' says Master McGrath.

And Rose stood uncovered, the great English pride,
Her master and keeper were close by her side;
They have let her away and the crowd cried: 'Hurrah!'
For the pride of all England – and Master McGrath.

As Rose and the Master they both ran along,
'Now I wonder,' says Rose, 'what took you from home;
You should have stopped there in your Irish demesne,
And not come to gain laurels on Albion's plain.'

'Well, I know,' says McGrath, 'we have wild heather
    bogs
But you'll find in old Ireland there's good men and
    dogs.
Keep your breath for the race and don't waste it on
    jaw,
And stuff that up your neb,' says Master McGrath.

Then the hare she went on just as swift as the wind
He was sometimes before her and sometimes behind,
Rose gave the first turn according to law;
But the second was given by Master McGrath.

The hare she led on with a wonderful view,
And swift as the wind o'er the green field she flew.
But he jumped on her back and he held up his paw –
'Three cheers for old Ireland,' says Master McGrath.

Anonymous

More drink. In the refrain, 'Bainne, an bó is na gamhna'
means 'Milk, the cow and the calves.'

BALLINAMONA

In the sweet County Limerick one cold winter's night,
Oh the turf fires were burning when I first saw the
   light,
And a crazy old midwife went tipsy with joy,
As she danced round the floor with her slip of a boy –
     Singing *Bainne, an bó is na gamhna,*
     And the juice of the barley for me.

When I was a young lad of eight years or so,
With my turf and my primer to school I did go,
To a dirty old schoolhouse without any door,
And the schoolmaster lying dead drunk on the floor –
     Singing *Bainne, an bó is na gamhna,*
     And the juice of the barley for me.

At booklearnin' I wasn't a genius I'm thinkin',
But soon I could beat the schoolmaster at drinkin',
At wakes and at weddings for nine miles around,
In a corner blind drunk I was sure to be found –
     Singing *Bainne, an bó is na gamhna,*
     And the juice of the barley for me.

Till one morning the priest read me out from the altar,
And said I would end all my days in a halter,
I'd dance a merry jig between Heaven and Hell,
And his words they did scare me the truth I now tell –
     Singing *Bainne, an bó is na gamhna,*
     And the juice of the barley for me.

So the very next morning my way I did make,
Along to the vestry the pledge for to take,
I peeped in the window saw three priests in a bunch,
'Round a great roarin' fire drinkin' tumblers of punch –
     Singing *Bainne, an bó is na gamhna,*
     And the juice of the barley for me.

So from that day to this I have lived all alone,
Jack of all trades and master of none,

The sky is me roof, the earth is me floor,
And I'll spend all me days drinkin' poteen galore –
    Singing *Bainne, an bó is na gamhna*,
    And the juice of the barley for me.

Anonymous

This unusual song, from a Glasgow broadside, gives a vivid – though occasionally obscure – glimpse of late nineteenth-century international relations in the city's tenements.

THE BATTLE ON THE STAIR

Says Mrs Doyle to Mrs Grant,
You'd better clean the stairs!
Ye've missed yer turn for mony a week,
The neighbours a' did theirs!
Says Mrs Grant to Mrs Doyle,
I'll tell ye Mrs Doyle,
You'd better mind your ain affairs
And clean the stair yoursel'.
It's a disagreeable thing
A row upon the stairs,
Flyting, scolding, scandle and clash
Is a row upon the stairs.

Says Mrs Grant to Mrs Doyle,
I'm sure it's no my turn,
You've got a cheek to order me,
There's not a woman born
That keeps a cleaner house than me,
And mark ye, Mrs Doyle,
Just wipe your mouth before you speak,
And gang and clean yoursel'.

Says Mrs Doyle – Ye dirty slut,
Who was it stole the beef?
What do you say? cries Mrs Grant,
Do you mean that I'm a thief?
Pay me the sixpence I lent you,
To treat big I at M'Gine,
And where's the blankets I lent you
The last time you lay in?

Says Mrs Doyle to Mrs Grant,
You very well do know,
The sixpence that you lent to me
I paid you long ago,
And your dirty ragged blanket,
As all the neighbours says,
Walked off home the other night,
Drawn there by bugs and fleas.

Says Mrs Grant to Mrs Doyle,
How dare ye speak to me;
The holey stockings on your legs,
Are shameful for to see.
My holey stockings Mrs Grant,
Looks better in the street
Than your goodman's old blutcher boots
You wear to hide your feet.

Says Mrs Doyle to Mrs Grant,
I'd be ashamed to speak,
Your husband's wages they were seized
For debt the other week.
The ear-rings you got from the Jew
On tick, the other day,
Is like the clubman's shawl you got,
I'm sure you'll never pay.

Says Mrs Grant to Mrs Doyle,
You'd better haud your jaw,
The very shift upon your back
Is just as black's the craw.
You lazy wretch, cries Mrs Doyle,
It's true, there is no doubt,
You went and drunk with Rob the snob,
The time your man was out.

Says Mrs Doyle to Mrs Grant,
You brazen looking slut;
To wash or clean the dirty stairs
I will never stir a foot
Before I'd lift a scouring clout
The dirty stairs to clean.
I'd see them turn as black as you,
You drunken pawnshop queen.

The Irish blood of Mrs Doyle,
It then began to rise,
She made a rush upon her foe
To tear out both her eyes,
The Highland pluck it did get up,
And now said Mrs Grant,
Look neighbours, she has struck me first,
I'll give her what she wants.

At length the police took them both,
As I have heard them say,
While they were fined ten shillings each,
Upon the following day,
Or go ten days to Bridewell
For to settle their affairs,
Where they would learn to clean their cells
As well as clean their stairs.

Brendan Behan
(Attrib.)

*More verses have been attributed to Brendan Behan (1923-
1964) than he could possibly have written. This is one of
them, recalled by his brother Brian: the IRA had recently
attacked an equestrian statue in the Phoenix Park.*

'IRELAND'S STRUGGLE'

'Neath the horse's prick
A dynamite stick
Some gallant hero did place.
For the cause of our land
With a light in his hand
Bravely the foe he did face.
Then without showing fear
He kept himself clear
Expecting to blow up the pair.
But he nearly went crackers
All he got was the knackers
And made the poor stallion a mare.
This is the way
Our heroes today
Are challenging England's might:

With a stab in the back
And a midnight attack
On a horse that can't even shite!

In The History of the Ginger Man (1994), JP Donleavy
remembers Behan singing this verse to the tune of 'Kevin
Barry':

'WOULD YOU?'

Would you live on women's earnings,
      Would you give up work for good?
Would you lead a life of prostitution?
      You're goddamn right I would.

Dominic Behan

*Unlike many politically motivated songwriters, Brendan's
brother Dominic (1928-1989) was a witty and successful
lyricist. In the 1960s, a folk group called the Ludlow Trio
gave him an Irish Number One hit with this neat hymn to
our island status.*

THE SEA AROUND US

They say that the lakes of Killarney are fair,
No stream like the Liffey could ever compare;
If it's water you want you'll find nothing more rare
Than the stuff they make down by the ocean.

       Chorus:
  The sea, oh the sea is the gradh geal mo croidhe,
  Long may it stay between England and me,
  It's a sure guarantee that some hour we'll be free
  Oh thank God we're surrounded by water!

Tom Moore made his waters meet fame and renown,
A great lover of anything dressed in a crown;
In brandy the bandy old Saxon he'd drown,
But throw ne'er a one into the ocean.

The Scots have their whisky, the Welsh have their
    speech,
And their poets are paid about tenpence a week
Provided no hard words on England they speak;
Oh Lord! What a price for devotion!

The Danes came to Ireland with nothing to do
But dream of the plundered old Irish they slew;
'Yeh will in your Viking,' said Brian Boru,
And he threw them back into the ocean!

Two foreign old monarchs in battle did join,
Each wanting his head on the back of a coin:
If the Irish had sense they'd drowned both in the Boyne
And partition throw into the ocean!

*Dominic Behan often wrote about the London Irish: this
ironically jaunty marching song salutes the army of Irish
labourers who helped to make England what it is today.*

MCALPINE'S FUSILIERS

As down the glen came McAlpine's men
With their shovels slung behind them;
It was in the pub they drank the sub
And up in the spike you'll find them;
They sweated blood and they washed down mud
With pints and quarts of beer,
And now we're on the road again
With McAlpine's Fusiliers.

I stripped to the skin with the Darky Flynn
Way down upon the Isle of Grain;
With the Horseface Toole I knew the rule
No money if you stop for rain;
When McAlpine's god was a well filled hod
With your shoulders cut to bits and seared,
And woe to he who looks for tea
With McAlpine's Fusiliers.

I remember the day that the Bear O'Shea
Fell into a concrete stairs;
What the Horseface said, when he saw him dead,

Well, it wasn't what the rich call prayers.
'I'm a navvy short,' was the one retort
That reached unto my ears,
When the going is rough, well you must be tough
With McAlpine's Fusiliers.

I've worked till the sweat near had me bet
With Russian, Czech and Pole;
On shuddering jams up in the hydro dams
Or underneath the Thames in a hole;
I grafted hard and I've got me cards
And many a ganger's fist across me ears:
If you pride your life, don't join, by Christ,
With McAlpine's Fusiliers.

John Betjeman

*In these pages we include a scatter of verses that are written
about rather than by the Irish. John Betjeman (1906-1984)
spent some years in Dublin, read the* Church of Ireland
Gazette *and liked to imagine that he was in some way spir-
itually one of us – he even took to signing his name 'Seán Ó
Betjemán'. In the simplicity of this bitter-sweet ballad he
captures the various elements of an Irish country town as
no native has ever done.*

THE SMALL TOWNS OF IRELAND

The small towns of Ireland by bards are neglected,
They stand there all lonesome on hill top and plain.
The Protestant glebe house by beech trees protected
Stands close to the gates of his Lordship's demesne.

But where is his Lordship, who once in a phaeton
Drove out twixt his lodge gates and into the town?
Oh his tragic misfortunes I will not dilate on;
His mansion's a ruin, his trees are cut down.

His impoverished descendant is living in Ealing,
His daughters must type for their bread and their
    board,
O'er the graves of his forbears the nettles are stealing
And few will remember the sad Irish Lord.

Yet still stands the Mall where his agent resided,
The doctor, attorney and such class of men.
The elegant fanlights and windows provided
A Dublin-like look for the town's Upper Ten.

'Twas bravely they stood by the Protestant steeple
As over the town rose their roof-trees afar.
Let us slowly descend to the part where the people
Do mingle their ass-carts by Finnegan's Bar.

I hear it once more, the soft sound of those voices
When fair day is filling with farmers the Square,
And the heart in my bosom delights and rejoices
To think of the dealing and drinking done there.

I see thy grey granite, oh grim House of Sessions!
I think of the judges who sat there in state
And my mind travels back to the monster processions
To honour the heroes of brave Ninety-Eight.

The barracks are burned where the Redcoats
    oppressed us,
The gaol is broke open, our people are free,
Though Cromwell once cursed us, St Patrick has
    blessed us –
The merciless English have fled o'er the sea.

Look out where yon cabins grow smaller to smallest,
Straw-thatched and one-storey and soon to come
    down,
To the prominent steeple, the newest and tallest,
Of Saint Malachy's Catholic Church in our town:

The fine architecture, the wealth of mosaic,
The various marbles on altars within –

To attempt a description were merely prosaic,
So, asking your pardon, I will not begin.

Oh my small town of Ireland, the rain drops caress
    you,
The sun sparkles bright on your field and your Square,
As here on your bridge I salute you and bless you,
Your murmuring waters and turf-scented air.

*Here, Betjeman paints with cinematic precision the absurd
tragedy of Oscar Wilde.*

THE ARREST OF OSCAR WILDE AT THE
CADOGAN HOTEL

He sipped at a weak hock and seltzer
    As he gazed at the London skies
Through the Nottingham lace of the curtains
    Or was it his bees-winged eyes?

To the right and before him Pont Street,
    Did tower in her new built red,
As hard as the morning gaslight
    That shone on his unmade bed,

'I want some more hock in my seltzer,
    And Robbie, please give me your hand –
Is this the end or beginning?
    How can I understand?

'So you've brought me the latest Yellow Book:
    And Buchan has got in it now:
Approval of what is approved of
    Is as false as a well-kept vow.

'More hock, Robbie – where is the seltzer?
    Dear boy, pull again at the bell!
They are all little better than *cretins*,
    Though this *is* the Cadogan Hotel.

'One astrakhan coat is at Willis's –
    Another one's at the Savoy:
Do fetch my morocco portmanteau,
    And bring them on later, dear boy.'

A thump, and a murmur of voices –
('Oh why must they make such a din?')
As the door of the bedroom swung open
    And TWO PLAIN CLOTHES POLICEMEN came in:

'Mr Woilde, we 'ave come for tew take yew
    Where felons and criminals dwell:
We must ask yew tew leave with us quoietly
    For this *is* the Cadogan Hotel.'

He rose, and he put down *The Yellow Book.*
    He staggered – and, terrible-eyed,
He brushed past the palms on the staircase
    And was helped to a hansom outside.

*The desire of a certain type of bourgeois townee to claim
knowledge of Irish has inevitably given rise to mockery in the
Gaeltacht and elsewhere. In the 1960s the poet composed this
squib for a friend over afternoon tea in St Stephen's Green.*

'THE DINGLE PENINSULA'

Up and down the Peninsula
The Dub-a-lin people go,
Some of them talking the Irish
(But talking it terrible slow.)

Anonymous

*In countless pantos and reviews at the Gaiety Theatre,
Jimmy O'Dea (1899–1965), Ireland's great comic actor of the
mid-twentieth century, put on an apron, took out his teeth,
and sang this favourite song:*

BIDDY MULLIGAN

I'm a buxom fine widow, I live in a spot,
    In Dublin they call it the Coombe
And my shop and my stall is laid out on the street
    And my palace consists of one room.
At Patrick Street corner for forty-five years

I stood there – I'm telling no lie –
And while I stood there sure no body would dare
    To say black was the white of my eye.

      Chorus:
  You may travel from Clare to the County Kildare,
    From Drogheda right back by Macroom,
  But where would you see a fine widow like me,
    Biddy Mulligan, the Pride of the Coombe,
    My boys,
    Biddy Mulligan, the Pride of the Coombe?

I sell apples and oranges, nuts and split peas,
    Bananas and sugar stick sweet,
Of a Saturday night I sell second hand clothes
    And the floor of my stall is the street.
I sell fish of a Friday laid out on a dish
    Fresh mackerel and lovely ray
I sell lovely herrings, such lovely fresh herrings,
    That once swam in dear Dublin Bay.

Now I have a son Mick and he plays on the flute
    He belongs to the Longford Street Band,
And it would do your heart good for to see them
  march out
    When the band goes to Dollymount Strand.
In the Park of a Sunday I cut quite a dash
    All the neighbours look on in surprise
At my grand paisley shawl and my bonnet so tall
    Would dazzle the sight of your eyes.

Hilda Blennerhassett
(Attrib.)

An all too accurate prophetic verse from 1902 on the likely effects of the 1903 Wyndham Act. It was preserved in a scrapbook compiled by a young member of a Kerry landed gentry family, Hilda Blennerhassett, who may well have written it. (One of her family's seats bore the eloquent name of Ballyseedy. Reborn as a hotel, it now prefers to spell itself Ballyseede.)

'HE WAS AN IRISH LANDLORD'

He was an Irish Landlord
Loyal to King and true
Fought in England's battles,
Fought in the van right through.

Now he is robbed and plundered,
Turned out of house and land,
All by the British Parliament
Urged on by the rebel band.

Alas for his faith and valour,
Alas for the flag he bore
Right to the front for England
On many a distant shore.

The man who shot the Landlord,
The man with the blackened face,
The man who houghed the cattle
Is the man to take his place.

Oh England think and ponder
Before it is too late
What would it be with Ireland
Wholly a rebel State.

Charles J Boland

*The Clonmel writer Charles Boland was a contemporary of
Percy French, whose work this song strongly resembles. It
even takes the tune of French's 'Hannigan's Aunt'.*

THE TWO TRAVELLERS

'All over the world,' the traveller said,
 'In my wanderings I have been;
An' there's nothing remarkable, living or dead,
 But these two lookin' eyes have seen.
From the haunts of the ape an' marmozet,
 To the lands of the Fellaheen.'
Says the other, 'I'll lay you an even bet
 You were never in Farranaleen.'

'I've hunted the woods of Seringapatam,
 An' sailed in the Polar Seas.
I fished for a week in the Gulf of Siam
 An' lunched on the Chersonese.
I've lived in the valleys of fair Cashmere,
 Under Himalay's snowy ridge.'
Says the other impatiently, 'Looka here,
 Were you ever at Laffan's Bridge?'

'I've lived in the land where tobacco is grown,
 In the suburbs of Santiago;
An' I spent two years in Sierra Leone,
 An' in Terra Del Fuego.
I walked across Panama all in a day,
 Ah me, but the road was rocky!'
The other replied, 'Will you kindly say,
 Were you ever at Horse-and-Jockey?'

'I've borne my part in a savage fray,
 When I got this wound from a Lascar;
We were bound just then from Mandalay
 For the isle of Madagascar.
Ah! the sun never tired of shining there,
 An' the trees canaries sang in.'
'What of that?' says the other, 'Sure I've a pair,
 And there's lots more over in Drangan.'

'I've hunted the tigers in Turkestan,
 In Australia the kangaroos;

An' I lived six months as medicine man
    To a tribe of the Katmandoos.
An' I've stood on the scene of Olympic games,
    Where the Grecians showed their paces.'
The other replied, 'Now tell me, James,
    Were you ever at Fethard Races?'

'Don't talk of your hunting in Yucatan,
    Or your fishing off Saint Helena;
I'd rather see young lads hunting the wran
    In the hedges of Tubberaheena.
No doubt the scenes of a Swiss canton
    Have a passable sort of charm,
But give me a sunset on Slievenamon
    From the road by Hackett's Farm.

'An' I'd rather be strolling along the quay,
    An' watching the river flow,
Than growing tea with the cute Chinee,
    Or mining in Mexico.
An' I wouldn't much care for Sierra Leone,
    If I hadn't seen Killenaule,
An' the man that ne'er saw Mullinahone
    Shouldn't say he had travelled at all.'

Anonymous

Benedict Kiely (1919–2006) included this curious fable in his
delightful book of rambles through Ireland's songs and verses,
And As I Rode By Granard Moat (Lilliput Press, 1996).

THE BOYS FROM BALLYSODARE

A dreadful dream I fain would tell
I dreamed I died and went to Hell.
And there, upon the topmost landing
Some prime Collooney boys were standing.
Then gazing round I wondered where
Dwelt the scamps from Ballysodare.

And musing thus, I scanned each face,
And from within that dreadful place,
Prisoners of every nationality
And chaps renowned for all rascality,
My quest was vain. They were not there.
The rowdy rakes of Ballysodare.

'Sir Nick,' quoth I, 'on every hand
I see your spoils from every land.
No doubt they well deserve their fate,
Their sins I wouldn't dare deflate,
But, might I ask you, is it fair
To quite pass over Ballysodare?'

'Ha, Ha,' quoth Nick, with sinister mirth,
'There's not a place on all the earth
Exempt from my bold operations,
Resist, who can, my machinations.
I'll take you lower still, and there
You'll find the bucks from Ballysodare.'

Still down we went to lower regions,
Encompassed by perspiring legions
From Straid, Kilvarnet and Killoran,
As well as Sligo and Bundoran.
Gaunt faces wore a look of worry.
Contingents, those, from Tobercurry.

At length we reached a dungeon rude
In Limbo's lowest latitude,

And there I saw in apprehension
A saucepan grim, of vast dimension,
Upon a roaring furnace boiling
While stoking imps around were toiling.

With conscious pride Old Nick drew near
The huge utensil. In the rear,
I peered with horror o'er his shoulder.
Despite the heat my blood ran colder.
He raised the lid and said 'In there
I boil the boys from Ballysodare.'

Anonymous

One of many versions of this Cork City street song.

THE BOYS OF FAIRHILL

Here's up them all says the boys of Fairhill.

The smell on Patrick's Bridge is wicked:
How does Father Mathew stick it?
Here's up them all says the boys of Fairhill.

The Blarney hens don't lay at all,
And when they lays they lays 'em small.
Here's up them all says the boys of Fairhill.

The Blackpool girls are very rude:
They go swimming in the nude.
Here's up them all says the boys of Fairhill

Blackpool boys are very nice:
I have tried them once or twice.
Here's up them all says the boys of Fairhill.

If you come to Cork you'll get drisheen,
Murphy's stout and pig's crubeens.
Here's up them all says the boys of Fairhill.

Well, Christy Ring he hooked the ball,
We hooked him up, balls and all.
Here's up them all says the boys of Fairhill

The smell on Patrick's Bridge is wicked.
How does Father Mathew stick it?
Here's up them all says the boys of Fairhill.
Here's up them all says the boys of Fairhill.

Anonymous

This fine 'stage-Irish' comic ballad's title (inverted) gave
Flann O'Brien his name; our rendering combines the best of
several variants, and includes verses added by the greatest
ballad-monger of them all, Colm Ó Lochlainn (1892–1972).

BRIAN O'LINN

Brian O'Linn was a gentleman born,
His hair it was long and his beard unshorn,
His teeth were out and his eyes far in –
'I'm a wonderful beauty,' says Brian O'Linn.

Brian O'Linn had no breeches to wear,
He got an old sheepskin to make him a pair,
With the fleshy side out and the woolly side in –
'They'll be pleasant and cool,' says Brian O'Linn.

Brian O'Linn had no shirt to his back,
He went to a neighbour's, and borrowed a sack,
Then he puckered the meal bag in under his chin –
'Sure they'll take them for ruffles,' says Brian O'Linn.

Brian O'Linn was hard up for a coat,
So he borrowed the skin of a neighbouring goat,
With the horns sticking out from his oxters, and then –
'Sure they'll take them for pistols,' says Brian O'Linn.

Brian O'Linn had no hat to put on,
He stuck on a pot that was under the shed,
He murdered a cod for the sake of his fin –
''Twill pass for a feather,' says Brian O'Linn.

Brian O'Linn had no brogues for his toes,
He hopped in two crab-shells to serve him for those.
Then he split up two oysters that match'd like a twin –
'Sure they'll shine out like buckles,' says Brian O'Linn.

Brian O'Linn had no watch to put on,
So he scooped out a turnip to make him a one.
Then he placed a young cricket in-under the skin –
'Sure they'll think it is ticking,' says Brian O'Linn.

Brian O'Linn to his house had no door,
He'd the sky for a roof, and the bog for a floor.
He'd a way to jump out, and a way to swim in –
' 'Tis a fine habitation,' says Brian O'Linn.

Brian O'Linn went a-courting one night,
He set both the mother and daughter to fight;
To fight for his hand they both stripped to the skin –
'Sure! I'll marry you both,' says Brian O'Linn.

Brian O'Linn, his wife and wife's mother,
They all lay down in the bed together,
The sheets they were old and the blankets were thin –
'Lie close to the wall,' says Brian O'Linn.

Brian O'Linn went to bring his wife home,
He had but one horse, that was all skin and bone –
'I'll put her behind me, as nate as a pin –
And her mother before me,' says Brian O'Linn.

Brian O'Linn, his wife and wife's mother,
Were all going home o'er the bridge together,
The bridge it broke down, and they all tumbled in –
'We'll go home by water,' says Brian O'Linn.

Anonymous

*Another song with many versions – probably the most
familiar is the one sung by The Dubliners, though this one
has some lively extra verses.*

THE BRITISH ARMY

When I was young I had a twist
For punching babies with me fist;
Then I thought I would enlist,
And join the British Army.

Chorus:
Toora loora loora loo
They're looking for monkeys up at the zoo,
Says I: 'If I had a face like you
I'd join the British Army.'

When I was young I used to be
As fine a man as ever you'd see
Till the Prince of Wales he said to me:
'Come and join the British Army.'

Sarah Comden baked a cake;
'Twas all for poor oul Slattery's sake.
She threw herself into the lake
Pretending she was barmy.

Corporal Daly went away;
His wife got in the family way,
And the only thing that she could say
Was: 'Blame the British Army.'

Corporal Kelly's a terrible drought;
Just give him a couple of jars of stout,
He'll beat the enemy with his mouth
And save the British Army.

Kilted soldiers wear no drawers:
Mary won't you lend them yours?
The poor must always help the poor,
God help the British Army.

We'll beat the enemy without fuss
And leave their bones out in the dust –
I know for they quite near beat us,
The gallant British Army.

So if you're young and in your prime,
Fond of every kind of crime,
I promise you a jolly good time,
Inside the British Army.

Final chorus:
Toora loora loora loo
I made me mind up what to do:
I'll work me ticket home to you
And fuck the British Army.

Anonymous

Nineteenth-century ballads sold in the city streets were often, like today's CD sleeves, ungrammatical, misspelt and badly printed. Such concerns are clearly of no consequence whatever in this tragic saga.

BROTHER BILL AND JAMIMA BROWN

I was at a railway station, upon the Dublin line,
I first met my Jamima – why should I call her mine?
Her eyes were bright, her hair was light, her dress a
  morning gown;
A travelling box beside her: wrote on it – Jamima
  Brown.

> Chorus:
>   I used to take her everywhere, to all the sights in
>   town,
>   But now she left me in dispair, did naughty Jamima
>   Brown.

At a baby linnen building up in Grafton Street
I first met my Jamima, so charming & so sweet,
She look'd the queen of a sewing mashine, I spent
  there many a crown
On collors & stays & Babies' caps, to gaze on Jamima
  Brown

One night I went to meet her, the weather being
  warm,
I seen her fondly leaning on a smart young fellow's
  arm;
Against my will I felt quite ill, inquiring with a frown,
'Who's that?' 'It's only Brother Bill,' said naughty
  Jamima Brown.

I sayes, 'My dear Jamima, if you'd with me agree,
Upon tomorow-evening to come unto the play,
Or to the exebition or any place in the town?'
'I feel obliged indeed, kind sir,' said naughty Jamima
  Brown.

'I want to ask a favour. I hope you won't be cross,
Or think it bad behaviour, but Father had a loss,

Will you kindly lend us fifty pounds? My Brother will
    be bound.'
'Of course I would.' Could I refuse my life to Jamima
    Brown?

I gave to her the fifty pounds but it was all no use,
For in a short time after, you'll find she cook'd my
    goose.
She hooked it away with Brother to another part of
    the town
And left me in the lurch to look for naughty Jamima
    Brown.

Years after that when passing by a shop in Dublin Town,
Amidst heaps of greens & kidney-beans stood Jamima
    Brown.
She was weighing of potatoes, throwing copper in the
    till –
Three lovely little children the image of Brother Bill!

I stood there with astonishment as on her I did gaze,
And when that she beheld me she stood all in amaze.
Her broken vow, I see it now, but not my fifty pounds:
The shop was bought but I was sold by naughty
    Jamima Brown.

          Chorus:
    I used to take her everywhere, to all the sights in
        town,
    But now she left me in dispair, did naughty Jamima
        Brown.

Harry T Browne

*Known as 'John o' the North' when wearing his poetic hat,
Harry Browne (1887-1973) was a freelance journalist,
writing for the* Larne Times *and later the* Belfast Tele-
graph. *Here he tackles the dichotomy between mythology
and geomorphology.*

THE GIANTS' CAUSEWAY

The Giants' Causeway, I used to hear them say,
Was built by Finn Mac Cool on a long ago day.

(Finn he was a giant, and the size o' ten
An' he lived in a castle down in Glenariff Glen.)
But Science laughs at this idea of its creation
And says it is a Crystallized Basaltic Formation –
For we live, an' we learn, as we go along,
But for once, by the hokey, Science could be wrong.

Ned Buckley

*In 1926 an army show-jumping team contested Ireland's
first Nations Cup at the Royal Dublin Society. These
'Jumping Irishmen' went on to achieve 22 cup wins around
the world during the 1930s. In Mallow, County Cork, the
'Bard of Knocknagree,' Ned Buckley (1880-1954), celebrated
their success.*

OUR ARMY JUMPING TEAM

I love to see the 'Cork Exam'
    Pictorial reviews,
And well do I each picture scan
    Ere I read any news;
Though each and all I've long admired,
    None served me as a theme;
Now by your group I feel inspired –
    'Our Army Jumping Team.'

'Tis grand to have an army and
    A navy of our own,
Unyoked by 'empty formulas'
    To a foreign king or throne.
Tone and Lord Edward bled for this,
    But never did they dream
That you should bring us all such bliss –
    'Our Army Jumping Team.'

They're christened gen'rals, officers
    And commandants as well,
Although they never were baptised
    In war by shot or shell –
Among them there are no Tims or Pats –
    'Tis Seamus, Shawn or Liam.
Ah! Who would dare to call you 'flats',
    'Our Army Jumping Team?'

They jumped in the United States
 In nineteen twenty nine.
This year they went to Germany
 And jumped across the Rhine.
And don't our exiles – maid and boy –
 With pride and glory beam
To see you proudly riding by –
 'Our Army Jumping Team?'

Although the times are very bad,
 We can't feel in the dumps
When wires and wireless homeward bring
 News of your faultless jumps.
Let farmers jump with rage at the
 Low prices for eggs and cream;
Their 'lep' is small compared with yours –
 'Our Army Jumping Team.'

The counties of our country once
 Were two dozen and eight;
Six of them are in 'bondage' still;
 The rest is a Free State.
There is a wall between them drawn,
 But there are some who deem
That you will 'clear' that partition,
 'Our Army Jumping Team.'

Michael Courtenay Burke

A stirring propaganda verse composed in 1936 by the Rev.
Michael C Burke of St Paul's Presbytery, Arran Quay, Dublin.

THE SUMMONS:
IRELAND'S ANTI-COMMUNIST ANTHEM

Men of Erin! Men of Erin!
Hearken to the clarion call,
Ireland sounds a note of warning
To her children one and all.
Deadly vipers creep amongst us,
List! They're hissing in the grass,
Dealing deftly dire destruction,
Spitting venom as they pass.

Men of Erin! Men of Erin!
Victims one by one expire,
Save, oh! save your weaker brothers
From the serpent's deadly fire.
Voices from the past are calling:
Guard the Faith for which we fell,
Glorious heritage of Patrick
Let no soul to Satan sell.

Men of Erin! Men of Erin!
Rome has spoken, hear her voice,
Pius, Peter's true successor,
Bids us now to make our choice.
God or Satan? Rome or Russia?
One or other, never 'twain.
We choose Christ, away with Satan,
Russia's loss and Ireland's gain.

Men of Erin! Men of Erin!
Answer then the Pope's appeal,
Join in one great solid phalanx,
Crush the serpents 'neath your heel.
Drive them forth, O Men of Erin!
E'en as Patrick did of yore;
Drive them back to godless Russia,
Sons, your Mother asks no more.

Hubert Butler

This wonderful poem is the longest in this book. Among many other things, it is a comment on the state of modern Ireland. It appeared in 1972 at the end of Ten Thousand Saints, *a book of extraordinary scholarship by Hubert Butler (1900–1990). In an introductory note, he writes: 'The hagiographical details of this poem are accurate. St Odran, the hero, was a famous saint of Iona. It is said that St Columba, finding that demons were infesting a site where he wished to build, discovered that only by burying a holy man alive could they be exorcised. St Odran volunteered, but after three days Columba decided to dig him up again for news of Heaven. St Odran, on being uncovered, instead of giving suitable information said: "There is no wonder in Death and Hell is not as it is reported." Thereupon*

Columba cried out furiously: "Earth, earth upon the mouth
of Odran that he may blab no more!" And he was covered
up again.

'Odran, in this poem, talks of rejoining "the gods"; he
had not, at the time, read O'Brien's Corpus Genealo-
giarum, *or he would have said "our ancestors".'*

THE SAINTS LEAVE IRELAND – A POEM

'How can we stop men sinning?' wailed the monks.
'We've filled a thousand gilded shrines with bones,
rekindled many an undying fire that died,
renewed St Colman's thumb, St Lactan's arm;
we've edited the lives of ninety saints
and placed among St Patrick's next-of-kin
the forebears of the just who pay their dues;
we've put such curses in St Findlug's mouth
that ulcers budded in the King of Creeve.
And many a time, our chronicles relate,
arms withered, tongues dropped out, eyes lost their
    sight,
when evil men infringed our grazing rights
or made foul jests about our private lives.
But still men sin, they fornicate, they lie,
they dodge, they quibble, and distort the truth.
Ah, saints of Ireland, serve us, who have served!'

The saints said nothing and a hundred years
went by before it all began again.
'How can we stop men sinning?' wailed the monks,
'We've christened all the temperance clubs and guilds
with names of saints. We've built St Moling's school,
St Flann's Infirmary, St Ronan's Bank.
We've edited the saints for boys and girls,
omitting all that's coarse, grotesque, unclean.
And now at last in eighteen fifty-six,
through five years' raffles, carnivals, appeals,
we've reared St Findlug's splendid church at Creeve,
(it cost us all of forty thousand pounds),
copied from one the Bishop saw at Rome,
but up-to-date, with scenes from Findlug's life
in washable Durescin in the nave
and angels holding lacquered gasoliers.
Nearby to mask the hot-water pipes a screen
of costliest malachite and porphyry,

donated by the Mayor of Boston's niece.
And in the sacristy the vestment press
even for the altar-boys is richly scrolled
by boarders of St Findlug's orphanage.
Upon the tympanum mid rich mosaic,
by Messrs Meyer of Munich, Patrick stands,
enthroning Findlug in the See of Creeve,
(he's in Carrara by Maguires of Cork),
while St Lugitha holds the title-deeds.
But still men sin, they fornicate, they lie,
they dodge, they quibble, and distort the truth.
Ah, saints of Ireland, serve us, who have served!'

The saints said nothing and a hundred years
went by before it all began again.
'How can we stop men sinning?' wailed the monks.
'We've taken the lead in sacred scholarship;
we've edited the lives with copious notes
and saints that even the Bollandists accept
we've sometimes queried and ourselves condemned
the passages where solar myth has farced
the text. Why, Canon Keefe, page ninety-four,
note eight, declares St Findlug never lived
and that St Patrick never went to Creeve.
The episode (see Z.C.P. vol. 5) is based
on faulty reading of defective texts.
We do not hide the truth from those who read
the learned monthlies for the Honours Course.
But why confuse the simple, or offend
the kinsmen of the Mayor of Boston's niece,
who lavished masses for her soul's repose?
Henceforward, though, our Bishop is averse
from dedications to the obscurer saints.
He recommends the Roman Calendar.
Though Roman saints are often odd, like ours,
they're better known than our poor Findlug is
and have good standing with the Bollandists,
while much more up-to-date for nursing-homes
are names like Bernadette and Fatima.
But still men sin, they fornicate, they lie,
they dodge, they quibble and distort the truth.
Ah, saints of Ireland, serve us, who have served!'

They moaned like this from habit. All supposed
the saints would take no notice, as before.
But Odran, always tactless and sincere,

poked up his head above the sod and said:
'You don't believe in us. It's just pretence!
Look at the footnotes, never mind the text!
When scholars hint, the vulgar show their hands.
They do not honour us. It's time to leave.
Because I was St Patrick's charioteer,
a bookie used my name to mask his frauds.
St Lachtan's Dairy waters all the milk;
St Ita's Laundry tears the sheets to shreds.
Does Brendan care a rap for Training Ships
or Seamen's Missions? Does the Fire Brigade
need Lassar's patronage? It's all pretence!
You're using us to gild the status quo,
to lend a fake romance to platitude,
to clothe some prelate's lust for consequence,
some builder's greed in pitchpine and cement.'
Then bawled the fiercest of the saints, Fecheen:
'I'm patron of some Convalescent Home,
I, who once seized de Lacy by the leg,
bending to steal the head-stone from my grave.
He ran to Multyfarnham raving mad.'
And Bridget said: 'When Strongbow lay abed,
I flogged him with my crozier till he died.
Ask Canice how de Peipo's archers fared,
who cut his grove at Finglas. Let us go!'

Then all around the coast the sacred rocks
began to float, Cuanna's, Declan's, Mogue's.
St Farnan launched his mighty oaken cross,
posting four saints at each extremity
to chant the psalms. Cauldrons and altar-stones
and floating dolmens teemed in every bay,
St Gobban's anvil, St Molua's tub.

And for the saints that had no private craft
St Brendan brought his fleet to Dingle Bay,
skippered by Ternoc, Malo and Finbarr.
From every townland, lis and rath the saints
drifted and stowed their sacred gear aboard.
And Caeman, Patrick's chamberlain, took charge
and listed all the items in the hold:
St Finnchu's meat-hook and St Gobnait's bees,
the relics Onnchu carried from Clonmore,
two flying croziers and one jaundiced bell,
ten thousand casks of water turned to wine,
great bales of meat made fish and fish made meat.
And meanwhile Ailbe, swineherd of the Pope,
marshalled the sacred livestock on the deck,
the stags that carried bibles on their horns,
the wolves that suckled saints, the dogs that preached,
the lambs that bleated hymns in thieves' insides,
Molaisse's badger, St Columba's crane,
three cocks that crowed for Matins, fourteen birds
that made their nests in cowls. Then fleas,
one case (St Nannan's), and St Finan's lice.
And while they listed, St Molua wept:
'We've lived beside them fifteen hundred years,
bearing the burden that their gods had borne.
We've cheered their loneliness and eased their pain
and veiled with poetry many an ugly deed.
How can we leave with all these precious things?
How will they fare?' St Dubhlitter, the clerk,
replied: 'There's less than you'd suppose down there.
That bale of curses that St Ruan brought
was put near Patrick's blessings in the hold.
They cancelled out precisely. Even the saints
are much reduced. That double bang you heard
was Ternoc meeting Naile on the deck.
Talking of Invernaile's rights and dues
in mutual malediction both dissolved.
Those little puffs of smoke were homonyms,
meeting and merging. Fifteen Colmans fused,
ten Lassars, six misprints jumped overboard.
And fifty, badly mauled by Canon Keefe
as late interpolations, all expired.
Let us be sailing now e'er worse befall.'
And Odran, peering down into the hold,
declared: 'There's nothing much in all this junk
they need regret. The lazy ones, of course,

will always want their cheeses made from stones.
But those with minds and hearts, by reason's light,
in brotherhood ...' but all the saints began
to yawn affectedly: 'Why Mrs Humphrey Ward
said all of that in eighteen eighty-eight.
It's old hat now. Professor E.O. James
has plucked the Golden Bough.' And Findlug said:
'In his last Lenten Pastoral at Creeve,
our bishop showed how modernism is dead.'
But Odran, barely listening, bumbled on:
'I think we saints, in general, symbolise
those inner conflicts, tribal, personal,
the conscious mind has failed to reconcile
and hence externalised. And we survive
through muddled sentiment and failing nerve.'
He whispered absently in Findlug's ear:
'Look up that reference in Canon Keefe!'
St Findlug flinched, turned pale, began to quote
more Lenten Pastoral, abruptly stopped,
then sullenly said: 'Right! But where'll we go?'
And Odran answered: 'To rejoin the gods,
fresh of our flesh, conceived from nothingness,
our kinsmen, whom we routed and replaced,
and now, replaced ourselves, rejoin as friends.
There Lug will take Molua by the hand,
and Bran will welcome Brendan as his mate.
Sardus will call me brother, Hercules
will greet St Erc and from their golden thrones
the Phrygian gods in reverence will rise
to meet the Holy Virgin of Kildare.'
Then Findlug muttered gruffly: 'Let's be gone!'
And soon the great Armada sailed away,
skirting the Dingle coast through Blasket Sound.
And were they bangs or murmurs of the sea?
And was it mist that veiled the fleet from sight
beyond Kilshannig Point? And did they reach,
with saints and stock and sacred gear intact,
the haven of the gods? I do not know.

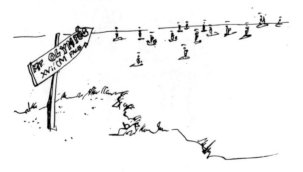

Anonymous

A ballad remembered by the tailor in Eric Cross's classic memoir, The Tailor and Ansty *(1942).*

THE BUTTERMILK LASSES

Come all you young fellows, whoever you be,
Draw nigh with attention and listen to me
It's on the new fashion I'm going to dilate,
That is worn by the buttermilk lasses of late.

Those donkey-bred girls, they must imitate
Each fashion that's worn by the ladies of state.
Their hair they embellish with ribbons and toys,
In order I'm sure for to please the young boys.

And every old woman that has got a dame,
She employs her whole efforts to keep up the game.
She sells them the eggs for to purchase a veil,
And pledges the blanket if all else should fail.

The sour buttermilk they sell by the score,
To purchase a cape or a silk parasol.
It's a jacket and bustle they then must provide,
And a pair of clasped boots their coarse ankles to
    hide.

For fear they are not in full show to be seen,
They must get a silk bonnet in red, blue and green.
You would think in your heart without a word of a lie,
That with ribbons and feathers they're ready to fly.

The finishing strokes are the brown bonny hats,
And the hair decorated with ribbons and plaits.
They're such numerous fashions it's hard to explain,
It fails my exertions them all to retain.

But the latest invention I almost forgot,
Which indeed is the strangest one of the whole lot.
The hoops which are worn, as I understand,
To make them both portly and stately and grand.

For to braze out the gowns, both of muslin and silk
That they purchase the same for the price of the milk.
No person on earth would imagine or think,
That they're fed on potatoes and sour buttermilk.

You'll see these young lasses on each market day,
With their boots in their hands and they trudging
        away.
To spare the light 'lastic that costs half a crown,
They don't put them on till they goes near the town.

It's then they do make a great show on the street,
Though at home they have beds without blanket or
        sheet.
Straw wads with a rug that's both worn and old,
And a cheap English blanket to keep out the cold.

Perhaps they have got but one shirt on their back,
And that without washing, both dirty and black.
And on each of their heels you will find a large kibe,
With a number of cracks that I cannot describe.

At home in the corner you'll find them each day,
With their heels in the ashes and they chatting away.
With the dog at the saucepan, the cat at the spoon,
The hens on the table, and the pig in the room.

Now to conclude and to finish with them,
I hope that these young girls will not me blame.
Because it's in order for to let them know –
That they're a laugh to the public wherever they go.

   and an extra verse composed by the tailor himself:

Now all you young maidens, don't listen to me
For I will incite you to immoralitee
Or unnatural vice or in similar way
Corrupt or deprave you or lead you astray.

Raymond Calvert

The composer of 'Willam Bloat' was a prosperous figure in the Belfast linen trade in the mid twentieth century. This, his only published poem, became extremely popular. It quickly entered the general ballad repertoire and was in consequence often enthusiastically 'improved' by its performers. One of them, indeed, invented a far more effective final couplet for the poem than Calvert would ever have allowed himself to pen:
> *For the razor blade was Dublin made*
> *But the sheet was Belfast linen.*

THE BALLAD OF WILLIAM BLOAT

In a mean abode on the Shankill Road
Lived a man called William Bloat.
He had a wife, the curse of his life,
Who continually got his goat.
So one day at dawn, with her nightdress on,
He cut her bloody throat.

With a razor gash he settled her hash,
Oh never was crime so quick,
But the steady drip on the pillow slip
Of her lifeblood made him sick,
And the pool of gore on the bedroom floor
Grew clotted cold and thick.

And yet he was glad that he'd done what he had,
When she lay there stiff and still,
But a sudden awe of the angry law
Struck his soul with an icy chill.
So to finish the fun so well begun,
He resolved himself to kill.

Then he took the sheet off his wife's cold feet,
And twisted it into a rope,
And he hanged himself from the pantry shelf.
'Twas an easy end, let's hope.
In the face of death with his latest breath,
He solemnly cursed the Pope.

But the strangest turn to the whole concern
Is only just beginnin'.
He went to Hell but his wife got well,
And she's still alive and sinnin',
For the razor blade was foreign made,
But the sheet was Irish linen.

Anonymous
('Tom Moore')

A tasty piece of recent Roscommon verse.

CARROTS FROM CLONOWN

The Spanish love their onions,
The French love their snails,
And if you're up in Iceland,
For breakfast you'll have whales;
Italians like spaghetti
And in long strings get it down,
But in Curraghabull you're sure to find
Some carrots from Clonown.

         Chorus:
Oh they're neat, they're grand to eat;
You can have them for your supper or your tay;
These fine big juicy carrots are so easy to get down
So everyone be sure and get some carrots from
   Clonown.

There is a lovely carrot,
The finest in the town
A fine big juicy carrot
And they grow it in Clonown;
You can boil it, you can stew it,
You can fry it on the pan –
It gives a woman beauty
And put muscles on a man.
They grow them up in Gorrybog,
In heaps of ass manure,
For all disease going
Sure carrots are the cure.
A woman up in Clonmacnoise
Was bald, her head went bare –
She ate some Clonown carrots –
Now her head is full of hair.

I heard about a woman,
Who was in great misery,
Married for some forty years
Couldn't have a family;
She'd been to all the doctors
And took pills – a dozen tins –
She ate the blooming carrots –
And next morning she had twins!
God help the poor small farmer,
He never can relax,
The Government are after him
To pay his yearly tax;
The men who run the EEC
For prices hold the reins –
Let's feed them Clonown carrots
And it might improve their brains.

Anonymous

*Despite the unknown poet's modesty, this colourful portrait
of city life by the river deserves better than to be consigned
to an appendix in Colm Ó Lochlainn's* More Irish Street
Ballads. *The verses appeared in the* Cork Examiner *on
Christmas Eve 1870, some decades before James Joyce's
'Rosalie the Coal Quay Whore' touted for her own 'furtive
swine' in Dublin.*

THE CHANT OF THE COAL QUAY

Were I sublimer than the Grecian rhymer,
Than Peristratus or bold Bonaparte,
Could I when lyrical like Moore that miracle
Endue my dialect with tuneful art,
I'd pen a ditty of the beauteous city
So wise and witty 'twould beget renown,
And like thrush or curlew I'd extend that purlieu
The Coal Quay market in my native town.

O! that's the dwelling where 'tis easy telling
If your sense of smelling is not up to snuff,
You'll find perfume there from flowers that bloom
    there
Sure you'd want six noses to smell enough.
'Tis there the sages of the learned pages
Your sight engages on each bookstand,
The Rule of Foster, great Paradise Lost, or
The Comic Songster – all second hand.

In there the animals in great congregation,
Show great rotation, both horse and hen,
With organ monkeys, dogs, ducks and donkeys,
And Poor Law Guardians and Aldermen.
You'll find great pleasure in jovial measure
While ballad singers in full voice combine,
With whispering lovers and cattle drovers,
A-reconnoiterin' their furtive swine.

GK Chesterton

*Yeats was extensively parodied throughout his career –
sometimes even by confirmed English literary folk like
Chesterton (1874–1936).*

'OLD KING COLE' *from*
VARIATIONS ON AN AIR COMPOSED ON HAVING
TO APPEAR IN A PAGEANT AS OLD KING COLE

Of an old King in a story
    From the grey sea-folk I have heard,
Whose heart was no more broken
    Than the wings of a bird.

As soon as the moon was silver
    And the thin stars began,
He took his pipe and tankard,
    Like an old peasant man.

And three tall shadows were with him
    And came at his command;
And played before him for ever
    The fiddles of fairyland.

And he died in the young summer
    Of the world's desire;
Before our hearts were broken
    Like sticks in a fire.

CHILDREN'S RHYMES

What used to be called 'street rhymes' are now more often heard in playgrounds or in housing estates. We can represent only a very few of them here. The first five below appear in Colette O'Hare's What Do you Feed your Donkey on: Rhymes from a Belfast Childhood *(Collins, 1978), the next two in* Orangeism *by Kevin Haddick-Flynn (Wolfhound Press, 1999), and the last two come from Leslie Daiken's pioneering little book,* Out Goes She *(Dolmen Press, 1963).*

Charlie Chaplin went to France
To teach all the cannibals how to dance,
With a heel, toe, a burlie-o
Miss the rope and out you go.

* * *

Barney Hughes's bread,
Tuppence a loaf,
And sticks to your belly like lead.
Not a bit of wonder
You rift like thunder.
Barney Hughes's bread.

* * *

I sent McCann out
For a can of stout.
McCann came running in,
And said me can was running out.

* * *

Holy Mary Mother of God
Pray for me and Tommy Todd;
I'm a Fenian and he's a Prod,
Holy Mary Mother of God.

* * *

Ah Ma, give us a penny
To see the big giraffe.
He's got a pimple on his willie
Ah Ma, give us a penny
To see the big giraffe.

* * *

Slaughter, Slaughter, Holy Water
We will kill the Papists one by one
We will tear them asunder
Until they lie under
The Protestant boys who follow the drum.

* * *

A Rope, a Rope, to hang the Pope
A pennyworth o' cheeze tae choke him
A pint o' lamp oil tae wash it down
A big hot coal tae roast him.

* * *

Auld Granny Gray
She let me out to play
I can't go near the wa-ter
To hunt the duck away.
Over the garden wall
I let the babby fall
Me mother came out
And gev me a clout

And knocked me over
A bottle of stout.

* * *

Lazy Mary will you get up,
Will you get up, will you get up,
O Lazy Mary will you get up,
And cook yer auld wan's breakfast?

Michael Coady

*'The Carrick Nine' is unique: a modern ballad purportedly
'salvaged from a rubbish skip' in Carrick-on-Suir, County
Tipperary. Here we reprint the text alone, but for further
illumination (and considerable entertainment) it is very
much worth seeking out* One Another *(Gallery Press,
2003), by the poet and writer Michael Coady (b. 1939). In
that book, under the umbrella title of 'Textament', the
verses are rewardingly accompanied by a map and a schol-
arly socioliterary analysis of the work, entitled 'Domains In
Flux: charting context and subtext of "The Carrick Nine".'
Air: 'Preab 'san Ól'.*

THE CARRICK NINE

One pleasant morning in this new millennium
    The summer sun was beaming down,
As a hardy skipper and his companions
    Cast off and sailed out from Carrick town.
They embarked with no premeditation
    Or contemplation of piracy,
They were well-provisioned against dehydration,
    With no inclination to mutiny.

The tide was full and their craft was shipshape
    And decked out bravely in blue and white,
They little thought as they swung downriver
    That this June day wouldn't turn out right.
While other men were slaves to duty
    And tied down to production-lines,
They had the freedom of the river
    This Monday morning of their lives.

'Farewell,' they cried, 'to Carrick Castle,
　　The hill, the bridges and the town,
And *au revoir* to our wives and lovers,
　　Expect us after the sun goes down.
The day is opening out before us,
　　Who know what's waiting around the bend?
The sky is blue and the birds are singing,
　　Long enough we'll all be dead!'

The lower Suir is a noble river,
　　Broad and deep in each bend and reach.
They'd a skipper skilled in navigating
　　Cross-currents where three counties meet.
They struck up shanties like 'Carrickfergus',
　　'A Hard Day's Night' and 'Nancy Spain',
Helped on by copious draughts of cider
　　That served to keep their spirits raised.

By Fiddown Bridge they were in fine fettle
　　And there decided to sail on,
They throttled up for their destination –
　　The Déise city of Waterford.
The Latin motto of that metropolis
　　Means the city that was never sacked –
The Carrick Nine were set to challenge
　　Its reputation as *urbs intact'*.

On they went by Rockett's Castle
　　Then swung north in the Long Reach
Where they say a Viking longship
　　Lies buried fifteen fathoms deep;
Past Grannagh Castle sacked by Cromwell
　　Then east by the rock of Bilberry
Until standing high on the horizon
　　Were Gracedieu and Mount Misery.

When they reached the city all hands were famished
　　With liquid rations almost drained,
Then their lookout spied upon the quayside
　　A large consignment of kegs of ale.
The Nine were not men prone to plunder,
　　They were no bloodthirsty privateers,
But that apparition was a fierce temptation
　　To mortal men with a lust for beer.

They'd a keg on board and another hoisted
    When suddenly all hell broke loose;
That yard was under intense surveillance
    And a Garda squad car sped into view.
'Cast off me hearties!' the skipper shouted,
    'We'll quench our thirst on Tinhalla Quay,
Where our forefathers often landed salmon
    And brewed up gallons of strong black tea!'

The Carrick Nine ploughed off upriver
    Thinking that they were safe afloat,
But the men in blue were out to get them –
    They straight-away commandeered a boat.
So here beginning was a chase most thrilling
    That would continue for several hours,
This naval tussle would test the muscle
    And sailing skills of the civil powers.

The pursuing Gardaí grew alarmed as
    The Carrick craft seemed to pull ahead;
They radioed for reinforcements
    And declared a high security alert.
They suspected big-time operators
    Dealing in cargoes of contraband –
There fleeing raiders must be captured
    And brought to justice upon the land.

The Harbour Board was soon alerted
    And the South-East Fishery patrol,
An Slua Muirí and a helicopter
    Went on standby in Waterford.
Police were summoned from around the region
    With urgent orders to waste no time:
Thirty lawmen came swiftly speeding
    To meet the threat of the Carrick Nine.

The wildlife never knew such action
    In the calm expanse of that waterway;
Swans and salmon were in a panic
    And trout were traumatized that day.
Boats came racing and making waves as
    Angry expletives were employed –
Words deleterious and names nefarious
    Flew fast and furious across the tide.

As the chase proceeded it became apparent
    There was no escape for the Carrick craft,
For it was trapped in a pincer movement
    With the Law advancing both fore and aft.
Boathooks were brandished at close quarters
    There were some dangerous attempts to ram,
One Garda tumbled into the river
    But happily came to no harm.

Pollrone's the place where the nine were captured
    It'll be remembered forevermore;
Statements were taken and charges drafted –
    This escapade would end up in court.
The Carrick Nine made their way homeward,
    Sick, sore and sorry to face their wives;
Their trip had ended in disaster
    But luckily with no loss of lives.

When it came to court the lawyers wrangled
    About jurisdiction and piracy,
The saline content of river water
    And whether 'High Seas' embraced estuary.
Statutes were dusted dating back to
    The Great Armada and Francis Drake,
But the accused men pleaded the affair was simply
    A harmless spree and a big mistake.

In his summing up the judge was scathing
    About the waste of Garda time
And all the manpower that had been mustered
    To apprehend the Carrick Nine.
He imposed fines and applied probation,
    The sentences were rather light,
Since the only losses were a keg of Smithwick's
    And a sergeant's cap that sank out of sight.

Outside the court there was pandemonium
    And loud commotion as the men walked free.
The media went into feeding frenzy
    With microphones and photography.
There were mobiles trilling and reporters milling
    To grab some in-depth interviews;
This had the makings of a movie
    Or a Prime Time special after the News.

The names of all could be related
    But I'll just mention their captain, Ben,
He made the papers and raised the flag for
    A famous family of fishermen.
Carrick people know their boatmen
    Are not wanting when there's need,
They've often come to people's rescue
    In times of river emergency.

Fair play also for those who're sworn
    To be our guardians of the peace,
None of us could walk in safety
    Without their presence on our streets.
So spare a thought for those policemen
    Who were not trained for naval tasks,
And ne'er before set foot on water
    To apprehend a pirate craft.

Now to conclude and close my story
    Concerning history and river lore,
God's blessing on our intrepid mariners
    Who boldly went where none did before.
Their dash and daring was quite amazing
    As delineated in these lines,
Sing on posterity to ensure longevity
    For the name and fame of the Carrick Nine.

Anonymous

*An old ballad popularised by Tommy Makem (b. 1932), the
'other' member of the Clancy Brothers.*

THE COBBLER

Oh, me name is Dick Darby, I'm a cobbler;
I served me time at old camp;
Some call me an old agitator
But now I'm resolved to repent.

    Chorus:
With me ingtwing of an ingthing of an idoh,
With me ingtwing of an ingthing of an iday,
With me rooboooboo rooboooboo randy,
And me lab stone keeps beating away.

Now, my father was hung for sheep stealing;
My mother was burned for a witch;
My sister's a dandy housekeeper,
And I'm a mechanical switch.

Ah, it's forty long years I have travelled
All by the contents of me pack;
Me hammers, me awls and me pinchers,
I carry them all on me back.

Oh, my wife she is humpy, she's lumpy;
My wife she's the devil, she's black,
And no matter what I may do with her,
Her tongue it goes clickety-clack.

It was early one fine summer's morning,
A little before it was day,
I dipped her three times in the river,
And carelessly bade her 'Good day!'

Anonymous

*Colm Ó Lochlainn picked up this oddity from a relative
in Waterford.*

THE COD LIVER OIL

I'm a young married man,
And I'm tired of my life,
For lately I married
An ailing young wife.
She does nothing all day,
Only sit down and sigh,
Saying, 'I wish to the Lord
That I only could die.'

Till a friend of my own
Came to see me one day,
And told me my wife
Was just pining away;
But he afterwards told me
That she would get strong
If I'd buy her a bottle
From Doctor de Jongh.

So I bought her a bottle
'Twas just for to try,
And the way that she scoffed it,
You'd swear she was dry;
I bought her another,
It went just the same,
Till I own she's got Cod
Liver Oil on the brain.

My house it resembles
A big doctor's shop,
With bottles and bottles
From bottom to top;
And when in the morning
The kettle's a-boil,
Ye'd swear it was singing out
'Cod Liver Oil!'

O Doctor, dear Doctor,
O Doctor de Jongh,
Your Cod Liver Oil
Is so pure and so strong,
I declare to my life,
I'll go down in the soil,
If my wife don't stop drinking
Your Cod Liver Oil.

Brian Coffey

In his younger days at least, Brian Coffey (1905–1995) was one of Ireland's few surrealist poets. This animated example of Irish avant-garde verse appeared in 1937.

KALLIKLES

'As if a brick had fallen on my head
from a great height, I fell in love;
someone come from behind with a shove
kicked me career and all down the water-shed.

'Stung now, I find it profits to reflect
on the diverse things may happen to man,
much in the way a wife must suspect
from empty pockets another also-ran.

'I think the roses never grow so red
as near a dye-works. And I remember
I wanted to be a sailor. When I'm dead
let it rain stink, if it wants, in December.

'But to continue meditating on life:
there are a number of ways of irritating people;
observe the big black woman with the knife
chasing Poe's raven up the steeple.

'You may wonder why the grass is green.
Nothing is green but thinking makes it so.
You may ask why even dogs do dream.
Pray tell me what results you have to show.

'Thus, you will observe often a man set at wine
in a four-square tavern for no better reason
than that he saw the Silk of the Kine
in a night-club accusing him of high treason.

'So we can all recall a time spent on sardine-oil
when the green leaves seemed greener than usual.'
'PADDY!'
          'Love's at the door, Sir, promising turmoil;
I'll be going now, if you don't mind, quiet-like, casual.'

Anonymous
('Adolescens')

A mock-archaic account from 1942 of evening activities at St Columba's College, a boarding school in the foothills of the Dublin mountains.

THE COLLEGE'S SATURDAY NIGHT

The glare on Kilmashogue awoke the Burghers of
    Dundrum,
Who heard reverberations as of a Mighty Drum.
The Mothers whispered gently, as their children woke
    in fright,
'Hush! Hush! My Sweet, be not afeard, 'tis College
    Gala Night.'
And in the Pubs look quickly up the Drinkers, Young
    and Old,

And Mumble in their Beards, and think of fearsome
    tales are told
Of what the Mad Young Collegers do when their
    Thirst for Knowledge
Has for One Night at least been slaked, and one and
    all the College
Begins the Gay Mad Revelrie that happens once a
    week.
No more doth German, Maths or French or even
    Extra Greek
But Saturday Night Activities hold their triumphant
    sway.
'Begone Dull Care!,' the College cries, and screams
    'Let us be Gay.'
In Sensuous Whirl of Carpentry, or Paint's Seductive
    Gleam,
Or Extra Artists' Flashing Brush, Confusion reigns
    supreme.
How lucky are they when they have such Gay
    Delights as these
To gratify their jaded tastes, their Free Young Hearts
    to please.
The Kindness of Authority by this is clearly seen,
Not Once, but Often they enjoy a lecture from a
    Dean.

Anonymous

*This eccentric early history of the country, kindly sent to us
by an acquaintance, was apparently written in about 1800
by a wandering poet – or 'file' (verse 9).*

A COMPLETE ACCOUNT OF THE VARIOUS
COLONIZATIONS OF IRELAND
AS DELIVERED BY THE SAGE FINTAN

Should any enquire about Eirinn,
It is I who can tell him the truth,
Concerning the deeds of each daring
Invader, since Time was a youth.

First Cassir, Bith's venturesome daughter,
Came here o'er the Eastern Sea;
And fifty fair damsels she brought her –
To solace her warriors three.

Bith died at the foot of his mountain,
And Ladra on top of his height;
And Cassir by Boyle's limpid fountain,
Ere rushed down the Flood in its might.

For a year, while the waters encumber
The Earth, at Tul-Tunna of strength,
I slept, none enjoyed such sweet slumber
As that which I woke from at length.

When Parthalan came to the island,
From Greece, in the Eastern land,
I welcomed him gaily to my land,
And feasted the whole of his band.

Again, when Death seized on the strangers,
I roamed the land, merry and free,
Both careless and fearless of dangers,
Till blithe Nemed came o'er the sea.

The Firbolgs and roving Fir-Gallions,
Came next like the waves in their flow;
The Fir-Donnans arrived in battalions,
And landed in Erris – Mayo.

Then came the wise Tuatha Dé Danann,
Concealed in black clouds from their foe;
I feasted with them near the Shannon,
Though that was a long time ago.

After them came the Children of Mile,
From Spain, o'er the Southern waves:
I lived with the tribes as their File
And chanted the deeds of their braves.

Time ne'er my existence could wither,
From Death's grasp I always was freed:
Till Patrick, the Christian, came hither
To spread the Redeemer's pure creed.

My name it is Fintan, the Fair-man,
Of Bochra, the son, you must know it;
I lived through the Flood in my lair, man,
I am now an illustrious poet.

Matthew Concanen

When A Match at Football, or The Irish Champions, *an
ambitious mock-heroic poem by Matthew Concanen (1701-
1749) appeared in 1721, Alexander Pope's* The Rape of the
Lock *was only a decade old, and the Irishman's achieve-
ment was ignored by posterity. But literary fashion is
always a game of two halves, and – who knows? – some
day the work may be the centrepiece of the Historical Soccer
Studies course at the University of Gorey ...
Here is a short extract:*

'A TACKLE ON TERENCE'
(*from*) A MATCH AT FOOTBALL

First Paddy struck the ball, John stopt its course,
And sent it backward with redoubl'd force;
Dick met, and meeting smote the light machine,
Reptile it ran, and skimm'd along the green,
'Till Terence stopp'd – with gentle strokes he trolls
(Th' obedient ball in short excursions rolls),
Then swiftly runs and drives it o'er the plain;
Follow the rest, and chase the flying swain.

So have I seen upon a frosty day
(By fowlers frighted, or in quest of prey),
Skim through the air, whole coveys of curlew,
One only leading, and the rest pursue.

Paddy, whose fleeter pace outstript the rest,
Came up, and caught the champion by the vest;
Between his legs, an artful crook he twin'd,
And almost fell'd him ere he look'd behind.
Norah with horror saw the destin'd wile,
Grew pale, and blush'd, and trembled for a while;
But when she saw him grasp the warrior's hand,
And face to face the grappling rivals stand,
What diff'ring pangs her anxious bosom tear,
Now flush'd with hope, now chill'd with sudden fear?
Paddy, to see the champion disengaged,
For so well-form'd a trip, with fury rag'd,
Bounds to pursue the ball; but Terence stopt,
Athwart him flung his leg, and down he dropt.

So some tall pine which many years has stood,
The pride of trees, and mistress of the wood;
Braves for a while the strokes, and seems to foil
The piercing axe, and mock the peasant's toil;
'Till lopp'd at length by one fell dexterous wound,
It falls and spreads its ruins all around …

TW Connor

*TW Connor, who died in 1936, enjoyed international success
as a writer of music-hall songs and burlesque monologues:
we think (and hope) that he – she? – was of Irish extraction
at least, but have failed to uncover any clinching biograph-
ical details. Information will be welcomed. These verses
from 1895 surely never sought immortality, but earn it in the
last two lines.*

SHE WAS ONE OF THE EARLY BIRDS

It was at the Pantomime
That Mabel and I did meet,
She was in the ballet, front row,
And I in a five shilling seat.
She was dressed like a dicky bird,
Beautiful wings she had on

With a figure divine, I wished she were mine –
On her I was totally gone.

She was a sweet little dicky bird,
'Chip, chip, chip,' she went.
Sweetly she sang to me
Till all my money was spent.
Then she went off song –
We parted on fighting terms –
She was one of the early birds,
And I was one of the worms.

John Costello

In 1860 the editor of The Drogheda Argus *wrote these
verses to celebrate a new stand at the local racecourse.*

BELLEWSTOWN HILL

If respite you'd borrow from turmoil or sorrow,
I'll tell you the secret of how it is done;
'Tis found in this statement of all the excitement
That Bellewstown knows when the races come on.
Make one of a party whose spirits are hearty,
Get a seat on a trap that is safe not to spill,
In its well pack a hamper, then off for a scamper,
And Hurroo for the glories of Bellewstown Hill.

On the road how they dash on, Rank, Beauty and
    Fashion,
It Banagher bangs, by the table of war,
From the coach of the Quality, down to the Jollity
Jogging along on an old low-backed car.
Though straw cushions are placed, two feet thick at
    the laste,
Its jigging and jumping to mollify, still
The cheeks of my Nelly are shakin' like jelly
From the jolting she gets as she jogs to the Hill.

In the tents play the pipers, the fiddlers and fifers,
Those rollicking lilts such as Ireland best knows;
While Paddy is prancing, his colleen is dancing
Demure, with her eyes quite intent on her toes.

More power to you, Mickey! faith your foot isn't
   sticky,
But bounds from the boards like a pea from a quill.
Oh. 'twould cure a rheumatic – he would jump up
   ecstatic
At 'Tatter Jack Walsh' upon Bellewstown Hill.

Oh, 'tis there 'neath the haycocks, all splendid like
   paycocks,
In chattering groups that the Quality dine;
Sitting cross-legged like tailors the gentlemen dealers
In flattering spout and come out mighty fine.
And the gentry from Navan and Cavan are havin',
'Neath the shade of the trees, an Arcadian quadrille.
All we read in the pages of pastoral ages
Tells of no scene like this upon Bellewstown Hill.

Arrived at the summit, the view that you come at
From etherealized Mourne to where Tara ascends,
There's no scene in our sireland, dear Ireland, old
   Ireland,
To which Nature more exquisite loveliness lends.
And the soil 'neath your feet has a memory sweet
The patriots' deeds they hallow it still;
Eighty-two's Volunteers (would today see their peers?)
Marched past in review upon Bellewstown Hill.

But hark! there's a shout – the horses are out –
'Long the ropes, on the strand, what a hullabaloo!
To old Crockafotha, the people that dot the
Broad plateau around are all for a view.
'Come, Ned, my tight fellow, I'll bet on the Yellow!'
'Success to the Green! we'll stand by it still!'
The uplands and hollows they're skimming like
   swallows
Till they flash past the post upon Bellewstown Hill.

Anonymous

*A chapbook song of the 1780s, taken from Andrew
Carpenter's ground-breaking collection,* Verse in English
from Eighteenth-Century Ireland *(1998). As Carpenter
points out,* A chusla se sthere *(verse 2) is a common Irish*

endearment in garbled form, and asafoetadu *(verse 4) a*
garlic-flavoured gum.

THE COUGHING OLD MAN

Each female so pretty in country and city,
I pray you will pity a languishing maid,
That is daily vexed and nightly perplexed,
All by my old husband – I wish he were dead.
He's cross grain'd and crooked and doating stupid,
And has no more sense than a young sucking calf,
Altho' he lies by me he ne'er can enjoy me,
For still when he is noodling he is killed with the cough.

The very first night that he came to bed to me,
I longed for a trial at Venus's game,
But to my sad vexation and consternation,
His hautboy was feeble & weak in the main.
For instead of pleasing he only kept teazing;
To him then I turned my back in a huff,
But still he did cry, 'twill do by-and-by,
A chusla se sthere! I am killed with the cough.

This doating old creature a remnant of nature,
His shins are so sharp as the edge of a knife,
His knees they are colder than snow on a mountain,
He stands more in need of a nurse than a wife;
I by him sit weeping whilst he lies a sleeping,
Like a hog in a sty he does grunt and puff,
A wheezing and harking both sneezing and farting,
And worse than all that he's killed with the cough.

His breath it does stink like asafoetadu,
His blobbring and slobbring I can't bear,
For each night when I lie beside him,
He must have a spitting cup placed on his chair;
His nose and his chin are joined together,
His tawny old skin is yellow and tough,
Both trembling and shaking like one in the ague,
Still smothering and spitting and killed with the cough.

For sake of cursed money my father has undone me,
By making me wed this doating old man,
Altho' some might shame me, what Maid can blame
    me,

To crown him with horns as soon as I can;
What signifies treasure without any pleasure,
I'm young and would have enjoyed enough,
And not to be tied to a gouty old fellow,
That's withered and worn and killed with the cough.

Since fortune to me has proved so cruel,
In brief my intention to you I'll relate.
If he does not alter and fare the better,
No longer on him I mean to wait.
I'll have a look out for some rousing young fellow,
That's able to give me some reason to laugh;
If such I can find than I'll swap my old cuckold,
And pitch to the vengeance himself and his cough.

Anonymous

*A famous old rebel song from the end of the eighteenth cen-
tury. Various terms may need explanation: 'Hessians' (verse
1) were – or were named after – German mercenaries in
English service; 'gallus' (verse 3), from 'gallows', here simply
means 'very'; to take 'leg-bail' (verse 5) was to escape from
custody; to 'cant' (verse 6) was to sell by auction, while in
the final verse 'gommach' means an eejit and 'Dhrimindhu'
(Irish: druimeann dubh) is not only a black cow with a
white back but also a nickname for Ireland.*

THE COW ATE THE PIPER

In the year ninety-eight, when our troubles were great,
It was treason to be a Milesian.
I can never forget the big black whiskered set
That history tells us were Hessians.
In them heart breaking times we had all sorts of
    crimes,
As murder never was rifer.
On the hill of Glencree not an acre from me,
Lived bould Denny Byrne, the piper.

Neither wedding nor wake was worth an old shake,
If Denny was not first invited,
For at emptying kegs or squeezing the bags
He astonished as well as delighted.

In such times poor Denny could not earn a penny,
Martial law had a sting like a viper –
It kept Denny within till his bones and his skin
Were a-grin through the rags of the piper.

'Twas one heavenly night, with the moon shining
    bright,
Coming home from the fair of Rathangan,
He happened to see, from the branch of a tree,
The corpse of a Hessian there hanging;
Says Denny, 'These rogues have fine boots, I've no
    brogues,'
He laid on the heels such a griper,
They were so gallus tight, and he pulled with such
    might,
Legs and boots came away with the piper.

So he tucked up the legs and he took to his pegs,
Till he came to Tim Kavanagh's cabin,
'By the powers', says Tim, 'I can't let you in,
You'll be shot if you stop out there rappin'.'
He went round to the shed, where the cow was in
    bed,
With a wisp he began for to wipe her –
They lay down together on the seven foot feather,
And the cow fell a-hugging the piper.

The daylight soon dawned, Denny got up and
    yawned,
Then he dragged on the boots of the Hessian:
The legs, by the law! he threw them on the straw,
And he gave them leg-bail on his mission.
When Tim's breakfast was done he sent out his son
To make Denny lep like a lamp-lighter –
When two legs there he saw, he roared like a daw
'Oh! daddy, de cow eat de piper.'

'Sweet bad luck to the baste, she'd a musical taste,'
Says Tim, 'to go eat such a chanter,
Here Pádraic, avic, take this lump of a stick,
Drive her up to Glenealy, I'll cant her.'
Mrs Kavanagh bawled – the neighbours were called,
They began for to humbug and jibe her,
To the churchyard she walks with the legs in a box,
Crying out, 'We'll be hanged for the piper.'

The cow then was drove just a mile or two off,
To a fair by the side of Glenealy,
And the crathur was sold for four guineas in gold
To the clerk of the parish, Tim Daly.
They went into a tent, and the luck-penny spent
(For the clerk was a woeful old swiper),
Who the divil was there, playing the Rakes of Kildare,
But their friend, Denny Byrne, the piper.

Then Tim gave a bolt like a half-broken colt,
At the piper he gazed like a gommach;
Says he, 'By the powers, I thought these eight hours,
You were playing in Dhrimindhu's stomach.'
But Denny observed how the Hessian was served,
So they all wished Nick's cure to the viper,
And for grá that they met, their whistles they wet,
And like devils they danced round the piper.

Maurice James Craig

*The architectural historian, poet and lover of mausoleums
and cats was born in Belfast in 1919. These sardonic verses so
appealed to Brendan Behan that he put them into his book of
chat about Ireland, Brendan Behan's Island (1962).*

BALLAD TO A TRADITIONAL REFRAIN

Red brick in the suburbs, white horse on the wall,
Eyetalian marbles in the City Hall:
O stranger from England, why stand so aghast?
May the Lord in His mercy be kind to Belfast.

This jewel that houses our hopes and our fears
Was knocked up from the swamp in the last hundred
    years;
But the last shall be first and the first shall be last:
May the Lord in His mercy be kind to Belfast.

We swore by King William there'd never be seen
An All-Irish Parliament at College Green,
So at Stormont we're nailing the flag to the mast:
May the Lord in His mercy be kind to Belfast.

O the bricks they will bleed and the rain it will weep,
And the damp Lagan fog lull the city to sleep;
It's to hell with the future and live on the past:
May the Lord in His mercy be kind to Belfast.

A lugubrious epigram from a 1948 collection.

THOUGHTS ON CAUSALITY

Run over by an ambulance?
Your case might well be worse,
For many a man has been by chance
Run over by a hearse.

Anthony Cronin

The image of the poet Anthony Cronin (b. 1928) attending Leopardstown Races with his friend the novelist Francis Stuart has attained a kind of mythic quality in literary circles; in this poem, however, as the 1940s reluctantly give way to the 1950s, the sport is confined to the bookies and pubs of central Dublin. The bookie's premises in South King Street was named after Fairway, winner of the St Leger in 1928. In 1949 Strathspey won the Cesarewitch, by which time the Irish grey Impeccable (b. 1944) had run the 15 wins of its illustrious career.

'FAIRWAY'S' FARAWAY

At six-to-four and five-to-two
The sun-flecked winners raced
Across the green grass far away
While up and down we paced.

At Kempton Park and Redcar,
Impeccable and Strathspey
With summer all around them
Galloped through cheers that day.
Torn tickets, cigarette stubs,
Two up and one to come,
A square of sunlight laid upon
Dirty linoleum.

The third leg third at ten-to-one,
We blink in the light once more.
Cool consolation waits beyond
MacArdle's open door.

A dray rolls down South King Street,
The setts are warm outside,
A faint sea breeze in Stephen's Green
Ruffles the typists' pride.

O endless August afternoons,
O grave reality:
Motes in the sun and melancholy
Stretch of eternity.

Jimmy Crowley

A modern song extolling the celebrated Cork delicacy. 'Me daza' in the chorus is Cork slang for 'very good', and the final Irish phrase means 'and we'll leave it there.' Verse 3 alludes to the fact that, only hours before his assassination, Michael Collins treated his family and entourage to a small barrel, or 'half tierce', of another famous local product, the powerful porter known as 'Clonakilty Wrastler'.

CLONAKILTY BLACKPUDDING

Way down in Clonakilty in the year of '89
The locomotive Banba came chugging down the line
On board sat Philip Harrington bound for culinary
    fame:
This place looks good to make me pud; I think I'll call
    the same –

Chorus:
Clonakilty Blackpudding, 'tis me daza, full of pep,
To put the lead back in your pencil and the spring
    back in your step.
Heaven knows what herbs and spices are inside the
    saucy skin
But it brings a smile to Erin's Isle – *agus fágfaimíd
    mar sin.*

The man who made the motorcars from Ballina-
    scarthy way,
Young Henry Ford who tempered gold from cold
    black steel, they say;
Said the painter in the foundry – Which color, Henry,
    pray?
'Tis equal, Jack, once you make it black like that tasty
    tack, said he.

And when the hills of Carbery with ricochets did ring
And the Black and Tans and Auxies stalked the
    column in the glen
Up spoke our own Big Fellow saying – Here's rations
    for ye, men!
There's a half a tierce of Wrastler, you can guess
    what's in the fin!

Salute, ye sons of rebel Cork, the warriors of yore
Who donned the blood and bandage in fame for ever
    more –
Blithe Christy Ring, brave Thady Quill, those hurling
    heroes bold –
What do you think sustained 'em, boys, and fortified
    their souls?

Final Chorus:
Clonakilty Blackpudding, 'tis me daza, full of pep,
To put the lead back in your pencil and the spring
    back in your step.
No one knows what Edward Twomey puts inside
    that saucy skin
But he brings a smile to Erin's Isle – *agus fágfaimíd
mar sin.*

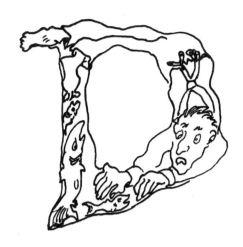

William Dawson

*For years after the kidnap in 1923 by anti-Treaty rebels of
Oliver St John Gogarty, Senator and Surgeon, this ballad,
written for the Arts Club, passed from hand to hand in
Dublin.*

THE LAY OF OLIVER GOGARTY

Come all ye bould Free Staters now and listen to my
    lay,
And pay a close attention, please, to what I've got to
    say;
For 'tis the Tale of a Winter's Night, last January year,
When Oliver St John Gogarty swam down the Salmon
    Weir.

As Oliver St John Gogarty one night sat in his home,
A-writin' of prescriptions or composin' of a poem,
Up rolled a gorgeous Rolls-Royce car and out a lady
    jumped
And at Oliver St John Gogarty's hall door she loudly
    thumped.

'O Oliver St John Gogarty,' said she, 'Now please
    come quick
For in a house some miles away a man lies mighty
    sick.'

Yet Oliver St John Gogarty to her made no reply,
But with a dextrous facial twist he gently closed one eye.

'O Oliver St John Gogarty, come let yourself be led,'
Cried a couple of maskèd ruffians, puttin' guns up to
    his head.
'I'm with you, boys,' cried he, 'but first, give me my
    big fur coat,
And also let me have a scarf – my special care's the
    throat.'

They shoved him in the Rolls-Royce car and swiftly
    sped away;
What route they followed Oliver St John Gogarty can't
    say,
But they reached a house at Islandbridge and locked
    him in a room,
And said, 'Oliver St John Gogarty, prepare to meet
    your doom.'

Said he, 'Give me some minutes first to settle my
    affairs,
And let me have some moments' grace to say my last
    night's prayers.'
To this appeal his brutal guard was unable to say nay,
He was so amazed that Oliver St John Gogarty could
    pray.

Said Oliver St John Gogarty, 'My coat I beg you hold.'
The half-bewildered scoundrel then did as he was told.
Before he twigged what game was up, the coat was
    round his head
And Oliver St John Gogarty into the night had fled.

The rain came down like bullets, and the bullets came
    down like rain,
As Oliver St John Gogarty the river bank did gain;
He plunged into the ragin' tide and swam with
    courage bold,
Like brave Horatius long ago in the fabled days of old.

Then landin' he proceeded through the famous
    Phaynix Park;
The night was bitter cold and what was worse,
    extremely dark;

But Oliver St John Gogarty to this paid no regard,
Till he found himself a target for our gallant Civic
    Guard.

Cried Oliver St John Gogarty, 'A Senator am I!
The rebels I've tricked, the river I've swum and sorra
    the word's a lie.'
As they clad and fed the hero bold, said the sergeant
    with a wink,
'Faith, then, Oliver St John Gogarty, ye've too much
    bounce to sink.'

Anonymous

A curiosity, remembered in Today We Will Only Gossip
(1964), the autobiography of Beatrice, Lady Glenavy.

'DE VALERA HAD A CAT'

De Valera had a cat
Who sat upon the fender,
Every time she heard a shot
She shouted 'No surrender'.

Anonymous

*The first of two starkly contrasting historical views of
Dublin, this Victorian street ballad is a rose-tinted view of
the capital of a prosperous Ireland, a city apparently in love
with gambling.*

'THE DELIGHTS OF DUBLIN'

Tipp'rary breeds a hardy lot,
    Tight-fisted with their money;
From Suir to Shannon shrewd and hot,
    They smile as sweet as honey!
Grass heifers Meath, Roscommon ewes
    Will give you all in plenty;
From Cork fine girls you may choose,
    Fat, fair, and under twenty!

But the Dublin girl that's born an' bred,
 Above all Ireland holds her head,
Stiff upper lip's her beauty.
  No holy poke, she likes a joke,
She shies at nayther drink nor smoke,
 An' at cards she knows her duty.
Each afternoon in Grafton Street,
 She's gorgeous in her raiment;
Puts on her bit at Leopardstown,
 And sweetly takes her payment!
Here's Granua Aile, boys! Drink her down!
 Quick end to all her troublin'!
May beauty, wit, an' wisdom crown
 Her Parliament in Dublin!

If Down an' Derry men are shrewd,
 'Tis Sweet Kildare for courting!
If Antrim beats the North for sense,
 East Cork's the place for sporting!
A Connaught man is like a hare
 So sly, so fond of dodging!
The Wexford man is slow and sure,
 Each pound in bank he's lodging!
But the Dublin boy that's born an' bred,
 Above 'em all high holds his head,
For swagger, sport, an' cunning!
 He's neither North, South, East, nor West,
But a blend of all that each holds best,
 An' the tips he gets are stunning:
To Fairyhouse each Eastertide

With Madge or Tess or Nancy,
Six on each outside car, he'll ride,
    An' freely back his fancy!
Here's Granua Aile, boys! Drink her down!
    Quick end to all her troublin'!
May beauty, wit, and wisdom crown
    Her Parliament in Dublin!

Anonymous

*Although it was the eighteenth century when this was
written (or rather adapted from John Bancks' 'Description
of London'), the Dublin portrayed here was little different
two centuries later – and perhaps even now things have not
changed as much as we like to think.*

DESCRIPTION OF DUBLIN

Mass-houses, churches, mixt together;
Streets unpleasant in all weather.
The church, the four courts, and hell contiguous;
Castle, College green, and custom-house gibbous.

Few things here are to tempt ye:
Tawdry outsides, pockets empty:
Five theatres, little trade, and jobbing arts,
Brandy, and snuff-shops, post-chaises, and carts.

Warrants, bailiffs, bills unpaid;
Masters of their servants afraid;
Rogues that daily rob and cut men;
Patriots, gamesters, and footmen.

Lawyers, Revenue-officers, priests, physicians;
Beggars of all ranks, age and conditions,
Worth scarce shews itself upon the ground;
Villainy both with applause and profit crown'd.

Women lazy, drunken, loose;
Men in labour slow, of wine profuse:
Many a scheme that the public must rue it:
This is Dublin, if you knew it.

Anonymous
('KO')

Writers of light verse often mock the posturings of more 'serious' poets. These scornful lines were published in University College, Dublin, in the 1920s.

DITTY

I'm a poet, God help me, and I must cry!
Genius goes with a watery eye.
With a watery eye,
And a big bow tie;
I'm a poet, God help me, and I must cry!

Morgan Dockrell

A somewhat similar attitude to poetic pretension lies behind this recent satire by Morgan Dockrell (b. 1939), an indefatigable campaigner for the old virtues of rhythm and rhyme in poetry.

PRIZE TIPS ...

To write PRIZE POETRY these days
    Is really very easy.
Some major faults you must erase –
    Old habits slick and sleazy.

COMMANDMENT ONE: THOU SHALT NOT RHYME.
    Detestable tradition.
For RHYMING is the greatest CRIME
    In MODERN COMPETITION.

COMMANDMENT TWO: THOU SHALT NOT SCAN.
    This defect shows iniquity,
Revealing that abhorrent plan
    Of HONOURING ANTIQUITY.

COMMANDMENT THREE: REVERE OBSCURITY,
    Brings benefits immeasurable,
Since Modern Poets of MATURITY
    Do NOT write poems pleasurable.

So take these MODERN HINTS on board,
    Let old fads decompose.
Join with the shapeless, thoughtless horde
Who write TRUNCATED PROSE.
And when you've closed MIND, EARS and EYES
You qualify TO WIN A PRIZE.

A whiff of Realpolitik. This satire features Veronica Suther-
land, Her Excellency the British Ambassador to Ireland from
1995 to 1999, who radically reformed the guest list for the
annual Horse Show Party at Glencairn, the Ambassadorial
Private Residence. It was written after an article appeared
in The Times *highlighting the fact that the traditional*
Anglo-Irish guests were no longer to be made welcome there.

THEY HAVE THEIR EXITS

Ochone, ochone! Just hear our wails
To learn we're ousted for the Gaels!
No more that weakish G & T
By courtesy of HMG.
No more for us with wife and bairn
The Horse Show Party at *Glencairn*.

It matters not that Grandpa Tom
Was decorated at the *Somme,*
That George (his brother) didn't quail
Immersed in mud at *Passchendaele;*
That cousin Percy didn't shirk
His Duty, fleeing to *Dunkirk.*
Better for us to row by row
Have gathered in the GPO.
H.E. decides we've no more clout,
Which means that socially we're OUT.

Let's eavesdrop on our brusque H.E.: –

'No Anglo-Irish guests for me!
As pragmatists we serve the State;
Our former foes we cultivate.
Non-influential 'Friends' we ditch …
That's *Staatsräson,* it keeps us rich.'
(Prolonged applause the room now fills

To hail H.E.'s linguistic skills.)
'Hence I don't say, "For ties residual
To Glencairn drinks, old 'friends' I bid you all."
Our loyalty's akin to voting;
Not tied but permanently floating.
Ourselves the Greatest Losers, we
Shun "Friends" now low on Punts and P.
Our Policy is to betray
Supporters once they've had their day.
The New-Look-Lot? There's Seán O'Shea
With contacts in the IRA.
But don't let's worry, he can sign
Fat contracts on the dotted line…
Let's not enquire his New-Wealth Sources!
OUT with the chaps with tweeds and horses!
There's our new "Friend", Herr Baron Wank,
With contacts in the *Bundesbank*.
He's buying up Cork, is ex-SS,
Served time for Crimes … but I digress …
Old principles must always fade
When HMG considers TRADE.
OUT with those Anglo-Irish runts.
IN with the Paddies, full of *PUNTS*.
OUT with that bunch who still are trading
On Names and Pasts which fast are fading …'

She rants … and sycophantic cheers
From moneyed minions fill her ears.

JACUZZI FANTASY

In the Jacuzzi pool I sit
With youthful female forms in plenty,
Which makes me feel so young and fit,
I fantasize once more I'm TWENTY.

But common sense resumes its sway …
Time with his precious gifts is thrifty.
I seem to hear those females say:
'Who *is* that *ghastly* man of FIFTY?'

JP Donleavy

In The Ginger Man, *the first novel by JP Donleavy (b. 1926) published in Paris in 1955, the very Behanesque Barney Berry rolls up on 'a flood of song', which includes these two charming verses:*

'MARY MALONEY'

Mary Maloney's beautiful arse
Is a sweet apple of sin.
Give me Mary's beautiful arse
And a full bottle of gin.

... and ...

'DID YOUR MOTHER ...'

Did your mother come from Jesus
With her hair as white as snow
And the greatest pair of titties
The world did ever know?

Charles Donnelly

A Swiftian verse sketch of Niall Sheridan, a UCD friend of the poet (1914–1937).

MR SHERIDAN'S MORNING PRAYER

At my rising up I pray
For a middling fine day,
For an adequate reply
From the manna-dropping sky,
For a fire to warm my shins
When the evening light begins,
For a pint or two to quaff,
For a robustious belly laugh,
For a walk with other bards,
For upwards of a hundred yards;
Send these blessings, pure and small,
On myself, and on us all.

Anonymous

*A bawdy broadside from the mid-nineteenth century. Your
'kaylin' (see line 5) was your colleen or girlfriend, while, in
the fifth and seventh verses 'smugging', as James Joyce knew
– the word is in* A Portrait of the Artist as a Young Man
– was something you might want to do with her.

DORAN'S ASS

One Paddy Doyle lived near Killarney
    He courted a maid called Biddy Toole,
His tongue, I own, was tipped with blarney,
    Which seemed to him a golden rule.
From day to dawn Pat watched his kaylin,
    And often to himself would say –
'Sure Biddy is my only darling,
    And she's coming to meet me on the way.'

One heavenly night in last November,
    The moon shone gently from above,
What night it was I can't remember,
    But Paddy went to meet his love.
That night Pa had got some liquor,
    Which made his spirits light and gay –
'Arrah, what's the use of going quicker,
    When I know she'll meet me on the way?'

He took out his pipes and began a-hummin'
    As slowly onward he did creep,
Till fatigue and the whiskey overcame him
    And down he lay and fell asleep.
He was not long without a comrade,
    And one that could give out the pay,
For a big jackass soon smelt out Pat,
    And lay down beside him on the way.

As Paddy he lay in a slumber,
    Thinking on his Biddy dear,
He dreamed of comforts without number,
    A-coming with the ensuing year.
While groping about on the grass,
    His spirits feeling light and gay,
Instead of Biddy he grasped the ass,
    Crying, 'Sure I have her any way.'

Pat hugged and smugged his hairy messer,
    And threw his hat at worldly care;
Says he, 'She's mine, and heaven bless her
    But upon my soul she is full of hair.'
Paddy's mate took up the hat,
    Crying, 'Welcome straw instead of hay.'
'Arrah,' says Pat, 'are you going to give us that?
    Don't let me die in such a way.'

Now Pat got up and away he cut,
    At railway speed, or as fast I'm sure,
And he never stopped a hand or foot,
    Till he came slap bang to Biddy's door,
By this time it was coming morning,
    Pat fell on his knees and began to pray,
Crying 'Let me in my Biddy darling,
    For I'm kilt and murthered on the way.'

Then Paddy told her all quite civil,
    While she prepared the potheen glass,
How he had hugg'd and smugg'd the divil
    'Arrah,' says she, 'that was Doran's ass.'
'Och,' says Pat, 'I think it was,'
    So they both got wed the following day.
But he ne'er got back the old straw hat,
    That the jackass eat upon the way.

Arthur Conan Doyle

*In other anthologies, Sherlock Holmes' inventor (1859–1930)
has sometimes been claimed as a son of Ireland. These lines
show that at least he appreciated our fighting skills.*

THE IRISH COLONEL

Said the King to the Colonel:
    'The complaints are eternal,
    That you Irish give more trouble
Than any other corps.'

Said the Colonel to the King:
    'This complaint is no new thing,
    For your foemen, Sire, have made it
A hundred times before.'

Martin Doyle

A selection of the epigraphs that appear above each section of agricultural advice in a little book entitled Hints Originally Intended for the Small Farmers of the County of Wexford, *first published in 1830 under the pen-name of Martin Doyle. The author, in reality a Protestant clergyman called William Hickey (1787?–1875), signally fails to disguise what is evidently his main interest outside farming – women.*

CONDITION AND QUALITY OF LAND

Hence let wise Farmers understand,
The need of draining swampy land;
The soil which too much wet has got,
Is worthless as a guzzling sot.

PREPARATION OF THE SOIL

The soil with anxious skill prepare,
Or 'twill not recompense your care,
But with pernicious weeds be fraught,
Like mind neglected and untaught.

THE ARRANGEMENT OF THE FARM ...

Arrange your house in order due,
Your garden, gates and fences too;
Neglect's offensive, and what's worse,
It helps to make an empty purse.

COTTAGE CLEANLINESS ...

Then banish first the slattern's vice,
Or vain is Martin's good advice,
No more with dirt offend my sense,
I can't with decency dispense –
Be always clean, 'tis done with ease,
Yourselves 'twill serve, your patrons please.
And know all ye who want good wives,
The lazy slattern never thrives.

MILK …

To enter well on house and lands,
A fitting capital demands,
Of prudence too, a proper spice,
But void of grasping avarice,
Such as poor Tim Delaney knew,
Who chose the double portioned shrew.

ON THE FOLLY OF KEEPING HORSES,
ON VERY SMALL FARMS

Let little farmers mind their spades,
Nor think of keeping four-legged jades;
The proverb long ago decides,
Which way a mounted beggar rides.

COW-FEEDING …

This number, if I do not err,
Will great advantages confer:
Of yore, ere stall fed beasts were known
Fresh meat held half the year alone;
Now, every month a stock supplies,
And hence, the farmer's profits rise.
No cattle starve – no waste is found,
Milk, meat, cheese, butter, all abound,
And, smiling plenty to secure,
Increasing dunghills give manure.

MANGEL WURZEL, &c &c

This section introduces to your notice
A plant, whose name uncouth to English throat is,
From Germany the Mangel Wurzel came,
And well deserves its widely spreading fame.

BEANS – TO BE SOWN IN DRILLS AND KEPT
FREE FROM WEEDS

On weeding land, poor Pat small care bestows,
Tho' weeds are farmers' most pernicious foes,
What pure delight to careful eyes it yields
To see the Scottish lasses in the fields,
Sans shoe or stocking, handling tidy hoes

And cutting every weed that shews its nose!
Yet to my mind, the Wexford maid surpasses
In beauty, tho' not industry, Scotch lasses.

DAIRY MANAGEMENT

Beware the fate of Mr Synge,*
From England if your maids you bring;
Then how shall Irish damsels please,
Unblest with art of making cheese?
Why – but one mode can I discern,
And that is – send them there to learn.

*A note here explains that the unfortunate Mr Synge (of Glenmore
Castle, County Wicklow) had brought home an English dairy-maid
who, 'unable to resist the love-making of some cheese-eating Eng-
lishman', had gone back to England to marry him.

Paddy Drury

*Paddy Drury was born about 1880 in North Kerry, where,
despite the opinions expressed below, he lived all his life as a
jobbing labourer (and poet).*

KERRY PLACES

Knockanure both mane and poor,
A church without a steeple
With bitches and whores lookin' over half-doors
Criticisin' dacent people.
Ballyduff for wakes and snuff;
And Bedford Road for asses;
Abbeyfeale for flour-meal,
Cahirmee for horses.
Ballygologue for thieves and rogues
But Listowel for kiss-me-arses!

Anonymous

*A classic (though periodically updated) ballad of the
fighting Irish.*

THE DUBLIN FUSILIERS

Well, you've heard about the indians with their
    tommyhawks and spears
And of the U.N. warriors, the heroes of recent years,
Also I might mention the British Grenadiers –
Well none of them were in it but the Dublin Fusiliers.
You've heard about the Light Brigade and of the deeds
    they've done,
And of the other regiments that many vic'tries won;
But the pride of all the armies, Dragoons and Cara-
    biniers
Was that noble band of warriors, the Dublin Fusiliers.

Chorus:
    With your left foot and right about face, this is the
        way we go,
    Charging with fixed bayonets, the terror of ev'ry
        foe,
    A glory to old Ireland, as proud as buccaneers,
    And a terror to Creation are the Dublin Fusiliers.

Well, you've heard about the wars between the Rus-
    sians and the Brits;
The tsar one day was reading an ould copy of Titbits,
And when the General came to him and threw himself
    down in tears:
'We'd better run back like blazes, here's the Dublin
    Fusiliers.'
The tsar commanced to tremble and he bit his
    underlip.
'Begorra boys' says he, 'I think we'd better take the tip,
For devils come from Dublin and to judge from what I
    hears,
They're demons of militia men, the Dublin Fusiliers.'

Well, the sergeant cried, 'Get ready lads, lay down
    each sword and gun.
Take off your shoes and stocking, boys, and when I
    tell yous, run.'

They didn't stop, but started and amidst three ringing
    cheers
Came a shower of bricks and bullets from the Dublin
    Fusiliers.
The time that Julius Caesar tried to land down at
    Ringsend
The coastguards couldn't stop them, so for the
    Dublins they did send,
But just as they were landing, lads, we heard three
    ringing cheers
'Get back to Rome like blazes, here's the Dublin
    Fusiliers.'

Lord Dunsany

*Still underrated as a prose writer, Lord Dunsany (1878–1957)
was never a great poet. However, in one of his autobio-
graphical volumes,* While the Sirens Slept *(1944), he is
proud of these parody limericks, written as real great poets
'might have done it, if they had been on board':*

'THERE WAS A YOUNG THING ON A SHIP'

Milton
There was a young thing in a ship
Foredoomed since the Fall to the trip;
    Not the fall of the leaves
    But that error of Eve's,
That mortal, deplorable slip.

Edgar Allan Poe
There was a young thing in a ship
With a lecherous look on her lip;
    And a sinister star
    Looking on from afar
Sent a curse on the whole of the trip;
Put a doom on that elegant ship.

Wordsworth
There was a young thing in a ship
Who, afraid of the harsh winter's nip,
    Some more underclothes wore
    Than she had done before.
None taught her this wild scholarship.

Browning
There was a young thing in a ship;
Mark the curve of her ankle and lip,
    And her labels on boxes
    And skins of strange foxes.
There's a tale for who follows the tip.

W B Yeats
There was a young thing in a ship
Who had seven pale smiles on her lip,
    That were once seven drakes
    On some magical lakes
Where the wild beer makes musical drip.

Swinburne
There was a young thing in a ship
Where the sea was afoam to the lip
    Of the languorous land
    At the north wind's command,
And the gods were inert in its grip.

Euclid
There was a young thing in a ship
Whose lip, with each angle or tip,
    To another's was equal,
    As was proved in the sequel,
By imposing his lip on her lip.

Omar Khayyam
There was a young thing in a ship
Who said let us carouse, let us sip
    The red wine of the sun;
    For the night comes when none
Shall carry a cup to a lip.

Tennyson
There was a young thing in a ship
A mere rose-bud, a delicate slip,
    So artless she knew
    Not the wheel from the screw,
So simple she did nought but skip.

Walt Whitman
There was a young thing in a ship
Who knew perfectly well what she was after;

>For I am not fettered by metre or rhyme,
>   camaradoes,
>   I am the strong white American man
>And am bound by none of the shackles of moribund
>   civilizations.

Paul Durcan

The poet (b. 1944) sighs over the sad plight of the intellectual.

ASHPLANT, NEW YEAR'S EVE, 1996

Year in year out, I tramp Sandymount Strand.
Is there no one to talk to in Ireland?

Anonymous

Also known as 'The Traveller all over the World', a version of this curious adventure was a favourite of the late Frank Harte (1933–2005). In the first verse 'sit ye síos-in-aice-liom' means 'sit down beside me', and in the last, 'Top-of-Coom' is a pub in Kerry, at 1033 feet (315 metres) above sea level definitively the highest one in Ireland.

THE EARTHQUAKE

Come all you fellow travelling men of every rank and
 station
And hear this short oration which as yet remains untold;
I might have been an Austrian, a German or a
 Bulgarian
But sit ye síos-in-aice-liom, and the truth I will unfold.
You'll hear of great disunity unveiled to the
 community,
So take this opportunity of listening to me;
You'll hear of foreign nations and of youthful
 expectations
And of a few relations in that beauty spot Glenlea.

Well I went to see the world's stage when only sixteen
 years of age,
A steerage passage I engaged on a ship called the Iron
 Duke;

I went on board at Dublin's Wall, all southward bound
    for the Transvaal,
I had a friend from Annascaul, and one from
    Donnybrook.
Our noble ship had scarcely steamed when in my
    mind sad memories gleamed –
I thought of all my neighbours dear and their loving
    company,
I thought of my two brothers and our love for one
    another,
I thought of my grey-haired mother there at home in
    Sweet Glenlea.

We landed safe but suddenly in that British spot, Cape
    Colony;
In search of manual labour I travelled near and far:
I crossed the Orange River, among Hottentots and
    Kaffirs,
And I was made Grand Master on the Isle of Zanzibar.
A Dutchman high who admired me ways took me to
    see the Himalays,
And boys-o-boys was I amazed, they're awful high to
    see;
We wandered on through Hindustan, along the River
    Ganges
And though it was a grand place, still the fairest was
    Glenlea.

This Dutchman suffered, his health declined, but he
    heard of cures in Palestine,
He persuaded me with him combine and along with
    him to go.
We landed safe at Jaffa and we journeyed to Jerusalem,
The ancient city of Hebron and the walls of Jericho.
The surrounding mountains' highest peaks, just like
    McGillicuddy's Reeks,
And from their summit you could see the Lake of
    Gallilee,
Likewise the River Jordan and the province of Samaria,
But though it sounds contrary – the fairest was Glenlea.

These doleful times soon drifted by till this faithful
    Dutchman friend and I
Were forced to part and say goodbye, perhaps to meet
    no more;

I stood forlorn upon the quay as the ship that bore
    him sailed away,
His memory in my mind will stay till life's long days
    are o'er.
Still Providence had willed its way and therefore
    conscience must obey:
I went on board and sailed away when my friend did
    me forsake,
But often meditation made me turn for recreation
And go home in contemplation to that beauty spot
    Glenlea.

In Palestine I made some coin, I heard of San
    Francisco's mine,
For to invest me capital I thought a good idee:
I landed safe in 'Frisco when the trees were blooming
    beautiful –
It was on that same evening that there was a great
    earthquake.
I was in my bed and sleeping sound, I woke to find
    things moving round,
But after that I heard no sound, no pain affected me,
And on the following morning when I'd recovered
    consciousness
I wrote of all the consequence to my home in sweet
    Glenlea.

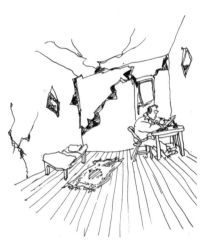

I told them in the letter how I lost the situation,
It was my earthly station and I wanted to go home,
And I hoped their generosity would aid my
    transportation,
And I went on relating how misfortune made me roam.
I got the cash to pay my way without disaster or delay
And landed safe at Queenstown Quay, on board the
    Chimpanzee,
And after an excursion of some five long hours
    duration
I reached the little station on the road to sweet Glenlea.

As we approached the terminus I viewed with
    consternation
The awful congregation there assembled in the rain,
And I hoped some other personage of worldly
    estimation
To heed their expectation was coming in by train.

As I scanned each individual's face, friends and
    neighbours, old time mates,
Assembled in their hundreds with a welcome home
    for me,
Oh! they shouted with elation and they shook with
    great vibration
The surrounding elevation on the road to sweet
    Glenlea.

And now I live contentedly among these friends and
    neighbours,
Endowed with all the favours of good fortune and
    delight,
And I've found among the multitude a charming little
    creature –
She's full of admiration, she's my lovely Irish wife;
And when we meet at Sunday's noon, at that cozy
    spot called Top-of-Coom,
Where songs and stories would illume the hearts of
    you and me,
Among that grand old company of lovely friends and
    neighbours
We're never tired of praising that beauty spot Glenlea.

Anonymous

In Col. WC Trimble's Collected Poems, *where these
stirring verses appear as an unsigned addendum, he
modestly remarks: 'I am asked to include a ballad about the
local regiment of Ulster Volunteer cavalry which escorted
Sir Edward Carson, M.P., K.C., to the great meeting at
Enniskillen, on 18th September, 1912.'*

THE ENNISKILLEN HORSE

Come all ye loyal Irishmen,
    Wherever ye may be,
And let my joyful news to you
    Resound from sea to sea;
'Tis of the Enniskillen Day
    That I would sing to you,
And of the things amazing there
    Appeared unto our view.

The first thing we observèd was
 The 'Jack' was everywhere,
Its red and white and glorious blue
 A-waving in the air;
And then there came that wond'rous sight
 To wise men and to loons,
The marching of the cavalry,
 Of Trimble's bold Dragoons.

If you could see those gallant lads,
 On horses fine astride,
Like David's chosen men of old,
 Best in the country side;
They sat like Grecian heroes
 All on their chargers fine,
And carried lances in their hands,
 And kept straight in a line.

The Colonel he rode at the head
 As proud as he could be
Of such a splendid regiment,
 Fermanagh's chivalry;
And Colonel Trimble drilled his men,
 The way they rode that day,
And bade the trumpeter to sound
 Before they marched away.

Then there was Colonel Doran,
 A gentleman you know,
And Mr Geoffrey Irvine,
 And Mr Kerr from Coagh;
And Mr Dominick Archdale,
 And Mr Dick Strathearn,
And Mr Willie Harvey of the town
 That sits upon the Erne.

Likewise the splendid sergeants
 And troopers every one,
They were the finest set of men
 That e'er the sun shone on.
They rode in great and grand array,
 And four men were abreast,
And everyone remarked that day
 How splendidly they 'dressed.'

Some fifty and two hundred men
    Rode to Portora gate,
The people cheered, and cheered again,
    As they rode on in state;
And then they formed into a line
    As straight as by rule,
And back right through the town again
    Marched to the Model School.

Then came the great Sir Edward
    Whom they went forth to meet,
They took his carriage straight in charge,
    And brought him up the street,
The cheers were heard on every side,
    Sir Edward said – 'Again
He never would behold the like
    Of Trimble and his men.'

Now here's unto our cavalry,
    That do not fear the foe,
They're sure to make some history
    Wherever they may go.
There's one thing that is pretty plain –
    Ye'll have some sultry noons
Before ye see the like of them,
    Of Trimble's bold dragoons.

They say their squadrons number two,
    And that there will be four,
And that they'll get the pick of all
    The youth of Erne's shore;
And if you want a regiment
    Of men without poltroons,
You cannot get the equal of
    Bold Trimble's fine Dragoons.

Now to conclude my narrative
    And finish up my song,
We're proud of these Fermanaghmen
    That unto us belong;
We'll say hurray for many a day
    And cheer till we be hoarse
For Trimble's gallant Yeomanry,
    The Enniskillen Horse.

Anonymous

This comes from a slim volume published in 1918. Mysteriously entitled Secret Springs of Dublin Song, *it contained parodies and verse satires directed at Yeats, Æ, George Moore and other Irish writers. The unsigned contributions have been variously attributed to Æ himself, Lord Dunsany, Ernest A Boyd, Seumas O'Sullivan, Oliver St John Gogarty and Susan Mitchell (who wrote the introduction).*

FAME

If I live to be very old
    They will know me then for a poet.
When my blood is sombre and cold,
If I live to be very old,
    They will shout, 'We know it. We know it,'
And I will be vexed by the riot,
And turn from my sloppy diet
To pray for a little quiet.

George Farquhar

With this song, which he wrote when almost on his deathbed, the penniless Farquhar (1677–1707) ribbed the fashionable audience who would attend his last play, The Beaux' Stratagem.

'A SONG OF TRIFLES'

A trifling song you shall hear,
Begun with a trifle and ended:
All trifling people draw near,
And I shall be nobly attended.

Were it not for trifles, a few,
That lately have come into play;
The men would want something to do,
And the women want something to say.

What makes men trifle in dressing?
Because the ladies (they know)
Admire, by often possessing,
That eminent trifle, a beau.

When the lover his moments has trifled,
The trifle of trifles to gain:
No sooner the virgin is rifled,
But a trifle shall part 'em again.

What mortal man would be able
At White's half an hour to sit?
Or who could bear a tea-table,
Without talking of trifles for wit?

The court is from trifles secure,
Gold keys are no trifles, we see:
White rods are no trifles, I'm sure,
Whatever their bearers may be.

But if you will go to the place,
Where trifles abundantly breed,
The levee will show you His Grace
Makes promises trifles indeed.

A coach with six footmen behind,
I count neither trifle nor sin:
But, ye gods, how oft do we find
A scandalous trifle within.

A flask of champagne, people think it:
A trifle, or something as bad:
But if you'll contrive how to drink it,
You'll find it no trifle, egad!

A parson's a trifle at sea,
A widow's a trifle in sorrow:
A peace is a trifle to-day,
Who knows what may happen to-morrow?

A black coat a trifle may cloak,
Or to hide it, the red may endeavour:
But if once the army is broke,
We shall have more trifles than ever.

The stage is a trifle they say,
The reason, pray carry along,
Because at every new play,
The house they with trifles so throng.

But with people's malice to trifle,
And to set us all on a foot:
The author of this is a trifle,
And his song is a trifle to boot.

Robert Farren

*The lives of the saints have been an unending source of
delight for many Irish writers, including Robert Farren
(1909-1984). Since its first publication in the early 1940s,
'The Pets' has deservedly been much anthologized. Here it
is again:*

THE PETS

Colm had a cat,
and a wren,
and a fly.

The cat was a pet,
and the wren,
and the fly.

And it happened that the wren
ate the fly;
and it happened that the cat
ate the wren.
Then the cat died.

So Saint Colm lacked a cat,
and a wren,
and a fly.

But Saint Colm loved the cat,
and the wren,
and the fly,

so he prayed to get them back,
cat and wren;
and he prayed to get them back,
wren and fly.

And the cat became alive
and delivered up the wren;
and the wren became alive
and delivered up the fly;
and they all lived with Colm
till the day came to die.

First the cat died.
Then the wren died.
Then the fly.

Anonymous

This reputedly Irish-American ballad gave its title (but not very much else) to James Joyce's last novel.

FINNEGAN'S WAKE

Tim Finnegan lived in Walkin Street,
 A gentleman Irish mighty odd,
He had a tongue both rich and sweet,
 And to rise in the world he carried a hod.
Now Tim had a sort of a tippling way,
 With the love of the liquor he was born,
And to help him on with his work each day,
 He'd a drop of the craythur ev'ry morn.

Chorus
Whack fol the dah, dance to your partner,
 Welt the flure, yer trotters shake,

Wasn't it the truth I told you,
    Lots of fun at Finnegan's Wake.

One morning Tim was rather full,
    His head felt heavy which made him shake,
He fell from the ladder and broke his skull,
    So they carried him home his corpse to wake.
They rolled him up in a nice clean sheet,
    And laid him out upon the bed,
With a gallon of whiskey at his feet,
    And a barrel of porter at his head.

His friends assembled at the wake,
    And Mrs Finnegan called for lunch,
First they brought in tay and cake,
    Then pipes, tobacco, and whiskey punch.
Miss Biddy O'Brien began to cry,
    'Such a neat clean corpse, did you ever see,
Arrah, Tim avourneen, why did you die?'
    'Ah, hould your gab,' said Paddy McGee.

Then Biddy O'Connor took up the job,
    'Biddy,' says she, 'you're wrong, I'm sure,'
But Biddy gave her a belt in the gob,
    And left her sprawling on the floor;
Oh, then the mighty war did rage;
    'Twas woman to woman and man to man,
Shillelagh law did all engage,
    And a row and a ruction soon began.

Then Micky Maloney raised his head,
    When a naggin of whiskey flew at him,
It missed and falling on the bed,
    The liquor scattered over Tim;
Bedad he revives, see how he rises,
    And Timothy rising from the bed,
Says, 'Whirl your liquor round like blazes,
    Thanam o'n dhoul, do ye think I'm dead?'

Gabriel Fitzmaurice

Fitzmaurice (b. 1952) is a prolific writer of verses, often for children. This short exchange comes from his 2001 book, Dear Grandad.

WHAT'S A TOURIST?

'Children, what's a tourist?
Can anyone tell me now?'

'Please sir, a man with a camera
Taking photos of a cow!'

Richard Flecknoe

One of the earliest poems here (published 1653), this can be read as a philosophical argument for drunkenness. Probably however it was not intended to be one: Flecknoe, who died in 1678, was a Jesuit priest of unsullied reputation, and has never been accused of being a wit.

OF DRINKING.

The fountains drink caves subterren,
    The rivulets drink the fountains dry;
Brooks drink those rivulets again,
    And then some river gliding by;
Until some gulphing sea drink them,
And ocean drinks up that again.

Of ocean then does drink the sky;
    When having brew'd it into rain,
The earth with drink it does supply,
    And plants do drink up that again.
When turned to liquor in the vine,
'Tis our turn next to drink the wine.

By this who does not plainly see,
    How into our throats at once is hurl'd –
Whilst merrily we drinking be –
    The quintessence of all the world?
Whilst all drink then in land, air, sea,
Let us too drink as well as they.

WP Fogarty

Written in the 1930s during a row over a decision to
modernize the Book of Common Prayer.

PRIVATE JUDGMENT

The Canon says: 'Yes',
And the Dean says: 'No'.
And the Curate says: 'Both are wrong.'
And away they all go
(With a Hey nonny no!)
To the service of Evensong.

The Bishop says: 'Aye',
And the Canon says: 'Nay',
And the Curate says: 'Couple of frauds.'
And away they all go
(With a Hey nonny no!)
To the service of Matins and Lauds.

* * *

The Canon, the Bishop, the Curate, the Dean,
Arm in arm to church they go.
But the world and his wife
Keep out of the strife
And go to a Picture Show!

Edward Forbes

More verses have been written about oysters than you might
imagine. Here is one of the odder and more revolting of
them. AP Graves put it into an 1893 anthology, Songs of
Irish Wit and Humour, *a book whose entries often*
distinctly lack either quality. But this one is something
special. (Incidentally, the ill-treated 'natives' in the last
verse are Irish oysters.)

THE ANATOMY OF THE OYSTER

Of all the conchiferous shell-fish,
    The oyster is surely the king:
Arrah, Mick, call the people who sell fish,

And tell them a dozen to bring.
For it's I that intind to demonstrate
　　The creature's phenomena strange:
Its functions – to set every one straight,
　　And exhibit their structure and range
　　　　In sweet rhyme!

Now, boys, I beseech, be attentive –
　　On this Carlingford fasten your eyes,
As I spread it before you so pensive,
　　Its gape opened wide with surprise.
See that small purple spot in the centre,
　　That's its heart, which is all on the move;
For though looking as deep as a Mentor,
　　It is tenderly beating with love
　　　　All the while.

Like a Chesterfield pea-coat, its liver,
　　Of fusty brown Petersham made,
It folds round its stomach to give a
　　Supply of fresh bile when there's need;
And though we, when we swallow our oyster,
　　Like it raw and by cooks undefiled,
The creature itself is much choicer,
　　Preferring its condiments biled –
　　　　It's so nice.

The fringes that circle its body,
　　Which epicures think should be cleared,
Are the animal's lungs – for, 'tis odd, he,
　　Like a foreigner, *breathes through his beard!*
And among all its memorabilia,
　　Than this structure there's none half so queer,
Though Sharpey may say they are *cilia,*
　　A *wiser* contrivance to 'speer' –
　　　　Let him try!

Now, these are the facts in the history
　　Of an oyster, I'd on you impress;
I've sarved them up plain without mystery –
　　To cook them would just make a mess.
So now, boys, we'll fetch in the whiskey,
　　Since the water is hot on the hob,
Whilst we stir up our native so frisky
　　By sticking a knife in its gob!
　　　　Dear old fish!

Percy French

*Though William Percy French (1854–1920) fills fewer than
two of the 4000+ pages in* The Field Day Anthology of
Irish Writing *(1991), those who can forgive his benign stage-
Irishry might reasonably judge him to have been Ireland's
greatest writer of light-hearted songs. This is a small
selection from his work.*

ABDULLA BULBUL AMEER

The sons of the prophet were hardy and bold,
And quite unaccustomed to fear,
But the bravest by far in the ranks of the Shah,
Was Abdulla Bulbul Ameer.

This son of the desert, in battle aroused,
Could spit twenty men on his spear.
A terrible creature, both sober and soused,
Was Abdulla Bulbul Ameer.

If you wanted a man to encourage the van,
Or to harass the foe from the rear,
Or to storm a redoubt, you had only to shout
For Abdulla Bulbul Ameer.

There are heroes aplenty and men known to fame
In the troops that were led by the Czar;
But the bravest of these was a man by the name
Of Ivan Skavinsky Skivar.

He could imitate Irving, play euchre and pool
And perform on the Spanish guitar.
In fact, quite the cream of the Muscovite team
Was Ivan Skavinsky Skivar.

The ladies all loved him, his rivals were few;
He could drink them all under the bar.
As gallant or tank, there was no one to rank
With Ivan Skavinsky Skivar.

One day this bold Russian had shouldered his gun
And donned his most truculent sneer:
Downtown he did go, where he trod on the toe
Of Abdulla Bulbul Ameer.

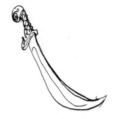

'Young man,' quoth Bulbul, 'has life grown so dull,
That you're anxious to end your career?
Vile infidel! Know, you have trod on the toe
Of Abdulla Bulbul Ameer.

So take your last look at the sunshine and brook
And send your regrets to the Czar;
By this I imply you are going to die,
Mr Ivan Skavinsky Skivar.'

Quoth Ivan, 'My friend, your remarks, in the end,
Will avail you but little, I fear,
For you ne'er will survive to repeat them alive,
Mr Abdulla Bulbul Ameer!'

Then this bold mameluke drew his trusty chibouque
With a cry of 'Allah Akbar!'
And with murderous intent, he ferociously went
For Ivan Skavinsky Skivar.

Then they parried and thrust and they side-stepped
    and cussed
Till their blood would have filled a great pot.
The philologist blokes, who seldom crack jokes,
Say that hash was first made on that spot.

They fought all that night, 'neath the pale yellow moon;
The din, it was heard from afar;
And great multitudes came, so great was the fame
Of Abdul and Ivan Skivar.

As Abdul's long knife was extracting the life –
In fact, he was shouting 'Huzzah!' –
He felt himself struck by that wily Kalmuck,
Count Ivan Skavinsky Skivar.

The sultan drove by in his red-breasted fly,
Expecting the victor to cheer;
But he only drew nigh to hear the last sigh
Of Abdulla Bulbul Ameer.

Czar Petrovich, too, in his spectacles blue
Rode up in his new crested car.
He arrived just in time to exchange a last line
With Ivan Skavinsky Skivar.

A loud-sounding splash from the Danube was heard
Resounding o'er meadows afar;
It came from the sack fitting close to the back
Of Ivan Skavinsky Skivar.

There's a tomb rises up where the blue Danube flows;
Engraved there in characters clear;
'Ah stranger, when passing, please pray for the soul
Of Abdulla Bulbul Ameer.'

A Muscovite maiden her lone vigil keeps,
'Neath the light of the pale polar star;
And the name that she murmurs as oft as she weeps
Is Ivan Skavinsky Skivar.

The sons of the prophet were hardy and bold,
And quite unaccustomed to fear,
But the bravest by far in the ranks of the Shah,
Was Abdulla Bulbul Ameer.

THE CYCLES OF TIME

She rode a stranger's donkey
    The day when first we met,
On the razor back of an ancient Jack
    Her childish form was set;
And standing by her side was one
    Who strove, but all in vain,
To rouse that donkey from his sleep,
    And start him off again.
I saw her but a moment,
    But methinks I see her still,
As she urged that most lethargic beast
    To mount Killiney Hill.

When next we met, a tricycle
    Her slender figure bore;
It seemed to me her sunny face
    Was redder than before;
And as she plugged along the path,
    With wild defiant air,
I noticed how the breeze had tossed
    Her long luxuriant hair.

She made me 'skip the gutter:'
    Yet methinks I see her now
On that heavy old two-tracker,
    With the dew upon her brow.

No heavy two-track tricycle
    Was there when next we met;
On wobbly wheel she glided by
    Upon a bicyclette;
Her face had all the whiteness –
    Her voice the anxious tone –
Of one who knows not what may hap
    If she should meet a stone.
She passed me by like winking,
    And methinks I see her yet,
A racing down that greasy road
    Upon a bicyclette.

And once again I saw that form:
    No bicyclette was there;
An alien hand propelled her in
    The family bath chair.
I saw she'd had an accident,
    And so I quickly said –
'I've taken my diploma out,
    So let me lend my aid.'
I saw her broken ankle,
    And I helped the bone to set
And now I'm her companion
    When she rides her bicyclette.

SONG OF WILLIAM, INSPECTOR OF DRAINS

Let others betake them to Western Plains
And ease the redman of his ill-gotten gains;
No tomahawk ever shall injure the brains
Of William, the Local Inspector of Drains.

He mounts his tall trap, gives his charger the reins,
And gallops away through the green country lanes,
The Board pays the posting – the balance remains –
With William, the Local Inspector of Drains.

He finds out the holding and what it contains,
Then maps out his system in furlongs and chains,
And points out positions for 'miners' and 'mains' –
Such wisdom has William, Inspector of Drains.

He plunges through marshes long haunted by cranes,
Unmindful of how the dark bog-water stains;
Traducers assert that this ardour he feigns,
They little know William, Inspector of Drains!

He stays in his quarters, of course, if it rains,
And wakes the piano's voluptuous strains,
And if of delay the bold tenant complains,
He's sat on by William, Inspector of Drains.

The fair maids of Cavan (this William maintains),
Tho' I think one should take it with salt, a few grains,
Have left in a body their woe-begone swains
For William, the Local Inspector of Drains!

'Tis an onerous post – but the writer refrains
From dwelling at length on its pleasures and pains,
It may not last long, but as yet he remains
      Yours faithfully,
              WILLIAM,
              Inspector of Drains

'ARE YE RIGHT THERE, MICHAEL?'
A LAY OF THE WILD WEST CLARE

You may talk of Columbus's sailing
    Across the Atlantical sea
But he never tried to go railing
    From Ennis as far as Kilkee.
You run for the train in the mornin',
    The excursion train starting at eight,
You're there when the clock gives the warnin',
    And there for an hour you'll wait.

And as you're waiting in the train,
You'll hear the guard sing this refrain:–

'Are ye right there, Michael? are ye right?
Do you think that we'll be there before the night?
      Ye've been so long in startin',
      That ye couldn't say for sartin –
Still ye might now, Michael, so ye might!'

They find out where the engine's been hiding,
      And it drags you to sweet Corofin;
Says the guard, 'Back her down on the siding,
      There's the goods from Kilrush comin' in.'
Perhaps it comes in in two hours,
      Perhaps it breaks down on the way;
'If it does,' says the guard, 'be the powers,
      We're here for the rest of the day!'

And while you sit and curse your luck,
The train backs down into a truck!

'Are ye right there, Michael? are ye right?
Have ye got the parcel there for Mrs White?
      Ye haven't! Oh, begorra!
      Say it's comin' down to-morra –
And it might now, Michael, so it might!'

At Lahinch the sea shines like a jewel,
      With joy you are ready to shout,
When the stoker cries out, 'There's no fuel,
      And the fire's taytotally out.
But hand up that bit of a log there –
      I'll soon have ye out of the fix;
There's a fine clamp of turf in the bog there;'
      And the rest go a-gatherin' sticks.

And while you're breakin' bits of trees,
You hear some wise remarks like these:–

'Are ye right there, Michael? are ye right?
Do ye think that ye can get the fire to light?'
      'Oh, an hour you'll require,
      For the turf it might be drier –'
'Well, it might now, Michael, so it might!'

Kilkee! Oh, you never get near it!
      You're in luck if the train brings you back,
For the permanent way is so queer, it

Spends most of its time off the track.
Uphill the ould engine is climbin',
   While the passengers push with a will;
You're in luck when you reach Ennistymon,
   For all the way home is down-hill.

And as you're wobbling through the dark,
You hear the guard make this remark:–

'Are ye right there, Michael? are ye right?
Do you think that ye'll be home before it's light?'
   ' 'Tis all dependin' whether
    The ould engine howlds together –'
'And it might now, Michael, so it might!'

SHLATHERY'S MOUNTED FUT

You've heard o' Julius Caesar, an' the great Napoleon,
   too,
An' how the Cork Militia beat the Turks at Waterloo;
But there's a page of glory that, as yet, remains uncut,
An' that's the martial story o' the Shlathery's Mounted
   Fut.
This gallant corps was organised by Shlathery's eldest
   son.
A noble-minded poacher, wid a double-breasted gun;
An' many a head was broken, aye, an' many an eye
   was shut,
Whin practisin' manoeuvres in the Shlathery's
   Mounted Fut.

   An' down from the mountains came the squadrons
    an' platoons,
   Four-an'-twinty fightin' min, an' a couple o' sthout
    gossoons,
   An' whin we marched behind the dhrum to
    patriotic tunes,
   We felt that fame would gild the name o'
    Shlathery's Light Dhragoons.

Well, first we reconnoithered round O'Sullivan's
   Shebeen –
It used to be 'The Shop House,' but we call it, 'The
   Canteen;'

But there we saw a notice which the bravest heart
    unnerved –
'All liquor must be settled for before the dhrink is
    served.'
So on we marched, but soon again each warrior's
    heart grew pale,
For risin' high in front o' us we saw the County Jail;
An' whin the army faced about, 'twas just in time to
    find
A couple o' policemin had surrounded us behind.

    Still, from the mountains came the squadrons and
        platoons,
    Four-an'-twinty fightin' min, an' a couple o' sthout
        gossoons;
    Says Shlathery, 'We must circumvent these
        bludgeonin' bosthoons,
    Or else it sames they'll take the names o'
        Shlathery's Light Dhragoons.'

'We'll cross the ditch,' our leader cried, 'an' take the
    foe in flank,'
But yells of consthernation here arose from every
    rank,
For posted high upon a tree we very plainly saw,
'Threspassers prosecuted, in accordance wid' the law.'
'We're foiled!' exclaimed bowld Shlathery, 'here ends
    our grand campaign,
'Tis merely throwin' life away to face that mearin'
    dhrain,
I'm not as bold as lions, but I'm braver nor a hin,
An' he that fights and runs away will live to fight agin.'

    An' back to the mountains went the squadrons and
        platoons,
    Four-an'-twinty fightin' min an' a couple o' sthout
        gossoons;
    The band was playing cautiously their patriotic
        tunes;
    To sing the fame, if rather lame, o' Shlathery's
        Light Dhragoons.

THE FOUR FARRELLYS

In a small hotel in London I was sitting down to dine,
When the waiter brought the register and asked me if
    I'd sign.
And as I signed I saw a name that set my heart astir –
A certain 'Francis Farrelly' had signed the register.
I knew a lot of Farrellys and out of all the crew
I kept on 'sort of wonderin'' which Farrelly were you.
And when I'd finished dinner I sat back in my chair,
Going round my native land to find, what Farrelly you
    were.

South
Were you the keen-eyed Kerryman I met below
    Kenmare,
Who told me that when Ireland fought 'the odds were
    never fair.'
If Cromwell had met Sarsfield, or met Owen Roe
    O'Neill,
It's not to Misther Gladstone we'd be lookin' for repeal.
Would have Ireland for the Irish, not a Saxon to be
    seen,
And only Gaelic spoken in that House in College
    Green.
Told me landlords wor the Divil! their agints ten times
    worse,
And iv'ry sort of government for Ireland was a curse!
Oh! if you're that Francis Farrelly, your dreams have
    not come true,
Still, Slainthe! Slainthe! Fransheen! for I like a man like
    you!

North
Or were you the Francis Farrelly that often used to say
He'd like to blow them Papishes from Darry walls
    away?
The boy who used to bother me that Orange Lodge to
    join,
And thought that history started with the Battle o' the
    Boyne. –
I was not all with ye, Francis, the Pope is not ma
    friend,
But still I hope, poor man, he'll die without that
    bloody end. –

And when yer quit from care yerself, and get to
    Kingdom Come,
It's no use teachin' you the harp – you'll play the
    Orange drum!
Och! man, ye wor a fighter, of that I had no doubt,
For I seen ye in Belfast one night when the Antrim
    Road was out!
And many a time that evinin' I thought that ye wor
    dead,
The way them Papish pavin' stones was hoppin' off
    yer head.
Oh! if you're the Francis Farrelly who came from
    North Tyrone –
Here's lookin' to ye, Francis, but do leave the Pope
    alone!

East

Or were you the Francis Farrelly that in my college
    days
For strolling on the Kingstown Pier had such a curious
    craze?
D'ye mind them lovely sisters – the blonde and the
    brunette?
I know I've not forgotten, and I don't think you forget!
That picnic at the Dargle – and the other at the Scalp –
How my heart was palpitatin' – hers wasn't – not a
    palp!
Someone said ye married money – and maybe ye were
    wise,
But the gold you loved was in her hair, and the
    di'monds in her eyes!
So I like to think ye married her and that you're with
    her yet,
'Twas some 'meleesha' officer that married the
    brunette;
But the blonde one always loved ye, and I knew you
    loved her too,
So me blessin's on ye, Francis, and the blue sky over
    you!

West

Or were you the Francis Farrelly I met so long ago,
In the bog below Belmullet, in the County of Mayo?
That long-legged, freckled Francis with the deep-set,
    wistful eyes,

That seemed to take their colour from those ever-
    changing skies.
That put his flute together as I sketched the distant
    scene,
And played me 'Planxty Kelly' and the 'Wakes of
    Inniskeen.'
That told me in the Autumn he'd be sailin' to the West
To try and make his fortune and send money to the
    rest.
And would I draw a picture of the place where he was
    born,
And he'd hang it up, and look at it, and not feel so
    forlorn.
And when I had it finished, you got up from where
    you sat,
And you said, 'Well, you're the Divil, and I can't I say
    more than that.'
Oh! if you're that Francis Farrelly, your fortune may
    be small,
But I'm thinking – thinking – Francis, that I love you
    best of all;
And I never can forget you – though it's years and
    years ago –
In the bog below Belmullet, in the County of Mayo.

RBD French

*If Percy French is neglected by academics, his kinsman RBD
French (1904–1981) suffers from being neglected by everyone.
Known to all as RBD, he was an old-style 'Trinity man', a
gentle and gentlemanly lecturer in English whose
enthusiasms included amateur theatricals and the books of
PG Wodehouse. 'The Martyr' appeared in* TCD: A College
Miscellany *in 1935.*

THE MARTYR

*(Experiments upon the measurement of alcohol in the
breath are being conducted in the Biochemical Laboratory.)*

The chemist makes experiments
    Incessantly for good.
        No soothing note of tabors

Accompanies his labours,
His are no choral merriments,
    No strain of brass or wood.
But sad, remote, unguided,
    And weary unto death,
In trials never ended
    He analyses breath.

He loathes the taste of sherry,
    He scorns the lure of gin,
No whiskey makes him merry
    And yet he pours it in;
Then from his draught of liquor
    He turns to his machine,
And if he's made it long enough
And deep enough and strong enough
    His breath inside the test-tube
    Will turn the water green.

And so, with marked emotion,
    He fills the hated cup.
        No murmur or complaining
        Accompanies its draining,
In studious devotion
    He simply laps it up.
And thus from morn to luncheon
    And on to midnight strike
Drains glass and stein and puncheon
    With infinite dislike.

He's definitely anti
    Madeira and Medoc,
Abominates Chianti
    And loathes the sight of Hock.
Yet for the good of science
    He breathes and breathes anew,
And if he's taken wine enough
And old enough and fine enough
    His fragrant respirations
    Will turn the water blue.

An infinite variety
    Of bottles, jugs and jars,
        From burgundy to brandy,
        He has to keep them handy,
The cocktail of society,
    The bitter beer of bars.
And since to err is sinful
    He often finds it best
To take another skinful
    And make a second test.

And shall this noble toiling
    No honour have, nor praise?
The chemist's ceaseless oiling
    Be still undecked with bays?
No! In this humble anthem
    His praises I produce,
And if I've made them sweet enough
And warm enough and neat enough,
    Perhaps he'll let me help him
    To turn the water puce.

*French's polished verses particularly sparkled when he had a
serious target. As the Second World War approached, and
England still favoured appeasement, he found one:*

SACRIFICE

The cause of peace demands sacrifices from all of us.
  – Daily Press, ad nauseam.
The lights are going out. – Mr Churchill, 1938.

Well everyone was very nice, and, speaking as a Czech,
I feel it was a privilege to help avert the wreck.
We had not much to offer, and what we could do was
    small,
But in a way we were to blame for being there at all;
And sacrifice to keep the peace is eminently right,
So we did what we could when Hitler juggled with
    the light.

Admittedly, our little share is hardly worth a fuss –
It's insignificant to what the world gave up for us.

The Premier gave up fishing and the King gave up the
    Clyde,
Duff Cooper gave his office up; and Bonnet gave his
    pride,
And Hitler gave up Godesberg – at least they tell us so,
But we gave up Bohemia when the lights were getting
    low.

Then Flandin said the crisis was a Bolshevist intrigue,
And he gave up democracy, and all gave up the League.
And France gave up her promises; for clearly, it was
    meant
That they should bind her only to a relative extent.
Of course, one can't be literal in matters of the kind,
So we gave our defences up when Hitler pulled the
    blind.

And Franco gave some soldiers up that Mussolini
    loaned,
And Rome gave up the axis when the Foreign Office
    phoned.
The Germans gave up butter and they didn't even flinch,
And only Lord Craigavon said he wouldn't give an inch.
With all this sacrifice about we had to do our bit,
So we gave in to Hungary when still the lamps were lit.

And now the thought that worries us is what we
    ought to do
When next the world is called on for a sacrifice or two.
To pay our debt we'd give our all that England still
    might live,
But we have a sort of feeling we may not have much
    to give.
Yet perhaps it doesn't matter, since we know beyond a
    doubt
That no one will remember us when all the lamps are
    out.

*The angry (and perhaps unpublished) verses below were
written, as French explains in a note on the manuscript, 'in
the early summer of 1940, when it became known that quite
a number of Dublin notabilities were hastening to sign the
[Visitors'] book at the German Embassy.' Among those
mentioned here are the widow of the 1916 signatory, Tom*

Clarke, the (Papal) Marquess McSwiney of Mashanaglass,
the Blueshirt General Eoin O'Duffy, and various politicians
including Seán T O'Kelly and Eamon De Valera.
A further note remarks, by way of introduction: 'A German
paper says that when Hitler conquers England he will
depose the Royal House and have himself crowned in
Westminster Abbey, and 'Punch' has a poem on this subject.
But will he be content with one crown?'

1940

God grant I may be present
　　God send I have my wish
When Adolf the Unpleasant
　　Comes sailing past the Kish,
To hear the joy bells calling
　　And raise my loyal cheer
When Adolf the Appalling
　　Sets foot on Kingstown Pier.

And onward through the flurry
　　Moves that triumphal car
Where burghers in a hurry
　　Wave high the swastika
From Monkstown's sea-girt pleasance
　　To leafy Herbert Park
Where Adolf the Excrescence
　　Is met by Mrs Clarke.

And now with what complacence
　　Comes Dev to bend the knee,
And Cosgrave makes obeisance
　　And Dillon, and Sean T.
Mashanaglass, in topper
　　Will surely leave his card
When Adolf the Improper
　　Rides into Castle Yard.

Now heavy are our troubles
　　Beneath the Saxon heel
Till Goering and till Goebbels
　　Shall come to work us weal,
And bitter as the Arctic
　　Runs high our tide of woe
But Adolf the Cathartic
　　Shall purge us white as snow.

Come searching as the senna
    To rid us of our plague,
O looter of Vienna!,
    O conquerer of Prague!
Our sons shall tell the story
    When all our days are done,
Of Cardinal Macrory
    Anointing Adolf I.

And hard beside the mitre
    The scourge of pagan Spain
O'Duffy the Gauleiter
    Shall wear the sword again.
Our fetters shall be rusting
    Our murmurs shall be still
When Adolf the Disgusting
    Is crowned on Tara Hill.

RBD was never quite at home in independent Ireland. This song was written in the 1950s for a revue in the Players' Theatre, TCD.

GREEN LITTLE ISLAND:
THE IRA MAN, THE ORANGEMAN
AND THE DIM LITTLE GAEL

We're the boys that make the noise
In our smile-and-a-tear-little island.
We're the boys that can't keep mum –
We fire the gun – and bate the drum –
And keep it up till kingdom come
In our dear little, queer little island –
    In our high little, spry little,
        Feel rather dry little
            Twelfth of July little
                Island.

The IRA Man
Form your battalions and march with the van!
Physical force is your only man!
Raid the barracks and customs store
And we'll march to freedom through martyrs' gore!
    That's the way to win the day

In our sad little, mad little island –
   In our ever disorderly
      Blow-up-the-Borderly
         Rough little, tough little
           Island.

The Orangeman
We bate them at Derry, we won at the Boyne,
And we'll pay them again in the very same coin –
So up with King Billy – we'll give them the boot
As we march to the tune of the Old Orange Flute.
   That's the way to win the day
      In our proud little, loud little island –
         In our smile-and-a-frown little
           Protestant Crown little
            Up Portadown little
             Island.

The Dim Little Gael
Ireland Gaelic is Ireland pure –
So down with foreign litherachure!
To lead the world to the path of light
We're prepared to do anything – only fight!
   That's the way to win the day
      In our proud little, loud little island,
         In our deep-in-the-mist little
           Never-been-kissed little
            Dim little, prim little
             Island.

Together
So we're the boys that make the noise
In our out of the way little island –
We are the patriotic chaps
That keep the country on the maps
Until we get some peace (perhaps)
In our not very gay little island –
   In our nineteen-sixteen little
      Orange and green little
         God-save-the-Queen little island,
           In our swate little, nate little,
            Quite-out-of-date little –
             Let's emigrate little
              Island.

Anonymous

In the 1820s pamphlets were issued carrying the lyrics of many of the hit songs from the new 2000-seater Theatre Royal in Hawkins Street, Dublin. This one, sung there by a 'Mr Adams' in 1826, chronicles the misadventures of an Irish emigrant in London. Of its various obsolete terms, a 'whisky' (verse 1) was a light horse-carriage, 'pelf' (verse 2) was a very common word for 'money', and in the days before an official police force, a call of 'Watch!' (verse 3) might attract a member of the city street patrol.

'FROM GREAT LONDONDERRY'

From great Londonderry to London so merry,
    My own natty self in a waggon did ride;
In London so frisky, folks ride in a whisky,
    At Connaught they carry their whiskey inside.
I jump'd from the waggon, and saw a Green Dragon:
    I spy'd a Blue Boar when I turn'd to the south;
At the Swan with two Throttles I tippled two bottles,
    And bothered the beef at the Bull and the Mouth.

        Chorus:
  Ah! Paddy, my honey! look after your money
    'Tis all botheration from bottom to top.
  Sing didderoo daisy, my jewel now be aisy,
    This London agrah! is the devil's own shop.

The great city wax-work was all a mere tax-work,
    A plan to bamboozle me out of my pelf;
Says I, Mrs Salmon, c'up none of your gammon,
    Your figures are no more alive than yourself.
I ax'd an old quaker the way to Long Acre;
    With thee and with thou he so bothered my brain,
After fifty long sallies, thro' lanes and blind alleys,
    I found myself trotting in Rosemary-lane.

At night, O, how silly, along Piccadilly,
    I wander'd, when up comes a beautiful dame.
Huzza! says the lady, how do you do, Paddy?
    Says I, pretty well, ma'am, I hope you're the same.
A great hulking fellow, who held her umbrella,
    Then gave me a terrible thump on the nob;
She ran away squalling: I, Watch! Watch! was bawling;
    But the devil a *watch* was there left in my fob.

Anonymous

Over the years this popular song about a spalpeen, or casual farm labourer, has appeared in various guises, on early ballad-sheets, in a 1909 collection by PW Joyce, and in Colm Ó Lochlainn's invaluable More Irish Street Ballads (1965), *from which this version is taken. In Donagh Mac Donagh's* Ballads With Music *the italicised word in verse 2 is annotated as 'niggard'; who are we to argue?*

THE GALBALLY FARMER

One evening of late as I happened to stray,
To the County Tipp'rary I straight took my way,
To dig the potatoes and work by the day,
    I hired with a Galbally farmer.
I asked him how far we were bound for to go,
The night it was dark and the north wind did blow,
I was hungry and tired and my spirits were low,
    For I got neither whiskey nor cordial.

This niggardly miser he mounted his steed
To the Galbally mountains he posted with speed;
And surely I thought that my poor heart would bleed
    To be trudging behind that old *naygur*.
When we came to his cottage I entered it first;
It seemed like a kennel or ruined old church:
Says I to myself, 'I am left in the lurch
    In the house of old Darby O Leary.'

I well recollect it was Michaelmas night,
To a hearty good supper he did me invite,
A cup of sour milk that would physic a snipe –
    'Twould give you the trotting disorder.
The wet old potatoes would poison the cats,
The barn where my bed was was swarming with rats,
'Tis little I thought it would e'er be my lot
    To lie in that hole until morning.

By what he had said to me I understood,
My bed in the barn it was not very good;
The blanket was made at the time of the flood;
    The quilt and the sheets in proportion.
'Twas on this old miser I looked with a frown,
When the straw was brought out for to make my
    shake down.
I wished that I never saw Galbally town,
    Or the sky over Darby O Leary.

I worked in Kilconnell, I worked in Kilmore,
I worked in Knockainy and Shanballymore,
In Pallas-a-Nicker and Sollohodmore,
    With decent respectable farmers:
I worked in Tipperary, the Rag, and Rosegreen,
At the mount of Kilfeakle, the Bridge of Aleen,
But such woeful starvation I never yet seen
    As I got from old Darby O Leary.

Anonymous

*Like the last, a famous song with many variants. This text
tries to reconcile the best of them.*

THE GALWAY RACES

As I rode out through Galway Town to seek for
    recreation
On the seventeenth of August, me mind being
    elevated,
There were multitudes assembled with their tickets at
    the station,
And me eyes began to dazzle and I going to see the
    races.

There were passengers from Limerick and passengers
    from Nenagh,
Passengers from Dublin and sportsmen from Tipperary,
There were passengers from Kerry and all quarters of
    the nation,
And our member Mr Hardy for to join the Galway
    Blazers.

There were multitudes from Aran and members from
    New Quay shore,
The boys from Connemara and the Clare unmarried
    maidens,
People from Cork City who were loyal, true and faithful
And brought home the Fenian prisoners from dying in
    foreign nations.

And it's there you'll see confectioners with sugar
    sticks and dainties,
The lozenges and oranges, the lemonade and raisins;
The gingerbread and spices to accommodate the ladies,
And a big crubeen for thruppence to be suckin' while
    you're able.

And it's there you'll see the gamblers, the thimbles
    and the garters,
And the sporting Wheel of Fortune with the four and
    twenty quarters,
There was others without scruple pelting wattles at
    poor Maggy,
And her father well contented and he looking at his
    daughter.

And it's there you'll see the pipers and the fiddlers
    competing,
The nimble-footed dancers and they trippin' on the
    daisies.
There was others shoutin' cigars and lights, and bills
    for all the races
With the colours of the jockeys, and the price and
    horses' ages.

And it's there you'll see the jockeys and they mounted
    on most stately,
The pink and blue, the red and green, the Emblem of
    our nation,
When the bell was rung for starting, all the horses
    seemed impatient,
I thought they never stood on ground, their speed was
    so amazing.

There was half a million people there of all
    denominations,
The Catholic, the Protestant, the Jew and
    Presbyterian.
There was yet no animosity, no matter what
    persuasion,
But fáilte and hospitality, inducing fresh acquaintance.

Mr Gavan
(attrib.)

*Though Athy is in County Kildare, these verses may be
another product of Galway. Colm Ó Lochlainn mentions a
music sheet from the 1870s where they are credited to a
certain 'Mr Gavan, the celebrated Galway poet.' In verse 6
'chaneys' (from 'china') means 'crockery'.*

LANIGAN'S BALL

In the town of Athy one Jeremy Lanigan
Battered away till he hadn't a pound,
His father he died and made him a man again,
Left him a farm and ten acres of ground.
He gave a grand party to friends and relations,
Who did not forget him when come to the wall,
And if you but listen, I'll make your eyes glisten,

At the rows and the ructions of Lanigan's Ball.

Myself to be sure got free invitations,
For all the nice girls and boys I might ask,
And just in a minute both friends and relations
Were dancing as merry as bees round a cask.
Miss Judy O'Daly, that nice little milliner,
Tipped me the wink for to give her a call
And soon I arrived with Peggy McGilligan,
Just in time for Lanigan's Ball.

There was lashings of punch and wine for the ladies,
Potatoes and cakes, there was bacon and tea,
There were the Nolans, Dolans, O'Gradys
Courting the girls and dancing away.
The songs they went round as plenty as water,
From the Harp that once sounded in Tara's old Hall,
To sweet Nelly Gray and the Rat-catcher's daughter,
All singing together at Lanigan's Ball.

They were doing all kinds of nonsensical polkas
All round the room in a whirligig,
But Julia and I soon banished their nonsense
And tipped them a twist of a real Irish jig.
Och mavrone, how the girls they got mad on me
And danced till you'd think the ceilings would fall,
For I spent three weeks at Brooks's Academy,
Learning steps for Lanigan's Ball.

The boys were as merry, the girls all hearty,
Dancing away in couples and groups,
Till an accident happened young Terence McCarthy,
He put his right leg through Miss Finnerty's hoops.
The creature she fainted and cried 'Meelia murther',
Called for her brothers and gathered them all;
Carmody swore that he'd go no further
Till he'd have satisfaction at Lanigan's Ball.

In the midst of the row Miss Kerrigan fainted,
Her cheeks at the same time as red as the rose,
Some of the lads decreed she was painted,
She took a small drop too much I suppose.
Her sweetheart Ned Morgan so powerful and able,
When he saw his fair colleen stretched by the wall,
He tore the left leg from under the table,
And smashed all the chaneys at Lanigan's Ball.

Boys, oh boys, 'tis then there was ructions,
Myself got a lick from big Phelim McHugh,
But soon I replied to his kind introduction,
And kicked up a terrible hullabaloo.
Ould Casey the piper was near being strangled,
They squeezed up his pipes, bellows, chanters and all,
The girls in their ribbons they all got entangled,
And that put an end to Lanigan's Ball.

Anonymous

An early nineteenth-century political street song, which
reads almost as if it is in code – though everyone at the time
would have understood that the hag was actually Ireland.

THE GAY OLD HAG

Will you come a boating, my gay old hag,
Will you come a boating, my tight old hag,
Will you come a boating, down the Liffey floating?
I'll make a pair of oars of your two long shins.

Crush her in the corner the gay old hag,
Crush her in the corner the tight old hag,
Crush her in the corner and keep her snug and warm,
Put powder in her horn, she's a fine old hag.

Napoleon's on dry land, says the gay old hag,
Napoleon's on dry land, says the tight old hag,
Napoleon's on dry land, with a sword in his right hand,
He's a gallant Ribbon man, says the gay old hag.

My mother's getting young, says the gay old hag,
My mother's getting young, says the gay old hag,
My mother's getting young and she'll have another
        son
To make the orange run, says the gay old hag.

Remember '98, says the gay old hag,
When our Boys you did defeat, says the gay old hag,
Then our Boys you did defeat, but we'll beat you out
        compleat,
Now you're nearly out of date, says the fine old hag.

Anonymous

*For over two centuries, the lives of the Irish saints have
inspired many irreverent retellings. This one, which is
presumably about St Kevin – his rocky 'bed' can still be seen
at Glendalough – is one of the most famous:*

THE GLENDALOUGH SAINT

In Glendalough lived an old saint,
Renowned for his learning and piety.
His manners were curious and quaint,
And he looked upon girls with disparity.

But as he was fishin' one day,
A catchin' some kind of trout, sir,
Young Kathleen was walkin' that way
Just to see what the saint was about, sir.

You're a mighty fine fisher', says Kate,
''Tis yourself is the boy that can hook them,
But when you have caught them so nate,
Don't you want some young woman to cook them?'

'Be gone out of that', said the saint,
'For I am a man of great piety,
Me character I wouldn't taint,
By keeping such class of society.'

But Kathleen wasn't goin' to give in,
For when he got home to his rockery,
He found her sitting therein,
A-polishing up of his crockery.

He gave the poor creature a shake,
Oh, I wish that the peelers had caught him:
He threw her right into the lake,
And of course she sank down to the bottom.

It is rumoured from that very day,
Kathleen's ghost can be seen on the river,
And the saint never raised up his hand
For he died of the right kind of fervour.

AD Godley

*Alfred Godley (1856–1925), a childhood friend of Percy French,
went on to become an eminent classical scholar at Oxford.
This 'Oirish' ballad was written shortly after Charles
Stewart Parnell (here 'Doolan') was imprisoned in 1881.*

THE ARREST

Come hither, Terence Mulligan, and sit upon the floor,
And list a tale of woe that's worse than all you heard
    before:
Of all the wrongs the Saxon's done since Erin's shores
    he trod
The blackest harm he's wrought us now – sure
    Doolan's put in quod!

It was the Saxon minister, he said unto himself,
I'll never have a moment's peace till Doolan's on the
    shelf –
So bid them make a warrant out and send it by the
    mail,
To put that daring patriot in dark Kilmainham gaol.

The minions of authority that document they wrote,
And Mr Buckshot took the thing upon the Dublin
    boat:
Och! sorra much he feared the waves, incessantly that
    roar,
For deeper flows the sea of blood he shed on Ireland's
    shore!

But the hero slept unconscious still – 'tis kilt he was
    with work,
Haranguing of the multitudes in Waterford and Cork, –
Till Buckshot and the polis came and rang the front
    door bell
Disturbing of his slumbers sweet in Morrison's Hotel.

Then out and spake brave Morrison – 'Get up, yer
    sowl, and run!'
(O bright shall shine on History's page the name of
    Morrison!)
'To see the light of Erin quenched I *never* could
    endure:

Slip on your boots – I'll let yez out upon the kitchen
    doore!'

But proudly flashed the patriot's eye and he sternly
    answered – 'No!
I'll never turn a craven back upon my country's foe:
Doolan aboo, for Liberty! ... and anyhow' (says he)
'The Government's locked the kitchen-door and taken
    away the key.'

They seized him and they fettered him, those minions
    of the Law,
('Twas Pat the Boots was looking on, and told me
    what he saw) –
But sorra step that Uncrowned King would leave the
    place, until
A ten per cent reduction he had got upon his bill.

Had I been there with odds to aid – say twenty men to
    one –
It stirs my heart to think upon the deeds I might have
    done!
I wouldn't then be telling you the melancholy tale
How Ireland's pride imprisoned lies in dark
    Kilmainham gaol.

Yet weep not, Erin, for thy son! 'tis he that's doing well,
For Ireland's thousands feed him there within his
    dungeon cell, –
And if by chance he eats too much and his health
    begins to fail,
The Government then will let him out from black
    Kilmainham gaol!

*Godley also poked fun at the sentimental posturing of the
post-Parnellite Irish Parliamentary Party at Westminster.*

PHASES OF THE CELTIC REVIVAL

Erin aboo! though the desolate ocean
    Sever my steps from the Gem of the Sea,
Why do I cry in a voice of emotion
    'Slainte, mavourneen acushla machree'?

Lo! 'tis the National Spirit is on me –
　　Lo! in the Strand as I peaceably go,
Thinking of wrongs that the Saxon has done me,
　　Dreaming afar of the County Mayo.

How shall Ierne her sentiments utter,
　　How shall Hibernians their feelings express,
Robed by a Sassenach tailor and cutter?
　　Bring me, O bring me the National Dress!

Doomed by the Saxon his fashions to follow,
　　Long at the feet of his vestments I sat;
Now for a coat that is tailed like a swallow –
　　Stick a dudeen in the brim of my hat:

Ragged and torn be the frieze of my breeches,
　　Garter my shins with a hayrope or two –
Thus went the Chiefs of whom History teaches,
　　Parnell and Grattan and Brian Boru!

Erin! if e'er 'mid the wealth that is London's
　　Lightly I recked of the pride of Clonmel,
Snared for a while by the alien's abundance,
　　Won by the Westminster Palace Hotel –

'Twas not my heart her allegiance forsaking,
　　'Twas not affections that falter and fail:
'Twas that a coat of the Sassenach's making
　　Could not consort with the thoughts of the Gael!

Now, when my breast in the passions that stir it
　　(Phadrig! a tumbler, mo bouchal aroon!)
Feels the approach of the National Spirit
　　(Put in the sugar and mix with a spoon), –

Now, when I glow with a Nation's afflatus,
　　Garments I'll wear that my ardour denote:
Tyrants who crush us, and foemen who hate us,
　　Tread, if you dare, on the tail of my coat!

*Two impeccably turned examples of traditional light verse
at its best, both of them dreaming of escape from the
shackles of university life:*

THE PARADISE OF LECTURERS

When you might be a name for the world to acclaim,
  and when Opulence dawns on the view,
Why slave like a Turk at Collegiate work for a wholly
  inadequate screw?
Why grind at the trade – insufficiently paid – of
  instructing for Mods. and for Greats,
When fortunes immense are diurnally made by a
  lecturing tour in the States?

Do you know that in scores they will pay at the doors
  – these millions in darkness who grope –
For a glimpse of Mark Twain or a word from Hall
  Caine or a reading from Anthony Hope?
We are ignorant here of the glorious career which
  conspicuous talent awaits:
Not a master of style but is making his pile by the
  lectures he gives in the States!

With amazement I hear of the chances they lose – of
  the simply incredible sums
Which a Barrie might have (if he did not refuse) for
  reciting *A Window in Thrums*:
Of the prospects of gain which are offered in vain as a
  sop to the Laureate's pride:
Of the price which I learn Mr Bradshaw might earn by
  declaiming his excellent Guide.

Columbia! desist from soliciting those who your
  bribes and petitions contemn:
Though plutocrats scorn the rewards you propose,
  there are others superior to them:
Why burden the proud with superfluous pelf, who
  wealth in abundance possess,
When indigent Worth (I allude to myself) would go
  for substantially less?

For Europe, I know, to oblivion may doom the fruits
  of my talented brain,
But they're perfectly sure of creating a boom in the
  wilds of Kentucky and Maine:
They'll appreciate *there* my illustrious work on the
  way to make Pindar to scan,
And Culture will hum in the State of New York when
  I read it my essay on Ἄυ!

I've a scheme, which is this: I will start for the West as
    a Limited Lecturing Co.,
And the public invite in the same to invest to the tune
    of a million or so:
They will all be recouped for initial expense by
    receiving their share of the 'gates',
Which I venture to think will be truly immense when
    I lecture on Prose in the States.

Thus Merit will not be permitted to rot – as it does –
    on Obscurity's shelf:
Thus the national hoard shall with profit be stored
    (with a trifle of course for myself):
For lectures are dear in that fortunate sphere, and are
    paid for at fabulous rates, –
All the gold of Klondike isn't anything like to the
    sums that are made in the States!

SWITZERLAND

In the steamy, stuffy Midlands, 'neath an English
    summer sky,
When the holidays are nearing with the closing of July,
And experienced Alpine stagers and impetuous
    recruits
Are renewing with the season their continual disputes
Those inveterate disputes
On the newest Alpine routes –
And inspecting the condition of their mountaineering
    boots,

You may stifle your reflections, you may banish them
    afar,
You may try to draw a solace from the thought of
    'Nächstes Jahr' –
But your heart is with those climbers, and you'll
    feverishly yearn
To be crossing of the Channel with your luggage
    labelled 'Bern,'
Leaving England far astern
With a ticket through to Bern,
And regarding your profession with a lordly
    unconcern.

They will lie beside the torrent, just as you were wont
   to do,
With the woodland green around them and a
   snowfield shining through:
They will tread the higher pastures, where celestial
   breezes blow,
While the valley lies in shadow and the peaks are all
   aglow –
Where the airs of heaven blow
'Twixt the pine woods and the snow,
And the shades of evening deepen in the valley far
   below.

*'Motor Bus' is Godley's best-known verse. However, as Latin
disappears from our schools, this ingenious grammatical*
aide memoire *seems destined to be forgotten too.*

MOTOR BUS

What is this that roareth thus?
Can it be a Motor Bus?
Yes, the smell and hideous hum
Indicat Motorem Bum!
Implet in the Corn and High
Terror me Motoris Bi:
Bo Motori clamitabo
Ne Motore caedar a Bo –
Dative be or Ablative
So thou only let us live:
Whither shall thy victims flee?
Spare us, spare us, Motor Be!
Thus I sang; and still anigh
Came in hordes Motores Bi,
Et complebat omne forum
Copia Motorum Borum.
How shall wretches live like us
Cincti Bis Motoribus?
Domine, defende nos
Contra hos Motores Bos!

Oliver St John Gogarty

A generation after AD Godley, Oliver St John Gogarty (1878–1957) was also steeped in the classics, but he had a far more puckish and bawdy sense of humour. His verse acrostic welcoming the soldiers back from the Boer War (THE WHORES WILL BE BUSY') is well known, but less familiar is this innocent-seeming verse, which he persuaded the very high-minded magazine Dana to publish in 1905. It is perhaps sufficient to say that horticulture is not really its main concern:

MOLLY

Molly through the garden
    Laughed and played with me,
And the gate unbarred in
    To the rosery.

Just she said to show me
    How the roses grew,
And when she would show me,
    Ask me if I knew

Which of all was fairest,
    Crescent bud or rose,
Till I guessed the rarest
    She would not disclose.

Laughing little lady,
    All her features shone
Like a star whose body
    And whose soul are one.

So I went intending
    To please her if I could,
Pondering then, and bending,
    Pointed to the bud.

But the moment after
    Saw her face illume
With a peal of laughter
    Reaching for the bloom.

One of the last of the late AN Jeffares' many scholarly books
was his glorious The Poems & Plays of Oliver St John
Gogarty *(2001), which includes many of the fugitive verses*
that circulated around Dublin for years. Here are four short
examples testifying to the writer's fascination with medical
aspects of sex – in the first one, for example, G.P.I. stands
for General Paralysis of the Insane, a diagnosis given to
those in the last stages of syphilis:

SUPPOSE

Suppose the Pope had G.P.I.
What would you say to that?
To his Infallibility
Would you write, NIL OBSTAT?
And gladlier kiss the Pontifical toes
If the Pontifex hadn't got a bridge to his nose?

But symptoms grow intensified
And the meninges thicker,
Do you think he'd be satisfied
With merely being Vicar,
Nor wake one day with the terrible boast:
I'm Father, Son and the Holy Ghost?

SING A SONG OF SEXPENCE

The King was in his countinghouse
Counting up his pelf;
The Queen was in her parlour
Playing with herself;
The Maid was in the garden
Trying to show the Groom
The vagina not the rectum
Is the entrance to the womb.

Mercury was a kill-or-cure treatment for some venereal
diseases. Gogarty adds a verse to the renowned ballad (see
page 27).

BRIAN O'LYNN

Brian O'Lynn had the pox and the gleet,
And he stunk like a privy in Mecklenburg Street,
Great globules of mercury dropped from his chin.
'Be Jasus, I'm rotten,' said Brian O'Lynn.

*An epigram prompted by a fatality involving a neon sign in
Dublin.*

ON A FALLEN ELECTRICIAN

Here's my tribute to 'lectrician Joe,
Who fell to his death through the O in Oxo.
He's gone to a land which is far far better
And he went, as he came, through a hole in a letter.

*Having been a Senator 1922-6, Gogarty left the country for
good in 1937, disgusted by many aspects of the new Ireland,
not least the 1929 Censorship of Publications Act.*

GOOSEY GOOSEY GANDER CENSORED
'TO RIDICULE THE IRISH CENSORS'

Goosey Goosey Gander
Where do you mmmmm
Upstairs and mmmmmmm
In a lady's mmmmmmm?

*Oddly, 'Ringsend', one of Gogarty's most celebrated works,
was considered to be 'light verse' when it was written, but is
so no longer. He said that he wrote it after reading Tolstoy.*

RINGSEND

I will live in Ringsend
With a red-headed whore,
And the fan-light gone in
Where it lights the hall-door;

And listen each night
For her querulous shout,
As at last she streels in
And the pubs empty out.
To soothe that wild breast
With my old-fangled songs,
Till she feels it redressed
From inordinate wrongs,
Imagined, outrageous,
Preposterous wrongs,
Till peace at last comes,
Shall be all I will do,
Where the little lamp blooms
Like a rose in the stew;
And up the back-garden
The sound comes to me
Of the lapsing, unsoilable,
Whispering sea.

Oliver Goldsmith

*Goldsmith (1728–1774) is of course very much part of
poetry's accepted canon, but since he, Swift and a few
others show in their work all the virtues that we were
seeking for* Ireland's Other Poetry, *it would have been
foolish to exclude them. Their influence on subsequent 'non-
serious' Irish verse is in any case undeniable.*

*Almost all his work was written in London, where he
lived on his wits and his writings. The spectre of poverty
hovered over Grub Street, and though Goldsmith himself
never quite starved, he remained acutely aware of those
who did:*

DESCRIPTION OF AN AUTHOR'S BED-CHAMBER

Where the Red Lion, staring o'er the way,
Invites each passing stranger that can pay;
Where Calvert's butt, and Parsons' black champagne,
Regale the drabs and bloods of Drury Lane;
There in a lonely room, from bailiffs snug,
The Muse found Scroggen stretch'd beneath a rug.
A window, patch'd with paper, lent a ray,
That dimly show'd the state in which he lay;

The sanded floor that grits beneath the tread;
The humid wall with paltry pictures spread;
The royal Game of Goose was there in view,
And the Twelve Rules the royal martyr drew;
The Seasons, framed with listing, found a place,
And brave Prince William show'd his lamp-black face.
The morn was cold; he views with keen desire
The rusty grate unconscious of a fire:
With beer and milk arrears the frieze was scored,
And five cracked tea-cups dress'd the chimney-board;
A night-cap deck'd his brows instead of bay,
A cap by night – a stocking all the day!

Goldsmith's most famous short poem.

AN ELEGY ON THE DEATH OF A MAD DOG

Good people all, of every sort,
    Give ear unto my song,
And if you find it wondrous short,
    It cannot hold you long.
In Islington there was a man,
    Of whom the world might say,
That still a godly race he ran,
    Whene'er he went to pray.
A kind and gentle heart he had,
    To comfort friends and foes;
The naked every day he clad,
    When he put on his clothes.
And in that town a dog was found,
    As many dogs there be,
Both mongrel, puppy, whelp, and hound,
    And curs of low degree.
This dog and man at first were friends;
    But when a pique began,
The dog, to gain his private ends,
    Went mad, and bit the man.
Around from all the neighbouring streets
    The wond'ring neighbours ran,
And swore the dog had lost his wits,
    To bite so good a man.
The wound it seem'd both sore and sad
    To every Christian eye;

And while they swore the dog was mad,
　　They swore the man would die.
But soon a wonder came to light,
　　That show'd the rogues they lied:
The man recover'd of the bite –
　　The dog it was that died.

Oliver Goldsmith was one of the very few poets ever to notice that booksellers, upon whom writers then depended for their livelihood, can be human too.

EPITAPH ON EDWARD PURDON

Here lies poor Ned Purdon, from misery freed,
　　Who long was a bookseller's hack:
He lived such a damnable life in this world,
　　I don't think he'll wish to come back.

Tony Lumpkin's party piece from Goldsmith's greatest work, She Stoops to Conquer *(1773).*

SONG

Let school-masters puzzle their brain,
　　With grammar, and nonsense, and learning;
Good liquor, I stoutly maintain,
　　Gives *genus* a better discerning.
Let them brag of their heathenish gods,
　　Their Lethes, their Styxes, and Stygians:
Their Quis, and their Quaes, and their Quods,
They're all but a parcel of Pigeons.
Toroddle, toroddle, toroll.

When Methodist preachers come down
　　A-preaching that drinking is sinful,
I'll wager the rascals a crown
　　They always preach best with a skinful.
But when you come down with your pence,
　　For a slice of their scurvy religion,
I'll leave it to all men of sense,
　　But you, my good friend, are the pigeon.
Toroddle, toroddle, toroll.

Then come, put the jorum about,
 And let us be merry and clever;
Our hearts and our liquors are stout;
 Here's the Three Jolly Pigeons for ever.
Let some cry up woodcock or hare,
 Your bustards, your ducks, and your widgeons;
Out of all the birds in the air,
 Here's a health to the Three Jolly Pigeons.
  Toroddle, toroddle, toroll.

*It may have been the song above that prompted Colm Ó
Lochlainn's suggestion that 'The March of Intellect', found
in a Dublin songbook of the early 1800s, was one that
Goldsmith wrote while he was at TCD in the 1740s. The idea
seems unlikely – the (admittedly Irish) word 'botheration',
in the last verse, for instance, would predate the OED's
earliest citation by over fifty years. Perhaps the poet was
someone of similar education who had read Goldsmith.
Either way, it's good fun, and deserves to be read today.*

THE MARCH OF INTELLECT

Oh! Learning's a very fine thing,
 As also is wisdom and knowledge,
For a man is as great as a king,
 If he has but the airs of a college,
And nowadays all must admit,
 In learning we're wonderful favoured,
For you scarce o'er your window can spit,
 But some learning man is be-slavered
  – Sing tol de rol ol de rol ay.

We'll all of us shortly be doomed
 To part with our plain understanding,
For intellect now has assumed,
 An attitude truly commanding!
All ranks are so dreadfully wise,
 Common sense is set quite at defiance,
And the child for its porridge that cries
 Must cry in the Language of Science.
  – Sing tol de rol ol de rol ay.

The weaver it surely becomes
 To talk of his web's involution

For doubtless the hero of thrums
    Is a member of some institution;
He speaks of supply and demand
    With the ease of a great legislator,
And almost can tell you off-hand,
    That the smaller is less than the greater.
      – Sing tol de rol ol de rol ay.

The tailor, in cutting his cloth,
    Will speak of the true Conic Section,
And no tailor is now such a Goth
    But he talks of his trade's genuflection,
If you laugh at his bandy-legged clan,
    He calls it unhandsome detraction
And cocks up his chin like a man,
    Though we know that he's only a fraction!
      – Sing tol de rol ol de rol ay.

The blacksmith 'mid cinders and smoke,
    Whose visage is one of the dimmest –
His furnace profoundly will poke
    With the air of a Practical Chymist;
Poor Vulcan has recently got
    A lingo that's almost historic,
And can tell you that iron is hot,
    Because it is filled with caloric.
      – Sing tol de rol ol de rol ay.

The mason in book-learned tone,
    Describes in the very best grammar
The resistance that dwells in the stone,
    And the power that resides in the hammer,
For the son of the trowel and hod
    Looks as big as the frog in the fable
While he talks in a jargon as odd
    As his brethren the builders of Babel.
      – Sing tol de rol ol de rol ay.

The cobbler that sits at your gate
    Now pensively points his hog's bristle
Though the very same cobbler of late
    O'er his work used to sing and to whistle;
But cobbling's a paltry pursuit
    For a man of polite education –
His work may be trod under foot

Yet he's one of the Lords of creation.
    – Sing tol de rol ol de rol ay.

Oh! Learning's a very fine thing!
    It is almost treason to doubt it –
Yet many of whom I could sing
    Perhaps might as well be without it,
And without it my days I will pass
    For to me it was ne'er worth a dollar,
And I don't wish to look like an ass
    By trying to talk like a scholar.
      – Sing tol de rol ol de rol ay.

Let schoolmasters bother their brain
    In their dry and their musty vocation;
But what can the rest of us gain
    By meddling with such botheration?
We cannot be very far wrong
    If we live like our fathers before us,
Whose learning went round in a song,
    And whose cares were dispelled in the chorus.
      – Sing tol de rol ol de rol ay.

Anonymous

*Through the central decades of the twentieth century,
Dublin Opinion (Masthead: 'Humour is the Safety Valve
of a Nation') was Ireland's answer to* Punch. *Many
contributions were unsigned, but between them the
proprietors Charles E Kelly and Tom Collins supplied most
of the content, both words and pictures. The following
throwaway comment is the first of a handful of verses we
take from this now half-forgotten treasure trove.*

GPO DOOR

Augustus Eusebius Locke
In error was firm as a rock.
He always went in by *amach*
And always went out by *isteach*.

George Granville, Lord Lansdowne

Though Alexander Pope called him 'Granville the Polite',
Samuel Johnson thought his work 'profane': the charms of
the lower orders have always been a problem for the
aristocracy …

TO CHLOE

Bright is the day, and as the morning fair,
Such Chloe is – and common as the air.

AP Graves

Alfred Percival Graves (1846-1931) was the son of a Bishop of
Limerick and a lifelong editor and maker of anthologies.
Still, some of his verses, in which he attempted (and failed)
to convey genuine Irish form and feeling in English retain a
peculiar charm. James Joyce used to recite his most famous,
'Father O'Flynn'. Here, however, is another real oddity that
deserves to be better known:

THE ROSE OF KENMARE

    I've been soft in a small way
    On the girleens of Galway,
And the Limerick lasses have made me feel quare;
    But there's no use denyin',
    No girl I've set eye on
Could compate wid Rose Ryan of the town of Kenmare.
      O, where
    Can her like be found?
      No where,
    The country round,
    Spins at her wheel
      Daughter as true,
    Sets in the reel,
      Wid a slide of the shoe
        a slinderer,
        tinderer,
        purtier,
        wittier colleen than you,
      Rose, aroo!
    Her hair mocks the sunshine,

And the soft, silver moonshine
Neck and arm of the colleen completely eclipse;
Whilst the nose of the jewel
Slants straight as Carran Tual
From the heaven in her eye to her heather-sweet lip.
O, where, etc.

Did your eyes ever follow
The wings of the swallow
Here and there, light as air, o'er the meadow field glance?
For if not you've no notion
Of the exquisite motion
Of her sweet little feet as they dart in the dance.
O, where, etc.

If y' inquire why the nightingale
Still shuns th' invitin' gale
That wafts every song-bird but her to the West,
Faix she knows, I suppose,
Ould Kenmare has a Rose
That would sing any Bulbul to sleep in her nest.
O, where, etc.

When her voice gives the warnin'
For the milkin' in the mornin'
Ev'n the cow known for hornin', comes runnin' to her pail;
The lambs play about her
And the small bonneens snout her
Whilst their parints salute her wid a twisht of the tail.
O, where, etc.

When at noon from our labour
We draw neighbour wid neighbour
From the heat of the sun to the shelter of the tree,
Wid spuds fresh from the bilin',
And new milk, you come smilin',
All the boys' hearts beguilin', alannah machree!
O, where, etc.

But there's one sweeter hour
When the hot day is o'er,
And we rest at the door wid the bright moon above,
And she's sittin' in the middle,
When she's guessed Larry's riddle,
Cries, 'Now for your fiddle, Shiel Dhuv, Shiel Dhuv.'

O, where
Can her like be found?
   No where,
The country round,
Spins at her wheel
   Daughter as true,
Sets in the reel,
   Wid a slide of the shoe
      a slinderer,
      tinderer,
      purtier,
      wittier colleen than you,
   Rose, aroo!

Arthur Griffith

*Alongside his political and editorial activities, Arthur
Griffith (1871–1922) was a fluent composer of humorous
verses. In many of them he expressed his contempt for the
English, the Anglo-Irish and, to put it bluntly, Protestants
and Jews. This entertaining ballad (whose ending is
marred, characteristically, by a gratuitous snipe at Jewry) is
part of a lively verse tradition of 'traveller's tales', in which
Ireland's inland waterways are the unlikely setting for
exotic adventures.*

THE THIRTEENTH LOCK

A bright-born day in merry, merry May,
And a weeping group stands by,
To bid adieu to the gallant crew,
That sails as the sun mounts high.
Leaning over the waves are the mariners brave,
Who reck not of storm or rock,
And they laugh and smoke and jest and joke,
Though they're bound for the Thirteenth Lock, yo ho!
They're bound for the Thirteenth Lock.

'O, skipper stay,' quoth a mariner gray
Who stood nigh Marrowbone Lane,
'I'm a sailor old and I trow as bold
As roves on this angry main.
Thirteen, be still! 'tis a number ill,

Beware, young man, don't mock!'
Right scornfully laughed the captain, 'See!
I'm bound for the Thirteenth Lock, yo ho!
I'm bound for the Thirteenth Lock.'

'O, Pat, beware!' cried a damsel fair,
'Sail not today my dear,
We warn, don't scorn, 'tis Friday morn,
The day true mariners fear.
And what would I do, Pat, if I lost you?
Sure my heart couldn't stand the shock.'
Full merrily laughed the captain, 'See,
I'm bound for the Thirteenth Lock, yo ho!
I'm bound for the Thirteenth Lock.'

'Cease, love, those sighs, dim not your eyes
With beauty-killing tears.
You may be bound I'll come back sound,
So calm your woman's fears,
And I'll bring to thee a chimpanzee,
A parrot, a jabberwock,
A kangaroo and a cockatoo
From the wilds of the Thirteenth Lock, yo ho!
From the wilds of the Thirteenth Lock.'

The ship set sail while a piercing wail
Rang out from the womankind.
'Port yer helm a-lee,' quoth the captain he,
'And we'll catch the southern wind.
Spur up your steed to its fiercest speed,
'Tis long past twelve o'clock.
We should sight the shore of Inchicore,
Then, ho! for the Thirteenth Lock, yo ho!
Ho! for the Thirteenth Lock.'

But never the shore of Inchicore
Could the man at the masthead see,
Though he craned his neck. To the quarter deck
He came and thus spake he:
'Skipper, 'tis true that I'm your crew,
Your mate, cook – all in stock,
But I'm hanged if I'll steer for a place so queer
As this cursed Thirteenth Lock, yo ho!
As this cursed Thirteenth Lock.'

'Let us change our way till another day,
And smoke and spin a yarn;
On the evening's tide we'll at anchor ride
In the bay of Dolphin's Barn.'
Then the skipper quick gave a mighty kick
And the mariner felt the shock,
And the crew found a grave 'neath the deep blue wave
On the way to the Thirteenth Lock, yo ho!
On the way to the Thirteenth Lock.

'Thus ever,' quoth he, 'perish mutiny,'
And turned him round with a smile,
About and around, and lo! he found
A shape behind the while,
With fiery eyes and horns of size
And a tail that might Peter shock.
At the skipper's gape up spake the shape:
'I'm bound for the Thirteenth Lock, yo ho!
I'm bound for the Thirteenth Lock.'

By the harbour sands a maiden stands,
With her gaze fixed out to sea;
But she'll watch in vain, for never again
Will he come with that chimpanzee.
And Israel stands, wringing both his hands,
His face like a marble block,
For the skipper bold borrowed half his gold,
Ere he sailed for the Thirteenth Lock, yo ho!
Ere he sailed for the Thirteenth Lock.

Griffith naturally disliked 'West-Brits' and 'Castle
Catholics', indeed, anyone who valued Ireland's links with
England. People like that tended to live in clusters in south

County Dublin – an alternative Ireland he dubbed
'Shoneenia' (after Seoinín, or 'little John Bull'). These
verses purport to have been written by a Professor Atkinson
of TCD (who had recently summed up the Irish language
and its literature as 'largely silly or indecent'). The
Irishman *in verse 2 is the* United Irishman, *the newspaper*
Griffith founded in 1899.

LUCINDA

Oh! lovely Lucy Lanigan, my distant twinkling star!
She walks in beauty every day through haughty, blue
    Rathgar,
She wears a frock from Chester and a London blouse
    and hat,
And she owns a British pugdog and a doaty Manxland
    cat.
        Oh! Lucinda!
        My beaming, gleaming star,
        I would that I were good enough
        To dwell in dear Rathgar.

Lucinda's so respectable the only songs she'll sing
Are 'Genevieve,' 'They Follow Me' and 'Heaven Bless
    the King!'
She reads the penny novelettes, the *Leader* too, she'll
    scan –
But she shudders at the mention of the horrid
    Irishman.
        Oh! Lucinda!
        My beaming, gleaming star,
        I would that I were good enough
        To dwell in dear Rathgar.

Her pa's a nice old gentleman, he lives beyond the gates
Of Dublin, where his business is, that he may dodge
    the rates.
Her ma collects old clothes and tracts for heathens in
    Hong Kong,
And her brother says 'Bay Jove!' and plays at croquet
    and ping-pong.
        Oh! Lucinda!
        My beaming, gleaming star,
        I would that I were good enough
        To dwell in dear Rathgar.

Then farewell, Oh! Lucinda, although my heart must
    break,
I'll go down to the Dodder and I'll jump in for your
    sake,
For they say, and, faith, I'll risk it, that when they've
    crossed the bar,
The souls of all the *seoiníní* foregather in Rathgar.
        Oh! Lucinda!
        I'm off to Donnybrook
        To drown myself to live for you
        And be your faithful spook.

*Stage-Irish theatricals of the sort popularised by Boucicault
were yet another of Griffith's targets: here he derides
Charles Hyland, manager of the Gaiety Theatre, as well as
the unionist newspapers of Dublin and for good measure
various grandee Trinity College dons – Apollo, Tony, Old
Morality were respectively nicknames for Professors
Mahaffy, Traill and the despised Atkinson.*

VALUABLE RECIPE FOR THE EMERALD ISLE

Would you be deemed a man of wit
And in Shoneenia make a hit,
Sit down and write a funny play;
I'll tell you shortly what's the way;
First take a Cockney without 'h's',
Dress him in what he calls 'knee-braiches',
And crownless hat with pipe in band,
And put a blackthorn in his hand;
Then make him say to all his neighbours:
'Och! tare-an'-ouns' and 'Oh! be japers!'
Take next an 'Arriet and attire her
Just as old Charteris would admire her;
Then make her squeal and kick and prance,
And there you've got an Irish dance.
Lug half a dozen others in
Whose business is to jump and grin,
Next sprinkle nicely through the play
Suggestions culled from Rabelais,
And jests in Britain still much told
That in Boccaccio's days were old,
And garnish well with 'Pillalu,'

'Bedad,' 'Begorra,' 'Wirrasthrue,'
Shure, musha, if you're shtuck for chaff,
'Ochone' will allus rise a laugh.
Drop in some whiskey and shillelagh,
And whoo, hurroo, 'twill make up gaily!
Now take your play and with it go
To Chancery-lane or Westland Row,
Herr Schwartzengard or Signor Ninni
Will find you notes for half a guinea;
And next assume a winning smile and
Pop off at once to Mister Eyland.
Should that great man your play befriend
Your troubles then are at an end;
Nor should you fear financial knocks as
Smut always pays in Dublin boxes.
Should Shakespeare, Ibsen, Molière come
The Dublin boxes stay at home,
But when there's coarseness and a ballet
The Dublin boxes nobly rally.
Should any wretched gallery gods
Presume to hiss what skunk applauds
The arm of Britain's mighty law
Will forth its 'venging truncheon draw
And knock the fellows on the noddles
For being such old mollycoddles.
The Reptile Press will sing your praises,
(Champagne's required, though, in some cases)
And dons from College Green locality –
Apollo, Tony, Old Morality –
Will shake you gravely by the hand
And hail you credit to the land;
Stout matrons ask you up to share
In tea-and-talk on Merrion Square,
And ancient maidens boast 'He dines
With us in Dalkey and Rathmines.'

*In 1897 Griffith had seen the Boer War in person. In this
biting pro-Boer propaganda verse, published after his return,
he out-Kiplings Kipling.*

THE SONG OF THE BRITISH 'ERO

I'm Trooper Robin Rape, a sojer from the Cape
    A supporter of Hold Hengland's glorious cause
And I've taken one man's share in that little 'ere affair
    When we taught the Matabili British laws:
        Bless their eyes!
    When we taught the dum-dum heathen British
      Laws.

You should have seen the fun when we worked the
  Maxim gun
    And the niggers fell like locusts all around;
How our leaders' faces glowed when they saw the
  blood that flowed
    And we stabbed the dying devils on the ground;
        Save their souls!
    We stabbed the wriggling beggars on the
      ground.

We captured in the kraals all the blessed nigger gals;
    'Twas funny boys to listen to them sue
For mercy and release, but we made them hold their
  peace,
    And we treated them as British sojers do –
        Don't you know?
    We treated then as British 'eroes do.

I guess the Gawd-saved black will respect the Union
  Jack
    For the future, boys, where'er it may be seen
And we'll put a lump of lead through the blessed
  nigger's head
    Who doesn't learn to sing 'Gawd Save the
  Queen.'
        Dear old Queen!
    We'll teach the dogs to sing 'Gawd Save the
      Queen.'

Anonymous

About eighty years before Arthur Griffith was deploring the treatment of black people in South Africa, this strange song was being sung on the stage of the Theatre Royal in Dublin. It gives a rare glimpse of what ethnic minorities had to cope with in early nineteenth-century Ireland.

GUINNESS AND COMPANY'S DRAYMAN

Near St James's Gate on Thomas-street side,
    Lived a widow who much did lack man;
Her lily white hand she long denied,
    To one John Brown a black man.
This John Brown stuck to her tight,
    But her heart was another way man,
For her thoughts by day and her dreams by night
    Was on Guinness and Company's drayman.

This drayman was more than six feet high,
    A proper huge broad backed man;
She liked him best the reason why,
    He was twice as big as the black man:
His face was like the full moon just rose,
    More like a fat cook than a lay man,
His eyes they did sparkle and so did the nose
    Of Guinness and Company's drayman.

John Brown was a footman and wore a cocked hat,
    Of dressing he had the knack man,
Round his neck was tied a white cravat,
    Just to show off the face of the black man,
Of the shape of his legs, he took much pride,
    Though they had no shape to display man,
And he looked when he laughed with his mouth so
    wide,
    As if he could swallow the drayman.

'Now plainly,' says she, 'if my mind I tells?
    I don't wish your feelings to rack man,
But surely there is such a nasty smells,
    That comes from every black man,
You can't think how my nose it pains,
    Though I turns it another way man?'
Says Brown, 'Dan't so bad as the stink of the grains,
    From Guinness and Company's drayman.'

This black man Brown did not despair,
    He was a decent clack man,
Says he, 'Me know my face not fair,
    Dats cause me such a black man. –
Black nor white finger can't feel,
    In the dark 'tis all the same man,
But I think myself much more genteel,
    Than Guinness and Company's drayman.'

Says she, 'We never can make a match,
    Yourself you off may pack man;
I think I'd get in the arms of Old Nick
    If I went to bed with a black man.'
Says he, 'Oh! scratch that out of your head
    Tho' my colour is black I'm a gay man,
You'd find it much worse to go to bed,
    With Guinness and Company's drayman.'

Now talk of the devil he's sure to come:
    The door at that moment flew back man,
And there stood the drayman all so glum,
    And he looked rather blue at the black man.
'That there lady', says he, 'is free,
    If she likes to have you she may man,
But don't you come here telling lies of me,'
    Says Guinness and Company's drayman.

Poor Mr Brown looked petrified,
    His courage was not to come back man,
He moaned and groaned and softly sighed,
    'Me vish me vasn't a black man.'
His eyes did roll and his teeth did grin,
    Says she, 'You may go on your way man,'
'And don't let me catch you coming here again,'
    Says Guinness and Company's drayman.

Charles Halpine

Born in County Meath in 1829, Halpine began as a Young Irelander and ended as considerable figure in America, an eminent journalist, politician, newspaper proprietor and soldier. He fought in the American Civil War, rising to Brigadier-General, and founded the first regiment of Afro-Americans. In his spare time he was an accomplished comic versifier. Though, like most Irish-American writers of his day, he often descended into 'begorrah-speak', a case might even be made for it in this jaw-dropping meditation on the use of the Irish as fodder for cannon or bayonet (here, 'bagnet').

SAMBO'S RIGHT TO BE KILT

Some tell us 'tis a burnin' shame
To make the naygers fight;
And that the thrade of bein' kilt
Belongs but to the white:
But as for me, upon my sowl!
So liberal are we here,
I'll let Sambo be murthered instead of myself,
On every day in the year.
　　　　On every day in the year, boys,
　　　　And in every hour of the day;
　　　　The right to be kilt I'll divide wid him,
　　　　And divil a word I'll say.

In battle's wild commotion
I shouldn't at all object
If Sambo's body should stop a ball
That was comin' for me direct;
And the prod of a Southern bagnet,
So ginerous are we here,
I'll resign, and let Sambo take it
On every day in the year.
    On every day in the year, boys,
    And wid none o' your nasty pride,
    All my right in a Southern bagnet prod,
    Wid Sambo I'll divide!

The men who object to Sambo
Should take his place and fight;
And it's betther to have a nayger's hue
Than a liver that's wake and white.
Though Sambo's black as the ace of spades,
His finger a thrigger can pull,
And his eye runs sthraight on the barrel-sights
From undher its thatch of wool.
    So hear me all, boys darlin',
    Don't think I'm tippin' you chaff,
    The right to be kilt we'll divide wid him,
    And give him the largest half!

*Over thirty years after Halpine's death, his caddish
proposal of marriage was reprinted in AM and TD
Sullivan's 'Irish Readings' (1902).*

TRUTH IN PARENTHESIS

I love – oh! more than words can tell
    (Your ninety thousand golden shiners);
You draw me by a nameless spell
    (As California draws the miners);
You are so rich in beauty's dower
    (And rich in several ways beside it),
Had I your hand within my power
    (Across a banker's draft to guide it),
No cares my future life could dim.
(My tailor, too – what joy to him!)

Oh! should you change your name for mine
    (I've given my name – on bills – to twenty),
Existence were a dream divine
    (At least so long as cash was plenty);
Our home should be a sylvan grot
    (Bath, billiard, smoking-room, and larder),
And there, forgetting and forgot
    (My present need, I'd live the harder),
Our days should pass in fresh delights
(Lethargic days, but roaring nights).

Oh, say, my young, my fawn-like girl
    (She's old enough to be my mother),
Let 'Yes' o'erleap those gates of pearl
    (My laughter it is hard to smother);
Let lips that Love hath formed for joy
    (For joy if they her purse resign me)
Long hesitate ere they destroy
    (And to a debtor's jail consign me)
The heart that beats but to adore
(Yourself the less, your fortune more).

Consent – consent, my priceless love
    (Her price precise is ninety thousand);
I swear by all around, above,
    (Her purse-strings now, I feel, are loosened),
I have not loved you for your wealth
    (Nor loved at all, as I'm a sinner);
Oh, bliss! you yield; one kiss by stealth!
    (I'm sick – that kiss has spoiled my dinner).
Now early name the blissful day
(My duns grow clamorous for their pay).

Edwin Hamilton

Another tale of doomed love, also from Irish Readings.
*Edwin Hamilton (1849–1919), a comic dramatist and
storyteller, is now remembered only because* Turko the
Terrible, *a pantomime he adapted for the Dublin stage in
1871, is mentioned in* Ulysses.

TO MY FIRST LOVE

I remember
    Meeting you
In September
    Sixty-two.
We were eating,
    Both of us;
And the meeting
    Happened thus:
Accidental,
    On the road;
(Sentimental
    Episode.)
I was gushing,
    You were shy;
You were blushing,
    So was I.
I was smitten,
    So were you
(All that's written
    Here is true.)
Any money?
    Not a bit.
Rather funny,
    Wasn't it?
Vows we plighted,
    Happy pair!
How delighted
    People were!
But your father
    To be sure
Thought it rather
    Premature;
And your mother
    Strange to say,
Was another
    In the way.
What a heaven
    Vanished then!
(You were seven,
    I was ten.)
That was many
    Years ago –
Don't let any-
    body know.

Carl Hardebeck

*The blind composer Carl Hardebeck (1869–1945), though a
lover of traditional Irish music, disliked the pipes. This
tease was written before 1912, but first published in 1965, in
Ó Lochlainn's* More Irish Street Ballads.

THE PIPER WHO PLAYED BEFORE MOSES

There was an old piper, old and hoary,
Who lived in the town of Ballingorey,
And this was the piper who played before Moses,
And this the only tune that he could play –
Nya – a – a – – a – a – a – a – – – a – – a
Nya – – a – – a – – – a – – a – – – a – – a
Nya – a – – – a – – a – – – a – – – a – – a
Nya – a – a – – – a – – a – a – a – a.

Now this old piper, old and hoary,
Who lived in the town of Ballingorey,
He died one day and he went down below
And this was the tune that he did play –
Nya – a – a – – a – a – a – a – – – a – – a *[etc.]*

And when the Divil saw this old man
He said 'Put him down in the frying pan;
For this is the piper who played before Moses
And here's the only tune that he can play' –
Nya – a – a – – a – a – a – a – – – a – – a *[etc.]*

William Hargreaves

*Some might say that there is no excuse for this sort of
thing, but when Val Doonican sang this song in 1967, it
somehow charmed its way into people's hearts, and is
now impossible to forget. William Hargreaves was an
English song writer of the 1920s, whose most famous
composition before Doonican came along was 'Burlington
Bertie From Bow'.*

DELANEY'S DONKEY

Now Delaney had a donkey that everyone admired,
Tempo'rily lazy and permanently tired,
A leg at ev'ry corner balancing his head,
And a tail to let you know which end he wanted to be
    fed.
Riley slyly said, 'We've underrated it,
Why not train it?' then he took a rag:
They rubbed it, scrubbed it, they oiled and
    embrocated it,
Got it to the post, and when the starter dropped his
    flag ...

There was Riley pushing it, shoving it, shushing it,
Hogan, Logan and ev'ryone in town,
Lined up attacking it and shoving it and smacking it –
They might as well have tried to push the Town Hall
    down.
The donkey was eyeing them, openly defying them,

Winking, blinking and twisting out of place,
Riley reversing it, ev'rybody cursing it,
The day Delaney's donkey ran the halfmile race.

The muscles of the mighty never known to flinch,
They couldn't budge the donkey a quarter of an inch,
Delaney lay exhausted, hanging round its throat
With a grip just like a Scotchman on a five pound note.
Starter, Carter, he lined up with the rest of 'em,
When it saw them, it was willing then,
It raced up, braced up, ready for the best of 'em,
They started off to cheer it but it changed its mind
    again …

There was Riley pushing it, shoving it and shushing it,
Hogan, Logan and Mary Ann MacGraw,
She started poking it, grabbing it and choking it –
It kicked her in the bustle and it laughed 'Hee-haw!'
The whigs, the conservatives, radical superlatives,
Liberals and tories, they hurried to the place,
Stood there in unity, helping the community,
The day Delaney's donkey ran the halfmile race.

The crowd began to cheer it, then Rafferty, the judge,
He came to assist them, but still it wouldn't budge;
The jockey who was riding, little John MacGee,
Was so thoroughly disgusted that he went to have his
    tea.
Hagan, Fagan was students of psychology,
Swore they'd shift it with some dynamite:
They bought it, brought it, then without apology
The donkey gave a sneeze and blew the darn stuff out
    of sight …

There was Riley pushing it, shoving it and shushing it,
Hogan, Logan and all the bally crew,
P'lice, and auxil'ary, the Garrison Artillery,
The Second Enniskillens and the Life Guards too.
They seized it and harried it, they picked it up and
    carried it,
Cheered it, steered it to the winning place,
Then the bookies drew aside, they all commited
    suicide,
Well, the day Delaney's donkey won the halfmile race.

Mrs EAG Harker

*Irresistible verses found on a copied typescript deposited in
the National Library in 1982.*

'WHEN JUDAS ISCARIOT'

When Judas Iscariot rode off in his chariot
He left our poor dear Lord to die:
But Mary, unwary, became quite contrary,
And would not allow him to die.

The tomb-stone they rolled off, they never were told
   off,
They found there no body inside:
The Gospel they preached then, poor sinners to teach
   then,
They soon spread its truth far and wide.

At Easter the feast were, the hen's egg the symbol,
Our dear Lord is risen again:
No more can the devil o'ercome us with evil,
Our Lord is in heaven to reign.

Anne Le Marquand Hartigan

*Ten brilliantly thought-provoking words from the poet's 1982
collection, Long Tongue.*

HEIRLOOM

My Father said,
It's always good weather
In bed.

Michael Hartnett

A daydream in verse: from A Book of Strays, *a posthumous collection of poetic leftovers by the Limerick poet (1941–1999).*

IF I WERE KING OF ENGLAND ...

If I were King of England
and you were Prince of Wales
we'd have a lark on the Royal Ark
with females and with males.

Oh happy days in England!
Oh gorgeous nights in Wales!
I could wear the ball-gowns,
and you could wear the tails!

You could bring Myfanwy round
and I some Swansea friends
and we'd all strive together
to pursue each others' ends.

We'd quieten Northern Ireland,
allow none to hunt or shoot;
we'd put the 'gay' in Gaelic
and blow the Orange flute.

We'd pacify the churches,
get rid of all sects at once,
by ordering all the clergy
to dress up as nuns.

We'd drink the malt of Scotland
and make sure no drop was spilt,
and you could flaunt your sporran
and I could twirl my kilt.

With dishy footmen at the Palace
at night to see us bed-ward –
you, my sweet Prince Alice,
and I, your sweet Queen Edward!

Anonymous

This tale in verse is part of an Irish poetic tradition that is widespread but essentially private, in which sporting and other incidents are recounted, and names are named. Often, the passage of time has rendered these excursions obscure: this example is a lively one from County Meath, perhaps modelled on 'The Night before Larry Was Stretched'. A note to the poem explains: 'The Hatchet is a wretchet public-house, in the sheebeen style, on the Summerhill-road, half way from Dunboyne – the country flat, and quite bare of timber – all grass land. It takes its name from the signboard, which represents a man with a hatchet cutting a large tree, supposed to be the last in the district; and so the 'Hatchet' remained victorious.'

THE HATCHET:
FEBRUARY 2nd, 1857

The day that came after the snow, was fixed for the
    Meet at the Hatchet;
A most unpoetical name, and not easy in verse to
    attach it.
And the country well suits to its name, 'tis dreary, flat,
    ugly, and scald, sir,
But when sportsmen are after their game, by them it
    is 'beautiful' called, sir,
        Whether hunting the deer, hare, or fox.

The snow and the frost were so hard, few Meath-men
    sent on to the muster,
But Sam ever true to his card, determined to give
    them a 'buster';
A thaw setting in about noon, said, 'If possible I will
    be at it,
So go on with the horses and hounds – if it thaws,
    they'll remember the Hatchet,
        For there's always good scent after snow.'

The morning came round, all serene –
    the Meet it was small – more's the pity;
A few of the neighbours around, and a
    few sporting gents from the city;
The Coolestown furze is drawn blank,
    then quick they trot on to Culmullen:

When off t'other side of a bank 'Tally ho!' goes the
 sporting old villain,
  That gave them some good runs before.

The 'flyers' went off with a dash, that electrified all
 that were in it;
I have heard of some fuss 'bout a gate, but that was
 the critical minute;
But two men got off with the hounds, and I say it
 with unfeigned sorrow,
They were none of my young friends around, but one
 'Chamberlain' and 'torney Morrough,
  Who had all this 'grand burst' to themselves.

Off by Bret's and the Lawlesses' ground, to the
 Summerhill road, near the Hatchet,
Through Barrstown-Kilcloone they sweep round at a
 pace, I defy you to match it,
But when in Mulhussy's deep land, Morrough's grey I
 can tell had his fill, sir,
For he hardly was able to stand, when they earthed
 him just under Larch-hill, sir,
  In forty-three minutes – nine miles.

The rest of the men made their play, by road and by
 field as they best could,
Bold Matt Corbally showing the way in a manner that
 none of the rest could.
As for 'Reynell', I vow and declare, he'll not rise to the
 height of his glory,
Till they lick every man in the field, and there's no one
 to tell him the story;
  Not till then from his labours he'll cease.

Now to all my young friends I see round, an old
 comrade his moral would render,
Though he treads upon delicate ground, for with
 some here the subject is tender;
When after a long snow and frost, a sudden thaw
 comes, you should watch it,
Nor sleeping be found at your posts, and get
 yourselves nicked by the Hatchet;
  But mind send up your horses next time.

Seamus Heaney

*In its first three words alone, this lament by the Nobel
laureate (b. 1939) for our beautiful, discarded coinage earns
its keep.*

A KEEN FOR THE COINS

O henny penny! O horsed half-crown!
O florin salmon! O sixpence hound!
O woodcock! Piglets! Hare and bull!
O mint of field and flood, farewell!
Be Ireland's lost ark, gone to ground,
And where the rainbow ends, be found.

Mr Heaton

*Six incontestable lines picked up in 1904 by an English
traveller in Ireland, William Bulfin.*

'BACON IS BACON'

Bacon is bacon
And mutton is mutton
    Not bad to eat.

Bacon is bacon
And mutton is mutton
    But only beef is meat.

James Henry

*James Henry (1798–1876), Dublin doctor, classicist and poet,
had been forgotten until 2002, when his work was revived by
Christopher Ricks (in a handsome edition from the
estimable Lilliput Press!) Two samples:*

'ON A WINDY DAY'

I saw, in Dresden, on a windy day,
A man and woman walking side by side,

– I tell a plain fact, not a poet's story,
And to my reader's judgment leave the moral –
He on his arm was carrying his great coat,
She, upon hers, a heavy-laden basket;
When, lo! a blast of wind comes, and the man,
Attempting to put on his coat, lets fall
Out of his mouth, ah, misery! his cigar;
But the compassionate woman quickly sets
Her basket on the ground, and with her right hand
Helping the coat on, with the left picks up,
And puts into her own mouth, the cigar,
And whiffs, and keeps it lighting, till the man's
Ready and buttoned up, then gives it back,
And takes her basket, and, all right once more,
Away they go, the man with his cigar,
The woman with the man, well pleased and happy.

STRIKING A LIGHT AT NIGHT

'First for the Bible, then the printing-press,
Most for the Lucifer match, the Gods I bless;
Without the other two, at dead of night,
What were the first?' I said, and struck a light.

George D Hodnett

This celebrated song has fooled many people. Though it uses language and imagery from a much earlier period, it was written halfway through the twentieth century by the late and much-remembered Hoddie, pianist, composer and latterly itinerant jazz critic of the Irish Times.

MONTO

Well if you've got a wing O! take her up to Ring O!
Where the waxies sing O! all the day;
If you've had your fill of porter, and you can't go any
    further,
Give your man the order: 'Back to the Quay!'
And take her up to Monto, Monto, Monto,
Take her up to Monto, lan-ge-roo … to you!

You've heard of Buckshot Forster, the dirty old
   imposter
He got a mot and lost her, up the Furry Glen.
He first put on his bowler and he buttoned up his
   trousers,
And he whistled for a growler, and he says, 'My man,
Take me up to Monto, Monto, Monto,
Take me up to Monto, lan-ge-roo ... to you!'

You've heard of the Dublin Fusiliers, the bloody old
   bamboozeleers,
De Wet'll kill the chiselers, one, two, three:
Marching from the Linenhall, there's one for every
   cannonball,
And Vicky's going to send them all over the sea.
But first ... send them up to Monto, Monto, Monto,
Send them up to Monto, lan-ge-roo ... to you!

When Carey told on Skin-the-goat, O'Donnell caught
   him on the boat –
He wished he'd never been afloat, the filthy skite.
It wasn't very sensible to tell on the Invincibles,
Who stuck up for their principles, day and night
By ... goin' up to Monto, Monto, Monto,
Goin' up to Monto, lan-ge-roo ... to you!

Now when the Czar of Russia and the King of Prussia
Landed in the Phoenix in a big balloon,
They asked the polis band to play 'The Wearin' of the
   Green,'
But the buggers in the Depot didn't know the tune.
So they both went up to Monto, Monto, Monto,
They both went up to Monto, lan-ge-roo ... to you!

Now the Queen she came to call on us, she wanted to
   see all of us –
I'm glad she didn't fall on us, she's eighteen stone.
'Mister Neill, Lord Mayor,' says she, 'Is this all you've
   got to show me?'
'Why, no ma'am, there's some more,' says he, 'Pogue-
   ma-hone!'
And he took her up to Monto, Monto, Monto,
He took her up to Monto, lan-ge-roo ... to you.

Michael Hogan

Michael Hogan, The 'Bard of Thomond' (1826–1899), is best known for his wonderful poem, 'Drunken Thady and the Bishop's Lady' – too long, sadly, to be included here. This teaspoonful of venom was written after a proposed statue of Daniel O'Connell in Limerick was abandoned in favour of one commemorating the son of a local grandee:

'VERSES FOR THE UNVEILING OF A STATUE
TO VISCOUNT FITZGIBBON'

Here he stands in the open air,
The bastard son of the great Lord Clare;
They called him Fitzgibbon, but his name is Moore,
For his father was a cuckold and his mother was a hoor!

Rudi Holzapfel

The late poet, polymath and book-dealer, Rudi Holzapfel (1938–2005), seemed to be more at home with figures from the country's past, particularly his beloved James Clarence Mangan, than he was with the wideboys of modern Ireland:

CHURCHGATE COLLECTION

I will not give to Fianna Fáil.
Hypocrite hoodlums, one and all:
Nor will I give to Fine Gael,
Traitors, ethics up for sale:
Who'd ever give to the PD's?
Look at them! Great balls of sleaze …
Labour augurs even worse:
In your pocket for your purse.

The 'Dem. Left'? They're just Communists;
Vote for them and slash your wrists …
The 'Independents'? Oh, no, please …
Dependent on their salaries:
Sinn Féin are just bloody mad:
Media banned? They should be glad!
Nor could I now support the Greens: –
Eggheads, weirdos, New Age queens.

So do not stop me as I pass
On my way to Sunday Mass:
On sacred ground you've surely strayed
From the Faith that you betrayed.
Till we get someone decent in
Who boots out all the gombeen men,
I'll give to Politics the birch, –
My money's going to the Church.

Anonymous

*A grisly tale about Irish navvies in Britain – or more
exactly, Scotland: the Kelvingrove Museum, which opened in
1901, is in Glasgow.*

HOT ASPHALT

Good evening, all me jolly lads,
I'm glad to see you're well.
If you'll gather all around me now
The story I will tell,
For I've got a situation
And, begorrah and begob,
I can whisper I've the weekly wage
Of nineteen bob.
'Tis twelve months come October
Since I left me native home,
After helping in Killarney, boys,
To bring the harvest down,
But now I wear a gansey
And around me waist a belt:
I'm the gaffer of the squad
That makes the hot asphalt.

Chorus:
Well, we laid it in the hollows
And we laid it in the flat,
And if it doesn't last forever,
Sure I swear I'll eat me hat.
Well, I've wandered up and down the world,
But sure I never felt
Any surface that was equal
To the hot asphalt.

The other night a copper comes
And he says to me, 'McGuire,
Would you kindly let me light me pipe
Down at your boiler fire?'
And he planks himself right down in front
With hobnails up, till late,
And says I, 'Me dacent man
You'd better go and find your bate.'
He ups and yells, 'I'm down on you,
I'm up to all yer pranks.
Don't I know you for a traitor
From the Tipperary ranks?'
Boys, I hit straight from the shoulder,
And I gave him such a belt
That I knocked him into the boiler
Full of hot asphalt.

We quickly dragged him out again
And we threw him in the tub,
And with soap and warm water,
We began to rub and scrub,
But devil the thing, it hardened,
And it turned him hard as stone,
And with every other rub
Sure you could hear the copper groan.
'I'm thinkin',' says O'Reilly,
'That he's lookin' like Ould Nick,
And burn me if I'm not inclined
To claim him with me pick.'
'Now,' says I, 'it would be easier
To boil him till he melts,
And to stir him nice and easy
In the hot asphalt.

You may talk about yer sailor lads,
Ballad singers and the rest,
Your shoemakers and your tailors,
But we please the ladies best.
The only ones who know the way
Their flinty hearts to melt
Are the lads around the boiler
Making hot asphalt.
With rubbing and with scrubbing
Sure I caught me death of cold,
And for scientific purposes

Me body it was sold.
In the Kelvingrove Museum, me boys,
I'm hangin' in me pelt,
As a monument to the Irish
Making hot asphalt.

Crawford Howard

*A lively Orange fantasy from the 1970s or 1980s, which can
be sung to the tune of 'The Wearing of the Green'.*

THE ARAB ORANGE LODGE

A loyal band of Orangemen from Ulster's lovely land,
They could not march upon the Twelfth – processions
   was all banned,
So they flew off till the Middle East this dreadful law
   to dodge
And they founded in Jerusalem the Arab Orange Lodge.
Big Ali Bey who charmed the snakes he was the first
   recruit,
John James McKeag from Portglenone learned him till
   play the flute,
And as the oul' Pied Piper was once followed by the
   rats
There followed Ali till the lodge ten snakes in bowler
   hats.

They made a martial picture as they marched along
   the shore.
It stirred the blood when Ali played 'The Fez My
   Father Wore'
And Yussef Ben Mohammed hit the 'lambeg' such a
   bash
It scared the living daylights from a camel in a sash!
Now the movement spread both far and wide – there
   were lodges by the score;
The 'Jerusalem Purple Heroes' was the first of many
   more,
The 'Loyal Sons of Djeddah' and the 'Mecca Purple
   Star'
And the 'Rising Sons of Jericho' who came by motor
   car.

The banners too were wonderful and some would
    make you smile
King Billy on his camel as he splashed across the Nile –
But the Tyre and Sidon Temperance had the best one
    of them all
For they had a lovely picture of Damascus Orange
    Hall!
The Apprentice boys of Amman marched beneath the
    blazing sun,
The Royal Black Preceptory were negroes every one
And lodges came from Egypt, from the Abu Simbel
    Falls,
And they shouted 'No Surrender!' and 'We'll guard
    old Cairo's walls!'

But when the ban was lifted and the lodges marched
    at last
The Arabs all decided for till march right through
    Belfast
And they caused a lot of trouble before they got
    afloat,
For they could not get the camels on the bloody
    Heysham boat!
Now camels choked up Liverpool and camels blocked
    Stranraer
And the Sheik of Kuwait came along in his great big
    motor car,
But the 'Eastern Magic' L.O.L. they worked a crafty
    move –
They got on their magic carpets and flew into
    Aldergrove!

When they came to Castle Junction where once stood
    the wee Kiosk
They dug up Royal Avenue to build a flamin' mosque
And Devlin says to Gerry Fitt, 'I think we'd better go!
'There's half a million camels coming down from
    Sandy Row.'
The speeches at the 'field' that day were really
    something new,
For some were made in Arabic and some were in
    Hebrew,
But just as Colonel Nasser had got up to sing 'The
    Queen',
I woke up in my bed at home and found it was a dream!

Anonymous

*A view of the rumbustious festival once held each August
just outside Dublin by the banks of the River Dodder (which
in the early nineteenth century was apparently no more
than a trickle in summer). The Barrack Street rangers of
verse 4 were prostitutes who worked around the Royal
Barracks area. For another trip to the fair, see page 308.*

THE HUMOURS OF DONNYBROOK FAIR (I)

To Donnybrook steer all you sons of Parnassus –
    Poor painters, poor poets, poor newsmen and
      knaves,
To see what the fun is that all fun surpasses –
    The sorrows and sadness of green Erin's slaves.
Oh, Donnybrook jewel! full of mirth is your quiver,
    Where all flock from Dublin to gape and to stare
At two elegant bridges, without e'er a river:
    So, success to the humours of Donnybrook Fair!

O you lads that are witty, from famed Dublin city,
    And you that in pastime take any delight,
To Donnybrook fly, for the time's drawing nigh
    When fat pigs are hunted, and lean cobblers
      fight;
When maidens, so swift, run for a new shift;
    Men, muffled in sacks, for a shirt they race there;
There jockeys well booted, and horses sure-footed,
    All keep up the humours of Donnybrook Fair.

The mason does come, with his line and his plumb;
    The sawyer and carpenter, brothers in chips,
There are carvers and gilders, and all sorts of builders,
    With soldiers from barracks and sailors from
      ships.
There confectioners, cooks, and printers of books,
    There stampers of linen, and weavers, repair;
There widows and maids, and all sorts of trades,
    Go join in the humours of Donnybrook Fair

There tinkers and nailers, and beggars and tailors,
    And singers of ballads, and girls of the sieve;
With Barrack Street rangers, the known ones and
  strangers,

And many that no one can tell how they live:
There horsemen and walkers, and likewise fruit-
    hawkers,
        And swindlers, the devil himself that would dare,
With pipers and fiddlers, and dandies and diddlers, –
        All meet in the humours of Donnybrook Fair.

'Tis there are dogs dancing, and wild beasts a-prancing,
        With neat bits of painting in red, yellow, and gold;
Toss-players and scramblers, and showmen and
    gamblers,
        Pickpockets in plenty, both of young and of old.
There are brewers, and bakers, and jolly shoemakers,
        With butchers, and porters, and men that cut hair;
There are montebanks grinning, while others are
    sinning,
        To keep up the humours of Donnybrook Fair.

Brisk lads and young lasses can there fill their glasses
        With whiskey, and send a full bumper around;
Jig it off in a tent till their money's all spent,
        And spin like a top till they rest on the ground.
Oh, Donnybrook capers, to sweet catgut-scrapers,
        They bother the vapours, and drive away care;
And what is more glorious – there's naught more
    uproarious –
        Huzza for the humours of Donnybrook Fair!

Douglas Hyde

*Verses by a very youthful Douglas Hyde (1860–1949), who
later learned to be a proper poet, translator and President of
Ireland.*

'MAKING PUNCH'

What drink is so nice
    As a tumbler of punch
Hot with lemon and spice
    Just after one's lunch.

Lordpunch is the loveliest beverage can be
    'Tis the wholesomest sweetest and nicest of all

And the greatest restorer I ever did see
    After weakness or illness a shake or a fall.

Punch must not be made carelessly or badly
    If you would wish to thoroughly enjoy it
The water must not be boiling fierce and madly
    For if it is not so you will destroy it.

Give me punch both hot and strong
    And I'd ask for nothing more
I would drink all evening long
    Till I fell upon the floor.

Now I feel my head is going
    Round and round the room doth spin
One glass more to overflowing
    And I think I'll turn in.

Anonymous

Another Yeatsian spoof, from Secret Springs of Dublin
Song *(1918).*

IDEAL POEMS
Y... S

I
*(Michael Robartes to His Beloved, telling her how the
greatness of His Verse shall open to her the door of Heaven)*

This pearl-pale poem that I have pondered o'er,
Made of a mouthful of the twilight air,
And of one dream – the falling of your hair,
Shall open for you the eternal door.

II
*(Michael Robartes in the place of the distraught
struggles against the spell which binds him)*

Outworn heart, come out from her hair,
That brought upon you this lonely doom,
And bound you down in the padded room,
Away, come away, to less shadowy hair!

There are hairs that blossom on foreheads more fair:

Curls ever shining with tendrils gay,
That twine and untwine as the winds are at play.
Away, come away, to unshadowy hair.

Anonymous

*Occasionally, it might seem as if Mullingar, County West-
meath, is famous only for the beefiness of its heifers. But in
the mid nineteenth century, the town clearly had much more
to offer, with its fine workhouse, its state-of-the-art railway
station, its access to sundry rural and urban leisure
activities, and not least its slim-ankled ladies.*

IN PRAISE OF THE CITY OF MULLINGAR

Ye may strain your muscles
To brag of Brussels,
  Of London, Paris, or Timbuctoo,
Constantinople,
Or Sebastople,
  Vienna, Naples, or Tongataboo,
Of Copenhagen,
Madrid, Kilbeggan,
  Or the capital of the Rooshian Czar,
But they're all infarior
To the vast, suparior,
  And gorgeous city of Mullingar.

That fair metropolis,
So great and populous,
  Adorns the regions of sweet Westmeath,
That fertile county
Which nature's bounty
  Has richly gifted with bog and heath.
Them scenes so charming,
Where snipes a-swarming
  Attract the sportsman that comes from far;
And whoever wishes
May catch fine fishes
  In deep Loch Owel near Mullingar.

I could stray for ever
By Brosna's river,

And watch its waters in their sparkling fall,
And the ganders swimmin'
And lightly skimmin'
 O'er the crystal bosom of the Roy'l Canal;
Or on Thursdays wander,
'Mid pigs so tender,
 And geese and turkeys on many a car,
Exchangin' pleasantry
With the fine bold peasantry
 That throng the market at Mullingar.

Ye Nine, inspire me,
And with rapture fire me
 To sing the buildings, both old and new,
The majestic court-house,
And the spacious workhouse,
And the church and steeple which adorn the view;
Then there's barracks airy
For the military,
 Where the brave repose from the toils of war;
Five schools, a nunnery,
And a thrivin' tannery,
 In the gorgeous city of Mullingar.

The railway station
With admiration
 I next must mention in terms of praise,
Where trains a-rollin'
And ingines howlin'
 Strike each beholder with wild amaze.
And then there's Main Street,
That broad and clean street,
 With its rows of gas-lamps that shine afar;
I could spake a lecture
On the architecture
 Of the gorgeous city of Mullingar.

The men of genius,
Contemporaneous
 Approach spontaneous this favoured spot,
Where good society
And great variety
Of entertainment is still their lot.
The neighbouring quality
For hospitality

And conviviality unequalled are;
And from December
Until November
    There's still diварsion in Mullingar.

Now, in conclusion,
I make allusion
    To the beauteous females that here abound;
Celestial creatures
With lovely features,
    And taper ankles that skim the ground ...
But this suspends me,
The theme transcends me –
    My muse's powers are too weak by far;
It would take Catullus,
Likewise Tibullus,
    To sing the beauties of Mullingar.

Anonymous

Here is another of the many songs sung by Brendan Behan.
Of unknown authorship, it was already very popular in
the 1920s.

'AN INCIDENT NEAR MACROOM'

On the eighteenth day of November,
Just outside the town of Macroom,
The Tans on their old Crossley Tender
Came whirling along to their doom.

For the Boys of the Column were waiting
With handgrenades primed on the spot,
And the Irish Republican Army
Made a shite of the whole fucking lot.

Oh the sun in the West it was setting –
'Twas the close of a cold winter's day –
When the Tans we were wearily waiting
Came into the spot where we lay.

Over the hills came the echo,
The sound of the rifle and gun,

And the cheers from our lorries gave tidings
That the Boys of the Column had won.

So here's to the Boys of Kilmichael,
Of Rafferty, Kill and Macroom:
With canisters ready and lighting,
They sent many's the Tan to his doom.

Anonymous

A beautiful ballad, sold as a broadside in the 1850s.

IRISH CASTLES IN THE AIR

This world is all a bubble, no matter where we go,
There's nothing here but trouble, hardships, toil, and
      woe;
Go where we will, do what we may, we are never free
      from care,
And at the best this world is but a castle in the air.
And yet each being loves the land where he sported as
      a child:
The very savage loves his plain, his woods, and prairies
      wild;
And I, with a true Irish heart, still wish in Ireland there
To sit among her groves and build my castles in the air.

Old Ireland had her poet, and she loved him well I'm
      sure,
He was a true born Irishman, his name it was Tom
      Moore;
But of this world's sorrows we know he had his share,
For Moore was always building his castles in the air.
He sang the rights of Ireland, he sang against her
      wrongs,
And many loving Irish hearts they cherish yet his
      songs;
He made the Irish hearts rejoice, he bade them ne'er
      despair,
And for Ireland in the future he built castles in the air.

We boast of Dan O'Connell, too, who struggled hard
      and sore

To bring both peace and happiness to dear old Erin's
    shore,
And though his efforts were in vain, the spirit still was
    there
For Dan still struggled on and built his castles in the
    air.
And now though he's dead and gone we find both old
    and young
Will often quote the wit that flowed from Dan
    O'Connell's tongue;
The widow and the fatherless their sorrows he would
    share
And build for them in days to come bright castles in
    the air.

Old Ireland has her statesmen and artists many a one,
Her sculptors and her generals, who noble deeds have
    done;
Besides she boasts of Goldsmith, with talents rich and
    rare,
Whose standard works made thousands build their
    castles in the air.
Her mountains, lakes, and valleys, are lovely to
    behold,
Her daughters they are bright and fair, her sons are
    brave and bold;
No other country where I've been to me seems half so
    fair,
It's the land where I, in childhood, built my castles in
    the air.

Anonymous

*A robust nineteenth-century view of Irish political
shenanigans in America.*

THE IRISH JUBILEE

A short time ago an Irishman named Docherty
Was elected to the Senate by a very large majority.

Sure he felt so elected that he went to Denis Cassidy
Who owned a bar room of a very large capacity.

'Arra,' says Docherty, 'go over to the brewer
For a hundred kegs of lager beer and give it to the poor!

Then go over to the butcher's shop and order up a ton
of meat:
Be sure the boys and girls have got all they want to
drink and eat.

They made me their senator, to show them all me
gratitude,
They'll have the finest supper ever given in the
latitude.

Tell them the music will be furnished by O'Rafferty,
Assisted on the bagpipes by Felix Mick M'Cafferty.

Sure whatever the expenses are, remember I'll put up
the tin,
And anyone who doesn't come, be sure and do not let
them in.'

Now Cassidy at once sent out the invitations,
And anyone who came was a credit to the nation.

Some came on bicycles because they had no fares to
pay,
And all those that did not come, made up their minds
to stay away.

Two by three they all rushed in the dining hall,
Young men and old men and girls that were not men
at all,

Blind men and deaf men and men who had the
chickenpox,
Single men and double men and men who had their
glasses on,

Well in a few minutes nearly every chair was taken
Till the taprooms and mushrooms were packed to
suffocation.

When everyone was seated and we started to lay out
the feast
Cassidy says, 'Rise up and give us each a cake apiece.'

He then said as manager he would try and fill the chair.
We then sat down and all looked over the bill of fare ...

Well there was pig's heads, goldfish, mocking birds
   and ostriches,
Ice cream, cold cream, Vaseline and sandwiches,

Blue fish, green fish, fishhooks and partridges,
Fishballs, snowballs, cannonballs and cartridges.

We ate oatmeal till we could hardly stirabout,
Ketch-up and hurry-up, sweet-kraut and sauer-kraut,

Dressed beef and naked beef and beef with all its
   trousers on,
Soda crackers, fire crackers, Cheshire cheese with
   breeches on,

Beefsteaks and mistakes were down upon the bill of
   fare,
Roast ribs and spare ribs and ribs that we couldn't spare,

Reindeer, snowdeer and dear me and antelope,
The women ate so much melon, the men said they
   cantaloupe,

Red herrings, smoked herrings, herrings from old
   Erin's Isle,
Bangor loaf and fruit cake and sausages a half a mile,

Hot corn, cold corn, and corn cake and honey-comb,
Red birds and red books, sea bass and sea foam,

Fried liver, baked liver, Carter's little liver pills,
And everyone was wondering who was going to pay
   the bill.

Well we ate everything that was on the bill of fare,
And then we looked on the back to see if any more
   was there ...

Well for dessert we had ice picks, tooth picks and a
   piece of skipping rope,
And we washed them all down with a big piece of
   shaving soap.

The band played hornpipes, gaspipes and Irish reels,
And we danced to the music of 'The Wind that
    Shakes the Barley Fields',

Then the piper played ould tunes and spittoons so
    very fine,
Then in came fiddler Pat and gave to him a glass of
    wine.

Arra a finer set of dancers you never set your eyes
    upon,
And anyone who couldn't dance was dancing with
    their slippers on.

Some danced jig steps door steps and highland flings,
And Murphy took his penknife out and tried to cut the
    'Pigeon's Wings'.

*(When the dance was over Cassidy told us all to join hands
and sing this good old chorus:)*

Should Old Acquaintance Be Forgot, whoever you
    may be,
Lets think of the good ould times we had at the Irish
    Jubilee!

Anonymous

*There are still several versions of this old song doing the
rounds. It has in recent years become one of Ireland's most
popular 'belters'.*

THE IRISH ROVER

In the year of our Lord, eighteen hundred and six
We set sail from the Coal Quay of Cork;
We were sailing away with a cargo of bricks
For the Grand City Hall in New York.
We'd an elegant craft, she was rigged fore-and-aft
And oh, how the wild winds drove her:
She had twenty-three masts and withstood several
    blasts,
And they called her the Irish Rover.

There was Barney Magee from the banks of the Lee,
There was Hogan from County Tyrone,
There was Johnny McGurk, who was scared stiff of
    work,
And a chap from Westmeath called Malone.
There was Slugger O'Toole, who was drunk as a rule,
And fighting Bill Casey from Dover,
There was Dooley from Clare, who was strong as a
    bear,
And was skipper of the Irish Rover.

There was old Mickey Coote, who played hard on his
    flute
When the ladies lined up for a set,
He would tootle with skill for each sparkling quadrille
Till the dancers were fluttered and bet;
With his smart witty talk, he was cock of the walk
And he rowled the dames under and over:
They all knew at a glance when he took up his stance
That he sailed in the Irish Rover.

We had one million bags of the best Sligo rags,
We had two million buckets of stones,
We had three million sides of old blind horses' hides,
We had four million packets of bones,
We had five million hogs and six million dogs,
And seven million barrels of porter,
We had eight million bales of old billy goats' tails,
In the hold of the Irish Rover.

We had sailed seven years when the measles broke out
And the ship lost her way in the fog,
And the whole of the crew was reduced down to two,
'Twas myself and the Captain's old dog.
Then the ship struck a rock – Oh Lord! what a shock –
And then she heeled right over,
Turned nine times around, and the poor dog was
    drowned –
I'm the last of the Irish Rover.

Robert Wyse Jackson

JWJ: TCD Miscellany *had long been the main undergraduate periodical in Trinity when* The College Pen *appeared in 1929. It lasted for two years. As I leafed through the entire run for this anthology, I found hundreds of verses and prose pieces by my late father that I had not known about. Few of them were in any way serious. This gift from the past included the following useful advice on the pronunciation of the Campanile, Trinity's rarely-rung bell-tower:*

A SOCIAL PROBLEM

Bon ton decrees that it is vile
To speak about the Campanile,
Nor is it ever quite genteel
To babble of the Campanile;
The social climber who is wily
Will not pronounce it Campanile.

But there are trials for those who know
The way to say it *comme il faut.*

For poets, speaking *à la mode,*
Confess it is a grievous load
To find a *rhyme* for Campanile.
(The fact that it is damp in Ely
Is quite irrelevant – a mere
Depression over Cambridgeshire).

The College Pen *fought a vigorous rearguard action against 'modern poetry', and rejoiced when* TCD Miscellany *was hoodwinked into printing the following poem, commended by* TCD *staffers GE Gill and WB Stanford. The* Pen *promptly reprinted it, with this introductory note:*

'*We would like to publish the following verse with all due acknowledgements to our contemporary. We think if would be a pity if it did not get the fullest publicity, since it has been approved by the highest critics in College, and we append an ode to the author:*'

TRA OZ MONTES

I feel the gaunt woods straining
Grey against the pale mists of yesterday
Their blackened arms to youth
And the south with castanets of Jaen
In orange groves of Andalusia,
And crackling glare of light
On patios ochre-red in murmuring sleep.
I come
For time bears heavy on the beam of youth
And I see
Jetted in painted lips
The serenaded setting of mantillas.

The poem was signed 'Cahors'. The 'ode to the author' that followed was written by an unidentified 'S.H.H.'

VERY BLANK VERSE

Some critics think the test of every verse
Is whether it is well expressed and terse,
But *T.C.D.* says there is but one test
And thinks, it seems, obscurity is best.

Now G-ll and St-nf-rd say their every want is
Aesthetically filled by 'Tra oz Montes.'
To cultivated minds it would be treason
To say that it has neither rhyme *nor* reason.

Now Cahors sends this message to all men;
Although he's one of those who wield the 'Pen.'

He'd no poetic thoughts, so filled the gap
By ringing changes on a Spanish map.

So that is why I gladly sing the praise
On him who really can write senseless lays –
That unpoetic fat man there with slacks on
Is 'Cahors,' better known, perhaps, as J-cks-n.

*The subject of dieting, then known as 'banting,' was clearly
a Jacksonian concern:*

A FAT MAN'S TRAGEDY

This is the tale of Joshua Parr
Who was completely circular;
A man who would eat tea and cakes
Ad lib., without dyspeptic aches;
Who dined sufficiently for two;
An omnivorous person who
Exploited to the full the uses
Of tummy walls and gastric juices;
So that, with gastronomic bliss,
His silhouette looked just like this: –

The world one day perceived it strange
That Mr Parr began to change;
He gave up super *table d'hôtes*;
Perused Arbuthnot's healthful notes;
Eschewed plum-pudding, pork, and goose;
Had dinner of fresh lemon juice;
Had luncheon of some H2O;
Decided that his tea must go,
And breakfasted on nuts and lettuce.
The causa causans – He had met his
Divinity – and proverbs say
They shape our ends – and tums – away.
Because of this, his figure here
Inclines towards an ovoid sphere.

But as, alas, the maiden felt
That handsome men are slightly svelte,

And as unluckily she found
That Mr Parr was somewhat round,
It follows that he did not fit
The maiden's formula for 'It.'
Nevertheless, he thought it worth
His while to think about his girth
– Example how a man can grow
Still less and less is shown below.

|

At this point readers all must cease
To think our hero was obese:
Indeed he soon became so slim
That she began to gaze on him.

|

But love's young dream was not to be,
For tragedy steps in, you see;
When fat men bant they seem to be
Just asking for catastrophe.
The outcome was: *he grew so weedy*
He disappeared – as subter vide.

NIL

Most reputable persons say
That they have heard within the Bay
A bodiless and tragic moan
For ten or twelve or fourteen stone;
Such noises usually are
A certain sign of Mr Parr.

* * *

If any moral's to be found
    It must be, we suppose: –
'It's love that makes the world go round,
    – *But never adipose.*'

EPISODE

Uncle took a Beecham's Pill
When he was exceeding ill,
And I am very grieved to tell
He now is very, very well.
It all is very hard on me
Who was residuary legatee.

Seán Jackson

An editor's (alter) ego is responsible for the two helpings of nonsense that follow:

WHO WANTS TO BE A MILLINER?

Sit down and I'll tell you the tale
Of my wonderful ten-gallon hat.
(If it makes you feel sick or go pale –
Well, what do I care about that?)

It's trimmed with dunduckety silk
And ribbons that hang in the breeze;
It's perfect for boiling up milk
Or melting down chocolates or cheese.

I've used it instead of a boat
On a voyage to Mullinavat,
With a sail made out of a coat
And a crew of sixteen and a cat.

I wear it on Sundays in June
Whenever I'm lying in bed:
It catches the heat of the moon
And stops it from burning my head.

My spider is living inside
(His name is Augustus Malone);
I wanted to find him a bride
In case he was feeling alone.

But he whispered, 'I like to be here
Just crawling around on your head,

And I'm happy to sleep in your ear –
It's a perfectly comfortable bed.'

My hat does the job of a dish:
I put all my food on the top,
And, using my comb, eat a fish
Or turnips or snails or a chop.

You may mutter, 'It sounds very grim –
What a horrible way to have lunch,'
But the paintings that circle the brim
Are by Manet and Monet and … Munch.

So now I have told you the tale
Of the thing I love most in my life,
And if you felt sick (or went pale) –
You should take a good look at my wife.

ENCOUNTER WITH AN EILEEN

Was I drunk upon that dance-floor?
You seemed to glide on ice:
The more I felt the way you moved,
The more I thought you nice.

Your dress was shot with silver,
Your arms were slim and slight.
I really liked your husky voice,
And that you were not white.

Then, suddenly, I wanted you,
To keep you safe and warm.
We left and hurried to my house:
You floated on my arm.

I breathed, 'My darling, come upstairs,
I need you, let's begin it.'
I don't know what it was you said,
Perhaps, 'An extra minute.'

I went ahead to make the bed,
Brush teeth and thinning hairs.
But no. You'd gone. I found your note –
'Daleks don't climb stairs.'

Anonymous

Though the quick pace and multiple rhymes of this Belfast epiclet make it extremely difficult to sing or even recite, Tommy Makem performs it brilliantly.

JOHNNY MCELDOO

There was Johnny McEldoo and McGee and me
And a couple or two or three went on a spree one day.
We had a bob or two which we knew how to blew
And the beer and whiskey flew and we all felt gay.
We visited McCann's, McIllmann's, Humpty Dan's,
We then went into Swann's our stomachs for to pack.
We ordered out a feed which indeed we did need
And we finished it with speed but we still felt slack.

Johnny McEldoo turned red, white and blue
When a plate of Irish stew he soon put out of sight,
He shouted out 'Encore' with a roar for some more
That he never felt before such a keen appetite.
He ordered eggs and ham, bread and jam, what a cram!
But him we couldn't ram though we tried our level
    best,
For everything we brought, cold or hot, mattered not,
It went down him like a shot, but he still stood the
    test.

He swallowed tripe and lard by the yard, we got
    scared,
We thought it would go hard when the waiter
    brought the bill.
We told him to give o'er, but he swore he could lower
Twice as much again and more before he had his fill.
He nearly supped a trough full of broth. Says
    McGrath,
'He'll devour the tablecloth if you don't hold him in.'

When the waiter brought the charge, McEldoo felt so
    large
He began to scowl and barge and his blood went on
    fire.
He began to curse and swear, tear his hair in despair,
And to finish the affair called the shop man a liar.
The shopman he drew out, and no doubt, he did clout

McEldoo he kicked about like an old football.
He tattered all his clothes, broke his nose, I suppose
He'd have killed him with a few blows in no time at all.

McEldoo began to howl and to growl, by my sowl
He threw an empty bowl at the shopkeeper's head.
It struck poor Mickey Flynn, peeled the skin off his
　　chin
And the ructions did begin and we all fought and bled.
The peelers did arrive, man alive, four or five,
At us they made a drive for us all to march away.
We paid for all the mate, that we ate, stood a trate,
And went home to reminate on the spree that day.

Paul Jones

Many of the best verses by Charles Kelly and Tom Collins in
Dublin Opinion *appeared over the shared pseudonym of
Paul Jones. Such pieces, while firmly rooted in the comic
verse tradition, often had a certain elegiac tone. Here are
three by 'Jones' from the 1940s and 1950s:*

REPENTANT SON

I always laughed when father sang.
　　　It wasn't that his voice was bad,
For tunefully and clear it rang.
　　　It was the little ways he had.

The earnest eyes that simply shone,
　　　And gave the risibles a jolt,
When he lamented maidens gone
　　　Like 'Alice,' lost love of 'Ben Bolt.'

The way his mild grey eyes went roaming
　　　Down paths that he alone could see,
When mother played for 'In the Gloaming,'
　　　And, as encore, 'The Sands of Dee.'

The way his whiskers seemed to wag
　　　When half-way up the scale, he knew
He had the high note in the bag,
　　　Was slightly too much for me, too.

Long silent is the voice that rang.
    I number chief amongst his wrongs:
I always laughed when father sang,
    Except when he sang comic songs.

'BATTLE'S A COD'

Battle's a cod.
Why should I die
At somebody's prod
For somebody's lie?

I do not want
To be drubbed or to drub.
All the fights I want
I can get in a pub.

Every time I see
Those statesmen's faces
I could hang myself
In my own braces.

I have grown wise.
I will face no odds
For men with eyes
Like a dying cod's.

BALLADE OF VANISHED BEAUTY

Behind the house I bought was spread a field:
    Wide, sweet, and open to the laughing sun,
With buttercups for its Lucullan yield,
    A cloth of gold magnificently spun.
And over all its painted ways would run
    The barefoot children on their timeless track;
But that was yesterday, and all that's done –
    They've started building houses at the back.

There was an old white horse that kept his post
    In the deep hollow near the rotting fence,
And looked in purple twilights like the ghost,

Of some old warhorse, and old Froissart's tents
Would rise behind him ... Some man took him hence –
    I think it was the knacker come to knack –
The world is sicklied with impermanence:
    They've started building houses at the back.

They're rooting up the grass, the flower, the bush,
    They've laid the axe to the great sycamore.
The concrete-mixer conquers, and the thrush
    Must be some other person's troubadour.
Already half the field's a leprous sore,
    With grey blocks piling in an evil stack.
With stuff like oyster-soup the runnels pour:
    They've started building houses at the back.

Envoi
Prince, when I go from earth my score to pay,
    Put me in Hades' last, lost, farthest wrack,
And I shall be consoled that none can say:
    They've started building houses at the back.

Anonymous

Here is a very early example of a song whose pattern is still being replicated by today's ballad singers, though details may have changed over the years. It comes from Wiseheart's Songster's Olio for 8 July 1826.

KATTY FLANNIGAN

At the dead of the night, when by whiskey inspired,
And pretty Katty Flannigan my bosom had fired,
I tapped at her window, when thus she began,
Oh! what the devil are you at? Begone you naughty
    man.

I gave her a look, as sly as a thief,
Or when hungry I'd view a fine surloin of beef;
My heart is red hot, says I, but cold is my skin,
So pretty Mistress Flannigan, oh, won't you let me in?

She open'd the door, I sat down by the fire,
And soon was reliev'd from the wet, cold and mire,
And I pleas'd her so mightily, that long e'er 'twas day
I stole poor Katty's tender heart, and then I tripp'd
    away.

Patrick Kavanagh

*Patrick Kavanagh (1904–1967) wore his hatreds on his sleeve.
Because he admired* Ulysses, *this prolonged sneer is perhaps
the most impassioned of many Irish attacks upon the 'Joyce
Industry'. It was first published in John Ryan's* Envoy *(April
1951) in a special Joyce number commemorating the tenth
anniversary of his death. The target in verses 3, 4 and 5 is
the Belfast poet and cleric, WR ('Bertie') Rodgers (1909–1969),
who had done two acclaimed radio broadcasts on James Joyce
for the BBC in 1950. The last verse must refer to Kavanagh
himself: in 1954 he was among the group of writers who
were the first to commemorate Bloomsday in Dublin.*

WHO KILLED JAMES JOYCE?

Who killed James Joyce?
I, said the commentator,
I killed James Joyce
For my graduation.

What weapon was used
To slay mighty Ulysses?
The weapon that was used
Was a Harvard thesis.

How did you bury Joyce?
In a broadcast Symposium.
That's how we buried Joyce
To a tuneful encomium.

Who carried the coffin out?
Six Dublin codgers
Led into Langham Place
By W. R. Rodgers.

Who said the burial prayers? –
Please do not hurt me –
Joyce was no Protestant,
Surely not Bertie?

Who killed Finnegan?
I, said a Yale-man,
I was the man who made
The corpse for the wake man.

And did you get high marks,
The Ph.D.?
I got the B.Litt.
And my master's degree.

Did you get money
For your Joycean knowledge?
I got a scholarship
To Trinity College.

I made the pilgrimage
In the Bloomsday swelter
From the Martello Tower
To the cabby's shelter.

*The Dublin Verse-Speaking Society had been started in 1938
by the poets Austen Clarke and Robert Farren. It did not
find favour in all quarters:*

JUSTIFIABLE HOMICIDE

'I killed a verse speaker,' said the Playboy,
'Through my radio he attacked me with that cry
So banshee-like I followed him through Dublin
And split him down the middle with my loy.'

Richie Kavanagh

*Richie Kavanagh revels in Ireland's new liberalism. He is a
master of the comic song that just about squeezes inside the
bounds of acceptability. This was a big hit in 2006.*

CHICKEN TALK

First time I heard a naughty word, was when I was a
    child.
I heard it from the chickens, me granny she went wild.
Me granny says, 'Now Johnny, the chickens they don't
    curse.'
'Be gore,' says I to granny, ''twas the chicken said it
    first.'

Chorus:
Fock fock fock fock, fock fock, fock off
Fock fock fock fock, fock fock, fock off
Now this is chicken talk
Fock fock fock fock, fock fock, fock off
This is what they say,
When the chickens they do lay.
Fock fock fock fock, fock fock, fock off
Fock fock fock fock, fock fock, fock off.

Then up the yard me granny came and let an awful
    shout.
She says to me 'Now Johnny, shut that f'en chicken's
    mouth.'
I ran the chicken up the yard, across and all around.
And yet the bleddy chicken wouldn't stop that f'en
    sound.

Then granny started cursing, but the chicken said it
    first.
The more that granny shouted, the more the chicken
    cursed.
Granny said, 'I never seen the like in all my life.
I never had a chicken that caused so much strife.'

    So let's all sing along.
    Let's sing the chicken song.
    Fock fock fock fock, fock fock, fock off
    Fock fock fock fock, fock fock, fock off
    Quack quack quack quack,went the duck.
    But the chicken still said fock.
    Fock fock fock fock, fock fock, fock off.
    Fock fock fock fock, fock fock, fock off …

James Kearney

*This song (Air: 'The Rakes of Mallow') features a rare
sighting of the great blind balladeer, Zozimus. The ballad
sheet, dated 1851, bears the remark: 'This very comical song
was written and sung by J. Kearney, in the character of
'Owney,' at the Castle Tavern, Dublin.' Of the various
slang terms, the 'moth' in verse 3 was a woman (more
recently a 'mot'), while in verse 5 'Snibs was watching all*

*our tickers,' probably means that pickpockets were eyeing
their watches. The flamboyant Louis Jullien (verse 3) was a
popular travelling bandleader.*

THE BALL OF DANDYORUM.

All you that are here attend, I pray,
And you shall hear, without delay,
About a party great and gay,
The type of all decorum.
The nobility met one and all,
Last week, down in the Music Hall,
At a Masquerade and Fancy Ball,
That was gave by Dandyorum.
      Tooral ooral, &c

Large placards soon the fun announced,
The ladies got their gowns well flounced,
And as through jigs and reels they bounced,
Like ribbons they all tore 'em.
Michael's Lane, and Meath Street too,
Was search'd for clothes, black, brown, and blue,
To dress this awful motley crew
For the ball of Dandyorum.
      Tooral ooral &c

For tickets they had such demand,
His committee soon had it planned
To go and engage with Jullien's band,
They sent them off before 'em.
They made me Usher of the Rod,
Till the lush began to make me nod,
Then on the buniony toes I trod
Of the moth of Dandyorum.
      Tooral ooral, &c

Zozimus came drest as a Turk,
Peg the man was Paddy from Cork,
Lord Howth, as a tinker, wanted work,
He tied my bib before him.
A quadrille or waltz he'd not go through,
But he roared for kettles old or new;
When he got no hammering to do,
He hammered Dandyorum.
      Tooral ooral, &c

There were oyster men and cockle pickers,
Snibs was watching all our tickers,
Spaniards, Turks, and herring-feckers
Dancing Tullochgorum.
Major White and Mickey Maw
Were dressed as two limbs of the law,
With clients they kept up such jaw,
I complained to Dandyorum.
    Tooral ooral, &c

Dandyorum called them two blackguards,
That led to an exchange of cards,
They brought pistols down to one of the yards
But first they drank a jorum.
They pulled the triggers bold and stout,
But devil a bullet would come out,
They were loaded both with stirabout
By the friends of Dandyorum.
    Tooral ooral, &c

The Major's shot took no effect,
But Dandy's hit him in the neck,
And left his clothes a pretty spec,
With the stirabout all o'er him.
When Mickey seen the Major's job,
For spite he tore his foolish nob,
And he swore by his martial slipper gob
He'd swallow Dandyorum.
    Tooral ooral, &c

The report of both the pistol shots
Frightened the life out of all the moths,
They ran, and down went pans and pots,
That was making up the jorum.
The Music Hall began to fill
With Peelers, and to show their skill,
To the station house, their last quadrille,
Was led by Dandyorum.
    Tooral ooral, &c

In the morning we were marched in state
Before the sitting magistrate,
And the Peeler that was on the beat
Showed how the moths all tore him.
Old Bag-wig says, you've broke the peace,

You must get a run in the Bastile chaise,
To round the rack for fourteen days –
O, more luck! says Dandyorum.
        Tooral ooral, &c

Peadar Kearney

*In this popular song, sometimes called 'The Liffeyside',
Peadar Kearney (1883-1942) cunningly mentions with pride
his greatest success, 'The Soldier's Song', at present
Ireland's National Anthem.*

FISH AND CHIPS

As down by Anna Liffey,
        My love and I did stray,
Where in the good old Liffey mud
        The sea-gulls sport and play
We caught the whiff of ray and chips
        And Mary softly sighed,
'Oh! John, come on for a Wan an' Wan,
        Down by the Liffey side.'

So down to Rabaiotti's
        Together we did go,
And the rapture then that filled our hearts
        No poet e'er could know.
We started atin' double wans,
        And Mary softly sighed,
'I'd live for ever atin' chips
        Down by the Liffey side.'

Then up along by George's Street
        The loving pairs to view,
While Mary swanked it like a queen
        In a skirt of royal blue.
Her coat was newly turned and
        Her blouse was newly dyed,
You could not match her round the block
        Down by the Liffey's side.

And on her old melodeon
        So sweetly she did play

'Good-by-ee and don't sigh-ee'
    And 'Rule Britann-i-ay',
But when she turned Sinn Féiner
    I nearly burst with pride,
To hear her sing 'The Soldier's Song'
    Down by the Liffey side.

So on Sunday morning early
    To Meath Street we will go,
And before good Father Murphy
    We there will make our vow:
He'll join our hands in wedlock banns
    And soon we'll be outside,
With the whole afternoon for our honeymoon
    Down by the Liffey side.

James Kelly

*James Kelly (1895–1978) was for many years employed as the
Glenarm, County Antrim, roadmender in the mid twentieth
century, and lived in a small house in Altmore Street, where
all the action of the village took place.*

DOWN THE STREET WHERE JIMMY LIVES

Oh what a happy place it is
Down the street where Jimmy lives
All is a bustle an' a buzz
Life goes on as it really is
Legs of mutton fry and fizz
It's there God takes away an' gives
Down the street where Jimmy lives.

There are roadmen there and sausage makers
Glaziers and painters an' undertakers,
All in the street where Jimmy lives.
The undertaker is close at hand
And he'll hurry you off till the promised land
Down the street where Jimmy lives.

There are rabbits in hutches, chicken in pens
Bubbly turkeys an' crowing hens
All in the street where Jimmy lives.

At eight o'clock there's always a fuss
As sparks fly out frae the morning bus,
Down the street where Jimmy lives.

An' afore the people are right out o' bed
There are carts come roun' wi' loads of bread
An' the noise o' the mill would turn your head
Down the street where Jimmy lives.

There's men wi' wives an' men wi' none
Jimmy himsel' lives quite alone,
He hasnae a queen to take the throne
Down the street where Jimmy lives.

The little boys hang by their heels
Over the bridge fishing for eels
An' the sailor lads when they've nowt tae do
Drink wi' Jack till they're roaring fu'
An' rise the steam in the Heather Dew.
That's the street where Jimmy lives.

THE OL' BLACK CAN

Oh alas what can I do
My ol' black can is split in two
There's nothing left to make the brew
For Sam an' me.

At night I cannae sleep a wink
When on your blackened sides I think
Misfortune's cup maun Jamie drink
What will the future be?

'Twas in the year o' forty-eight,
I cannae noo recall the date
When you were made by John McCrate
All sound and watertight.

Your handle had become quite loose
For you were still in constant use,
And mind you, you stood some abuse,
An' often kicked aboot the hoose.

Wi' hearts aflow we had gaped wi' pride
To watch you bubblin' o'er the side,
For often's time you did provide
Many's the hasty bite.

But with a mighty thunderclap
That nearly blew the stove tae jap
You flew aroon' my heid in scrap
An' left me broken hearted.

For when I heard that fatal blast
I knew your bubblin' days were past.
You done it dirty at the last
An' nearly scalded Sam an' me.

But since you were made o' tin
The tide was full and I pitched you in,
You could either sink or swim
There was nae yin for tae mourn.

You are tin an' I am clay
An' that is all there is to say
For some day I'll be pitched away
Never to return.

Anonymous

*In the 1960s the arrival of the first native Irish television
station brought exciting new cultural influences to parts
of the country formerly dependent on storytellers and
traditional music for their entertainment. This tuneful
acrostic drilled itself into the hearts, minds and stomachs
of the people:*

'KENNEDY'S BREAD'

K for Kennedy's
E for Energy
N for Nice and Nourishing
E for Enjoyment
D for delicious
YS means You're Satisfied –
Kennedy's Breeeeeeeeaaaaaaaadddd!!

Brendan Kennelly

*The benign presence of Brendan Kennelly (b. 1936) is a
refreshingly puckish influence on modern Irish poetry. This
incendiary squib comes from his 1995 Bloodaxe collection,*
Poetry My Arse.

TO NO ONE

Her husband passed on the street outside.
She watched, said softly to no one:
'The things you'd see passin' the window
When you wouldn't have a gun.'

At last! Judas tells it as it really was:

UNDER THE TABLE

There was a bomb-scare at the Last Supper.
We were tucking in to the bread and wine
When the phone rang in an abrasive manner
And someone said in a Cork accent at th'other end of
    the line

Dat dere was a big hoor of a bomb in de room, boy.
Unpardonable, I thought. Nothing excused it.
Zebedee found the bomb in a bag under the table.
Jesus defused it.

After that opening shock the evening went well.
Peter got sloshed and showed his old
Tendency to pull rank.

I told him, in the vaults of my mind, to go to hell
And brooded on my tentative efforts to open
An account in a Swiss Bank.

YOUR WAN'S ANSWER

If Bishops could
Get pregnant
Abortion would
Be a sacrament.

Anonymous

*An anti-enlistment song composed after the Crimean War of
1854-5. 'Kimeens', in verse 3, is from the Irish caimíní,
tricks, 'whaled' in verse 9 means something like 'thrashed',
and 'cleaveens' (verse 10) are in-laws.*

THE KERRY RECRUIT

One morning in March I was digging the land,
With my brogues on my feet and my spade in my hand,
And says I to myself, 'Such a pity to see
Such a fine strapping lad footing turf round Tralee.'

> Chorus:
> Wid me too ra na nya and me too ra na nya
> Wid me too ra na noo ra na noo ra na nya

So I buttered my brogues, shook hands with my spade,
Then went off to the fair like a dashing young blade,
When up comes a sergeant, he asks me to 'list:
'Arra, sergeant a grá, stick a bob in me fist.'

'O! then here is the shilling, as we've got no more,
When you get to head-quarters you'll half a score.'
'Arra, quit your kimeens,' says I, 'sergeant, good-bye,
You'd not wish to be quartered, and neither would I.'

Well the first thing they gave me it was a red coat
With a wide strap of leather to tie round my throat.
They gave me a quare thing – I asked what was that,
And they told me it was a cockade for my hat.

The next thing they gave me they called it a gun,
With powder and shot and a place for my thumb.
Well first she spit fire and then she spit smoke,
She gave a great lep and my shoulder near broke.

Well the first place they sent me was down by the quay,
On board of a warship bound for the Crimea:
Three sticks in the middle all rowled round with
    sheets –
Faith, she walked on the water without any feet.

When at Balaclava we landed quite sound,
Both cold, wet and hungry, we lay on the ground.
Next morning for action the bugle did call,
And we had a hot breakfast of powder and ball.

Sure it's often I thought of my name and my home
And the days that I spent cutting turf, och mavrone,
The balls were so thick and the fire was so hot,
I lay down in the ditch, boys, for fear I'd be shot.

Well we fought at the Alma, likewise Inkermann,
And the Russians they whaled us at the Redan.
In scaling the walls there, myself lost my eye,
And a big Russian bullet ran off with my thigh.

'Twas there I lay bleeding, stretched on the cold
    ground –
Heads, legs and arms were all scattered around.
I thought if my mam and my cleaveens were nigh
They'd bury me decent and raise a loud cry.

Well a doctor was called and he soon staunched my
    blood,
And he gave me an elegant leg made of wood,
They gave me a medal and ten pence a day –
Contented with Sheela, I'll live on half-pay.

Rudyard Kipling

Kipling's gentle portrait, published in Barrack-Room
Ballads, *1892, of one of the many Irish ex-soldiers then
trying to live on tiny army pensions, and reduced to begging
for letters to deliver for a few pence.*

SHILLIN' A DAY

My name is O'Kelly, I've heard the Revelly
From Birr to Bareilly, from Leeds to Lahore,

Hong-Kong and Peshawur,
Lucknow and Etawah,
And fifty-five more all endin' in 'pore.'
Black Death and his quickness, the depth and the
    thickness,
Of sorrow and sickness I've known on my way,
But I'm old and I'm nervis,
I'm cast from the Service,
And all I deserve is a shillin' a day.
        Shillin' a day,
        Bloomin' good pay –
        Lucky to touch it, a shillin' a day!

Oh, it drives me half crazy to think of the days I
Went slap for the Ghazi, my sword at my side,
When we rode Hell-for-leather
Both squadrons together,
That didn't care whether we lived or we died.
But it's no use despairin', my wife must go charin'
An' me commissairin' the pay-bills to better,
So if me you be'old
In the wet and the cold,
By the Grand Metropold won't you give me a letter?
        Give 'im a letter –
        'Can't do no better,
        Late Troop-Sergeant-Major an' – runs with a
            letter!
        Think what 'e's been,
        Think what 'e's seen,
        Think of his pension an' –
        GAWD SAVE THE QUEEN.

As World War One grinds on, Kipling (1865–1936) meditates,
as only Kipling can, on the fighting Irish:

THE IRISH GUARDS
1918

We're not so old in the Army List,
    But we're not so young at our trade,
For we had the honour at Fontenoy
    Of meeting the Guards' Brigade.
'Twas Lally, Dillon, Bulkeley, Clare,
    And Lee that led us then,

And after a hundred and seventy years
    We're fighting for France again!
    Old Days! The wild geese are flighting,
      Head to the storm as they faced it before!
    For where there are Irish there's bound to be fighting,
      And when there's no fighting, it's Ireland no more!
        Ireland no more!

The fashion's all for khaki now,
    But once through France we went
Full-dressed in scarlet Army cloth,
    The English – left at Ghent.
They're fighting on our side to-day
    But, before they changed their clothes,
The half of Europe knew our fame,
    As all of Ireland knows!
    Old Days! The wild geese are flying,
      Head to the storm as they faced it before!
    For where there are Irish there's memory undying,
      And when we forget, it is Ireland no more!
        Ireland no more!

From Barry Wood to Gouzeaucourt,
    From Boyne to Pilkem Ridge,
The ancient days come back no more
    Than water under the bridge.
But the bridge it stands and the water runs
    As red as yesterday,
And the Irish move to the sound of the guns
    Like salmon to the sea.
    Old Days! The wild geese are ranging,
      Head to the storm as they faced it before!
    For where there are Irish their hearts are unchanging,
      And when they are changed, it is Ireland no more!
        Ireland no more!

We're not so old in the Army List,
    But we're not so new in the ring,
For we carried our packs with Marshal Saxe
    When Louis was our King.
But Douglas Haig's our Marshal now
    And we're King George's men,
And after one hundred and seventy years
    We're fighting for France again!
    Ah, France! And did we stand by you,

When life was made splendid with gifts and
  rewards?
Ah, France! And will we deny you
  In the hour of your agony, Mother of Swords?
Old Days! The wild geese are flighting,
  Head to the storm as they faced it before!
For where there are Irish there's loving and fighting,
  And when we stop either, it's Ireland no more!
    Ireland no more!

Anonymous

*Lines from a County Limerick election lampoon written in
1830 in support of Lieutenant Colonel Standish O'Grady,
the local 'tenants' candidate', who had been verbally
attacked by the Knight of Glin, John Fraunceis Fitz-Gerald.*

'THE KNIGHT OF GLIN'

His vices have made, and still make him so poor,
That bailiff or creditor is ne'er from his door,
And deep tho' in debt, yet he's deeper in sin,
That lecherous, treacherous knight of the Glin.

That hoary old sinner, this profligate rare,
Who gloats o'er the ruin of the virtuous and fair;
In gambling and drinking and wenching delights
And in these doth spend both his days and his nights.

Yet there is the man who's heard to declare
'Gainst O'Grady he'll vote if the priests interfere.
But the priests and O'Grady do not care a pin
For the beggarly, profligate knight of the Glin!

*To be quite fair, we ought perhaps to mention that in his
1826 poem on the Knight, Michael Stackpool could not
disagree more –*

'... No, no, he spends his wealth among the poor,
Dispensing happiness from door to door ...'

Anonymous
('HI Brouw')

A final solution to one of the perennial problems of philosophy, suggested in TCD Miscellany *in June 1920.*

LA FEMME SAVANTE

'But, Locke,' she said,
'Was not consistently empiricist.'
I wondered wearily: –
'Why do philosophers persist?'
And: – 'Surely she were better dead?'
So then I rose
And strangled her …
And now the evenings pass more cheerily.

Osbert Lancaster

The English cartoonist, Osbert Lancaster (1908–1986), expertly anatomises the gloom of post-Emergency Dublin. From his Façades and Faces *(1950).*

EIREANN AFTERNOON

The distant Seychelles are not so remote
Nor Ctesiphon as ultimately dead

As this damp square round which tired echoes float
Of something brilliant that George Moore once said:
Where, still, in pitch-pine snugs pale poets quote
Verses rejected by the Bodley Head.
For in this drained aquarium no breeze
Deposits pollen from more fertile shores
Or kills the smell of long unopened drawers
That clings for ever to these dripping trees.
Where Bloom once wandered, gross and ill-at-ease,
Twice-pensioned heroes of forgotten wars
With misplaced confidence demand applause
Shouting stale slogans on the Liffey quays.

Charles Lever

We make no apology for including here a hearty helping of
Charles Lever (1806–1872). The most popular Irish novelist
of the Victorian era, with a reputation to rival Charles
Dickens, Lever was convicted in absentia of gross stage-
Irishry, and was ignored for most of the twentieth century.
But as this anthology should make evident, his verses shared
closely the spirit of the songs that he heard in the streets
and theatres of Dublin as he grew up. If Charles Lever's
worst sin was his attempt to reproduce Irish speech patterns
in print, then he should be forgiven – after all, Roddy Doyle
does it too.

Most of Lever's verses are found embedded in his novels:
this first example is a footsoldier's protest from Charles
O'Malley *(1841), a tale of the Peninsular War:*

BAD LUCK TO THIS MARCHING

Bad luck to this marching,
Pipeclaying and starching;
How neat one must be to be killed by the French!
I'm sick of parading,
Through wet and cold wading,
Or standing all night to be shot in a trench.
To the tune of a fife
They dispose of your life,
You surrender your soul to some illigant lilt;
Now, I like 'Garryowen'
When I hear it at home,
But it's not half so sweet when you're going to be kil't.

Then, though up late and early
    Our pay comes so rarely,
The devil a farthing we've ever to spare;
    They say some disaster
    Befell the paymaster;
On my conscience I think that the money's not there.
    And, just think, what a blunder!
    They won't let us plunder,
While the convents invite us to rob them, 'tis clear;
    Though there isn't a village
    But cries, 'Come and pillage'
Yet we leave all the mutton behind for Mounseer.

    Like a sailor that's nigh land,
    I long for that island
Where even the kisses we steal if we please;
    Where it is no disgrace
    If you don't wash your face,
And you've nothing to do but to stand at your ease.
    With no sergeant t' abuse us,
    We fight to amuse us,
Sure it's better beat Christians than kick a baboon;
    How I'd dance like a fairy
    To see ould Dunleary,
And think twice ere I'd leave it to be a dragoon!

IT'S LITTLE FOR GLORY I CARE

It's little for glory I care;
    Sure ambition is only a fable;
I'd as soon be myself as Lord Mayor,
    With lashins of drink on the table.
I like to lie down in the sun,
    And drame when my faytures is scorchin',
That when I'm too ould for more fun,
    Why I'll marry a wife with a fortune.

And in winter, with bacon and eggs,
    And a place at the turf fire basking,
Sip my punch as I roasted my legs,
    Oh! the devil a more I'd be asking.
For I haven't a jaynius for work –
    It was never the gift of the Bradies, –

But I'd make a most illigant Turk,
 For I'm fond of tobacco and ladies.

'COUNTRY LIFE'

Smoking, sleeping, poteen drinking,
 And ogling the Curate's daughters,
Doing everything but thinking –
 Such is life in Country Quarters!

'WHAT AN ILLIGANT LIFE'

What an illigant life a friar leads,
 With a fat round paunch before him:
He mutters a prayer and counts his beads,
 And all the women adore him.
It's little he's troubled to work or think;
 Wherever devotion leads him,
A 'a pater' pays for his dinner and drink,
 For the Church – good luck to her! – feeds him.

From the cow in the field to the pig in the stye,
 From the maid to the lady in satin,
They tremble, wherever he turns an eye;
 He can talk to the devil in Latin!
He's mighty severe to the ugly and ould,
 And curses like mad when he's near 'em;
But one beautiful trait of him I have tould,
 The innocent craytures don't fear him.

It's little for spirits or ghosts he cares;
 For 'tis true, as the world supposes,
With an *ave* he'd make them march down-stairs,
 Av they dared to show their noses.
The devil himself's afraid, 'tis said,
 And dares not to deride him;
For 'angels make each night his bed,
 And then – lie down beside him.'

'DUBLIN CITY'

Och, Dublin city, there is no doubtin',
    Bates every city upon the say;
'Tis there you'd hear O'Connell spoutin',
    An' Lady Morgan makin' tay.
For 'tis the capital o' the finest nation,
    Wid charmin' pisintry upon a fruitful sod,
Fightin' like divils for conciliation,
    An' hatin' each other for the love of God.

'A SUITABLE APPOINTMENT'

And they lookede aboute for a rudelie manne,
    That was valiante at knife and forke,
And who never desertede flagon nor canne,
    And him made they Mayor of Corke.

'OH, MARY BRADY'

Oh, Mary Brady, you are my darlin,
You are my looking-glass, from night till morning;
I'd rayther have ye without one farthen,
Nor Shusey Gallagher and her house and garden.

In the 1880s, the verse above, from Charles O'Malley, *was
adapted by a Bray chemist, James Vance, for his little daughter
to send as a valentine to a certain schoolboy sweetheart:*

O Jimmie Joyce you are my darling
You are my looking glass from night till morning
I'd rather have you without one farthing
Than Harry Newell and his ass and garden.

MICKEY FREE'S ANCESTRY

Oh! once we were illigint people,
    Though we now live in cabins of mud;
And the land that ye see from the steeple
    Belonged to us all from the Flood.

My father was then King of Connaught,
    My grand-aunt Viceroy of Tralee;
But the Sassenach came, and, signs on it!
    The devil an acre have we.

The least of us then were all earls,
    And jewels we wore without name;
We drank punch out of rubies and pearls –
    Mr Petrie can tell you the same,
But, except some turf mould and potatoes,
    There's nothing our own we can call;
And the English – bad luck to them – hate us,
    Because we've more fun than them all!

My grand-aunt was niece to Saint Kevin,
    That's the reason my name's Mickey Free!
Priest's nieces – but, sure, he's in heaven,
    And his failin's is nothin' to me.
And we still might get on without doctors,
    If they'd let the ould island alone;
And if purple-men, priests, and tithe-proctors,
    Were crammed down the great gun of Athlone.

'A PLEA'

Open, ye bogs, and swallow down
That horrid place called Philipstown;
And if you've room for any more
Then swallow dirty Tullamore.

CS Lewis

It tends to be overlooked that C S Lewis (1898–1963) was a native of Belfast, and therefore as Irish as anybody. He is of course best remembered for the Chronicles of Narnia: *this is an extract from his 'Narnian Suite'.*

MARCH FOR STRINGS, KETTLEDRUMS, AND
SIXTY-THREE DWARFS

With plucking pizzicato and the prattle of the
   kettledrum

We're trotting into battle mid a clatter of
    accoutrement;
Our beards are big as periwigs and trickle with
    opopanax,
And trinketry and treasure twinkle out on every part
    of us –
      (Scrape! Tap! The fiddle and the kettledrum).

The chuckle-headed humans think we're only petty
    poppetry
And all our battle-tackle nothing more than pretty
    bric-a-brac;
But a little shrub has prickles, and they'll soon be in a
    pickle if
A scud of dwarfish archery has crippled all their
    cavalry –
      (Whizz! Twang! The quarrel and the javelin).

And when the tussle thickens we can writhe and
    wriggle under it;
Then dagger-point'll tickle 'em, and grab and grip'll
    grapple 'em,
And trap and trick'll trouble 'em and tackle 'em and
    topple 'em
Till they're huddled, all be-diddled, in the middle of
    our caperings –
      (Dodge! Jump! The wriggle and the summersault).

When we've scattered 'em and peppered 'em with
    pebbles from our catapults
We'll turn again in triumph and by crannies and by
    crevices
Go back to where the capitol and cradle of our people
    is,
Our forges and our furnaces, the caverns of the earth –
      (Gold! Fire! The anvil and the smithying).

Fergus Linehan

*Fergus Linehan has for many years been writing songs and
verses for the stage and elsewhere. 'The Blackbird' dates
from his student days, while 'The Shaving Ghost' is a more
recent composition.*

THE BLACKBIRD

One day as I went down the road to town,
What did I see but a blackbird hanging upside down,
I said: 'Sweet bird, why do you sing your song?'
She said to me: 'A no good gentleman blackbird done
    me wrong.

'Oh I was young, 'twas in the month of May,
When earwigs squirm and snails come out to play,
His fine feathers, they quite beguil-ed me,
He said to me: "Come on up to me come on up to my
    nest,
I've some very fine etchings there for you to see."

'But in that nest, slap up against the wall,
Was a great big double bed and damn all else at all,
I said to him: "Where are those etchings that your
    nest adorn?"
He looked at me (most peculiar like)
And he said: "Is it yesterday morning you're after
    being born?"

'Ochone, ochone, ochone 's wirrasthru,
Which means what happened next,
I'm not going to describe to you,'
And thus she sang, as she hung there by her little
    skinny legs:
'He left me all alone with a nestful of fatherless eggs.

'And that is why I roam the whole wide world
    through,
Catching slugs and worms and sometimes catching
    the flu,'
And so she sang, that poor godforsaken blackbird hen,
    It only goes to show …
That there's no good at all to be got out of men!

THE SHAVING GHOST

Sweet God on high the Shaving Ghost,
Oh he's the boy would scare you,
At dead of night his tricks he played,
With razor sharp, with cut-throat blade,
And if he met you, you'd be flayed,
For he would never spare you.

He lived, if you could call it that,
Inside a dark old hall sir,
Amid most awful screams and shouts,
He'd cut off ears, he'd cut off snouts,
Then nail up all the bloody gouts,
In rows along the wall sir.

The shaving ghost, the shaving ghost,
Come on until I shave ya!

He'd cut your throat in half a sec,
Or so the stories stated,
And in his mansion of the dead,
In every single dusty bed,
He kept a ghastly severed head,
That he'd decapitated.

A traveller boy got lost one night,
That mansion he espied it,
So tired he didn't give a damn,
He forced a creaking window jamb,
Which dropped behind him with a slam,
And he was trapped inside it.

The shaving ghost, the shaving ghost,
Come on until I shave ya!

The shaving ghost came down the stairs,
A sight would never lave ya,
He wore a long old blood-stained cloak,
He held a cracked old mirror broke,
He grinned and all the words he spoke,
'Come on until I shave ya!'

'But sir I'm much too young to shave,'
The boy felt consternation,

For all his youth, though, he was brave,
He wasn't ready for the grave,
The ghost said: 'Come on 'til I shave,'
He'd not much conversation.

The shaving ghost, the shaving ghost,
Come on until I shave ya!

The shaving ghost whipped out his blade,
Bad thoughts began to harbour,
The boy said: 'One small nick and ye
Will not get any tip from me,'
The ghost paused, with uncertainty,
For he had been a barber.

A ray of early sun shone in,
The boy, not discommoded,
Grabbed up the mirror from its place,
And shone it in the ghost's pale face,
The ghost yelled, with a fierce grimace,
And bloodily exploded.

The traveller boy was covered in
Gore, flowing like a river,
Two eyeballs lay there at his feet,
Ten fingers and a lot of teeth,
Some bowels and kidneys underneath,
And several lumps of liver.

The dripping boy wiped up the mess,
His face and clothes all smear-ded,
And when he'd got himself half dry,
Broke down the door and said goodbye,
And told himself: 'I think when I
Grow up, I will be bearded!'

The shaving ghost, the shaving ghost,
Come on until I shave ya!

Anonymous
('TC')

A fizzy alphabetical jeu d'esprit *from* Dublin Opinion,
August 1958.

LITTLE EMILY OF DEE

When little M L E of D
    Went out the town to view
Wrapped up against the I C wind
    That down the High Street blew,

There passed her in a lowlier pram
    Another bright-eyed baby,
And, as his name was Abraham,
    They called him little A B.

And, as the months succeeded months,
    Their young affection grew,
'I C U, M L E,' he would lisp,
    And 'A B,' she would coo.

But, when the twain grew up, alas!
    They could not wedded B:
'Twas plain that her rich Papa was
    Poor A B's N M E.

'I N V U,' the poor lad Z
    'I N V U,' Z E,
'For P T's sake,' Z M L E
    'O do not N V me!

O go and ask Papa for me
    And hear what he may say
Tell him I love U with a love
    That never will D K.'

Papa has looked upon the lad,
    His eyes are small and B D,

'My M L E will wed rich George.
        I do not like the needy.

In fact,' his B D eyes grew grim,
        His face with anger pale,
'If I C U round here again
        I'll have U clapped in J L.'

'No matter what my father says
        I'll be no bride of Georgie's
For he is nearly A T and
        Takes part in tavern R G's.'

'O, M L E, my love to B,
        I am not rich nor clever.
I only want to B with U
        For F R and for F R.'

'If I no more may B with U,
        With U no more may B,
Then I must go and throw myself
        Into the cruel C.'

U C the lovers standing there,
        A teardrop in each eye,
And from the C the evening breeze
        Comes gentle as a sigh.

Now I V twines round A B's mound
        Beneath an L M tree,
And willows wave above the grave
        Of little M L E.

Anonymous

Among the predecessors of Dublin Opinion *was a shortlived
Dublin comic magazine,* Zozimus, *named after the city's
famous songwriter. This macabre lament appeared in 1872.*

THE LONELY MAN

Here I sit, so sad and lonely,
        In my solitary room,

With my night-lamp here beside me,
  But it can't dispel the gloom.

For to me all things are gloomy,
  Nothing now gives me delight;
Now I'm longing for the morning –
  When it comes, I'd wish for night.

Time was when I was the gayest –
  Yes, the gayest of the gay;
That was when poor Ben was living,
  Now he's in the cold damp clay.

Yes, he's dead and gone for ever,
  And the grass waves o'er his head,
And the little Robin Redbreast
  Sings above his narrow bed.

That's the reason I am gloomy –
  I will ne'er be gay again;
How could I be ever happy
  In this wide world without Ben?

Reader, I had better tell you,
  Ere I put away my pen,
How it was that death deprived me
  Of my only friend, poor Ben.

Our Ben came from a far off place,
  Called the Isle of Newfoundland;
One morn he bit me, and I hung him
  From my umbrella stand!

Anonymous

*We know nothing whatever about this delightful story in
verse, given to us by a friend. The date is perhaps 1900 or so
– before petrol-driven launches apparently – though it could
be earlier or a good deal later.*

A LONGFORD LEGEND

Oh! 'Tis of a bold major a tale I'll relate,
Who possessed a fine house and a charming estate,
Who, when possible, always his pleasure would take
From morning till night in a boat on his lake.
So a steam-launch he bought from a neighbouring peer,
And learnt how to start her, to stoke, and to steer;
But part of the craft he omitted to learn –
How to ease her, and to stop her, and back her astern.

Well, one lovely spring morn from their moorings
     they cast,
The furnace alight and the steam in full blast.
As they cruised through the lake, oh! what pleasure
     was theirs!
What congratulations! what swagger! what airs!
'Evening's come,' says the major; 'let's home for the
     night.
I'll pick up the mooring and make her all right;
Whilst you, my gay stoker, your wages to earn,
Just ease her, and stop her, and back her astern.'

'Do what?' asked the stoker, 'Why, stop her, of course!'
'Faith! it's aisier stopping a runaway horse!
Just try it yourself!' The field officer swore!
But that was no use, they were nearly on shore!
He swore at himself, at the boat, and the crew;
He cursed at the funnel, the boiler, and screw,
But in vain! He was forced from his mooring to turn,
Shouting, 'Ease her, and stop her, and back her astern!

It was clear that on shore they that night would not
     dine,
So they drank up the brandy, the whisky and wine;
They finished the stew and demolished the cake
As they steamed at full speed all the night round the
     lake.

Weeks passed; and with terror and famine oppressed,
One by one of that ill-fated crew sank to rest;
And grim death seized the major before he could learn
How to ease her, and stop her, and back her astern.

And still round the lake their wild course they pursue,
While the ghost of the major still swears at the crew,
And the ghosts of the crew still reply in this mode,
'Just ease her, and stop her yourself – and be blowed!'
Here's the moral: Imprimis, whene'er you're afloat,
Don't use haughty words to your crew on your boat;
And ere starting, oh! make this your deepest concern –
Learn to ease her, and stop her, and back her astern.

Anonymous

Caustic verses from the eighth number of Zozimus. *Before editing* The Nation *and becoming an MP, the poet TD Sullivan wrote for the magazine – this unsigned attack on the hereditary aristocrats of Ireland reads like one of his.*

LORD TOMNODDY

My Lord Tomnoddy's the son of an earl,
His hair is straight, but his whiskers curl;
His lordship's forehead is far from wide,
But there's plenty of room for the brains inside,
He writes his name with indifferent ease,
He is rather uncertain about the 'd's,'
But what does it matter if two, or one,
To the Earl of Fitznoodle's eldest son?

My Lord Tomnoddy to college went –
Much time he lost, much money he spent;
Rules, and windows, and heads he broke,
Authorities wink'd – 'young men will joke!'
He never peeped inside of a book –
In two years' time a degree he took;
And the newspapers vaunted the honours won
By the Earl of Fitznoodle's eldest son.

My Lord Tomnoddy came out in the world,
Waists were tightened, and ringlets curl'd;

Lavinia langished, and matrons smil'd.
'Tis true, his lordship is rather 'wild;'
In very queer places he spends his life –
There's talk of some children by nobody's wife;
But we mustn't look close into what is done
By the Earl of Fitznoodle's eldest son.

My Lord Tomnoddy must settle down –
There's a vacant seat in the family town!
It's time he should sow his eccentric oats.
He hasn't the wit to apply for votes;
He cannot e'en learn his election speech;
Three phrases he speaks – a mistake in each!
And then breaks down – but the borough is won
For the Earl of Fitznoodle's eldest son.

My Lord Tomnoddy prefers the Guards
(The House is a bore); so – it's on the cards –
My Lord is a cornet at twenty-three,
A Major at twenty-six is he –
He never drew a sword except on drill;
The tricks of parade he has learnt but ill –
A lieutenant-colonel at thirty-one
Is the Earl of Fitznoodle's eldest son.

My Lord Tomnoddy is thirty-four;
The earl can last but a few years more.
My lord in the Peers will take his place:
Her Majesty's counsels his words will grace.
Office he'll hold and patronage sway;
Fortunes and lives he will vote away;
And what are his qualifications? One: –
He's the Earl of Fitznoodle's eldest son!

Anonymous

*This grand old song has here been augmented and clarified
with lines borrowed from another very closely related one on
the same subject, called 'The Black Cavalry'.*

THE LOUSE HOUSE OF KILKENNY

Oh, the first of me downfall, I set out the door;
I straight made me way on for Carrick-on-Suir.

Going out by Rathronan 'twas late in the night,
Going out the West Gate for to view the gaslight.

Chorus:
Radley fal the diddle ay,
Radley fal the diddle airo.

I went to the town's hall to see the big lamp,
And who should I meet but a bloody big tramp;
I finally stepped over and to him I said:
'Will you kindly direct me to where I'll get a bed?'

'Twas then he directed me down to Cooks Lane,
To where old Buck St John kept an old sleeping cage.
From out of the door was a small piece of board
Hung out on two nails with a short piece of cord.

I looked up and down till I found out the door,
And a queerer old household sure I ne'er saw before,
Then the Missus came out and these words to me said:
'If you give me three coppers, sure I'll give you a bed.'

Well, I then stood aside with me back to the wall,
And the next thing I saw was an oul cobbler's stall,
And there was the cobbler and he mending his brogues,
With his hammers and pinchers all laid in a row.

Then she brought me upstairs and she put out the light,
And in less than five minutes I had to show fight,
And in less than five more sure the story was worse,
The fleas came around me and brought me a curse.

'Twas all around me body they formed an arch;
'Twas all around me body they played the Death march;
For the bloody oul major gave me such a nip,
That he nearly made away with half of me hip.

Now I'm going to me study, these lines to pen down,
And if any poor traveller should e'er come to town,
And if any poor traveller should be nighted like me –
Beware of Buck St John and his black cavalry.

Samuel Lover

*Samuel Lover (1797–1868), painter, professional comic writer
and prolific anthologist (the lowest literary calling of them
all), has taken much stick for spreading stage-Irishry. See
what you make of these two.*

THE BIRTH OF SAINT PATRICK

On the eighth day of March it was, some people say,
That Saint Pathrick at midnight he first saw the day;
While others declare 'twas the ninth he was born,
And 'twas all a mistake between midnight and morn;
For mistakes *will* occur in a hurry, and shock,
And some blam'd the babby – and some blam'd the
    clock –
Till with all their cross questions sure no one could
    know,
If the child was too fast – or the clock was too slow.

Now the first faction fight in owld Ireland, they say,
Was all on account of Saint Pathrick's birthday,
Some fought for the eighth – for the ninth more
    would die,
And who wouldn't see right, sure they blacken'd his
    eye!
At last, both the factions so positive grew,
That *each* kept a birthday – so Pat then had *two*,
Till Father Mulcahy, who showed them their sins,
Said, 'No one could have two birthdays, but a *twins*.'

Says he, 'Boys, don't be fightin' for eight or for nine,
Don't be always dividin' – but sometimes combine;
Combine eight with nine, and seventeen is the mark,
So let that be his birthday.' – 'Amen,' says the clerk.
'If he wasn't a *twins*, sure our hist'ry will show –
That, at least, he's worth any *two* saints that we
    know!'
Then they all got blind dhrunk – which complated
    their bliss,
And we keep up the practice from that day to this.

PADDY'S PASTORAL RHAPSODY

Here's a health to you, my darlin'
Though I'm not worth a farthin';
For when I'm drunk I think I'm rich,
I've a feather-bed in every ditch.

James M Lowry

*This extraordinary example of technicolour Celtic
illumination was written by a now quite forgotten
poet/versifier, who graduated from TCD in 1871.*

THE LAST OF THE LEPRECHAUNS

Shillelagh Conn Mulligan Bryan O'Toole
Was chief of the party who fought for Home Rule,
Whilst his rival in love and in politics too
Was Deelish-MacDermot-O'Donel-Aboo.

Of the Amnesty faction this Deelish was chief,
Who sought for political pris'ners' relief.
'They're a parcel of knaves and their leader's a fool.'
Said Shillelagh Conn Mulligan Bryan O'Toole.

Now Shillelagh and Deelish both loved the same girl,
With eyes of the azure and hair of the curl;
As sweet as a rose and as fair as the dawn,
Was Eily Mavourneen Dhudeen Colleen Bawn.

But her father, old Tirlogh MacDonagh O'Byrne,
A chieftain, whom nought from his purpose could turn,
Had promised the hand of Dhudeen Colleen Bawn
To The Desmond O'Doherty Shaun Leprachaun.

'Twas June, and the mistletoe hung on the bough,
And holly and ivy were gleaming, I trow,
On tower and turret, where, rising to view,
Stood the castle of Kilballywhackwirrasthrue.

There dwelt the fair Dhudeen, her uncle its lord,
Whom rich men all hated, whom poor men adored;
Much feared by the great, but beloved by the serf,
Was Blatherumbloodanounsthunderandturf.

The fair summer moon shone serenely and pale
On the forms of two lovers who roamed through the
   vale:
They were Eily Mavourneen Dhudeen Colleen Bawn.
And The Desmond O'Doherty Shaun Leprachaun.

'Oh, say, dost thou love me?' the Leprechaun cried,
'My Kippeen! My Caubeen!! My Sassenach pride!!!'
'I am thine, only thine,' sighed Dhudeen Colleen Bawn;
'I'm thy Soggarth Alanna, thine own Omadhaun.'

The words were scarce spoken, when, with a loud
   shout,
Shillelagh O'Toole from the hedge bounded out,
And following, sprang with a fiendish hurroo,
The Deelish-MacDermot-O'Donel-Aboo.

'We swear that the Dhudeen will ne'er be thy bride,'
Cried each chieftain, advancing with menacing stride.
'Die, villain! Die, traitor!! Die, lying upstart!!!'
And two daggers were plunged in the Leprachaun's
   heart.

Said Shillelagh to Deelish, 'Let fate now decide
Between us who gets the Dhudeen for his bride.
A Camac I'll toss up: if 'heads,' she is mine,
But if on the contrary 'harps,' she is thine.'

Aloft flew the Camac. Then fell with a thud,
And the emerald sod was empurpled with blood,
The blood of a chieftain, the chief of Home Rule,
The blood of the dauntless Shillelagh O'Toole.

For fate had decided that 'heads' was the word,
And Deelish drew swift from the scabbard his sword,
Crying: 'Heads let it be, thou incompetent fool!'
As he cut off the head of Shillelagh O'Toole.

Then suddenly, mortally wounded, he reeled,
By whose hand the historian has never reveled;
But dead as Queen Anne and bold Brian Boru,
Fell Deelish-MacDermot-O'Donel-Aboo.

Then rang through the night a wild cry of despair,
Like the shriek of the Banshee when roused from her
   lair;

'Acushla-macree! Faugh-a-balla!! Crubeen!!!'
'Twas the death-cry of Eily, fair Eily Dhudeen.

A moss-covered cromlech still points out the place,
And the traveller who reads this inscription may trace,
HERE LYES EILY MAVOURNEEN DHUDEEN
  COLLEEN BAWN,
WITH YE DESMOND O'DOHERTY SHAUN
  LEPRACHAUN.

*Clearly, Lowry could turn his hand to anything. This one,
from his 1906 collection* A Lay of Kilcock, *seems to owe a
little to the song* 'Eibhlín a Rún'.

TOTTIE DE VERE

Yes, we must parted be,
  Tottie De Vere,
Dear as you are to me,
  Tottie De Vere.
Dear in the double sense
Of vulgar pounds and pence,
Fact, I must say expense –
  Tottie De Vere.

Who made the fivers fly?
  Tottie De Vere.
Woo liked the champagne dry?
  Tottie De Vere.
Who, when the play was o'er,
Went for Scott's oyster store,
And eat at least three score?
  Tottie De Vere.

Who collared all my cash?
  Tottie De Vere.
Who was it made me smash?
  Tottie De Vere.
Who laughed, with eyes so blue,
When the various bills came due,
Marshall and Snellgrove's too?
  Tottie De Vere.

But now thou'rt cold to me,
    Tottie De Vere,
Since I've no gold for thee,
    Tottie De Vere.
So without much regret
You and I part, my pet,
But I shall ne'er forget,
    Tottie De Vere.

Edward Lysaght

*That beshamrocked monument to the forgotten, the 1893
Cabinet of Irish Literature (four volumes), remarks that,
as a struggling barrister in London, Edward Lysaght
(1763–1810) fled back to Ireland when he discovered that his
wife's father, 'whom he had believed was a wealthy Jew, was
only a bankrupt Christian'. Once safely home, he 'occupied
his leisure hours in verse-making, and the production of
many a witty skit now utterly lost.' 'Pleasant Ned', as he
unsurprisingly became known, made verses like these ones,
in which 'Sweet Chloe' warns about the effects of alcohol
upon a man's amorous 'delights'.*

LOVE *VERSUS* THE BOTTLE

Sweet Chloe advised me, in accents divine,
    The joys of the bowl to surrender;
Nor lose, in the turbid excesses of wine,
    Delights more ecstatic and tender;
She bade me no longer in vineyards to bask,
Or stagger, at orgies, the dupe of a flask,
For the sigh of a sot's but the scent of the cask,
    And a bubble the bliss of the bottle.

To a soul that's exhausted, or sterile, or dry,
    The juice of the grape may be wanted;
But mine is reviv'd by a love-beaming eye,
    And with fancy's gay flow'rets enchanted.
Oh! who but an owl would a garland entwine
Of Bacchus's ivy – and myrtle resign,
Yield the odours of love for the vapours of wine,
    And Chloe's kind kiss for a bottle?

Somhairle MacAlastair

*When the Irish fascist 'General' Owen O'Duffy led his 700
disciples home again after an absurd attempt to join the
anticommunist side in the Spanish Civil War, they were
greeted with a wave of mockery: Brendan Behan was to call
them the only army ever to have returned from war with
more men than it had originally set out with. Professor
Hogan, William Lombard Murphy (the power behind the
Independent newspaper group) and Patrick Belton, a
disaffected TD, were among O'Duffy's few eminent
supporters. This song by 'Somhairle MacAlastair' (thought
to be the pseudonym of Diarmuid MacGiolla Phádraig) was
circulating before the drunken rabble had even set off.*

BATTLE SONG OF THE IRISH CHRISTIAN
FRONT: 'OFF TO SALAMANCA'

My name is Owen O'Duffy,
And I'm rather vain and huffy,
The side of every Bolshie I'm a thorn in.
But before the break of day,
I'll be marching right away,
For I'm off to Salamanca in the morning.

Chorus:
With the gold supplied by Vickers,
I can buy Blue Shirt and knickers,

Let the Barcelona Bolshies take a warning.
For I lately took the notion,
To cross the briny ocean
And I start for Salamanca in the morning.

There's a boy called Paddy Belton,
With a heart that's soft and meltin',
Yet the first to face the foemen, danger scorning,
Tho' his feet are full of bunions,
Yet he knows his Spanish onions,
And he's off to Salamanca in the morning.

Now the 'Irish Christian Front',
Is a Lombard-Murphy stunt.
(Hark! the ghostly voice of Connolly gives warning)
And Professor Hogan's pals,
Can don their fal-de-lals
And start for Salamanca in the morning.

When they get kicked out of Spain,
And they travel home again,
Let them hearken in good time to this, our warning.
If they try their Fascist game,
They'll be sorry that they came
Back from Salamanca in the morning.

Alec McAllister

*Much of the work of Alec McAllister (1917–1993) first saw
the light in the 'Corran', a quarterly magazine published by
Larne and District Folklore and Historical Society. He often
set his verses and monologues in the 1930s, using a language
that was, as here, rich in words specific to County Antrim.*

THE BREAKING OF MAGGIE

She was tall thin an' thirty, wi' glossy black hair
She had a wee bit o' land an' money tae spare.
The boys tried tae court her for mony a mile
But they never got more than their tay an' a smile.

Now, just at that time I was feeling my best
So I thought I would tackle along wi' the rest.

It happened to be in the spring o' the year,
Wi' the hens laying bravely an' the beef no sae dear.

Man, wi' feeding an' leisure, I hadnae a grumble
I just felt like haein' a bit o' a rumble,
So I sent my good shirt to the laundry on Monday
To hae everythin' ready for the following Sunday.

They starched it so stiff I wud houl' you a dollar
It tuk me two hours to get in till that collar,
I shined up my shoes in a way that wud please you
An' I had a crease in thon trousers by hookey wud
    shave you.
An' for the fear on the loanin I'd dirty my feet
They carried me out to the road on a sheet.

When I landed wi' Maggie my heart was on fire,
She was sitting there milkin' the cows in the byre,
I just walked right up an' I reached her my han'
Says I 'How are ye Maggie,' says she 'Rightly, Dan.'
I took a seat at the end o' the walk
An' Maggie an' me had a sensible talk.

I niver dae things in too much o' a hurry,
I done a rash thing yince, an' in sowl I was sorry.
I knew this could end up in two different ways
An' both scenes appeared very plain in my eyes.

I wud either be kissin an' callin her 'lassie'
Or else I'd be lying sprawled oot in the cassey.
Well she finished her cow an' prepared to retreat
So I buttoned my coat an' jumped to my feet.

Says I to mesel, 'Noo for the curfuffle,
I will conquer my task or I'll die in the scuffle.'
She saw what was coming an' just made a dart
But when I'm set on a thing I be wonderful smart.

I grabbed her goin' by me, an' she pulled an' she tore,
An' by the skin o' my teeth I got her jammed in the
    door.
I would have needed some help, there was plenty to
    do,
But I got her calmed down in a minute or two.

An' in twenty-five minutes, by the Mullingar goose,
I had her kissed twenty times, an' as quate as a moose!
I took an odd rest an' I spun her a joke
An' Maggie she laughed till I thought she wad choke!

An' Maggie that niver before had been kissed
Was just realising how much she had missed,
Says she 'You'll come in for a wee drop o' soup'
But I tripped ower the cow an' fell in the group.

When I got up I was clarried wi' dirt,
I near cried when I looked at my nice laundried shirt,
But I got mysel' washed an' well dried at the fire –
It's no place for courtin' among cows in a byre.

But that was the first night, an' we've had mony
    anither
An' noo we are plannin' tae be buried taegither!

Donagh Mac Donagh

A howl of political anger, from The Hungry Grass, *the
1957 collection by the Dublin poet (1912–1968).*

JUVENILE DELINQUENCY

Who threw the stone that brought the window down
What hand was glutted in the toffee jar
Who slipped behind the counter for half-a-crown
What dusty finger blasphemed on the motor car

And who Oh who was hurried from the class-room
Who was a barbed Saint Stephen feathered with guilt
Who took a hammer to the family heirloom
Who broke who tore who shattered and who split

Whose is the dirty face that snivels reform
Who promises a future bright safe whole and new
Who learns at last to wear the uniform
That masks the criminal record from the view?

John McDonald

Ulster folk poetry, for some reason, sometimes runs to extreme forms of fantasy (see 'The Arab Orange Lodge' earlier in this book). That indefatiguable literary truffler, James M Healy of Cork, put this fine specimen into his glorious Comic Irish Recitations, *whence we take it out again.*

THE ORANGEMAN'S HELL

It was Sammy McNello that done it
He's never done swingin' the lead,
And one bloody day as he swung it,
He struck me a belt on the head.

'Get up,' says he, tryin' to shift me,
'I never heard nothin',' he said,
'Are you deaf?' says he, trying to lift me;
But I wasn't deaf – I was dead.

Of course I went straight up to heaven
It's millions o' miles past the sun;
I arrived at quarter past seven
In the year of three thousand and one.

I met this big chap in the hallway,
And says I, 'I'm just in from Belfast.'
Says he, and his accent was Galway,
'So they let an oul' Prod in at last!'

I followed him down a long passage
Where it led to your man wouldn't tell,
But I very soon got the message,
When I seen a big sign sayin' Hell.

Says I, 'Ach, for God's sake have pity!
I repent all the wrongs o' me past.'
But he led me on intil a city
A place the dead spit o' Belfast.

'Is thon hell?' says I, quite astounded,
'Thon's it indeed,' says the lad;
'If thon's hell,' says I, lookin' round it,
'If thon's hell it can't be too bad.'

The city was just as I knew it.
All the oul' friendly places were there;
Street by street I went wanderin' through it,
And then into Donegal Square.

There nobly before me, God love it,
The oul' City Hall stood in state –
With the Tricolour flyin' above it,
And two civic guards at the gate!

It was only the start o' me torment,
I soon learned the terrible facts,
The Pope was now livin' in Stormont
And Paisley was cleanin' the jacks.

The head o' the great Orange Order
Had long ago give himself up;
Jack Lynch had abolished the border,
And Linfield was out of the Cup.

All the Fenians had lovely fat faces,
But the poor Prods were queueing for soup;
There were Papists in all the high places
And The Abbey was playin' at the Group.

By now I was damn nearly cryin'
Demented, me nerves was on edge;
I went down De Valera Street flyin',
And over the Vatican Bridge.

To the shipyards I galloped like lightnin'
I thought I'd find Orangemen there,
But what did I find! It was frightnin'!
Speakin' in Gaelic they were.

The whole blinkin' city was stinkin',
There was nowhere a poor Prod could go,
Oh, what desperate thoughts I was thinkin'
Then it came in a flash – Sandy Row!

I knew they'd be loyal to Lizzie,
And wouldn't leave me in the lurch;
But when I got there they were busy,
Buildin' a Catholic Church!

I stood lookin' on broken-hearted,
My thoughts – ach, there's no words could tell
For now all my hopes had departed,
I knew I was really in hell.

I went back to the fella that brought me,
He was havin' a snooze at the gate;
I tried to get out, but he caught me –
You can't get away from your fate.

Says I, 'I don't like where you sent me,
If I'd known it I'd never a came';
And says he, and him standin' fornint me,
'Are you not happy here? What a shame!'

'Up here every freedom is given,
You can wander about as you will;
It's just that there's some thinks it's heaven,
And then again, some thinks it's hell.

'It's all in the mind – sure it's tragic,
Hell's the things and the people you hate.
The more hate, the more Hell – sure it's logic,
But some finds that out when they're late.'

I'm a ghost now, ach, just a beginner,
But if I was a mortal again,
I'd be nice to the Micks and the Shinners,
And I'd write to the Pope now and then.

Every man born on earth is your brother
So don't write thon things on the wall,
Because if we loved one another,
This land could be heaven for all.

Patrick MacDonogh

This piece was written halfway through the twentieth century, but it could have been said about Dublin at any time since Jonathan Swift, whose eye for insincerity was shared by MacDonogh (1902–1961).

NO MEAN CITY

Though naughty flesh will multiply
Our chief delight is in division;
Whatever of Divinity
We are all Doctors of Derison.
Content to risk a far salvation
For the quick coinage of a laugh
We cut, to make wit's reputation,
Our total of two friends … by half.

Patrick MacGill

*A memorable curiosity by the Donegal novelist and 'Poet of
the Pick' (1889–1963) – who was clearly the model for Flann
O'Brien's 'Jem Casey'.*

FAIR LADIES

I put an ant in a Spider's web;
The Spider, a greedy, grasping sinner,
Collared the Ant for an early dinner,
Forgetting, of course, the Robin's neb!

On the apple-tree Miss Robin sat,
And the morning's tragedy horrified her –
Down she flew and gobbled the Spider,
Forgetting, of course, the watching Cat.

'Mew! My turn to do my bit,'
Said the Cat, place-proud, benignant, subtle –
Down through the branches shot like a shuttle,
Straight on the Robin and gobbled it.

I know no moral to take from that –
Yet think, a hoary, unshriven Sinner,
When I see sweet ladies eating their dinner,
Of the Ant, the Spider, the Robin and the Cat.

William McGonigall

William McGonigall (1825?–1902), the most famous 'bad poet' in the world, almost rivals Robbie Burns as the national poet of Scotland. It is intriguing to find that the Census of 1841–51 suggests that he left his native Ireland when he was ten; we hereby claim him as one of our own. His stage trademark, which he delivered in full Hibernian costume, was this song, of which every line was, according to a contemporary press notice, 'a masterpiece of Irish comic acting.'

THE RATTLING BOY FROM DUBLIN

I'm a rattling boy from Dublin town,
I courted a girl called Biddy Brown,
Her eyes they were as black as sloes,
She had black hair and an aquiline nose.

Chorus:
Whack fal de da, fal de darelido,
Whack fal de da, fal de darelay,
Whack fal de da, fal de darelido,
Whack fal de da, fal de darelay.

One night I met her with another lad,
Says I, Biddy, I've caught you, by dad;
I never thought you were half so bad
As to be going about with another lad.

Says I, Biddy, this will never do,
For to-night you've prov'd to me untrue,
So do not make a hullaballoo,
For I will bid farewell to you.

Says Barney Magee, She is my lass,
And the man that says no, he is an ass,
So come away, and I'll give you a glass,
Och sure you can get another lass.

Says I, To the devil with your glass,
You have taken from me my darling lass,
And if you look angry, or offer to frown,
With my darling shillelah I'll knock you down.

Says Barney Magee unto me,
By the hokey I love Biddy Brown,
And before I'll give her up to thee,
One or both of us will go down.

So, with my darling shillelah, I gave him a whack,
Which left him lying on his back,
Saying, botheration to you and Biddy Brown,
For I'm the rattling boy from Dublin town.

So a policeman chanced to come up at the time,
And he asked of me the cause of the shine,
Says I, he threatened to knock me down
When I challenged him for walking with my Biddy
    Brown.

So the policeman took Barney Magee to jail,
Which made him shout and bewail
That ever he met with Biddy Brown,
The greatest deceiver in Dublin town.

So I bade farewell to Biddy Brown,
The greatest jilter in Dublin town,
Because she proved untrue to me,
And was going about with Barney Magee.

Iggy McGovern

Iggy McGovern (b. 1948), who in his leisure hours is a
physicist at TCD, won the 1996 Odyssey Joycean Light Verse

Competition with this poem. He explained that it was
'inspired by the titles in Joyce's Pomes Penyeach and
Joyce's little-known interest in soccer.'

POMES INDIGEST

I was watching the needleboats at San Sabba
Dreaming I was on the beach at Fontana
A-courting Miss Tilly, admiring her dimples,
When who should arrive but thirteen German simples
Singing tutto e sciolto (or totally scuttered)
'Eine Rose Gegeben Zu Meine Tochter'
Then shouts of 'olé' and 'ober der moon'
Rap versions of 'Sie Veeps Ober Rahoon'
Sure that sort of rubbish went out with the Flood
And the loss of my nightpiece just boiled up my blood:
'Yez better piss off up the ould Bahnhofstrasse
Unless yez would like a good kick up the asse!'
Now I was alone and I hadn't a prayer
Except for a memory of the players
In a mirror at midnight, The Boys in Green
Big Jack and Alders and Quinno and Keane
And I scattered the lot of them over the beach
For they weren't the worth of a brass pfennig each.

In this subtle plea for the use of rhyme and metre in modern
poetry, McGovern offers a brilliant example of the formal
use of both. From his 2005 collection, The King of Suburbia.

TIME UP

Ho, Citizen of The Third Rock!
The Lords of Interstellar Time
are here to calibrate your clock,
the tick, the tock, the cheep, the chime,
the pound of flesh owed to Shylock,
the reason and the rhyme.

Your seasons are all out of rhyme:
you should be cleaving to the Rock
of Ages, yet you waste your time
in vain pursuit, against the clock,
of poetry; your paltry chime
has ended in gridlock.

We must insist you now padlock
the nursery door upon all rhyme
of unicorn and red-eyed roc,
the hick'ry-dick'ry mouse of time,
Wee Willie Winkie's eight o'clock,
Oranges 'n' Lemons chime.

Forget the Golden Treasury's chyme,
the out of date Rape of the Lock,
those ancient mariners of rhyme:
O Christ! It is the Inchcape Rock!
(a problem solved all in good time
by Harrison's fine clock).

When pumpkin-like at 12 o'clock
your forehead butts the front-door chime,
the wrong key jiggling in the lock,
the dogs take up the woof of rhyme,
the hand that makes the cradle rock
will coldly ask: What time

do you call this? – it's borrowed time!
There is no ten-to-three stopp't clock
so let go of that wine-keg's chime;
no visitation from Porlock
and no amount of see-saw rhyme
can stay the pendulum's rock.

Long past the time of seaside rock
and schoolbook rhyme. Let us unlock
the graveyard, chime the old church clock.

Shane MacGowan

Again and again, the lyrics of Shane MacGowan (b. 1957)
resonate with dark poetry. This song offers a new definition
of Irish heroism.

THE SICK BED OF CUCHULAINN

McCormack and Richard Tauber
Are singing by the bed
There's a glass of punch below your feet
And an angel at your head

There's devils on each side of you
With bottles in their hands
You need one more drop of poison
And you'll dream of foreign lands

When you pissed yourself in Frankfurt
And got syph down in Cologne
And you heard the rattling death trains
As you lay there all alone
Frank Ryan brought you whiskey
In a brothel in Madrid
And you decked some fucking blackshirt
Who was cursing all the Yids
At the sick bed of Cuchulainn
We'll kneel and say a prayer
And the ghosts are rattling at the door
And the devil's in the chair

And in the Euston Tavern
You screamed it was your shout
But they wouldn't give you service
So you kicked the windows out
They took you out into the street
And kicked you in the brains
So you walked back in through a bolted door
And did it all again
At the sick bed of Cuchulainn
We'll kneel and say a prayer
And the ghosts are rattling at the door
And the devil's in the chair

You remember that foul evening
When you heard the banshees howl
There was lousy drunken bastards
Singing Billy's in the bowl
They took you up to midnight mass
And left you in the lurch
So you dropped a button in the plate
And spewed up in the church

Now you'll sing a song of liberty
For blacks and paks and jocks
And they'll take you from this dump you're in
And stick you in a box
Then they'll take you to Cloughprior

And shove you in the ground
But you'll stick your head back out and shout
'We'll have another round'
At the graveside of Cuchulainn
We'll kneel around and pray
And God is in His heaven
And Billy's down by the bay

MJ MacManus

*The journalist M J MacManus (1888–1951) produced several
volumes of comic verses and prose pieces. Unlike Arthur
Griffith or Brian O'Higgins, his satire was gentle, but he often
hit the mark all the same. In verse 4 below, the obsolete slang
word, 'knutty' – the 'k' is sounded – means snappily dressed.*

THE O'FLANAGAN-BROWNES

Mrs Matilda O'Flanagan-Browne
Is one of the smartest smart women in town,
She lives in the most stylish road in Rathgar,
Has a daughter and son and a limousine car.

At Charity Balls she is well to the fore
(The Society columns will tell what she wore),
She's a patron of drama and art – though, perhaps,
Now and then she commits a grammatical lapse.

Percy Fitzclarence O'Flanagan-Browne
Is one of the gayest young men about town,
His Fair Isle pullover is simply a dream,
His tobacco is scented, he uses face-cream.

There's no one in Trinity nearly so knutty,
There's no one whose jokes are so brilliantly smutty;
His tutor believes he is wasting his fees
Yet he must be quite clever – he reads *Ulysses*.

Hyacinth Gladys O'Flanagan-Browne
Is the leader of fashion, the talk of the town,
Her cigarette-holder is ten inches long,
She knows a good cocktail, her language is strong.

The sums that she pays every year for her clothes
And schoolgirl complexions the Lord only knows;
But though she must spend a small fortune on dress
No one in Dublin contrives to wear less.

Mr James Michael O'Flanagan-Browne
Was the landlord of many slum districts in town,
Places by none recommended for health
But splendid for keeping slum landlords in wealth.

James Michael is dead, I am happy to say,
And lies under marble up Glasnevin way;
But his widow and Percy and Hyacinth are
Still quite the best people in happy Rathgar.

A BALLADE OF PORTADOWN

*'The Irishman who does not know Portadown does
not know Ireland.' – Rev. Andrew McKechnie.*

I've dreamed a while on Tara's hill,
I've listened to the bands at Bray;
At Dromahair I felt a thrill
Recalling Mr Yeats's lay.
At Dingle once I spent a day,
I wooed a lass at Edgeworthstown,
I've travelled far, but strange to say
I've never been to Portadown.

Of Dublin I have had my fill,
I sigh no more for Bantry Bay;
I don't suppose I ever will
In Cavan spend another day.
At Clonakilty golf I play,
I once got drunk in Galway Town,
And yet – deplore the fact who may –
I've never been to Portadown.

At Sligo cockles made me ill,
At Blarney Guinness made me gay,
Of Scarva I have memories still
And pipes that played an Orange lay.
At Skibbereen I tried to pray
When Black-and-Tans oppressed the town,
But nobody can ever say
I cursed the Pope in Portadown.

Envoi
Prince, explain it how you will,
By dire neglect or fortune's frown,
This sad remembrance haunts me still –
I've never been to Portadown.

THE AUTHOR'S LAMENT

Although I am an author
(In a tin-pot sort of way)
I fear that I shall never
Make literature pay.

Alas! it is not given
To every mortal man
To write a scabrous novel
The libraries will ban.

Besides, the plays I've written
Are very much too flabby
To cause a nine-days' wonder
Or a riot at the Abbey.

And although I've made the motley
Occasionally fit well,
I never could write rubbish
So brightly as Miss Sitwell.

I *might* write clotted nonsense
By strenuous endeavour,
And make the puzzled critics
Ejaculate, 'How clever!'

I *could*, like Mr Joyce,
Confound the prim reviewer,

If my timid nose would let me
Dive headlong in a sewer.

But my work is undistinguished,
And my royalties are lean,
Because I never am obscure,
And not at all obscene.

POCKET-BOOK WISDOM

I took her to dine
In a café expensive.
She had the best wine,
When I took her to dine;
I wanted to shine
But now I am pensive.
I took her to dine
In a café expensive.

Louis MacNeice

His 1937 grumble about the consumer society, 'Bagpipe Music', is justly celebrated, and duly finds its place here, but some other mordant excursions by Louis MacNeice (1907–1963) also deserve an airing. These two were written shortly after the outbreak of World War Two:

NIGHT CLUB

After the legshows and the brandies
And all the pick-me-ups for tired
Men there is a feeling
Something more is required.

The lights go down and eyes
Look up across the room;
Salome comes in, bearing
The head of God knows whom.

DEATH OF AN ACTRESS

I see from the paper that Florrie Forde is dead –
Collapsed after singing to wounded soldiers,
At the age of sixty-five. The American notice
Says no doubt all that need to be said

About this one-time chorus girl; whose rôle
For more than forty stifling years was giving
Sexual, sentimental, or comic entertainment,
A gaudy posy for the popular soul.

Plush and cigars: she waddled into the lights,
Old and huge and painted, in velvet and tiara,
Her voice gone but around her head an aura
Of all her vanilla-sweet forgotten vaudeville nights.

With an elephantine shimmy and a sugared wink
She threw a trellis of Dorothy Perkins roses
Around an audience come from slum and suburb
And weary of the tea-leaves in the sink;

Who found her songs a rainbow leading west
To the home they never had, to the chocolate Sunday
Of boy and girl, to cowslip time, to the never-
Ending weekend Islands of the Blest.

In the Isle of Man before the war before
The present one she made a ragtime favourite
Of 'Tipperary', which became the swan-song
Of troop-ships on a darkened shore;

And during Munich sang her ancient quiz
Of *Where's Bill Bailey?* and the chorus answered
Muddling through and glad to have no answer:
Where's Bill Bailey? How do *we* know where he is!

Now on a late and bandaged April day
In a military hospital Miss Florrie
Forde has made her positively last appearance
And taken her bow and gone correctly away.

Correctly. For she stood
For an older England, for children toddling
Hand in hand while the day was bright. Let the wren
    and robin
Gently with leaves cover the Babes in the Wood.

BAGPIPE MUSIC

It's no go the merrygoround, it's no go the rickshaw,
All we want is a limousine and a ticket for the
     peepshow.
Their knickers are made of crêpe-de-chine, their shoes
     are made of python,
Their halls are lined with tiger rugs and their walls
     with heads of bison.

John MacDonald found a corpse, put it under the sofa,
Waited till it came to life and hit it with a poker,
Sold its eyes for souvenirs, sold its blood for whisky,
Kept its bones for dumb-bells to use when he was fifty.

It's no go the Yogi-Man, it's no go Blavatsky,
All we want is a bank balance and a bit of skirt in a
     taxi.

Annie MacDougall went to milk, caught her foot in
     the heather,
Woke to hear a dance record playing of Old Vienna.
It's no go your maidenheads, it's no go your culture,
All we want is a Dunlop tyre and the devil mend the
     puncture.

The Laird o' Phelps spent Hogmanay declaring he was
     sober,
Counted his feet to prove the fact and found he had
     one foot over.
Mrs Carmichael had her fifth, looked at the job with
     repulsion,
Said to the midwife 'Take it away; I'm through with
     over-production'.

It's no go the gossip column, it's no go the ceilidh,
All we want is a mother's help and a sugar-stick for the
     baby.

Willie Murray cut his thumb, couldn't count the
     damage,
Took the hide of an Ayrshire cow and used it for a
     bandage.
His brother caught three hundred cran when the seas
     were lavish,

Threw the bleeders back in the sea and went upon the
   parish.

It's no go the Herring Board, it's no go the Bible,
All we want is a packet of fags when our hands are
   idle.

It's no go the picture palace, it's no go the stadium,
It's no go the country cot with a pot of pink
   geraniums,
It's no go the Government grants, it's no go the
   elections,
Sit on your arse for fifty years and hang your hat on a
   pension.

It's no go my honey love, it's no go my poppet;
Work your hands from day to day, the winds will blow
   the profit.
The glass is falling hour by hour, the glass will fall for
   ever,
But if you break the bloody glass you won't hold up
   the weather.

William Maginn

When Irish comic writers are stuck for a subject, Saint
Patrick often comes to the rescue. Here, William Maginn
(1793–1842), a Corkman whose pleasures were (a) drinking
and (b) writing, neatly covers both interests. The
'mulligrubs' of verse 2 are collywobbles.

SAINT PATRICK OF IRELAND, MY DEAR!

A fig for Saint Denis of France –
    He's a trumpery fellow to brag on;
A fig for Saint George and his lance,
    Which spitted a heathenish dragon;
And the saints of the Welshman or Scot
    Are a couple of pitiful pipers;
Both of whom may just travel to pot,
      Compared with that patron of swipers,
        Saint Patrick of Ireland, my dear!

He came to the Emerald Isle
    On a lump of a paving stone mounted;
The steamboat he beat by a mile,
    Which mighty good sailing was counted.
Says he, 'The salt water, I think,
    Has made me most fishily thirsty;
So bring me a flagon of drink
    To keep down the mulligrubs, burst ye –
        Of drink that is fit for a saint.'

He preached, then, with wonderful force,
    The ignorant natives a-teaching;
With a pint he washed down his discourse,
    'For,' says he, 'I detest your dry preaching.'
The people, with wonderment struck,
    At a pastor so pious and civil,
Exclaimed – 'We're for you, my old buck!
    And we pitch our blind gods to the divil,
        Who dwells in hot water below!'

This ended, our worshipful spoon
    Went to visit an elegant fellow,
Whose practice, each cool afternoon,
    Was to get most delightfully mellow.
That day, with a black-jack of beer,
    It chanced he was treating a party;
Says the Saint – 'This good day, do you hear,
    I drank nothing to speak of, my hearty!
        So give me a pull at the pot!'

The pewter he lifted in sport
    (Believe me, I tell you no fable),
A gallon he drank from the quart,
    And then placed it full on the table.
'A miracle!' everyone said,
    And they all took a haul at the stingo;
They were capital hands at the trade,
    And drank till they fell; yet, by jingo,
        The pot still frothed over the brim!

Next day, quoth his host, ''Tis a fast,
    And I've naught in my larder but mutton;
And on Fridays, who'd make such repast,
    Except an unchristian-like glutton?'
Says Pat, 'Cease your nonsense, I beg,
    What you tell me is nothing but gammon;

Take my compliments down to the leg,
 And bid it come hither a salmon!'
  And the leg most politely complied!

You've heard, I suppose, long ago,
 How the snakes, in a manner most antic,
He marched to the County Mayo,
 And trundled them into th' Atlantic.
Hence, not to use water for drink,
 The people of Ireland determine:
With mighty good reason, I think,
 Since Saint Patrick has filled it with vermin,
  And vipers and such other stuff!

Oh! he was an elegant blade
 As you'd meet from Fairhead to Kilcrumper!
And though under the sod he is laid,
 Yet here goes his health in a bumper!
I wish he was here, that my glass
 He might by art magic replenish;
But since he is not – why, alas!
 My ditty must come to a finish,
  Because all the liquor is out.

Derek Mahon

The poet Derek Mahon (b. 1941) is also a fine critic. Here he makes some economical literary and social assessments:

ANGLO-IRISH CLERIHEWS

The Picture of Dorian Gray
Is still read today;
While other Victorian novels degenerate in the attic,
Its reputation remains static.

    * * *

Laetitia Prism,
A precursor of 'transformative' feminism,
Anticipated contemporary refigurations of sexuality
In, and I quote Lady Bracknell, 'a three-volume novel
 of more than usually revolting sentimentality'.

* * *

Constance Gore-Booth
Sipped champagne in her youth;
But Constance Markievicz
Drank from 'the foul ditch'.

* * *

Maud Gonne
Was no fonne;
If her husband came home late she would call out:
'You drunken, vainglorious lout!'

* * *

George Moore
Was a terrible boore;
Whenever he cried '*Ave!*'
People would turn away.

* * *

John Quinn
Preferred the Algonquin
To any other hotel –
Though he liked the Plaza as well.

* * *

John Quinn
Grew thinn
Financing the Irish Literary 'Racket'
Out of his own pocket.

* * *

'STRANGE MEETING'
for Lucy McDiarmid

Wilfred Owen
And Elizabeth Bowen
Never met;
And yet ...

Francis Sylvester Mahony

*Like William Maginn, Mahony (1804–1866) was a Corkman
and a drinker. Today most examples of his waspish and
erudite wit are almost unreadable, but these verses, written
under his pseudonym of 'Father Prout', remain justly
popular. In verse 3 'Adrian's Mole' is the Castel Sant'Angelo
in Rome, built as a mausoleum for the Emperor Hadrian.*

THE BELLS OF SHANDON

With deep affection
And recollection
I often think of
    Those Shandon bells,
Whose sounds so wild would,
In days of childhood,
Fling round my cradle
    Their magic spells.
On this I ponder,
Where'er I wander,
And thus grow fonder,
    Sweet Cork, of thee;
With thy bells of Shandon,
That sound so grand on
The pleasant waters
    Of the river Lee.

I've heard bells chiming
Full many a clime in,
Tolling sublime in
    Cathedral shrine;
While at a glibe rate
Brass tongues would vibrate –
But all their music
    Spoke nought like thine;
For memory dwelling
On each proud swelling
Of the belfry knelling
    Its bold notes free,
Made the bells of Shandon
Sound far more grand on
The pleasant waters
    Of the river Lee.

I have heard bells tolling
Old 'Adrian's Mole' in,
Their thunder rolling
    From the Vatican,
With cymbals glorious
Swinging uproarious
In the gorgeous turrets
    Of Notre Dame;
But thy sounds were sweeter
Than the dome of Peter
Flings o'er the Tiber,
    Pealing solemnly: –
O! the bells of Shandon
Sound far more grand on
The pleasant waters
    Of the river Lee.

There's a bell in Moscow,
While on tower and kiosk, o!
In St Sophia
    The Turkman gets,
And loud in air
Calls men to prayer
From the tapering summit
    Of tall minarets.
Such empty phantom
I freely grant them,
But there is an anthem
    More dear to me, –
'Tis the bells of Shandon,
That sound so grand on
The pleasant waters
    Of the river Lee.

Tommy Makem

After 'The Boys' blew up Nelson's Pillar in Dublin, several songs on the subject were soon written. For this one, Tommy Makem (b. 1932) cheekily borrows the air of 'The Sash my Father Wore.' In performance, does the last verb of verse 3, line 4, sometimes acquire an extra letter?

LORD NELSON

Lord Nelson stood in pompous state upon his pillar
    high
And down along O'Connell Street, he cast a wicked
    eye:
He thought how this barbaric race had fought the
    British crown
Yet they were content to let him stay right here in
    Dublin town.
So remember brave Lord Nelson, boys, he had never
    known defeat,
And for his reward, they stuck him up in the middle of
    O'Connell Street.

Well for many years, Lord Nelson stood and no one
    seemed to care.
He'd squint at Dan O'Connell, who was standing right
    down there:
He thought, 'The Irish like me or they wouldn't let
    me stay –
That is except those blighters that they call the I.R.A.'
So remember brave Lord Nelson, boys, he had never
    known defeat,
And for his reward, they stuck him up in the middle of
    O'Connell Street.

And then in 1966, on March the seventh day,
A bloody great explosion made Lord Nelson rock and
    sway.
He crashed and Dan O'Connell cried in woeful
    misery:
'There are twice as many pigeons now will come and
    sit on me.'
So remember brave Lord Nelson, boys, he had never
    known defeat,
And for his reward, they blew him up in the middle of
    O'Connell Street.

James Clarence Mangan

*For many years after he was safely dead, James Clarence
Mangan (1803–1849) enjoyed the status of 'Ireland's
National Poet'. However, his reputation depended on a tiny
percentage of his poems. Most of his early pun-laden
rhymes for Dublin's comic magazines, for example, have
now largely lost their savour with the passage of time, but
the clever technical exercise below remains entertaining. It
was written to 'the memory of the late lamented Mr John
Kenchinow, Butcher, of Patrick Street', and Mangan
claimed to have won a wager by confining himself to only
two rhymes, the butcher's name and his 'stall'.*

JOHNNY KENCHINOW

Come, get the black, the mourning pall,
    (The reason I will mention now),
And with it, Blockheads, Bards and all,
Assist to cover Dia's hall
    For the loss of Johnny Kenchinow.

'And is he gone!' cry one and all.
    To keep you in suspension now,
Is not my wish; yes, at the call
Of Death was lately doomed to fall
    Lamented Johnny Kenchinow.

If anyone refuse to yawl,
    Ye Bards, I will convince ye now,
That, though at first a stubborn Saul
Ye be, ere long, repentant Paul
    Shall weep for Johnny Kenchinow.

Alas! this world's a slippery ball
    And do I reprehension now
Deserve, for saying that a straw'll
At times compel a man to sprawl
    Like peerless Johnny Kenchinow?

Messina's Cobbler, him of Gaul,
    Nay, he whose home Valentia now
Is, never pierced with shining awl
A shoe more sure than Death's sharp claw'll
    Pierce us like Johnny Kenchinow.

Great man! to see thy empty stall –
    (A stall there's not a bench in now) –
Unnerves me quite. I scarce can scrawl
A word, while tears more sour than gall
    Flow for thee, Johnny Kenchinow.

What though thy legs were long and tall,
    Them is the wet clay drenching now;
And eke those hands, so wont to haul
The mutton from the well-soiled wall
    By thee built, Johnny Kenchinow.

Thy Widow's purse, of course, is small,
    So may the State a pension now
Allow her, as a threadbare shawl
And sieve-like shoes for respite call
    In vain from Johnny Kenchinow.

Her name, howe'er, no man dare maul;
    She is an upright wench, (and now,
I talk of wenches) none could squall
So loud by half, or rather bawl,
    At the wake of Johnny Kenchinow.

But Judy's praises here to drawl
    Is none of my intention now.
In sooth 'twere needless, and withal,
My Muse is ill disposed to brawl
    Of aught, save Johnny Kenchinow.

Ye far-famed wits whom rhymes enthrall,
    I pray you pay attention now:
Say, will ye come? Oh! yes, ye shall,
To view the worms that slowly crawl
    O'er the bed of Johnny Kenchinow.

And if the sight your souls appal,
    Pray tell me what must fence ye now
Against that grief, which doubtless all
Who read this woe-creating scrawl
    Must feel for Johnny Kenchinow.

The how of this is hard to fathom, but no harder than the why. Perhaps the clue is in the poem's epigraph from Pope: 'Order is Heaven's first law.'

A RAILWAY OF RHYME

Now will I try a most Hercule-	An
Achievement, which I guess I shan't a-	Ban-
don till I finish it, for if I	Can
Succeed, I'll count myself as great as	Dan
O'Connell, or that reverend wag, D-	E-an
Swift; and there never yet was such a	Fan-
tastical rhymer since the world be-	Gan,
From Cork to Rome, and thence to Ispa-	Han,
In Persian, Irish, or Ital-	Ian,
As Jonathan, whose name in Dutch is	Jan.
My fame will far exceed that of Mar-	K An-
tony, of Homer, Caesar, Corio-	Lan-
us, or, in short, of any mortal	Man,
Even Mendez Pinto, also called Fer-	Nan,
Whose book I'll read on getting a l-	O-an
Thereof, because I'm told it will ex-	Pan-
d my mind, and stuff and store it with a	Quan-
tity of facts true as the Alco-	Ran.
But first I calculate I'll munch a	Tan-
kard of strong ale, then dress like Don J-	U-an,
And stroll to Cohen's neat Cigar Di-	Van,
(Though smoking overmuch has made me	Wan,)
And there I'll hear folks talk much more like	Xan-
tippe than Socrates or John Bun-	Yan,
Of whom, however, I'm no parti-	Zan.

And what might a verse speaker make of this challenge, which Mangan claimed was a translation 'from the Turkish of Foozooli'?

STAMMERING OR TIPSY GHAZZEL

I am so – drunk – that I ca – ca – I cannot
    Make out – what – the – fun – is – at – all!
Ca – cannot say if – this pla – this pla – planet
    Be an – gu – lar – square – or – a ball.
Nin – pom – cooks – nin – com – poops – tell us that –
    Fancy

And Judg – ment – are 'drowned – in the – bowl;'
All around my – turban! – 'tis Necro – ma – mancy
 That – gets – the blind side of – the soul!
Happy's the – tippler – who – stammers no – nothing,
 Whose – tongue – when he – moistens it – lags!
I am – for one – too – too faw – fond of – clothing
 My – tipsy – ideas – in – rags.
I am – the pote – am the poet – Foo – zooli –
 A genius – and – no mis – mis – take –
Taking the – world – raaather coo – coo – coo –
 coolly,
 And com – monly wi – wide awake.
Any – chap – dying to view – to – to see me
 Will – catch me – at Stoo – Stiss – Stambool,
Where, – though I – seem now – somewhat – dreamy,
 He'll find – I'm not – qui – quite a – fool!

Bob Martin

*This song was heard at Dan Lowrey's Music Hall in the
1880s – did any school in Killaloe at the time really boast a
'Monsieur' teaching French?*

KILLALOE

When a boy straight up from Clare heard his mother
 called a *mère*
He gave Mossoo his fist between the eyes.
Says Mossoo with much alarm, Go and call for *Johnny
 Darm*,
There's no such name, said I, about the place.
Comment, he made reply. Come on yerself, says I,
And I scattered all the features of his face.

Oh boys, there was the fun, you should see him when
 'twas done,
His eyeballs one by one did disappear
And a doctor from the south took some days to find
 his mouth
Which had somehow got concealed behind his ear.
Then he swore an awful oath he'd have the law agin
 us both
And he'd lave both Limerick and Clare,

For he found it wouldn't do to teach French in Killaloe
Unless he had a face or two to spare.

Now I'm glad to find 'tis true ye are plased with Killaloe
And our conduct to the Teacher they did send;
But I've tould you all that passed, so this verse must be
    the last
That's the reason I have left it to the end.
We're all Irish tenants here and we're all prepared to
    swear
That to the Irish language we'll be true,
But we all wid one consent, when they ax us for the
    rent,
Sure we answer them in Frinch in Killaloe.

Anonymous

*The writer Terence de Vere White remembered his Roman
Catholic mother teasing his Church of Ireland father with
these lines:*

'MARTIN LUTHER WAS A FRIAR'

Martin Luther was a friar
Whom the devil did inspire
To break his vows and marry a nun –
And this the Protestant Church begun.

MJF Mathews

*An anatomy of divided loyalties, published in wartime
(March 1944) in* TCD Miscellany, *of which Michael
Mathews (c.1922-1965) had been editor the term before. The
title (from the Irish 'mar dhea') means something like the
sing-song 'I don't think so' or today's ironic '... Not!'.*

MORYAH

Would you talk a little less about O'Connell?
Have you finished quoting from 'The Great O'Neill?'
    Do you realise that Tone

Never kissed the Blarney Stone
And that Parnell was deficient in appeal?

What, you did your Christmas shopping through the
    medium?
You were under your O'Dearest in '16?
        You are intimate and pally
        With Professor Alf O'Rahilly
And you hate the sight of Senator John Keane?

You were born just forty paces from McBirney's?
You think 2RN should keep the ether clean?
        That we'd be a nation sooner
        If we bumped off every crooner
And danced sets around Tom Moore in College Green?

You can quote me every word of Emmet's speeches?
And you never stigmatize the G.A.A?
        So you wear an Easter Lily
        And you blew up Good King Billy,
And you welshed the bally Northerners at Bray?

So our standards are not those of other nations?
You think birth-control has blunted Cupid's dart?
        That MacLiammoir and Hilton
        Smell like putrifying Stilton,
And 'The Rugged Path' epitomises Art?

You're a decent bowsy after my own heart then;
Come and have a couple up in Inchicore!
        What!! You're building tanks in Jarrow
        And your leave is up to-morrow?
God Almighty, this *exthraordinary* war!

Hugh Maxton

While the critic, biographer and librarian WJ McCormack
(b. 1947) presents a charming, avuncular face to the world,
his poetic avatar, Hugh Maxton, is less forbearing:

TO A DUBLIN HOST

Very well unknown across my city,
I can't spare a damn for your polite, average

Criticism. In short, no more shitty
Invitations to speak as you please. Rage
Is one defence left to serenity.
Distend your hand to no classic savage.

FAXES TO THE CRITIC: III

Of course you're right
        And I am obscure
To be sure to be sure.
        Now, get out of the light.

Anonymous

Ah, nostalgia! From a mid-century Dublin Opinion
compilation.

MEMORY

Do you remember what I used to call you
        In the dear dusks of long-dead summer eves
While the soft breezes by the river rustled
        The sally leaves?

Do you remember what I used to call you,
        As I went thro' the cornfield joyously,
While you were lab'ring in the meadow grasses,
        'Pig-face McKee'?

Spike Milligan

*Though born in India, Spike (1918-2002) was a proud
Irishman by ancestry and passport.*

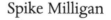

YOU MUST NEVER BATH IN AN IRISH STEW

You must never bath in an Irish stew
It's a most illogical thing to do
But should you persist against my reasoning
Don't fail to add the appropriate seasoning.

IT WOULD BE OBSCENE

It would be obscene
For the Queen
To turn green.
It would be much more patriotic to
Turn red white and blue.

Richard Milliken
(Attrib.)

*'The Groves of Blarney' is based on a song about Castle
Hyde in Fermoy, of which a typical verse reads:*

The richest groves throughout this nation and fine
    plantations you will see there;
The rose, the tulip, and sweet carnation, all vying with
    the lily fair.
The buck, the doe, the fox, the eagle, they skip and
    play by the riverside;
The trout and salmon are always sporting in the clear
    streams of sweet Castle Hyde.

*The Corkman Richard Milliken (1767–1815) is credited with
having written most of this parody. It became so popular
that it spurred many other Corkmen to write further similar
light topographical verses.*

THE GROVES OF BLARNEY

The groves of Blarney
They look so charming,
Down by the purling
    Of sweet silent streams;
Being banked with posies
That spontaneous grow there,
Planted in order
    By the sweet rock close.
'Tis there the daisy,
And the sweet carnation,
The blooming pink,
    And the rose so fair;
The daffodowndilly –
Likewise the lily,

All flowers that scent
    The sweet fragrant air.

'Tis Lady Jeffers
That owns this station,
Like Alexander,
    Or Queen Helen fair;
There's no commander
In all the nation
For emulation,
    Can with her compare.
Such walls surround her,
That no nine-pounder
Could dare to plunder
    Her place of strength;
But Oliver Cromwell
Her he did pommell,
And made a breach
    In her battlement.

There's gravel walks there,
For speculation,
And conversation
    In sweet solitude.
'Tis there the lover
May hear the dove, or
The gentle plover,
    In the afternoon;
And if a lady
Would be so engaging
As to walk alone in
    Those shady bowers,
'Tis there the courtier
He may transport her
Into some dark fort, or
    All under ground.

For 'tis there's a cave where
No daylight enters,
But bats and badgers
    Are forever bred;
Being mossed by nature,
That makes it sweeter
Than a coach and six,
    Or a feather bed.

'Tis there the lake is,
Well stored with perches,
And comely eels in
      The verdant mud;
Besides the leeches,
And groves of beeches,
Standing in order
      For to guard the flood.

'Tis there's the kitchen
Hangs many a flitch in,
With the maids a stitching
      Upon the stair;
The bread and biske',
The beer and whiskey,
Would make you frisky
      If you were there.
'Tis there you'd see
Peg Murphy's daughter
A washing *praties*
      Forenent the door,
With Roger Cleary,
And Father Healy,
All blood relations to
      My lord Donoughmore.

There's statues gracing
This noble place in –
All heathen gods
      And nymphs so fair:
Bold Neptune, Plutarch,
And Nicodemus,
All standing naked
      In the open air!
So now to finish
This brave narration,
Which my poor geni
      Could not entwine;
But were I Homer,
Or Nebuchadnezzar,
'Tis in every feature
      I would make it shine.

*Also said to be Milliken's work (though with even less
certainty than the verses above), this reads like Cork City's
answer to Dublin's 'The Night that Larry Was Stretched.'
'De Pool' is Blackpool, near where the Leitrim Street
Foundling Hospital, as well as the tanners and the glue-
boilers of verses 5 and 6, were to be found.*

DE GROVES OV DE POOL

Now de war, dearest Nancy, is ended,
    And the peace is come over from France,
So our gallant Cork city militia
    Back again to headquarters advance.
No longer a-beatin' dose rebels,
    We'll now be a-beatin' de bull,
And all oder genteel recreations
    Dat are found in de Groves ov de Pool.

Den out came our lovin' relations
    To see wor we livin' or no,
Besides all de jolly ould neighbours
    All around us who flock'd in a row.
De noggins of sweet Tommy Walker
    We lifted accordin' to rule,
And wetted our necks wid de native
    Dats brewed in de Groves ov de Pool.

When de reg'ment marched into de Commons,
    'Twould do your heart good for to see,
You'd tink not a man nor a woman
    Was left in Cork's famous city;
De boys dey came flockin' around us,
    Not a hat or wig stuck to a skull,
All to compliment dose Irish heroes
    Dat sprung from de Groves ov de Pool.

Wid our band out before us in order
    We played comin' in to de town,
We up'd wid de ould 'Boyne Water,'
    Not forgettin' 'De Croppies Lie Down;'
Bekase you may read in the newses
    Dat 'twas we made dose rebels so cool,
Who all tought, like Turks, or like Jewses,
    To murder de Boys ov de Pool.

O! sure dere's no nation in Munster
    Wid de Groves ov de Pool can compare,
Where dose heroes were all edicated,
    An' de nymphs are so comely an' fair,
Wid de gardens around entertainin'
    Wid sweet purty posies so full,
Dat is worn by dose comely young creatures
    Dat walks in de Groves ov de Pool.

Oh! many's de time, late an' early,
    Dat I wished I was landed again
Where I'd see de sweet Watercourse flowin',
    Where de tanners dere glory maintain;
Likewise dat divine habitation
    Where dose babbies are all sent to school,
Dat never had fader nor moder,
    But were found in 'de Groves ov de Pool.'

Come all ye young youths ov dis nation,
    Come fill up a bumper all round,
Drink Success to Blackpool navigation,
    And may it wid plenty be crown'd.
Here's success to de jolly hoop-coilers,
    Likewise to de shuttle an' spool;
To de skinners, an' worthy glue-boilers
    Dat lives in de Groves ov de Pool.

Ewart Milne

*Unfortunately, and sadly, Ewart Milne (1903–1987) has
never had a 'Complete Poems'. With his 1958 collection,*
Once More to Tourney, *he might be said to have single-
handedly redefined light verse. The following three poems
are from that remarkable book.*

COCKLES AND MUSSELS

'In the juvescence of the year'
Came Angela to the seashore,
With Molly Moloney
Dancing on the seashore.

And after them hurrying
And scurrying with hope
Came Big Bill Barnacle
With a long long telescope.

Came Bill with a friend
Who had not been to sea,
A student: a pal
With a Trinity degree.

The story is short
Which I have now to tell,
Molly and Angela
Wished to plunge in the swell

And undressed on the sands
Thinking no one was near
Among the cockles and mussels
In the juvescence of the year.

What happened next hour
We'll skip and just say
The tide it swep in
While the four were at play,

And the frocks made for dancing
And the Trinity hose
And the bell bottom trousers
Were devoured by the waves.

The moral I think is
You should never be found
In the juvescence of the year
Running stark naked around –

Or like Molly and Angela
And B. Barnacle and friend
You may have to get home
Covered only by hand –

And no painterly talent
Within miles to essay
An odd fig leaf or two,
Or a cloud to apply.

WHEN I CONSIDER

When I consider how the hair of your chest
is turrible hairy and tough
I reach a conclusion (you must wear a vest)
of hairiness I've now had enough
so come out from behind your forest my lad
come out for it's long past the hour
let me see whether thee has got aught else that be
but grass for an ass in a shower my lad
      but grass for an ass in a shower

When I consider the ugh of your nest
(and faesh it's a waesome sicht)
I reach the conclusion SAMS TOILETS ARE BEST
out of sight out of mind full of sweetness and light
so come clean from behind your audition my lad
come clean or Ben Brian Carew
(whose initials suggest he is wearing a vest)
will do something or other to you my lad
will make little snow bells out of you my lad
      snow bells snow bells at all out of you

A BALLAD OF CHRISTMAS DAYS

The First Day of Christmas and the family's raving mad,
Father's winding engines up he is a likely lad,
His age is all of eight or nine and he's growing
    younger and younger,
Of all the Father Christmases there's none with a
    beard like father.

The Second Day of Christmas and mother's gone
    demented,
The fire is out the sticks are damp and coal must be
    invented.
Santa Claus is coughing shuffling home in all the rain,
There'll be one Santa less I fear when the green comes
    out again.

The Third Day of Christmas and the colly birds look
    low,
Scotland Yard could never tell where all those turkeys
    go,
Lord send us quick a fine fat duck we'll toast in
    Mangan ale,
Christmas comes but once a year here's to you
    Granuaile!

The Fourth Day of Christmas and the house is all abed,
Simon Peter at the foot with Luke and Mark and
    Buster at the head,
Likewise Pa and Ma and Meg and me and Martha on
    the floor,
God save you Merry Gentlemen there's always room
    for more.

The Fifth Day of Christmas we spent down on the
    farm,
In hopes to find eight milkmaids we had brought the
    jugs for cream,
But the milk ran off in rubber tubes that were
    fastened to the cows,
When someone pressed a button like ten pipers was
    the noise.

The Sixth Day of Christmas we would a-hunting go,
First catch your rabbit net your hare so soft we went
    and so so,
All the conies had convulsions when they saw our
    Indian file,
And a partridge in a peartree smiled a pitying sort of
    smile.

The Seventh Day of Christmas father took us to the
    Zoo,
Where we met ten lords a-leaping all with bottoms
    painted blue,
Where we met a swan and swaness begging bread for
    swanlings five,
Besides a ring-tailed octaroon that tried to skin us all
    alive.

The Eighth Day of Christmas we tailed a shopworn
    goose,

They priced it up we priced it down it was no sort of
    use,
'Twas then we found that English hens were farther
    off than French,
We were nearly at our wit's end: we scraped the pot,
    the dish, the bench.

The Ninth Day of Christmas was where Pa and Ma
    fell out,
I held her bonnet high for Ma while Buster held Pa's
    coat,
They whacked and whaled and whaled and whacked
    the result it was a draw,
Ma had two lovely eyes of black and Pa was wounded
    in his jaw.

The Tenth Day of Christmas we retired once more to
    bed,
The rain came in in bucketfuls we had a slate loose
    mother said,
An Ark is what we chiefly need said Pa that's if we
    stay afloat,
Go and get your Christmas shovels boys or we're
    drownded in the moat.

The Eleventh Day of Christmas reduced us to a stroll,
In the park around the duckpond round and round we
    set our goal,
Now hold on tight to Buster, Ma, those ducks are
    there to swim,
See yonder turtle doves in blue have fixed their eyes
    on him.

The Twelfth Day of Christmas we took our Xmas
    Greetings down,
And traded them with barrow boys we chanced to
    meet in town,
The price was made and all agreed there was little
    cause to fear
We'd get the same cards back again on Christmas Day
    next year.

*Though long resident in Britain, until the last decade of his
life Milne struggled to extract his work from what he called
'the timeless stream of Irishness'. This unclassifiable
quatrain appeared in 1983, in* The Beau, *one of Dublin's
most interesting 'little magazines':*

LONG LIVE THE KING

Under the River Ouse at Bedford
Offa lies
Who made the Kingdom of the English
Then yawned and closed his eyes.

Susan Mitchell

*During the first decade of the twentieth century, when the
novelist George Moore was living in Dublin, Susan Mitchell
(1866–1926) made teasing him into an art form. In 1908 she
brought out her book,* Aids to the Immortality of Certain
Persons in Ireland: Charitably Administered, *from
which these verses come.*

GEORGE MOORE EATS A GREY MULLET

I sailed away from France, alas!
    My heart was wildly grieving,
For all a man of taste was gas-
    Tronomically leaving.
No woman from my heart I tore –
    The sex will always find me –
I fretted for no girl, but for
    A fish I'd left behind me.

The cooks of France, how great they be,
    And of their art so willing,
And in thy restaurant, Henri,
    I had spent many a shilling.
When on my plate that wondrous day,
    Le Bar, I first did find thee,
O France! why did I sail away
    And leave thy fish behind me?

Napoleon, great thy triumphs be
    That stick in British gullet,

But greater glory thine, Henri,
    Who cooked my first grey mullet!
Although I have left Rome, I wish
    That I in Rome could find me,
To eat my fish from Nero's dish,
    The fish I left behind me.

I've sought it over London town,
    And eke in Dublin city,
At many a table I've sat down,
    Nor found it, more's the pity.
O Irish maids, with eyes so meek,
    Should ardent glances blind ye,
Mine eyes seek not your hearts, they seek
    A fish I left behind me.

Ah! what a hero-heart I gave
    Without a thought of fooling,
To live in Dublin and to brave
    Bad cooks and English ruling.
But could I feed as once I fed,
    Regret should never find me,
For *Ave atque Vale* said
    To the fish I left behind me.

GEORGE MOORE BECOMES THE PRIEST OF APHRODITE

In good Victoria's humdrum days
    I started my career, Sir,
I from Mayo to France did go,
    Where I acted very queer, Sir.
But I my sins repenting sore,
    To pious Dublin came, Sir,
And though I find most things a bore,
    I stay here all the same, Sir.
But if you ask me to explain,
    I really cannot say, Sir,

Why I in Dublin still remain
    When I might go away, Sir.

Now I was christened in Mayo,
    Where Popery was in fashion,
But for that error long ago
    I have a great compassion.
I would be christened once again,
    And wear a robe with flounces,
Alas, I'm weighed by stones who then
    Was weighed by pounds and ounces.
But though my form no pretty nurse
    May bear to my baptism, Sir,
I have renounced my country's curse,
And left the Roman schism, Sir.

When I from Popery did recant,
    And left my dark condition,
To be a simple Protestant
    Was long my sole ambition.
But since my views on Saving Grace
    The Puritans found flighty,
Behold me now in Ely Place
    The priest of Aphrodite.
I'll set her image up on high,
    Within my garden shady,
And every day a wreath I'll lay
    Before my marble lady.

But even this does not explain,
    Nor can I really say, Sir,
Why I in Dublin still remain
    When I might go away, Sir.

Mary Monck

*A charming and gently risqué piece of whimsy by Mary
Monck (1677–1715), the daughter of an intermittently insane
Dublin aristocrat.*

A TALE

A Band of *Cupids* th' other Day
Together met to Laugh and Play,

When on a sudden, 'Come, who flies?' ⎫
Says one; 'But whither?' t'other cries. ⎬
'Why, whither, but to *Cloe*'s Eyes' ⎭
Reply'd a third. The wanton Crew
(Like swarms of Bees to Roses) flew
Around the beauteous *Cloe*'s Face,
And crowded hard to get a place.
This on her nether Lip does fix,
Whilst on her Cheek another sticks.
This swings upon her flowing Hair,
In her fair Eyes a lovely pair
Of Youths stand with their Torches lit;
Two others on her Eye-brows sit,
Each with his Bow; Amongst the Rest
One miss'd her Chin, and on her Breast
Fell head-long, but soon looking up did cry
'None of you've got so good a Place as I!'

James Montgomery

*Montgomery, later the first Irish Film Censor, had these
atmospheric verses about nautical bad language published in
Mrs Cruise O'Brien's 1915 Dublin Book of Recitations.*

THE CANAL BOAT

*Now this is a tale that the turf men tell, in the glow of the
    fo'c'sle light,
When the sad simoon sighs over Naas, and the Banshee
    blanches the night;
And they chant the lay in a minor kay (tho' it may be sung
    in a sharp)
To the muffled melodeon's morbid moan, or the twang of
    the wild Jew's harp.
I heard the tale in the town of Trim, from my aunt (may
    she rest in bliss),
It's sombre and sketchy, and vague and dim, like a Yeatsian
    epic of Usheen or Finn,
And the doggerel jingles like this: –*

A private canal boat from Naas,
        Was scudding along a lee shore;
The captain had nought on his face
        Save the whiskers he constantly wore.

But nothing like fear, for man, maid or peer
    Could be seen in the leer on the features he
        bore.

The captain's young wife, Maritana,
    Was aft with the 'crew' down the hatch;
She piously played the piana
    And he sang some sacred catch.
        (It's most edifying to know when you're
          buying
        Your turf, that there's somewhere a catch.)

The skipper collogued with Claude St John,
    A thoughtful young man from Blackrock,
Who guided the galloping ingin
    Attached to 'The Pride of Kilcock.'
They chatted on various topics – Volunteers,
    transmigration of souls,
        And whether the Portydown goal for the Pope
        was heated by gas or by coals.

They bragged about dinner in Stickfoot's, and what
    might be had à-la-carte,
        They prattled of Bergson and Plato, and neo-
        impressionist art –
When out shrieked the skipper, 'Avast there! ye son of
    a Sandymount midge,
        Shut up with yer Nietzsche, reverse the black
        mare, *the top sod is hittin' the bridge.'*

                              * * *

Now, strange to say, I never heard a boat-man spin this
    narrative;
        Aunt Julia always halted here and said, 'Be
        warned in time,
And never use the words he used, or anything
    comparative,
        Or like him, till the crack of doom, you'll expiate
        your crime.'

My uncle James – so justly famed for blasphemous
    celerity –
        Would not reveal the curse to me tho' bribed
        with foaming jars;

A jarvey, whom I interviewed, repulsed me with
   asperity.
      And as for me, I never frequent 'pubs' or even
        bars.

So what, that hardy mariner from Hazelhatch or
   Philipstown,
      Hurled at the oat-fed engine with a wild and
        fiendish yell,
(It may have been some primal thing from Druid ages
   handed down,
      It may have been – why speculate) alas! I cannot
        tell.

                *   *   *

But the fate of the Dutch man who sails round the
   Cape –
As legend informs us – in spiritual shape,
Was decreed on the pirate profane.
(If the story brings tears, I hope you'll excuse)
Their fate was so awful that many who cruise
In basins adjoining Ringsend,
When tossed in their crafts by that sulphurous gale
Which blows from the Gas Works, they hear a weird
   wail,
They shudder and shiver and think of 'the tale

... that the turf men tell, in the glow of the fo'c'sle light,
When the sad simoon sighs over Naas and the Banshee
   blanches the night;
And they chant the lay in a minor kay (tho' it may be sung
   in a sharp)
To the muffled melodeon's morbid moan, or the twang of
   the wild Jew's harp.'

Christy Moore

To reprint all the best lyrics of Christy Moore (b. 1945)
would make this book very long indeed – and some of them
change almost every time he sings them. Here are three of
his mini-epics to be getting on with. The first one celebrates
Ireland's best ever showing in the World Cup.

JOXER GOES TO STUTTGART

It was in the year of '88, in the merry month of June,
When the gadflies they were swarming and dogs
    howling at the moon,
With rosary beads and sandwiches for Stuttgart we
    began,
Joxer packed his German phrase book and jump leads
    for the van.

Some of the lads had never been away from home
    before.
It was the first time Whacker put his foot outside of
    Inchicore.
And before we left for Europe, we knew we'd need a
    plan,
So we all agreed that Joxer was the man to drive the
    van.

In Germany the Autobahn was like the Long Mile
    Road,
There was every make of car and van, all carrying the
    full load,
Ford transits and Hi-Aces, and an old Bedford from
    Tralee,
With the engine overheating from long-hauling duty-
    free.

There was fans from Ballyfermot, Ballybough and
    Ballymun
On the journey of a lifetime and the craic was ninety-
    one.
Joxer met a German's daughter on the bank of the
    River Rhine
And he told her she'd be welcome in Ballyfermot any
    time.

As soon as we found Stuttgart, we got the wagons in a
    ring,
Sean Óg got out the banjo and Peter played the
    mandolin.
There were fans there from everywhere, attracted by
    the sound
Of the first Fleadh Ceol in Europe, and Joxer passed
    the flagon round.

But the session it ended when we'd finished all the
    stout,
The air mattresses inflated and the sleeping bags rolled
    out,
As one by one we fell asleep, Joxer had a dream –
He dreamt himself and Jack Charlton sat down to pick
    the team.

Joxer dreamt they both agreed on Packie Bonner
    straight away
And that Moran, Whelan and McGrath were certainly
    to play,
Ah but tempers they began to rise, patience wearing
    thin,
Jack wanted Cascarino, but Joxer wanted Quinn.

The dream turned into a nightmare, Joxer stuck the
    head on Jack
Who wanted to bring Johnny Giles and Eamon
    Dunphy back.
The cock crew in the morning, it crew both loud and
    shrill
And Joxer woke up in his sleeping bag many miles
    from Arbour Hill.

Next morning none of the experts gave us the
    slightest chance,
They said the English team would lead us on a merry
    dance.
With Union Jacks those English fans for victory they
    were set
Until Ray Houghton got the ball and stuck it in the net.

What happened next is history, it brought tears to
    many eyes,
That day will be the highlight of many people's lives,

Well Joxer climbed right over the top and the last time
  he was seen
Was arm-in-arm with Jack Charlton, singing 'Revenge
  for Skibbereen.'

Now Whacker is back in Inchicore, he's living with his
  Mam
And Jack Charlton has been proclaimed an honorary
  Irishman
Do you remember that German's daughter on the
  bank of the River Rhine
Ah jeez, well didn't she show up in Ballyfermot last
  week ...

*This lyric, written after a visit in 1985 to Paddy Murphy's
pub in Brandon, is full of Kerry detail: in verse 2, for
instance, 'Kruger's' is a pub in Dunquin, which its colourful
owner, the late 'Kruger' Kavanagh, was proud to claim as
the most western watering-hole in Europe. Inishvickillane
(final verse) is one of the smaller Blaskets, famous both for
its ruined Oratory of Saint Brendan, and for Charles J
Haughey's ownership of the entire island. 'Fungi' is
Dingle's resident dolphin.*

SAINT BRENDAN'S VOYAGE

A boat sailed out of Brandon in the year of 501
'Twas a damp and dirty morning Brendan's voyage it
  began.
Tired of thinning turnips and cutting curly kale
When he got back from the creamery he hoisted up
  the sail.
He ploughed a lonely furrow to the north, south, east
  and west
Of all the navigators Saint Brendan was the best.
When he ran out of holy water he was forced to make
  a stop,
He tied up in Long Island, put America on the map.
Did you know that Honolulu was found by a
  Kerryman,
Who went on to find Australia then China and Japan?
When he was touching seventy he began to miss the
  crack,
And turning to his albatross he sez, 'I'm heading back.'

Chorus:
'Is it right or left for Gibraltar?
What tack do I take for Mizen Head?
I'd love to settle down near Ventry Harbour,'
Saint Brendan to his albatross he said.

To make it fast he bent the mast and built up mighty
    steam,
Around Tierra del Fuego and up the warm Gulf
    Stream.
He crossed the last horizon, Mount Brandon came in
    sight,
And when he cleared the customs, into Dingle for the
    night.
When he got the spuds and bacon he went to douse
    the drought,
He headed west to Kruger's to murder pints of stout,
Around by Ballyferriter and up the Connor Pass,
He freewheeled into Brandon, the saint was home at
    last.

The entire population came (281), the place was
    chock-a-block,
Love nor money wouldn't get your nose inside the
    shop.
The fishermen hauled up their nets, the farmers left
    their hay,
Kerry people know that saints don't turn up every day.
Everything was going grand till Brendan did announce
His reason for returning was to try and set up house.
The girls were flabbergasted at Saint Brendan's neck –
To seek a wife so late in life and him a total wreck.

Worn out by the rejection that pierced his humble
    pride,
'Begod,' said Brendan, 'if I run I'll surely catch the
    tide.'
Turning on his sandals he made straight for the docks
And hauling up his anchor he cast off from the rocks.
As he sailed past Inishvickillane there stood the
    albatross:
'I knew you'd never stick it out, 'tis great to see you,
    boss.'
'I'm baling out,' said Brendan, 'I badly need a break –
Two weeks of talking to Fungi is more than I can take.'

This song breaks all the rules, including those of this book.
Christy Moore apparently wrote it in about 1987 for the
(then very proper) Eurovision Song Contest; it is hardly
surprising that, as he has said, he 'never even got the
courtesy of a rejection slip.'

THE ROSE OF TRALEE (ME AND THE ROSE)

Listen for a while
And I'll tell you the story
of How I fell in love with The Rose Of Tralee

It was five o'clock in the morning, I was only after
    getting off the Stena
I was heading down the North Wall minding my own
    business
When a voice behind me went 'Where are you going
    at this hour of the morning?'
I turned round and who was standing behind me only
    the Rose of Tralee
And she wearing a grand new blue Bean-Garda's
    uniform
(I thought for a minute that she was a Super)

'Hey Rose! How's it going, Baby? Last time I saw you
    was upstairs in The Tent
Down below in The Dome with Gaybo in the Pretty
    Polly tights and all the beauty queens
From Tashkent, Istanbul, Bangkok and Liverpool, how
    are you keeping?'
'Can you account for your movements?' said she to me
'Jasus Rose, there is no need to be like that.
    Movements is it?
I'll give you all the movements you want. You'd better
    sharpen your pencil
You're going to be a busy little woman. Christy has a
    memory like a supergrass
He can remember things that never happened at all

'The first thing I can remember is the seventh of May
    1945 at the back of Donnolly's Hollow
It was the night before Pa Connolly drove the
    Roadstone lorry into the Seven Springs
And St Brigid started rolling out the tintawn across the
    Curragh of Kildare

Then I woke up one morning, Rose, I was after
    getting conscripted into the Altarboys
I was ringing the bell and swinging the Thurible. The
    smell of the incense would remind you
Of the inside of an Arab's tent and no sign of Gaddafi
    nowhere'
'Ita Missa Est,' says Rose. 'Gloria Tibi Domine,' says I,
    for I love to hear a bit of Latin
It reminds me of the Old Tridentine. Sure the nine
    first Fridays never killed anyone

'The next thing I knew I was serving my time to be a
    cornerboy in the Curragh Camp
I was trying to teach the sheep to talk Irish, Cúpla
    Focal, Céad Míle Fáilte, Tiocfaidh ár lá
Ah fuck you and your lá.
Then I got a job selling lambs balls to mushroom
    farmers that couldn't afford horse shite
One day I was walking across the Curragh of Kildare
    and I fell into an officer's mess
He was only home after six months in the LEB and the
    poor man was loaded
Then I met a fellow whose first cousin was married to
    a man whose sister's brother-in-law
Was going out with a girl whose grandmother used to
    fill hot-water bottles for Patrick Sarsfield
(Before the Battle of Clongorey). I had to go on the run

'I ran so fast that I ended up abroad in Paddington
Digging footings, scraping pots
Pulling cable, starting drotts
Boiling kettles, making tae
Digging deep, thrown away

'I was a disposable Paddy serving my time to be a co-
    pilot on a Kango hammer in Shepherd's Bush
I was doing 86 mph on a JCB down the Kilburn High
    Road
When the SPG flagged me down and held me under
    the PTA
Until I got away and went underground with the
    Green Murphy
Then one Thursday I was heading down the
    Hammersmith Broadway
And I met a man from Ballaghadereen in the County
    Roscommon

He was a demolition expert and Georgian houses
    were his speciality
"Any chance of the start?" said I
"What would you know about demolition?" said he
"I've been known to demolish large bottles," said I
"That'll do," said he

'Monday morning came and myself and Raymond
    Roland and Roger Sheelock and Liam Farrell
With Mairtín Byrnes and Tony Rohr we were painting
    a door
We gave it six coats and three coats more and that was
    just undercoat
The ganger was fond of a tune and Thursday never
    came too soon
We were getting four pounds a day and all we could eat
But it's an awful job trying to eat all day
Then I went looking for digs. Up the Chiswick High
    Road I knocked on the door
And this English lady came out and took one look at me
"Oooogh" said she "get away from my door there'll be
    no blacks nor Paddys getting in here."
So I let on I was a white South African
"O tar isteach" said she "Tá fáilte romhat a Buachall"
    She was a Mayo woman
"Come in outa that and make yourself at home but
    don't be blowing your nose in the blankets"

'Then I tried to join the British Army to better myself
I volunteered as a sub-contractor building houses with
    no doors or handles on them
"What ye bin doin' lately then, Paddy?" the recruiting
    officer said to me
"I was helping O'Brien to shift it, sir," said I
    "Spreading the toxic all over the Golden Vale
I was helping Paddy Gallagher cover Stephen's Green
    in concrete
I was helping Sam Stephenson block all the daylight
    out of Dublin
I was taking the bends out of the Liffey for Dr Smurfit
I was counting the golden beans for Dr O'Reilly
I was doling out the diddley-eye for Dr Darragh
I was taking the sweetener out of the Greencore
And vacuum packing T-bone steak for Larry Maith an
    Fear"

"Oh you're overqualified for the British Army" said he
And he put me on the first Stena out of Holyhead.
    Total exclusion

'And here I am arriving home after eight years in exile.
    Arais arís
This is some welcome for a returned immigrant. Céad
    Míle Fáilte my arse
With your pioneer pin and your fánne and your white
    star for not cursing
It would be more in your line to give me a lift in the
    panda.' And she did

There I was in the back of the White Squad heading
    into town looking for an early morning house
There's Paddy Slattery 'You're welcome home,
    Christy' (Big Slate!)
'Would you and your girlfriend like a drink?' Well she
    took off her cap and in she went
'I'll have a brandy with a small drop of port,' said she
    'I never drink pints when I'm on duty.'
Well she lowered it up, 'twas like throwing cold water
    into a barrel of sawdust
And no purse
'I'll see you tonight' said she 'and it'll be my twist.'

Well there I was, outside the GPO waiting for the most
    beautiful Kerry woman in the whole wide world
Here she comes, will you look at her, sashaying down
    the boulevard in her docs and her 501s
'Hey Rose! Over here!' 'What's on your mind big
    fellow?' (I was wearing my platforms)
'I wouldn't mind a bit of a dance.' So she took me to a
    disco in the Garda Club – Le Baton Rouge
Some spot. Wall to wall moustaches. Did you ever
    wonder what they do with all the hash?
'Twas like Woodstock – gay bikers on acid. Me and
    the rose we danced the night away
Five o'clock in the morning and she says to me 'Fancy
    coming back to my place, Lofty?'
Does a bear shite in the woods

Through Rathmines and Rathgar she got me siren
    going and the warning lights were flashing
Pulled in for two doner kebabs and the Leinster Leader

Back to her place two up two down. She pulled the
    cork out of the Blue Nun
And I got sick all over the Rottweiler
And then she put the music on
Lovely new CD … Daniel
'Oh then fare thee well sweet Donegal, the Rosses and
    Gweedore'
'O! Rose,'
'O! Daniel,'
'Agh! Here.'
'I suppose a rasher sandwich is out of the question?'

That's how I met up with The Rose of Tralee.

Thomas Moore

*A century and a half before Christy Moore was using satire
to point out political injustices and absurdities, that other
consummate songwriter Thomas Moore (1779–1852) was
doing the same. This was his reaction to a parliamentary
speech on colonial slavery delivered in March 1826 by Lord
Dudley and Ward, when 'His Lordship said that it took a
long time for a moral position to find its way across the
Atlantic. He was sorry that its voyage had been so long …'*

MORAL POSITIONS: A DREAM

T'other night, after hearing Lord Dudley's oration
    (A treat that comes once in the year, as May-day
      does),
I dreamt that I saw – what a strange operation! –
    A 'moral position' shipped off for Barbadoes.

The whole Bench of Bishops stood by, in grave
    attitudes,
    Packing the article tidy and neat; –
As their Reverences know, that in southerly latitudes,
    'Moral positions' don't keep very sweet.

There was Bath[ur]st arranging the custom-house
    pass;
        And, to guard the frail package from tousing and
            routing,
There stood my Lord Eld[o]n, endorsing it 'Glass,'
        Though – as to *which* side should lie uppermost
            – doubting.

The freight was, however, stowed safe in the hold;
        The winds were polite, and the moon looked
            romantic,
While off in the good ship 'the *Truth*,' we were rolled,
        With our ethical cargo, across the Atlantic.

Long, dolefully long, seemed the voyage we made; –
        For 'the *Truth*,' at all times but a very slow sailer,
By friends, near as much as by foes, is delayed,
        And few come aboard her, though so many hail
            her.

At length, safe arrived, I went through 'tare and tret' –
        Delivered my goods in the primest condition –
And next morning read, in the *Bridgetown Gazette*,
        'Just arrived, by "the *Truth*," a new Moral
            Position;

The Captain' – here, startled to find myself named
        As 'the Captain' (a thing which, I own it with
            pain,
I through life have avoided), I woke – looked ashamed –
        Found I *wasn't* a Captain, and dozed off again.

*As his friend Lord Byron did, Moore disparaged the once
free-thinking Southey for accepting the post of Poet
Laureate in 1813:*

EPITAPH ON ROBERT SOUTHEY

Beneath these poppies buried deep,
        The bones of Bob the bard lie hid;
Peace to his manes; and may he sleep
        As soundly as his readers did!

Through every sort of verse meandering,
    Bob went without a hitch or fall,
Through epic, Sapphic, Alexandrine,
    To verse that was no verse at all;

Till fiction having done enough,
    To make a bard at least absurd,
And give his readers *quantum suff.*,
    He took to praising George the Third.

And now, in virtue of his crown,
    Dooms us, poor whigs, at once to slaughter;
Like Donellan of bad renown,
    Poisoning us all with laurel-water.

And yet at times some awful qualms he
    Felt about leaving honour's track;
And though he's got a butt of Malmsey,
    It may not save him from a sack.

Death, weary of so dull a writer,
    Put to his books a *finis* thus.
Oh! may the earth on him lie lighter
    Then did his quartos upon us!

Sometimes, though, Moore was content just to write utter ...

NONSENSE

Good reader! if you e'er have seen,
When Phoebus hastens to his pillow,
The mermaids, with their tresses green,
Dancing upon the western billow:
If you have seen, at twilight dim,
When the lone spirit's vesper hymn
Floats wild along the winding shore:
If you have seen, through mist of eve,
The fairy train their ringlets weave,
Glancing along the spangled green; –
If you have seen all this, and more,
God bless me! what a deal you've seen!

Anonymous

This magazine parody of the 1870s deplores the (still deplorable) 1857 statue of Tom Moore in Dublin.

THE MOORE STATUE

There's not in this wide world a statue less neat
Than that placed where Westmoreland and College
    Streets meet;
Oh, the last ray of feeling and life must depart
Ere the gloom of that statue shall fade from my heart.

Yet it was not that some one had placed on a slab
A heavy-cloaked gentleman hailing a cab,
And noting its number with pen or with quill –
Oh, no, it was something more heart-rending still:

'Twas that statues of Burke and of Goldsmith were
    near,
Which made the queer figure look even more queer,
And showed how the worst works of art disimprove
When we see them contrasted with works that we
    love.

Oh, marvellous statue, how calm could we rest
If the waves of the Liffey rolled over thy breast?
Then the shame that we feel at your presence should
    cease,
And our hearts, nearing College Street, still be at peace.

Anonymous

*Hector McDonnell: 'Mrs McGrath' is to be found in Colm Ó
Lochlainn's wonderful book of ballads. He gives this more
extended version than the one that is usually sung, in which
the last three verses are often omitted. This is a great shame,
as they add greatly to the punch of the piece, and have a
ring of authenticity. It has for many years served me well
as a means of entertaining small boys, though I have
noticed it does not have the same resonance with small girls.
Ah well, boys will be boys.*

MRS McGRATH

Oh widow McGrath lived in Kilrush,
And she had the money very flush.
She had one son, her darling dear,
But she sent him away for to be a fusilier.

'Oh Mrs McGrath,' the sergeant said,
'Would you like to make a soldier out of your son
    Ted,
With a scarlet coat and a big cocked hat,
Now Mrs McGrath, wouldn't you like that?'

Now Mrs McGrath lived by the sea shore
For the space of seven long years or more,
Till she saw a big ship coming in the bay:
'Hollaloo Horraroo and I think it's he.'

'Oh captain dear where have ye been,
And have ye been sailing on the Meditereen,
And have ye any tidings of my son Ted,
Be the poor boy living or is he dead?'

Then up comes Ted without any legs
And in their place two wooden pegs –
She kissed him a dozen times or two
Crying, 'Holy Moses, it isn't you.'

'Oh were ye drunk or were ye blind
That you left your two fine legs behind?
Or was it walking upon the say
Wore your two fine legs from the knees away?'

'Oh I wasnae drunk and I wasnae blind,
When I left my two fine legs behind,
For a cannon ball on the fifth of May
Took my two fine legs from the knees away.'

'Oh Teddy me boy,' the widow cried,
'Them two fine legs were yer Mama's pride.
Those stumps of a tree will not do at all,
Why did ye not run from the big cannon ball?

'All foreign wars I do proclaim
Between Don John and the King of Spain,

And by herrings I'll make them pay the time
That they took those legs from a son of mine,

'And if I had my son back again
No more would I let him fight for the King of Spain,
For I'd rather have him as he used to be
Than the King of France and his whole navee.'

'Arrah mother ma'am do not make on so,
For I've fifty pounds for every toe,
And if I had another pair
I'd be off to the wars and I'd leave them there.'

Mary Myler

*It could happen to anyone! From a little book by the late
artist and writer (1939–2004), who is greatly missed in her
home town of Arklow.*

PUTTING MY FOOT IN IT

    I met a friend the other day
I said 'My God, you look so pale.'
It was only afterwards I found out
He had just spent six months in jail.

Anonymous

In some quarters, Irish admiration for Napoleon knew no bounds. Here is a mid-nineteenth-century broadside song.

NAPOLEON IS THE BOY FOR KICKING UP A ROW

Arrah, murther, but times is hard,
    And poverty makes no man civil,
Gutta percha has spoiled our trade,
    Shoemaking's gone to the devil.
Arrah, don't I mind the good ould time,
    That I was 'prentice to Mick McCarthy,
Sure, the money was plenty as paving stones
    In the days of General Bonaparte.

Chorus:
    Whack row de dow,
    Old Boney was the boy, you know,
    For kicking up a row.

He was the greatest man alive,
    He far exceeded Nebuchadnezzar,
The great Mogul or Brian Boroimhe,
    Or Hannibal or Julius Caesar.
He crossed the Alps in an open boat,
    Which made the heathen much enraged,
He defeated General Musselman,
    And conquered the pyramids of Egypt.

He swore he'd be an Emperor soon,
    And like the conqueror Alexander,
He'd blaze away both night and day
    Until the whole world was knocked under.
He said he'd blow up the broad Atlantic,
    And then knock down the walls of China,
But little thought he how soon he'd be
    A prisoner in St Helena.

To Elba's Isle he went for a while,
    But such solitude was not delighting
For he said he couldn't find peace in his mind
    Unless he was engaged in fighting,
So he must go, and he marched thro' snow,
    But they burned the place and that's what sold
      him,
And the reason why he didn't stop,
    Was the devil a house they'd left to hold him.

The French say it was by treason vile
    And British gold he was defeated –
He was sent off to a barren isle,
    Where he was murdered and ill-treated.
But his nephew's on the throne of France,
    And maybe when his plans are riper,
He'll treat Old England to a dance,
    And try to make her pay the piper.

Anonymous
('A Converted Saxon')

In the early 1830s the Dublin Penny Journal *gave space for
this perhaps ill-advised exercise in patronising praise,
purportedly from an English pen:*

THE NATIVE IRISHMAN

Before I came across the sea
    To this delightful place,
I thought the native Irish were
    A funny sort of race;
I thought they bore shillelagh-sprigs,
    And that they always said:

'Och hone, acushla, tare-an-ouns,
    Begorra,' and 'bedad!'

I thought they sported crownless hats
    With dhudeens in the rim;
I thought they wore long trailing coats
    And knickerbockers trim;
I thought they went about the place
    As tight as they could get;
And that they always had a fight
    With everyone they met.

I thought their noses all turned up
    Just like a crooked pin;
I thought their mouths six inches wide
    And always on the grin;
I thought their heads were made of stuff
    As hard as any nails;
I half suspected that they were
    Possessed of little tails.

                        ★ ★ ★

But when I came unto the land
    Of which I heard so much,
I found that the inhabitants
    Were not entirely such;
I found their features were not all
    Exactly like baboons';
I found that some wore billycocks,
    And some had pantaloons.

I found their teeth were quite as small
    As Europeans' are,
And that their ears, in point of size,
    Were not pecul-iar.
I even saw a face or two
    Which might be handsome called;
And by their very largest feet
    I was not much appalled.

I found them sober, now and then;
    And even in the street,
It seems they do not have a fight
    With ev'ry boy they meet.

I even found some honest men
    Among the very poor;
And I have heard some sentences
    Which did not end with 'shure.'

It seems that praties in their skins
    Are not their only food,
And that they have a house or two
    Which is not built of mud.
In fact, they're not all brutes or fools,
    And I suspect that when
They rule themselves they'll be as good,
    Almost, as Englishmen!

Anonymous

*Some say that in this famous ballad Nell Flaherty is really
Ireland and her drake Robert Emmet: it seems unlikely,
though it's true that her reaction to the loss of a domestic
fowl, however plump, is perhaps a little intemperate – and
note the bird's colouring in verse 2.*

NELL FLAHERTY'S DRAKE

My name it is Nell, quite candid I tell,
And I lived near Cootehill I will never deny.
I had a large drake, the truth for to speak,
That my grandmother left me and she goin' to die.
He was wholesome and sound, and he weighed
    twenty pound,
The universe round I would rove for his sake,
Bad wind to the robber, both drunken and sober,
That murdered Nell Flaherty's beautiful drake.

His neck it was green, and most to be seen,
He was fit for a queen of the highest degree.
His body was white that would you delight,
He was plump, fat and heavy, and brisk as a bee.
The dear little fellow, his legs they were yellow,
He'd fly like a swallow or dive like a hake;
But some wicked savage to grease his white cabbage
Has murdered Nell Flaherty's beautiful drake.

May his pig never grunt, may his cat never hunt,
That a ghost may him haunt in the dead of the night,
May his hen never lay, may his ass never bray,
May his goat fly away like an old paper kite.
That the flies and the fleas may the wretch ever tease,
And a bitter north breeze make him tremble and shake,
May a four-year-old bug make a nest in the lug
Of the monster that murdered Nell Flaherty's drake.

May his pipe never smoke, and his teapot be broke,
And to add to the joke may his kettle ne'er boil,
May he ne'er rest in bed till the hour he is dead,
May he always be fed on lobscouse and fish oil,
May he swell with the gout till his grinders fall out,
May he roar, bawl, and shout with a horrid toothache,
May his temples wear horns and all his toes corns,
The monster that murdered Nell Flaherty's drake.

May his spade never dig, may his sow never pig,
May each nit in his wig be as large as a snail,
May his door have no latch, may his house have no
    thatch,
May his turkey not hatch, may the rats eat his kale,
May every old fairy, from Cork to Dunleary,
Dip him snug and airy in some pond or lake,
Where the eel and the trout may dine on the snout
Of the monster that murdered Nell Flaherty's drake.

May his dog yelp and growl with hunger and cold,
May his wife always scold till his brain goes astray,
May the curse of each hag who e'er carried a bag
Light on the wag till his beard turns grey;
May monkeys still bite him and mad apes still fight him,
And everyone slight him, asleep and awake,
May weasels still gnaw him and jackdaws still claw him,
The monster that murdered Nell Flaherty's drake.

The only good news that I have to diffuse
Is that long Peter Hughes, and blind piper McPeak,
That big-nosed Bob Manson, and buck-toothed Bob
    Hanson,
Each man has a grandson of my darling drake.
My bird he had dozens of nephews and cousins
And one I must get or my poor heart would break,
To keep my mind easy or else I'll go crazy,
There ends the whole tale of Nell Flaherty's drake.

Anonymous

This withering verse is from the magazine Zozimus *in July 1870. It was inspired by a small-ad in the* Manchester Guardian, *which read: 'WANTED, A THOROUGH GENERAL SERVANT, no Irish need apply. – 70 Carter-street, Greenheys.'*

NO IRISH NEED APPLY

Wanted, a maid to scrape and scour,
To toil from morn till midnight hour,
To cook with hands quite undefiled,
And on a pinch to mind the child;
Betimes she must at table wait,
With graceful step remove each plate;
But as the wages will be high,
No horrid Irish need apply.

Wanted, a lady deeply read
In languages both quick and dead,
To take the charge of six young dears,
As teacher in their infant years;
To sit at table she may dare,
When guests are not assembled there;
Her breeding must be good and high –
No vulgar Irish need apply.

Wanted, a youth of pious mein,
At Slim's the grocer's on the Green,
At sanding sugar, watering rum,
An adept he must have become;
Inventive tact he must pursue
At times to frame a lie or two;
But as his eyes must turn on high
No sinful Irish need apply.

Wanted, a man with muscles strong,
With whip in hand, and cutting thong,
To lash the backs of canting knaves,
Who dare to make a nation slaves,
And then insult each feeling dear
They lack the honour to revere;
This crying want to well supply,
Let *none* but Irishmen apply.

Con O'Brien

*Time for something good to eat. In September 1930, this
paean to the most Irish dish of all appeared in the* Cork
Weekly Examiner. *In verse 2 'smack' means 'liking', while
'griskins' are pork steaks, and 'crubeens' salted pig's feet.*

BACON AND GREENS

The beef and the beer of the Saxon may build up
    good, strong, hefty men;
The Scot goes for haggis and porridge and likes a 'wee
    drap' now and then;
The German may spice up a sausage that's fit for great
    Kaisers and Queens,
But the Irishman's dish is my darling – a flitch of
    boiled bacon and greens.

They laughed at the pig in the kitchen when Ireland
    lay groaning in chains,
But the pig paid the rent, so no wonder our 'smack'
    for his breed still remains,
And what has a taste so delicious as 'griskins' and
    juicy 'crubeens',
And what gives us health, strength and beauty like
    bacon, potatoes and greens?

Let our curing factories cure flitches and mild
    flavoured 'cheeks',
But give me a farmer's smoked gammon that hung
    o'er the chimney for weeks,
Where the scent of the peat-fire perfumed it by just
    the most natural means,
And let butter-sauce stand for a relish – 'tis then you
    have bacon and greens.

The pig may not rank as a beauty, but still I maintain
    he looks well,
With rings on his nose and his short curly tail, don't
    you think he looks perfectly 'swell'?
And then taking mud-baths like 'swankies', his skin
    from infection he cleans,
But, alas! at the height of his glory he's made into
    bacon and greens.

The proof of the pudding is eating, and who can deny
    what I say?
Good food makes a brave, brainy nation, and, faith,
    we can prove it to-day:
Our lassies and lads still inherit a style never seen in
    'laddeens',
And their beauty and strength prove the merit of good
    Irish bacon and greens.

The chase and the fight were the glory of Erin's great
    chieftains of yore,
And when they set down to their feasting they dined
    on the head of the boar,
And the tongue was first served to the ladies who
    shone at those banqueting scenes,
While the warriors drained the big goblets to wash
    down the bacon and greens.

Just look round the world this moment and sons of
    those chieftains you'll see,
In war and in peace standing foremost, no matter
    wherever they be;
Where glory and danger are calling, you'll find no
    bosthoons or spalpeens
But you'll see the big, conquering manhood built up
    on our bacon and greens.

Flann O'Brien

For his short-lived comic paper, Blather *(1934–5), Flann O'Brien / Brian O'Nolan / Myles na gCopaleen (1911-1966) invented a new verse form. Here are two samples:*

STRANGE BUT TRUE

The extraordinary thing about cows is
That they never wear trowsis.

WE WOULDN'T SAY IT UNLESS WE KNEW

Of gay women the gayest
Is May Wayest.

In At Swim-Two-Birds *(1939), the poems of Jem Casey (Poet of the Pick and Bard of Booterstown) are described as 'the real old stuff of the native land, stuff that brought scholars to our shore when your men on the other side were on the flat of their bellies before the calf of gold with a sheepskin around their man.' Mr Shanahan, who recites this one, supplies a final verse of his own:*

THE WORKMAN'S FRIEND

When things go wrong and will not come right,
Though you do the best you can,
When life looks black as the hour of night –
A PINT OF PLAIN IS YOUR ONLY MAN.

When money's tight and is hard to get
And your horse has also ran,
When all you have is a heap of debt –
A PINT OF PLAIN IS YOUR ONLY MAN.

When health is bad and your heart feels strange,
And your face is pale and wan,
When doctors say that you need a change,
A PINT OF PLAIN IS YOUR ONLY MAN.

In time of trouble and lousy strife,
You have still got a darlint plan,
You still can turn to a brighter life –
A PINT OF PLAIN IS YOUR ONLY MAN.

– and Mr Shanahan's extra verse:

When stags appear on the mountain high,
With flanks the colour of bran,
When a badger bold can say good-bye,
A PINT OF PLAIN IS YOUR ONLY MAN.

*When Casey himself appears, he regales the company with
these stirring verses:*

A WORKIN' MAN

Come all ye lads and lassies prime
From Macroom to old Strabane,
And list to me till I say my rhyme –
THE GIFT OF GOD IS A WORKIN' MAN.

Your Lords and people of high degree
Are a fine and a noble clan,
They do their best but they cannot see
THE GIFT OF GOD IS A WORKIN' MAN.

From France to Spain and from Holland gay
To the shores of far Japan,
You'll find the people will always say
THE GIFT OF GOD IS A WORKIN' MAN.

He's good, he's strong and his heart is free
If he navvies or drives a van,
He'll shake your hand with a gra-macree –
THE GIFT OF GOD IS A WORKIN' MAN.

Your Lords and ladies are fine to see
And they do the best they can,
But here's the slogan for you and me –
THE GIFT OF GOD IS A WORKIN' MAN.

A WORKIN' MAN, A WORKIN' MAN,
Hurray Hurray for a Workin' Man,
He'll navvy and sweat till he's nearly bet,
THE GIFT OF GOD IS A WORKIN' MAN!

Some years later in the Irish Times, *Myles na Gopaleen emulated a satire of Horace to take on the persona of an eminent Dublin man of letters. Joseph Hone, mentioned in the last line, was the Irish biographer of both WB Yeats and George Moore.*

'AFTER HORACE'

Please give me, Lord, it's all I ask,
A fairly large-size brandy cask,
With brazen hoops about its girth
In case its belly burst from mirth,
And in this tree a tiny tap
To measure out the golden sap.
Not quick or profligately at all
But by the half-one or the ball
And please arrange to have it set
In some underelict maisonette,
The sort of place which if you please
Would cost six thousand without fees,
Located nearly anywhere
But Merrion or Fitzwilliam Square,
And preferably where I can dress
For night shows at the R.D.S.
Without the need for forking out
A dollar to a taxi lout.
Please also have the house contain
A wife of twenty and a wain,
Two servant girls from Swanlinbar,
A nurse, a gardener and a char,
And furniture to indicate
There's people there (or were of late)
And flowers and pictures placed with care
('What faultless taste!) – when I'm not there!
Mementoes also please provide,
In shape of tusk or rug or hide
To show a caller that my aim
Was formerly at biggish game.

Ferocious beasts whose lairs have been
Tropical, polar and marine.
A sport that called for skill and luck
And practically unbounded pluck.
I want to have as well as those
Incredibly expensive clothes,
Enormous jewels (not of paste) –
A hint at my Byzantine taste –
And naturally it's understood
No man in my position could
Afford to loll inside the back
Of lesser car than Cadillac.
One other point I'd like made clear –
It's not my wish that I appear
Just muscular and wealthy, far
From interested in *objets d'art*,
Or thinking that a Bach Chorale
Is used for horses, that Pascal
Grew pansies or that James Joyce bases
His fame on *Irish Names of Places* –
Remembering naught of letters save
That Gorgon Zola wrote *Le Rêve*.
I'd rather be, if you don't mind,
A man of quite another kind:
Let not the cups I won for golf
Exclude a love of Hugo Wolff,
Picasso can be reconciled
With hunting lions in the wild;
I do not feel my war with leo
Unfits me for the Archduke Trio
Or that, if I'm grown rich and fat,
I can't read Proust because of that.
I only ask to be allowed
To stand out brightly from the crowd,
Be famous, and have critics say
That I'm the sun that lit my day –
Though knowing well that never could
My genius be quite understood
And when I die, please raise no stone –
Just have me done by Joseph Hone.

Jane Vere O'Brien

From the Irish Statesman, *3 March 1928.*

A BALLAD

There was a King in Hesperland
Had seven hundred crown;
He gave a hundred to his love,
Who bought herself a gown.

She bought a gown of rushy green
Trimmed round with amethyst,
And when the king saw her therein
His heart beat in his breast.

She wore the gown both day and night
For many a rolling year
And still she was his heart's delight
And still she was his dear.

Upon a time the green did fade,
The amethysts fell off,
And when the silk and satin frayed
His Court began to scoff.

Then said she: 'O my Love and King,
Give me a hundred crown;
And for your better honouring,
I'll buy another gown.'

He answered: 'O, my Love in green,
I'll wed a Wife in red.'
There was a King in Hesperland,
But he is long since dead.

Harry O'Donovan

A favourite stage song written for the Gaiety's Jimmy O'Dea
(who sang it in drag as 'Biddy Mulligan'.)

THE CHARLADIES' BALL

You may talk of your outings, your picnics and parties,
Your dinners and dances and hoolies and all,
But wait till I tell you of the gas that we had
On the night that we went to the Charladies' Ball.
I went there as Queen Anne and I went with my man –
He was dressed as a monkey locked up in a cage –
There was pirets and pirots and Hottentots and what-
      nots
And stars that you'd see on the Music Hall stage.

Chorus:
At the Charladies' Ball, people said one and all,
'You're the belle of the ball, Mrs Mulligan.'
We had one-steps and two-steps and the divil
      knows what new steps,
We swore that we never would be dull again, by
      dad.
We had wine, porter and lemonade, we had
      cocktails and cocoa and all,
We had champagnes that night but we'd real pains
      next morning,
The night that we danced at the Charladies' Ball.

There was Cowboys and Indians that came from
      Drumcondra,
Sweet Francis Street fairies all diamonds and stars,
There was one of the Rooneys as the clock over
      Mooney's
And a telegram boy as a message from Mars.
Mary Moore from the Lots was the Queen of the
      Scots
With a crown out of Woolworth's perched up on her
      dome,
There was young Jemmy Whitehouse came dressed as
      a lighthouse
And a Camden Street Garbo that should have stayed
      home.

Chorus:
At the Charladies' Ball people said one and all,
'You're the belle of the ball, Mrs Mulligan.'
We had one-steps and two-steps and the divil
knows what new steps,
We swore that we never would be dull again, by
dad.
We had wine, porter and Jameson, we had cocktails
and cocoa and all,
We had rumbos and tangos, half-sets and
fandangos,
The night that we danced at the Charladies' Ball.

Mary Ellen O'Rourke was the Queen of the Dawn.
By one-thirty she looked like a real dirty night.
Mick Farren, the bester, came dressed as a jester –
He burst his balloon and dropped dead at the fright.
Kevin Barr came as Bovril, 'Stops that sinking feeling',
Astride of a bottle, pyjamas and all,
But he bumped into Faust, who was gloriously soused
And the two of them were sunk at the end of the hall.

Chorus:
At the Charladies' Ball people said one and all,
'You're the belle of the ball, Mrs Mulligan.'
We had one-steps and two-steps and the divil
knows what new steps.
We swore that we never would be dull again, by
dad.
We had wine, porter and Jameson, we had cocktails
and cocoa and all,
We'd a real stand-up fight but we fell down to
supper
The night that we danced at the Charladies' Ball.

Charles O'Flaherty

*An alternative portrait (see page 171) of Donnybrook Fair,
proverbial for its alcoholic brawling. This flight of fancy first
appeared in* Trifles in Poetry *(1821) by Charles O'Flaherty,
a pawnbroker's son who rose to become editor of the*
Wexford Evening Post. *He wrote it in 1815 for a Dublin
convivial society called 'The Hermits'; in the 1820s it was*

still being sung 'by Mr Rally, at the Harmonic Meetings'.
The song, which takes the tune of 'The Athlone Landlady',
graphically falls to pieces as the drink takes hold.

THE HUMOURS OF DONNYBROOK FAIR (II)

Oh! 'twas Dermott O'Nowlan M'Figg
That could properly handle a twig!
 He went to the Fair,
 And kick'd up a dust there,
In dancing the Donnybrook Jig,
   With his twig,
Oh! my blessing to Dermott M'Figg.

When he came to the midst of the Fair,
He was all in a *puagh* for fresh air,
 For the Fair very soon
 Was as full as the moon,
Such mobs upon mobs as were there,
   Oh! rare,
So more luck to sweet Donnybrook Fair.

The souls they came pouring in fast,
To dance while the leather would last,
 For the Thomas-street brogue
 Was there much in vogue,
And oft with a brogue a joke passed,
   Quite fast,
While the cash and the whiskey did last.

But, Dermott, his mind on love bent,
In search of his sweetheart he went,
 Peep'd in here and there
 As he walk'd thro' the Fair,
And took a small drop in each tent,
   As he went,
Och, on whiskey and love he was bent.

And who should he spy in a jig,
With a Meal-Man, so tall and so big,
 But his own darling Kate,
 So gay and so neat, –
Faith, her partner he hit him a dig,
   The pig!
He beat the meal out of his wig!

Then Dermott, with conquest elate,
Drew a stool near his beautiful Kate;
    'Arrah, Katty!' says he,
    'My own Cushlamacree!
Sure, the world, for beauty, you beat,
        Compleate,
So we'll just take a dance while we wait.'

The piper, to keep him in tune,
Struck up a gay lilt very soon,
    Until an arch wag,
    Cut a hole in his bag,
And at once put an end to the tune,
        Too soon,
Och, the music flew up to the moon.

To the fiddler says Dermott M'Figg,
'If you'll please to play "Shelagh na Gig,"
    We'll shake a loose toe,
    While you humour the bow,
To be sure you must warm the wig
        Of M'Figg,
While he's dancing a tight Irish jig.'

The Meal-Man he looked very shy,
While a great big tear stood in his eye,
    He cried, 'Lord how I'm kilt
    All alone for that jilt,
With her may the devil fly high
        In the sky,
For I'm murdered and I don't know for why.'

'Oh!' says Dermott, and he in the dance,
Whilst a step towards his foe did advance,
    'By the Father of men
    Say but that word again,
And I'll soon knock you back in a trance
        To your dance,
For with me you'd have but a small chance.'

'But,' says Kitty, the darling, says she,
'If you'll only just listen to me,
    It's myself that will show
    That he can't be your foe,
Though he fought for his cousin, that's me,'

Says she,
'For, sure, Billy's related to me.'

'For my own cousin-jarmin, Anne Wild,
Stood for Biddy Mulrooney's first child,
 And Biddy's step-son,
  Sure, he married Bess Dunn,
Who was gossip to Jenny, as mild
   A child,
As ever at mother's breast smiled.'

'And may be you don't know Jane Brown,
Who served goats' whey in sweet Dundrum town,
 'Twas her uncle's half-brother
  That married my mother,
And bought me this new yellow gown,
   To go down,
Where the marriage was held at Miltown.'

'By the powers!' then, says Dermott, ''tis plain,
Like the son of that rapscallion Cain,
 My best friend I've kilt,
  Though no blood there is spilt,
And the Devil a harm did I mean,
   That's plain,
But by me he'll be ne'er kilt again.'

Then the Meal-Man forgave him the blow,
That laid him a sprawling so low,
 And being quite gay,
  Asked them both to the Play,
But Kitty, being bashful, said 'No!,
   No! No!'
Yet he treated them all to the Show!

*These extra two verses gave added zest when the song was
performed by Mr Rally:*

Oh then how the girls did look
When the clergyman opened his book,
 'Till young Nelly Shine
  Tipt Dermott a sign,
Faith he soon popt her into a nook
   Near the Brook,
And there he fell kissing the cook.

For a while she began for to cry,
Was poor girl so undone as I,
    When the ladies came round,
      Caught them both on the ground,
Their fingers they clapt to their eyes
        So sly,
We're courting, said she, don't be shy.

Brian O'Higgins

*Brian O'Higgins (1882-1963), politician and ardent
propagandist for Irish separatism and for the Irish language,
was a prolific writer of light verses (often as 'Brian na
Banban'). The poem below is probably his; the four that
follow certainly are.*

*In the first decades of the last century, Dublin Castle
urged the police to learn Irish, as potential rebels were using
it as a sort of code. The Irish words in the chorus mean:
(line 1): 'Alas, alack'; (line 2): 'Do you understand me?';
(lines 3 & 4): 'I think it is and I think it isn't, But I am
learning the Irish.' Verse 3 reveals that the cook has given
her policeman boyfriend a sabotaged book, full of deliberate
errors. The last verse is simply a gloat.*

THE LIMB OF THE LAW

You can tell by my feet I'm a limb of the law,
The people of Dublin for me have no grá;
The hiss me and boo me when I pass them by,
'Sinn Féin', 'Up the Rebels' you'll hear them all cry.
Now you may think that's bad, but there's one thing
    that's worse:
This grand Irish language, on my soul 'tis a curse,
With their yibberin and yabberin like an old asses' bray,
The Castle expects me to know what they say,

        Chorus:
With 'Ochone' and 'Mo bhróin' you'll hear them all
    say,
'An dtuigeann tú mé?' and 'Sinn Féin, hooray!'
'Is dóigh liom go bhfuil is is dóigh liom nach é,
'Ach tá mé ag foghlaim na Gaeilge.'

Now I've a friend on the force and he's courting a cook
And what do you know but she bought him a book,
With Irish on this side and English on that,
So small I could carry it round in my hat.
Oh first learn the letters and then the whole phrase.
I'll have it all off in a couple of days.
Then their yibberin and yabberin I'll soon understand.
Such larnification will stagger the land.

Now this book I procured and to learn I must try;
'An bhfuil mé?' means 'Are you?', 'An bhfuil tú?' means
        'Am I?'
'Is dóigh liom', I think that I do understand,
'Mo lámh' is my foot and 'Mo chluas' is my hand.
'Tá mé ag foghlaim,' I'm learning, you see
If I keep on like this, an inspector I'll be.
I'm getting so big that I don't know the cat.
My head is two sizes too large for my hat.

Now with larnification I'm bloody near dead,
I lie on the floor 'cause I can't lie in bed.
I am walking and talking when I'm fast asleep.
When I hear 'Up the rebels!' my flesh starts to creep.
My friends all have left me, I've now just a few.
I'm walking around like a wandering Jew.'

*O'Higgins, like his friend Arthur Griffith, linked his hostility
to the English to Anti-Semitism. In 1907, Dublin hosted a
lavish 'Irish International Exhibition'. Some people wondered
how Irish it really was. (Air: 'The Top of Cork Road')*

THE GRAND INTERNATIONAL SHOW.

A fig for the mad-heads who prate Nationality,
We will be true to the old hospitality;
Fling to the dickens all childish formality –
        Open the gates, let the foreigners come!
What can poor clodhopping Ireland show?
She's vulgar and lazy, and stupid and slow.
        Let the Jew artificer
        From darkness release her,
        And flatter and fleece her,
        And wink at his chum!

Chorus:
Hurrah! for the grand International Show –
Jingoes and Germans and Jews in a row;
  Irish humility,
  Foreign civility,
  Shoddy gentility
  Guarding them all!

O, such a show! 'twill be surely the greatest one
Ever was held upon earth – since the latest one;
Highest in tone, and in motive the straightest one;
  (Run on the lines of the railways and trams).
First on the list is a king – off his throne,
  Then big shoddy dealers,
  And mud-flinging squealers,
  And broad-footed peelers,
  As gentle as lambs!

Beautiful samples of 'Henglish' society;
Tipsters and toffs in the grandest variety;
Irish Seoiníní, with Seoinín anxiety,
  Rushing to mix with the cross-channel mob.
Who ever saw such a noble display?
Princes (and pickpockets) pleasant and gay.
  Jews and Jewesses,
  And loyal addresses,
  And Royal caresses,
  And – all for a bob!

O'Higgins wasted no sympathy on the English, however
worthy their cause. This is the second of his 'Five War Songs'.

FROM THE TRENCHES

We were out picking blackberries
  Along the River Aisne,
When up came seven thousand Huns
  Without a bally sign.
They shelled us hard from where they lay
  Upon a bally hill,
But we were English Tommies
  And we meant to have our fill.

We gathered all the blackberries
    (About a bally ton),
And then we charged the savages
    And set them on the run.
We slaughtered near a thousand –
    Shot the beggars as they ran –
And never lost a blackberry,
    Not to speak about a man!

*An attack on WB Yeats from 1924, when he was a Senator
of the Irish Free State. His unscholarly transliterations from
the Irish had infuriated language purists.*

THE ISLE OF INNISFREE

I will arise and go now, and go to Innisfree,
    (If 'twere Inis Fraoigh now, I wouldn't know its
      name)
And in my hut of wattles I'll be spooning with the
  Shee,
    (Don't make it Sidhe, dear printer, for it wouldn't
      be the same.)

And in the Celtic twilight, I'll destroy the A B C
    Of Is and Tá and other things I'd dearly love to
      ban;
For Cáitlín Ní Uallacháin is different, do you see?
    To Cathleen, the Daughter of Houlihan.

The language of the Senate there shall fall upon my ear
    (I'll purchase me an aerial when my pension
      cheque is paid)
And with my own right hand I'll draw Three-Sixty
  Quid a year,
    To keep the Pot of Broth a-boil in the W.B-loud
      glade.

And when the vulgar Gaelic Tongue is dead as Finn
  McCool,
    (Don't print it Fion MacCumhaill, or 'twill baffle
      W.B.)
I'll teach Yeatsonian Irish, in a purely Pagan School,
    To keep the home fires burning in the Isle of
      Innisfree.

In July 1937, as the new King and Queen visited Northern Ireland, all the customs posts along the border mysteriously went on fire.

THE BONFIRE ON THE BORDER

'Twas on July the twenty-eighth
In the year of thirty-seven,
A fire was lit without a grate
And the flames leaped high to heaven.
Our King and Queen came sailing down
The Lough in the best of order,
And we welcomed them to Belfast town
With a bonfire on the Border.

The Queen put a muffler round her neck
Assisted by her weemin,
The King walked up and down the deck
Surrounded by his G-men.
He asked 'What is that glare I see?'
The reply was there in order:
'It's Ireland united in loyalty
With a bonfire on the Border!'

Some say the spark was Ulster's own
Some say it was extraneous,
A man in Down said it lit on its own
The combustion being spontaneous.
A lad who loves his King and Queen
And stands for Law and Order,
Says the flames were Orange, White and Green
In that bonfire on the Border.

They may prance and dance in Belfast Town,
They may croon 'Whereas' in Dublin;
They may sever the Empire from the Crown,
But they might as well not be troublin':
Neither Lay Tribunal nor Legal Bench,
Nor turnkey, tout or warder,
Nor all the Boyne water can ever quench
That bonfire on the Border!

Here's to the lads that played the game,
Here's to the minds that planned it,
Here's to the hands that lit the flame,

Here's to the winds that fanned it:
May it blaze again from shore to shore
Consuming our land's disorder:
May it leap and roar from shore to shore
Till it burns away the Border!

John O'Keeffe

From his 1781 play, The Agreeable Surprise, *the last one
to be written by the Dublin-born writer (1747–1833) before his
blindness (which was, he believed, traceable to an infection
picked up when he tumbled into the Liffey).*

JINGLE

Amo, amas,
I love a lass,
As cedar tall and slender;
Sweet cowslip's face
Is her nominative case,
And she's of the feminine gender.
Horum quorum,
Sunt divorum,
Harum, scarum, Divo,
Tag rag, merry derry, periwig and bobtail
Hic, hoc, harum, genitivo.

Patrick O'Kelly

*Apart from, possibly, 'Nell Flaherty's Drake' (on page 297),
this is the most satisfying piece of sustained invective in
Irish verse. Said to date from the 1750s, it made a laughing
stock of the County Cork village.*

THE CURSE OF DONERAILE

Alas! how dismal is my tale,
I lost my watch in Doneraile.
My Dublin watch, my chain and seal,
Pilfer'd at once in Doneraile.
May Fire and Brimstone never fail

To fall in show'rs on Doneraile.
May all the leading fiends assail
The thieving Town of Doneraile.
As light'nings flash across the vale,
So down to Hell with Doneraile.
The fate of Pompey at Pharsale,
Be that the curse of Doneraile.
May Beef, or Mutton, Lamb, or Veal
Be never found in Doneraile,
But Garlic Soup and scurvy Cale
Be still the food for Doneraile.
And forward as the creeping snail
Th' industry be, of Doneraile.
May Heav'n a chosen curse entail
On rigid, rotten Doneraile.
May Sun and Moon for ever fail
To beam their lights on Doneraile.
May ev'ry pestilential gale
Blast that curs'd spot called Doneraile.
May not a Cuckoo, Thrush or Quail
Be ever heard in Doneraile.
May Patriots, Kings and commonweal
Despise and harass Doneraile.
May ev'ry post, Gazette and Mail
Sad tidings bring of Doneraile.
May loudest thunders ring a peal
To blind and deafen Doneraile.
May vengeance fall at head and tail
From North and South at Doneraile.
May profit light and tardy sale
Still damp the trade of Doneraile.
May Fame resound a dismal tale
Whene'er she lights on Doneraile.
May Egypt's plagues at once prevail
To thin the knaves of Doneraile.
May frost and snow, and sleet and hail,
Benumb each joint in Doneraile.
May wolves and bloodhounds trace and trail
The cursed crew of Doneraile.
May Oscar, with his fiery flail,
To Atoms thresh all Doneraile.
May every mischief, fresh and stale,
Abide henceforth in Doneraile.
May all, from Belfast to Kinsale,
Scoff, curse, and damn you Doneraile.

May neither Flow'r nor Oatenmeal
Be found or known in Doneraile.
May want and woe each joy curtail,
That e'er was known in Doneraile.
May no one coffin want a nail,
That wraps a rogue in Doneraile.
May all the thieves that rob and steal
The Gallows meet in Doneraile.
May all the sons of Granuwale
Blush at the thieves of Doneraile.
May mischief big as Norway whale
O'erwhelm the knaves of Doneraile.
May curses, wholesale and retail,
Pour with full force on Doneraile.
May ev'ry transport wont to sail
A convict bring from Doneraile.
May ev'ry churn and milking pail
Fall dry to staves in Doneraile.
May cold and hunger still congeal
The stagnant blood of Doneraile.
May ev'ry hour new woes reveal,
That Hell reserves for Doneraile.
May ev'ry chosen ill prevail
O'er all the Imps of Doneraile.
May no one wish or pray'r avail
To soothe the woes of Doneraile.
May th' Inquisition strait impale
The rapparees of Doneraile.
May curse of Sodom now prevail,
And sink to ashes Doneraile.
May Charon's Boat triumphant sail,
Completely mann'd, from Doneraile.
Oh! may my couplets never fail
To find new curse for Doneraile.
And may grim Pluto's inner gaol
For ever groan with Doneraile.

*In desperation, Lady Doneraile eventually presented Patrick
O'Kelly with a replacement watch and seal, and so the
happy poet wrote an antidote, 'Blessings on Doneraile',
which began:*

How vastly pleasing is my tale,
I found my watch in Doneraile.
My Dublin watch, my chain and seal,

Were all restor'd at Doneraile.
May Fire and Brimstone ever fail
To hurt or injure Doneraile.
May neither friend nor foe assail
The splendid town of Doneraile ...

... and so on until the end. But nobody wanted to know.

Anonymous

Yet another song that is occasionally attributed to Brendan
Behan, probably on the grounds that as a very young man
he took part in the IRA's sabotage campaign in England:

THE OLD ALARM CLOCK

When first I came to London
In the year of thirty nine,
The city looked so wonderful
And the girls were so divine,
But the coppers got suspicious
And they soon gave me the knock –
I was charged with being the owner
Of an old alarm clock.

Oh, next morning down by Barber street
I caused no little stir:
The IRA were busy,
And the telephones did burr.
Said the judge, 'I'm going to charge you
With the possession of this machine,
And I'm also going to charge you
With the wearing of the green.'

Now says I to him, 'Your honor,
If you'll give me half a chance,
I'll show you how me small machine
Can make the peelers dance.
It ticks away politely
Till you get an awful shock,
And it ticks away the gelignite
In me old alarm clock.'

Said the judge, 'Now listen here, my man,
And I'll tell you of our plan.
For you and all your countrymen
I do not give a damn.
The only time you'll take is mine –
Ten years in Dartmoor dock –
And you can count it by the ticking
Of your old alarm clock.'

Now this lonely Dartmoor prison
Would put many in the jigs;
The cell it isn't pretty
And it isn't very big.
Sure I'd long ago have left the place
If I had only got
Ah, me couple o' sticks of gelignite –
And me old alarm clock.

Anonymous

A ballad sheet song. Culinary note: 'prog' (verse 4) means food, and 'burgoo' (verse 6) means porridge or stew.

THE OLD LEATHER BREECHES

At the Sign of the Bell on the road to Clonmel
Paddy Hegarty kept a neat shebeen;
He sold pig's meat and bread, kept a fine lodging bed,
And was liked in the country he lived in.
Himself and his wife, both struggled through life:
On weekdays Pat mended the ditches,
But on Sundays he dressed in a suit of the best,
And his pride was his old leather breeches.

For twenty-one years, at least so it appears,
His father these breeches had run in,
And the morning he died, he to his bedside
Called Paddy, his own darling son, in;
His advice then he gave ere he went to his grave,
As he bade him take care of his riches,
Says he, 'It's no use to step into my shoes,
But I'd like you'd leap into my breeches.'

Now last winter's snow left victuals so low
That Paddy was ate out completely,
With the snow coming down he could not get to
    town,
Thoughts of hunger did bother him greatly.
One night as he lay adreaming away
Of ghosts, fairies, spirits and witches,
He heard an uproar, just outside his door,
And he jumped up to pull on his breeches.

Says Brian McGurk, with a voice like a Turk,
'Come, Paddy, and get us some eating,'
Says Big Andy Moore, 'We'll burst open the door,
Sure this is no night to be waiting.'
The words were scarce spoke when the door it was
    broke,
And they crowded round Paddy like leeches,
And they swore by the hob, if they didn't get prog,
They would eat him clean out of his breeches.

Poor Paddy in dread slipped up to the bed
That held Judy his own darling wife in;
And there 'twas agreed that they should get a feed,
So he slipped out and brought a big knife in;
He cut out the waist of his breeches, the beast,
And he ripped out the buttons and stitches,
And he cut them in stripes, the way they do tripes,
And he boiled them his old leather breeches.

The tripes they were stewed, on a dish they were
    strewed,
And the boys all roared out, 'Lord be thankit,'
But Hegarty's wife was afraid of her life
And she thought it high time for to shank it;
To see how they smiled, for they thought Paddy boiled
Some mutton or beef of the richest,
But little they knew, it was leather burgoo
That was made out of Paddy's ould breeches.

As they messed on the stuff, says Darby, 'It's tough,'
Says Andy, 'You're no judge of mutton,'
When Brian McGurk, on the point of his fork,
Held up a big ivory button;
Says Paddy, 'What's that, sure I thought it was fat,'
Brian leps to his feet and he screeches,

'Be the powers above, I was trying to shove
Me teeth through the flap of his breeches.'

They all flew at Pat, but he cut out of that,
He ran when he saw them all rising;
Says Brian, 'Make haste, and go for the priest,
Be the holy Saint Patrick, I'm poisoned.'
Revenge for the joke they had, for they broke
All the chairs, bowls, and tables, and dishes,
And from that very night they'd knock out your
    daylight
If they'd catch you with old leather breeches.

Anonymous

*Both the Dubliners and the Clancy Brothers seem to perform
with particular relish in their recordings of this decidedly
misogynistic old song.*

THE OLD WOMAN FROM WEXFORD

Oh there was an old woman from Wexford and in
    Wexford she did dwell;
She loved her old man dearly but another one twice as
    well –
With me tiggery tiggery toram and me toram toram ta.

One day she went to the doctor some medicine for to
    find:
She said, 'Will you give me something for to make me
    old man blind?'
With me tiggery tiggery toram and me toram toram ta.

'Feed him eggs and marrowbones and make him suck
    them all,
And it won't be very long after till he won't see you at
    all.'
With me tiggery tiggery toram and me toram toram ta.

The doctor wrote a letter and he signed it with his
    hand;
He sent it round to the old man just to let him
    understand –

With me tiggery tiggery toram and me toram toram ta.

She fed him eggs and marrowbones and made him
    suck them all,
And it wasn't very long after till he couldn't see the
    wall –
With me tiggery tiggery toram and me toram toram ta.

Says he, 'I'd like to drown myself, but that might be a
    sin.'
Says she, 'I'll go along with you and help to push you
    in.'
With me tiggery tiggery toram and me toram toram ta.

The woman she stepped back a bit to rush and push
    him in,
And the old man quickly stepped aside and she went
    tumblin' in –
With me tiggery tiggery toram and me toram toram ta.

Oh how loudly she did yell and how loudly she did
    bawl,
'Yerra hold your whist, old woman, sure I can't see
    you at all.'
With me tiggery tiggery toram and me toram toram ta.

Now eggs and eggs and marrowbones may make your
    old man blind,
But if you want to drown him you must creep up
    close behind –
With me tiggery tiggery toram and me toram toram
    ta –
With me tiggery tiggery toram – and the blind man he
    could see.

Anonymous

*In this tongue-in-cheek ode from the eighteenth century,
which curiously appears to be made up of limericks whose
first lines do not rhyme, County Wicklow becomes a sort of
classical Arcadia.*

ON DEBORAH PERKINS
OF THE COUNTY OF WICKLOW

Some sing ye of Venus the goddess,
Some chant ye of rills, and of fountains;
    But the theme of such praise
    As my fancy can raise,
Is a wench of the Wicklow mountains.

Mount Ida they surely surpass,
With the Wood-nymphs' recess, and their lurkings;
    O! 'tis there that I play
    And wanton all day,
With little black Deborah Perkins.

King Solomon, he had nine hundred, at least,
To humour his taste, with their smirkings;
    But not one of 'em all,
    When she led up a ball,
Cou'd foot it like Deborah Perkins.

The fair Cleopatra, Anthony lov'd,
But, by heaven, I'd give him his jerkings;
    If that he was here
    And shou'd think to compare
That trollop, with Deborah Perkins.

Bacchus he priz'd Ariadne the sweet,
But I wish we were now at the firkins;
    I'd make him reel off,
    In contemptible scoff,
While I toasted plump Deborah Perkins.

Might I have all the girls at command,
That boast of their Dresden, or markings;
    I'd rather feed goats,
    And play with the coats
Of cherry-cheek'd Deborah Perkins.

A fig for the eclogues of Maro,
Or Ovid's fantastical workings;
    If I haven't their letters,
    I sing of their betters,
When I touch up young Deborah Perkins.

Conal O'Riordan

*Never let it be said that the Jesuits did not encourage young
Irish writers. In* Adam of Dublin, *a novel from 1920 by
Conal O'Riordan (1874–1948), the love-smitten thirteen-
year-old hero allows his teacher to see this:*

'ADAM'S FIRST POEM'

What a happy chap
Am I in your lap,
Where I have been,
Dear Josephine.

Behold my happiness,
If I may so express
Myself when I have been,
Not far from Josephine.

*Mr Flood, S.J., returns the poem with praise, having
'amplified' it as follows:*

Behold my happiness,
If I may so express
Myself when I have been
Near kind Miss Josephine!

Miss Josephine is kind,
Because her noble mind
Impels her to be so,
That heav'nwards she may go.

So therefore I'll not sigh
When I behold her die.
For God doth her require
To help to swell His choir
His high and heavenly choir
In the Land of Heart's Desire.

Anonymous

This much-loved nineteenth century ballad used to be the
party piece of many an Ulster Parish Priest. Hector
illustrated it for the Blackstaff Press in the 1980s, and fondly
remembers then going on Downtown Radio in Belfast. The
interviewer remarked that 'Regular listeners to this
programme will know this ballad well, as we had it sung for
us only last week by Cardinal Tomás Ó Fiaich.'

THE OULD ORANGE FLUTE

In the county Tyrone, near the town of Dungannon,
Where many's the ruction myself had a han' in
Bob Williamson lived, a weaver by trade,
And all of us thought him a stout-hearted blade.
On the Twelfth of July as it yearly did come,
Bob played on the flute to the sound of the drum.
You can talk of your harp, your piano or lute,
But nothing could sound like the Ould Orange Flute.

But Bob the deceyver, he took us all in,
For he married a Papish named Bridget McGinn,
Turned Papish himself, and forsook the Ould Cause
That gave us our freedom, religion and laws.
And the boys in the townland made comment upon it
And Bob had to fly to the province of Connaught.
He flew with his wife and his fixin's to boot,
And along with the others the Ould Orange Flute.

At the Chapel on Sundays to atone for past deeds,
He said 'Paters' and 'Aves' and counted his beads,
Till, after some time, at the priest's own desire,
He went with his ould flute to play in the choir.
He went with his ould flute to play in the Mass,
But the instrument shivered and sighed, Oh alas!
When he blew it and fingered and made a great noise,
The flute would play only 'The Protestant Boys'.

Bob jumped and he started and got into a splutter,
And threw the ould flute in the Bless'd Holy Water;
He thought that this charm might bring some other
      sound,
When he blew it again, it played 'Croppies Lie Down',
And all he could whistle and finger and blow,

To play Papish music he found it no go.
'Kick the Pope', 'The Boyne Water' and such like it
    would sound,
But one Papish squeak in it couldn't be found.

At a council of priests that was held the next day
They decided to banish the ould flute away;
For they couldn't knock heresy out of its head
And they bought Bob another to play in its stead.
So the ould flute was doomed, and its fate was
    pathetic;
It was fastened and burned at the stake as heretic.
While the flames rose around it, they heard a strange
    noise –
'Twas the ould flute still whistlin' 'The Protestant Boys'!

Anonymous

Charles Dickens and other theatre-going Londoners heard a good deal about the comic side of Ireland during the first few decades of the nineteenth century – this piece was apparently presented at Drury Lane by a certain Mr Johnstone.

PADDY MacSHANE'S SEVEN AGES

If my own botheration don't alter my plan,
I'll sing seven lines of a tight Irishman,
    Wrote by old Billy Shakespeare of Ballyporeen.
He said while a babe I lov'd whiskey and pap,
That I mewled and puk'd in my grandmother's lap;
She joulted me hard just to hush my sweet roar,
When I slipp'd through her fingers down whack on
    the floor,
    What a squalling I made sure at Ballyporeen.

When I grew up a boy, with a nice shining face,
With my bag at my back, and a snail-crawling pace,
    Went to school at old Thwackum's at
        Ballyporeen.
His wig was so fusty, his birch was my dread,
He learning beat *out* 'stead of *into* my head.
'Master Macshane', says he, 'you're a great dirty dolt,
You've got no more brains than a Monaghan colt;
    You're not fit for our college at Ballyporeen.'

When eighteen years of age, I was teas'd and perplext
To know what I should be, so a lover turn'd next,
    And courted sweet Sheelah of Ballyporeen.
I thought I'd just take her to comfort my life,
Not knowing that she was already a wife:
She ask'd me just once that to see her I'd come,
When I found her ten children and husband at home,
    A great big whacking chairman of Ballyporeen.

I next turn'd a soldier, I did not like that,
So turn'd servant, and liv'd with the great Justice Pat,
    A big dealer in p'ratoes at Ballyporeen.
With turtle and venison he lin'd his inside,
Ate so many fat capons, that one day he died.
So great was my grief, that to keep spirits up,
Of some nice whiskey cordial I took a big sup,
    To my master's safe journey from Ballyporeen.

Kick'd and toss'd so about, like a weathercock vane,
I pack'd up my awls, and I went back again
    To my grandfather's cottage at Ballyporeen.
I found him, poor soul! with no legs for his hose,
Could not see through the spectacles put on his nose;
With no teeth in his head, so death cork'd up his chin;
He slipp'd out of his slippers, and faith I slipp'd in,
    And succeeded poor Dennis of Ballyporeen.

Anonymous

*A peculiar theatrical song (air: 'The Irish Wedding') from
much the same period, which apparently went down well at
Dublin's Theatre Royal in the 1820s. The publishers of this
'Irish Ballad' followed the (then widespread) practice of
putting the puns in italics in case readers should miss them.*

PADDY'S BURIAL

An Irish lad
Is always mad,
Roaring, singing, swearing, O;
And Paddy Clem
Was just the same

From birth unto his burying, O.
'Twas at the sign of th' artichoke,
  The whiskey did o'ertake him, O;
He fell *asleep* and never *woke*,
  So Pat's friends met to *wake* him, O.
    With fillillilloo! Och, hubbubbubboo!
      My darling Pat, you're cruel O!
    Howl, hibbibbibboo, and fillillilloo!
      Why did you die, my jewel, O?

  When Paddy's bed,
  From foot to head,
Was hung with flow'rs and crosses O,
    His friends, Och hone!
    Began to groan,
  And pipe o'er Paddy's losses, O.
Dead Pat had lost all worldly joys,
  And grief was ev'ry soul in, O;
But *soon* by drinking *late*, the boys
  All got *dead*-drunk a-howling, O –
    Fillillilloo, &c.

  The morning came,
  And Paddy Clem
The undertaker fasten'd down;
    The mourners pressed,
    Genteelly dressed
  In mourning blue, and green, and brown.
They all went reeling from the door,
  The coffin after the moaners there,
All Paddy's friends, and forty more,
  And all of them chief groaners were.
    Fillillilloo, &c.

  And now the priest,
  Whose fist they *greast*,
To pray o'er Pat, when underground,
    He sung a *sarmon*,
    His clerk th' *Amen*,
  Which set them howling all around.
Then all began to fill the grave,
  And she jump'd in, and down she sat,
And swore, If I've a soul to save,
  I'll buried be *alive* like Pat.
    Och, Fillillilloo, &c.

Said Rourke, you flat,
Come out of that,
See how the rain is pouring down;
Said she, I'm *dry*,
Said Rourke, you *lie*;
Come out, or I will crack your crown.
For general fight the sign went round,
The mourners little caring, O,
For rain; so all the souls got drown'd,
And beat, at Paddy's burying, O.
With fillillilloo! Och, hubbubbubboo!
They all there fought a duel, O.
Howl, hibbibbibboo! &c.

Anonymous

*'The viewless wings of Poesy', as imagined in the ninth
issue of* Zozimus, *July 1870.*

PANEFUL

The other day in mood sublime
I hurried down through Grafton-street;
I little recked of scene or time,
Or whither led my wayward feet,
For mighty thoughts convulsed my soul,
And radiant visions thronged my brain;
My eyes in frenzy fine did roll;
I was in strong poetic vein.
On rushed I through the brainless crowd
(How doth the poet loathe the cad),
And thus I spoke my thoughts aloud
(For kept I silent, I'd go mad): –
'Resounding Seas, and blazing Stars,
And Hurricanes without control;
Earthquakes and Fiends, and awful Wars,
'Tis ye alone delight my soul!
For me the Common hath no joys,
The Earth's a Humbug – Man an Ass' –
But here I heard a fearful noise,
And found I'd smashed a pane of glass.

Anonymous

Whether this was originally an Irish verse or not is almost irrelevant, for we seem to have thoroughly adopted it.

THE PIG

It was a night in dark November
As I very well remember,
I strolled down Sackville Street in drunken pride,
But my knees were all a-flutter,
So I plumped down in the gutter
And a pig came up and lay down by my side.

So I lay down in the gutter
Thinking thoughts I could not utter,
When a colleen passing by did primly say,
'You can tell a man that boozes
By the company he chooses.'
And the pig got up and slowly walked away.

Anonymous

It is always best when a poem is longer than its title – as this is, just about; it comes from TCD Miscellany, *November 1937.*

PINDARIC ODE WRITTEN ON A WINTER
EVENING NOT FAR FROM SORREL HILL

On Sorrel Hill the Druid sat
And spat and spat and spat and spat
             And spat.

Anonymous

The Dublin Observer *published this spirited view of contrasting religious taboos in about 1830. The poem refrains from mentioning that the Archbishop of Canterbury is already in the enviable position of being able to avail himself of both wine and wife. A 'curtain lecture' (verse 3) was a wife's bedtime harangue.*

THE POPE AND THE SULTAN

The Pope sits in Saint Peter's chair,
And many a well-fed monk is there;
He quaffs at will the choicest wine –
I would Saint Peter's keys were mine!

But, no! 'tis never his to prove
The melting kiss of woman's love;
And who, to spend his hours alone,
Would choose to sway the world's own throne?

The Sultan hath his harem fair,
And many a sweet Circassian's there;
No curtain lecture gives his wife –
Gods! but that were a merry life!

But, stop! 'tis never his to know
Of rosy wine, the inspiring glow:
His Alcoran forbids the bowl –
Such lot would suit but ill my soul!

But could I mix the tulip's bloom
With the red rose's sweet perfume;
Could I but mingle Pope with Turk –
Methinks that were a glorious work!

I'd think whene'er I stole a kiss,
What Sultan could do more than this?
And, when laid senseless on the floor,
I'd cry, 'The Pope could drink no more!'

Thomas Hamblin Porter

A mock-heroic chronicle of the domestic economy of
Phoebus (the sun), written in about 1820 by an otherwise
obscure Trinity-educated cleric.

THE NIGHT-CAP

Jolly Phoebus his car to the coach-house had driven,
    And unharnessed his high-mettled horses of light;
He gave them a feed from the manger of heaven,
    And rubbed them and littered them up for the night.

Then down to the kitchen he leisurely strode,
    Where Thetis, the housemaid, was sipping her tea;
He swore he was tired with that damned up-hill road,
    He'd have none of her slops or hot water, not he.

So she took from the corner a little cruiskeen
    Well filled with the nectar Apollo loves best,
(From the neat Bog of Allen, some pretty poteen);
    And he tippled his quantum and staggered to rest.

His many-caped box-coat around him he threw,
    For his bed, faith, 'twas dampish, and none of the
        best;
All above him the clouds their bright-fringed curtains
    drew,
    And the tuft of his night-cap lay red in the west.

Simon Quin
(Attrib.)

Another of the new breed of descriptive verses from early
nineteenth-century Cork. This one comes in various
versions. The 'statue' in verse 2 is apparently the protruding
figurehead of a sunken ship, and in verse 3 'skeehories' are
haws or wild rose-hips (from the Irish 'sceachóir'); as for
'tender gob-stones', could they be edible molluscs of some
sort – cockles, perhaps?

THE TOWN OF PASSAGE

The town of Passage
Is neat and spacious,
All situated
    Upon the sea,
The ships a-floating,
And the youths a-boating
With their cotton coats on,
    Each summer's day.
'Tis there you'd see,
Both night and morning,
The men-of-war
    With fresh, flowing sails,
The bould lieutenants,
And the tars so jolly,

All steering for Cork
    In a hackney chaise.

'Tis there's a statue,
Drawn by nature,
Leaping from the mud
    To the dry land,
A lion, or leopard,
Or some fierce 'crature'
With a reading-made-easy
    In his hand.
There's a 'rendy-vou house'
For each bould hero
To take on,
    Whose heart beats high,
The colours a-dropping,
And the childer's rockets
All pinned across it,
    Hanging out to dry.

'Tis there's the strand, too,
That's deck'd with oar-weeds,
And tender gob-stones,
    And mussel shells;
And there's skeehories,
And what still more, is
Some comely, fresh flowing,
    Water rills.
'Tis there the ladies,
When break of day is,
Their tender loviers
    Do often pelt,
While some are airing,
And some are bathing,
Quite unadorned,
    To enjoy their health.

And there's a ferry-boat
That's quite convenient,
For man and horses
    For to take a ride,
And 'tis there in clover,
You may cross over
To Carrigaloe,
    At the other side.

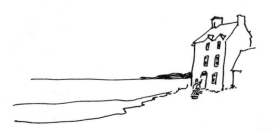

There may be seen, O!
The sweet Marino
With its trees so green, O!
    And fruit so red,
And lovely White Point,
And right forenent it
The Giant's Stairs,
    And ould Horse Head.

There's a house for lodgers,
At one Molly Bowen's
Where often goes in
    One Simon Quin,
Where without a coat on,
You'd hear him grope on
The door to open,
    And let him in;
Then straight up stairs –
One pair of windys,
With the slates alone
    'Twixt him and the sky,
Oh! 'tis there till morning,
The fleas all swarming
Do keep him warm
    Where he does lie.

Anonymous

*Both Colm Ó Lochlainn and Frank Harte included versions
of this lively ballad in their collections. This one combines
elements of both. As Harte points out, it can be roughly
dated by 'Brady's Loop-line Porter' (verse 8): the Loop-line
Railway Bridge across the Liffey was built in the 1890s.
'Carman Hall' (verse 4) is off Francis Street, Dublin 8.*

THE RAGMAN'S BALL

Come pay attention for a while, my good friends one
    and all,
And I'll sing to you a verse or two about a famous ball.
Now the ball was given by some friends who lived
    down in Ashe Street
In a certain house in the Liberties where the Ragmen
    used to meet.

Well the names were called at seven o'clock, every
    man was on the spot,
And to show respect for the management every
    ragman brought his mot.
I must admit that I brought mine at twenty-five
    minutes to eight,
And the first to stand up was Kieran Grace to tell me
    that I was late.

Then up jumps Humpy Soodelum, and he says, 'I
    think somehow,
By the way yiz are going on tonight, yiz are looking
    for a row;
Now look at here, Grace, if you want your face, you'd
    better not shout or bawl,
There's a lot of hard chaws to be here tonight, so
    respect the Ragman's Ball.'

Then we all sat down to some fish and chips, and
    every man was there,
Oh! and at the place of honour Billy Boland took the
    chair;
Well he swiped the chair and sold it to an old one in
    Carman Hall,
And he danced on the face of poor Kieran Grace the
    night of the Ragman's Ball.

Says my one, 'You're a quare one now, and Billy,
    you're hard to beat,'
When up jumps Liza Boland, and told her to hould
    her prate;
But my one made a clout at her, she missed and struck
    the wall,
And the two of them went in the ambulance the night
    of the Ragman's Ball.

Just to make the thing a swell affair, we all brought
    friends a few;
We brought up Blind Gort Whelan and Big Dan
    Kenny too;
And the gallant Jack Tar smoked his cigar, and slipped
    coming through the hall,
And he lost a new bag and all his swag the night of
    the Ragman's Ball.

To keep the house alive, my boys, we brought some
    music, too,
We brought up Tommy Reynolds and his old tin
    whistle too;
He played that night with all his might till coming on
    to dawn
But we couldn't find any to dance with Dan Kenny
    that night of the Ragman's Ball.

Well, for eating we had plenty, as much as we could hold,
We drank Brady's Loop-Line Porter till around the
　　floor we rolled,
In the midst of the confusion someone shouted for a
　　song,
When up jumped oul Dunlavin and sang, 'Keep rolling
　　your barrel along.'

So we all sat down to some ham parings when
　　everything was quiet,
Well, for broken noses I must say we had a lovely night;
Black eyes – they were in great demand, not to
　　mention split heads at all,
So if anyone wants to commit suicide let him come to
　　the Ragman's Ball.

Anonymous

This is one of the most evocative and effective of eighteenth-century Irish ballads. Mallow, County Cork, was then a fashionable spa town, Ireland's Bath. In the 'Long Room' there, dashing young men could drink chocolate (and other liquids), gamble, and speculate about which local beauties would attend that night's ball.

　The 'Sinking-fund' mentioned in verse 4 was a government contingency account, while in verse 7, 'racking' meant 'overcharging' and 'teizing' simply 'teasing'.

THE RAKES OF MALLOW

Beauing, belling, dancing, drinking,
　　Breaking windows, damning, sinking,
Ever raking, never thinking,
　　Live the Rakes of Mallow.

Spending faster than it comes,
　　Beating Bawds, and Whores, and Duns,
Bacchus' true begotten Sons,
　　Live the Rakes of Mallow.

One time nought but Claret drinking,
　　Then like Politicians thinking
To raise the Sinking-fund, when sinking,
　　Live the Rakes of Mallow.

One Time flush with Money Store,
　　Then as any poet poor,
Kissing Queens, and then the Whore,
　　Live the Rakes of Mallow.

When at home with Dadda dying,
　　Still for Mallow water crying,
But when there, good Claret plying,
　　Live the Rakes of Mallow.

Living short but merry Lives,
　　Going where the Devil drives,
Keeping Misses, but no Wives,
　　Live the Rakes of Mallow.

Racking tenants, Stewards teizing,
　　Swiftly spending, slowly raising,
Wishing to spend all our Days in
　　Raking thus at Mallow.

Thus to end a raking Life,
　　We grow sober, take a Wife,
Ever after live in strife,
　　Wish again for Mallow.

Anonymous

*In the 1940s and 1950s, the Irish Civil Service became the
object of a good deal of abuse, not least in* Dublin
Opinion, *which wondered whether the culture of 'jobs for
the boys' was really the cause that generations of Irish
patriots had fought and died for.*

THE REARING OF THE GREEN

Oh, I met with Napper Tandy and he took me by the
　　hand,
And he said, 'How's poor old Ireland, and how does
　　she stand?'
I said, 'Well, since you ask me, sir, the thing that
　　makes me nervous
Is, every second mother's son is in the Civil Service.'

Anonymous
('Pat')

Messages from the past are often ambiguous: as one looks back, was anything ever quite what it seemed? From TCD *Miscellany, March 1945.*

RETROSPECT

I remember, I remember a night of long ago –
There was me and cousin Margaret, and Dad and
    Uncle Joe.
There were crowds and crowds of people from the
    Bridge to College Green
All celebrating something – Was it Mafeking or the
    Queen?

There were grand illuminations – There were harps of
    green and white,
You'd have said that it was noonday, not the middle of
    the night.
And of course I didn't realise then, but now it's true I
    know
That a lot of lamps were shining very bright in Uncle
    Joe.

I was pushed and squashed and trodden on, but I was
    proud and grand,
And I wasn't really frightened as I clutched my father's
    hand.
And my bosom swelled with fervour, and I've not the
    slightest doubt
That I cheered when Uncle Joe did. What was it all
    about?

ER Rexfort

This is one of a rash of songs about Oscar Wilde that became popular after his sensational tour of the United States in 1882.

WILDE OSCAR WILDE

Oh, Lucy, my aesthetic darling,
My lily, my sunflower, my soul,

Thou star that enchantest the starling,
While moons with pale aureoles roll,
This night we shall sit in sweet sorrow,
And list to an aesthetic child;
I've ma-a-a-anaged two dollars to borrow
That we might go hear Oscar Wilde.

Chorus:
Oh, Ah, Ah, Oh, isn't it sweet to be utter!
Too utterly utterly sweet!
Oh kiss me! But say 'ere we go, dear,
We'd better get something to eat.

Would'st listen to something aesthetic,
Then put on thy gown of sage green,
Go rub off that rouge and cosmetic,
And try to look sallow and lean,
Let thy hair thy lank shoulders flow down on,
Stare off into infinite space,
How u-u-u-utterly you'll look with that gown on
When we glide up the hall to our place.

Oh, Lucy, how utter our bliss is,
Tonight when the stork is at roost,
When the star pelts the sunflower with kisses,
Aesthetics will take a big boost,
I shall clasp in lithe fingers a lily,
A sunflower swoon in thy hair,
Oh, I-I-I-I would be utterly happy
If I had knee breeches to wear.

Anonymous

Riddles of this sort are common in Irish – and indeed in early English – traditions. This one is remembered in The Tailor and Ansty – *and may have helped to get the book banned.*

A RIDDLE

My back it is deal,
My belly's the same,
            And my sides are well bound with good leather.

My nose it is brass,
There's a hole in my ass,
    And I'm very much used in cold weather.

Thorold Rogers

*JE Thorold Rogers (1825–1990) was an English MP and
economic historian. This jaundiced view of David la
Touche and the other political founders of the Bank of
Ireland was published, rather surprisingly perhaps, by the
Catholic Truth Society of Ireland in a 1919 collection of
'Popular and Patriotic Poetry'.*

THE BANK OF IRELAND,
FORMERLY THE IRISH SENATE HOUSE.

We all know that Judas was led to betray
    The Master he served for his own dirty pelf;
But he proved his repentance by casting away
    The cash he received and by hanging himself.

The Irish political traitors of old
    Higgled, bargained, and lastly, their country
        betrayed,
Judas got only silver; they stood for gold,
    And both won the scorn of the parties who paid.

Here the parallel ends; he repented, not they;
    He hanged himself – they were too shrewd to be
        rash,
For on the same spot where they settled the pay
    They erected a Bank and invested the cash.

Amanda M. Ros

*The wife of the stationmaster of Larne, Country Antrim,
Amanda M'Kittrick Ros (1860–1939) became famous as a
sort of prose McGonagall. Her poetry, too, was delightfully
inept, and never more so than when musing on the subject
of death.*

ON VISITING WESTMINSTER ABBEY A 'REDUCED DIGNITY' INVITED ME TO MUSE ON ITS MERITS

Holy Moses! Have a look!
Flesh decayed in every nook!
Some rare bits of brain lie here,
Mortal loads of beef and beer,
Some of whom are turned to dust,
Every one bids lost to lust;
Royal flesh so tinged with 'blue'
Undergoes the same as you.
Wealth and lands were theirs to boast,
Yachts lying nigh to every coast,
Homage from the million theirs
Clad in gold and gorgeous wares.
Here they lie who had such store,
Move a muscle – nevermore;
Dead as all before them died:
Richer man are you beside,
Begging as you walk your way,
Life still yours while dead are they:
All the refuse lying here
Has no life to give it cheer.
Alas! You stand above them all
Tho' poverty did you befall.
Life was thine, once noble lord!
Now you tramp on their record.
Tributes of 'Masonic Love'
Shall not passports prove Above.
Slabs of monumental art
Tell the sycophants' remarks.
Noble once, these dead folk now,
Darkness stamped have on their brow.
All portrays without – within
Lots of love and shoals of sin.
Famous some were – yet they died:
Poets – Statesmen – Rogues beside,
Kings, Queens, all of them do rot.
What about them? Now – they're not!

Mrs Ros could be very angry, particularly with critics and lawyers – this insult is reproduced as it appears in her Poems of Puncture *(1913), even down to the misspelling in the first line.*

EPITAPH ON LARGEBONES – THE LAWYER

Beneath me hear in stinking clumps,
Lies Lawyer Largebones all in lumps;
A rotten mass of clockholed clay,
Which grows more honeycombed each day.
See how the rats have scratched his face?
Now so unlike the human race;
I very much regret *I* can't
Assist them in their eager 'bent'.

Darby Ryan

*As the story goes, this celebrated satirical ballad was first
heard one Sunday in 1830 when Darby Ryan (1777-1856),
astride his horse, sang it to the congregation as they came
out of the village church in Bansha, County Tipperary. In
the first verse, the 'wizzen' is the throat – and 'Peelers' were,
of course, members of the Irish constabulary, named after
its founder, Robert Peel.*

THE PEELER AND THE GOAT

Oh the Bansha Peelers went out one night
On duty and patrolling O,
They met a goat upon the road
And took him for being a-strolling O,
With bay'nets fix'd they sallied forth
And caught him by the wizzen O,
And then swore out a mighty oath,
They'd send him off to prison O.

'Oh, mercy, sir!' the goat replied,
'And let me tell my story O
I am no Rogue, no Ribbonman,
No Croppy, Whig, or a Tory O;
I'm guilty not of any crime
Of petty or high treason O,

And our tribe is wanted at this time,
For this is the ranting season O.'

'It is in vain for to complain
Or give your tongue such bridle O,
You're absent from your dwellingplace
Disorderly and idle O.
Your hoary locks will not prevail,
Nor your sublime oration O,
For Peeler's Act will you transport,
On your own information O.'

'No penal laws I did transgress
By deeds or combination O,
I have no certain place of rest,
No home or habitation O.
But Bansha is my dwellingplace,
Where I was bred and born O,
I'm descended from an honest race,
That's all the trade I've learned O.'

I will chastise your insolence
And violent behaviour O;
Well bound to Cashel you'll be sent,
Where you will gain no favour O.
The magistrates will all consent
To sign your condemnation O;
From there to Cork you will be sent
For speedy transportation O.'

'This parish an' this neighbourhood
Are peaceable and tranquil O;
There's no disturbance here, thank God!
And long may it continue so.
I don't regard your oath a pin,
Or sign for my committal O,
My jury will be gentlemen
And grant me my acquittal O.'

'The consequence be what it will,
A peeler's power I'll let you know,
I'll handcuff you, at all events,
And march you off to Bridewell O.
And sure, you rogue, you can't deny
Before the judge or jury O,

Intimidation with your horns,
And threatening me with fury O.'

'I make no doubt but you are drunk,
With whiskey, rum, or brandy O.
Or you wouldn't have such gallant spunk
To be so bold or manly O.
You readily would let me pass
If I had money handy O,
To treat you to a poteen glass –
'Tis then I'd be the dandy O.'

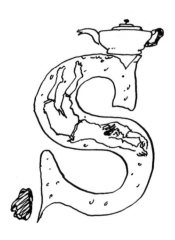

Anonymous

*HMcD: Years ago I got this wonderful skit of a ballad from
Tony McAuley, a great figure at the BBC in Belfast and a fine
folk singer.*

'A SAILOR COURTED A FARMER'S DAUGHTER'

A sailor courted a farmer's daughter
Who lived contagious to the town of Strabane.
With melodious words he did besought her
And begged her not to look at any other art or
    contagion of a man.

Now that farmer's daughter had a proud possession –
A silver taypot and two pound twelve in gold:
'Would ye marry me, my sweet salt water sailor,
If I had nothing in the world at all and wrapped all my
    possessions into a bundle and threw them into the
    bottom of the deep blue ocean cold?'

'I would marry you, my heart's contentment,
If you'd nothing in the world but your old mother's
    curse.'
So she wrapped all her possessions up into a bundle
    and threw them into the say,
And that ends my verse.

But that salt water sailor he could swim like a duckeen,
So he took off his clothes and dived down deep below,
And then swam away with the bundle laughing,
Thinking of all the grand times he was going to have
    drinking her fortune away with his friends and
    family when he got back to his own home just a
    mile and a half outside the town of Ballinasloe.

But that farmer's daughter nearly shite herself
    laughing,
For there was nothing in the bundle but an old
    petrallion of a stone.
Oh a sailor boyo courted a farmer's daughter –
But now he just wished he'd got the hell out of that
    and left the wee girl alone.

A SCATTERING OF LIMERICKS

'A YOUNG LADY REPORTER FROM YOUGHAL'

A young lady reporter from Youghal
Wore a newspaper dress at a ball
    But the dress caught on fire
    And burned her entire
Front page, sporting section and all.

*The limerick, of which the one above is an anonymous
specimen, is perhaps the quintessential light verse form. It
possibly owes its origin to a small group of alcoholics in or
around the Limerick village of Croom in the mid-eighteenth
century. Known as the 'Maigue poets', they took to abusing
each other in verses that are recognizably limericks, despite
being written in the Irish language. James Clarence Mangan
translated some of these into English in the 1840s; by then the
form had already became widespread in Britain, where it was
being made famous by Edward Lear and others.*

    *An entire book could be made of examples from Ireland:
we have room here for only a few, beginning with Mangan's
– relatively loose – translations from originals by the Maigue
poets Seán Ó Tuama ('the Merry', 1706–1775) and Aindreas
Mac Craith ('the Jolly Pedlar', 1708–1795?):*

O'TUOMY'S DRINKING SONG

I sell the best brandy and sherry,
To make my good customers merry;
 But, at times their finances
 Run short, as it chances,
And then I feel very sad, very!

Here's brandy! Come, fill up your tumbler,
Or ale, if your liking be humbler,
 And, while you've a shilling,
 Keep filling and swilling –
A fig for the growls of the grumbler!

I like, when I'm quite at my leisure,
Mirth, music, and all sorts of pleasure.
 When Margery's bringing
 The glass, I like singing
With bards – if they drink within measure.

Libation I pour on libation,
I sing the past fame of our nation,
 For valour-won glory,
 For song and for story,
This, this is my grand recreation!

ANDREW MAGRATH'S REPLY TO JOHN O'TUOMY

O, Tuomy! you boast yourself handy
At selling good ale and bright brandy,
 But the fact is your liquor
 Makes everyone sicker,
I tell you that, I, your friend Andy.

Again, you affect to be witty,
And your customers – more is the pity –
 Give in to your folly,
 While you, when you're jolly,
Troll forth some ridiculous ditty.

But your poems and pints, by your favour,
Are alike wholly wanting in flavour;
 Because it's your pleasure,
 You give us short measure,
And your ale has a ditch-water savour!

Vile swash do you sell us for porter,
And you draw the cask shorter and shorter;
    Your guests, then, disdaining
    To think of complaining,
Go tipple in some other quarter.

Very oft in your scant overfrothing
Tin quarts we found little or nothing;
    They could very ill follow
    The road, who would swallow
Such stuff for their inner man's clothing!

You sit gaily enough at the table,
But in spite of your mirth you are able
    To chalk down each tankard,
    And if a man drank hard
On tick – oh! we'd have such a Babel!

You bow to the floor's very level,
When customers enter to revel,
    But if one in shy raiment
    Takes drink without payment,
You score it against the poor devil.

When quitting your house rather heady,
They'll get nought without more of 'the ready.'
    You leave them to stumble
    And stagger, and tumble
Into dykes, as folk will when unsteady.

Two vintners late went about killing
Men's fame by their vile Jack-and-Gilling;
    Now, Tuomy, I tell you
    I know very well you
Would, too, sell us all for a shilling.

The Old Bards never vainly shall woo me,
But your tricks and your capers, O'Tuomy,
    Have nought in them winning –
    You jest and keep grinning,
But your thoughts are all guileful and gloomy!

* * *

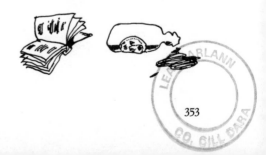

Nineteenth-century rhymesters sometimes used the limerick as just another verse form. There were several entertaining efforts along these (anonymous) lines. A 'jazey' (verse 2) was a type of bob wig.

THE HERO OF BALLINACRAZY

When I lived in sweet Ballinacrazy, dear,
The girls were all bright as a daisy, dear;
    When I gave them a smack,
    They whispered, good lack!
And cried, Paddy, now can't you be aisy, dear?

First I married Miss Dolly O'Daisy, dear,
She had two swivel eyes, wore a jazey, dear;
    Then to fat Miss Malone,
    Weighing seventeen stone;
Then to lanthorn-jaw'd skinny O'Crazy, dear.

Then I married Miss Dorothy Taisy, dear,
A toast once in Ballinacrazy, dear;
    Her left leg was good,
    But its fellow was wood,
And she hopped like a duck round a daisy, dear.

Then I married her sister, Miss Taisy, dear,
But she turned out so idle and lazy, dear;
    That I took from the peg
    My deceased lady's leg,
For to leather the live one when lazy, dear.

Then I picked up rich old Mother Hazy, dear,
She'd a cough, and employ'd Dr Blazy, dear,
    But some drops that he gave
    Dropp'd her into her grave,
And her cash very soon made me aisy, dear.

Then says I to old Father O'Mazy, dear,
'Don't my weddings and funerals plase ye, dear?'
    'Oh,' says he, 'you blackguard,
    Betwixt church and churchyard,
Sure, you never will let me be aisy, dear.'

Oh, ladies, I live but to plase ye, dear,
I'm the hero of Ballinacrazy, dear;
    I'll marry you all,

Lean, fat, short, and tall,
One after the other to plase ye, dear.

* * *

*Though the long poem of linked limericks was to have little
future, the solo five-line verse would go on to glory. The
early doyen of the form was of course Edward Lear
(1812-1888), among whose few works of Irish interest is the
following limerick about the McDonnell stronghold,
Dunluce Castle. It may not be his best:*

There was an old man of Dunluce
Who went out to sea on a goose,
  When he'd gone out a mile,
  He observed with a smile,
'It is time I returned to Dunluce.'

* * *

*The limerick lends itself particularly to the bawdy (and
further on in this section some of Gogarty's spicier effusions
may be found), but there have also been good limericks on
history, literary criticism and even theological philosophy.
The famous serve-and-volley exchange below, of which the
first has been attributed to Ronald Knox (1888-1957) and the
second to nobody, neatly summarises the central hypothesis
of the late Bishop of Cloyne:*

'GEORGE BERKELEY AND GOD: AN EXCHANGE'

There once was a man who said, 'God
Must think it exceedingly odd
  If He finds that this tree
  Continues to be
When there's no one about in the Quad.'

'Dear Sir:
Your astonishment's odd:
I am always about in the Quad
  And that's why the tree
  Will continue to be,
Since observed by,
   Yours faithfully,
    God.'

* * *

In the 1960s Odearest Mattresses offered prizes for limericks chosen for their weekly front page advertisements in the Irish Times. *Here are three representatives of the hundreds that were printed:*

'PATRICK KAVANAGH'
(Anonymous)

Just now with the advent of Spring
We agree that all poets must sing,
  For the poems I have made
  Put all verse in the shade,
For the 'spring' in ODEAREST'S the thing.

'MYLES NA GOPALEEN'
(Anonymous)

Omniscient omnipotent Myles
Writes a column in multiple styles,
  While chastising the nation
  He gets inspiration
From ODEAREST – a Buddha all smiles.

'AFTER THE FALL'
(JR Croft)

On ODEAREST a patient named Paul
Relaxed on receiving a fall.
  He got better, not worse,
  Took a turn for the nurse
And went off to the Jervis St Ball.

       ★ ★ ★

Also in the 1960s, while Robert Wyse Jackson was Bishop of Limerick, a limerick competition was held in the city. Under an assumed name, he sent in two, and was amazed to be awarded first place with this – decidedly limp – effort:

THE ORIGIN OF THE LIMERICK

A landlord from Maigueside, Ó Tuomy,
Hated verses long winded and gloomy,
  On the limerick he hit
  For its scarifying wit,
In a setting sufficiently roomy.

When told he had won, he recited the wrong entry to a
television interviewer, assuming it to be marginally the
better of the two:

THE MAIGUE POETS

The traditional poets of the Maigue
Knew nothing of White Horse or Haig,
    But uiscebah hot
    Distilled in a pot
Kept them merry, poetic and vague.

The subsequent confusion led to mutterings that the whole
thing must have been a fix, so the bishop felt it best to return
the £5 prize money ('to help with administration costs'). A
few days later, the postman brought him a bottle of Dimple
Haig whisky, sent by a grateful distillery. This was NOT
returned. Instead he thanked the firm in verse:

If those old poets of Maigue
Had known about your lovely Haig,
    Their uiscebah hot
    Distilled in a pot
Would all have been thrown in the Maigue.

Sadly, there were to be no more bottles.

* * *

Many years ago, another Church of Ireland cleric, the late
Canon Coslett Quin, came up with the following unique
limerick, which he had written in the dialect of his native
Antrim:

'AN ANTRIM LIMERICK'

There was a wee fellow frae Clough
Who was fu', an' fell in till a sheugh.
    But the glar an' the japs
    Came up till his chaps
So the puir crayture couldnae e'en say 'ogh'.

* * *

For some reason, James Joyce has often been subjected to limerickification. The present editors find that they have one each about him in their bottom drawers, and can think of no better occasion to take them out:

ULYSSES BY JAMES JOYCE
(Hector McDonnell)

The tragedy of poor Molly Bloom
Was to be trapped in a tale of such gloom
    About Dublin's decay
    And her husband's long day
Pondering on birth, faith, class, death, fried kidneys,
    strange odours, bodily functions, the privy and the
    womb.

JOYCE'S VOICES
(Seán Jackson)

There was nobody purer than Joyce
When he sang in his light tenor voice,
    But when Bloom and his Mrs
    Had their day in *Ulrs*,
His language was (fictionally) choice.

The writers of the following enchanting Joycean entries to yet another contest, the Galway Nora Barnacle House Limerick Competition, 1995, were both twelve years old:

'A CIVILIZED MAN'
(Elaine Ward)

James was born in 1882
And he never got the flu.
    He was an Irish writer
    But never a fighter.
And he was such a civilized man
That he wouldn't drink a can
And he never even beat up a man.

'AT THE LAKE'
(Andrea McGowan)

Joyce went out one day
In the sunny month of May

He went down to the lake
And wrote *Finnegans Wake*
And that's when his hair turned grey.

* * *

*Indeed, one of the delights of the limerick is how our
expectations of the form can be neatly thwarted to good
effect. Here are two anonymous examples that demonstrate
what may be achieved:*

'THE STING'

There was a young man of Tralee
Who was stung on the neck by a wasp.
    When they asked did it hurt
    He replied: 'Not a bit,
It can do it again if it likes.'

* * *

A RHYME OF LLANFAIR P.G.

When the soldiers passed through Llanfair-pwllgwyn-
   gyllgogerychwyrndropwll-llantysiliogogogoch,
'My kingdom,' I cried, 'for a gwllgwyngyll-
   gogerychwyrndropwll-llantysiliogogogoch.'
    They said to me: 'Fudge!
    Twenty miles you must trudge.'
So I cursed like a native of Fwllgwyngyllgogery-
   chwyrndropwll-llantysiliogogogoch.

* * *

After that example of overseas exotica from TCD
Miscellany, *we end this section with the ubiquitous
Gogarty, without a doubt the most successful Irish
perpetrator of the limerick – good ones are often attributed
to him on the flimsiest of evidence. Here is a small handful
of the best of them, taken from* The Poems & Plays of
Oliver St John Gogarty, *edited by AN Jeffares.*

THE YOUNG MAID OF MADRAS

There was a young maid of Madras
Who had a most beautiful ass.
    It was not round and pink,
    As you bastards might think:
It was grey with long ears and ate grass.

A PROFESSOR OF TRINITY HALL

A professor of Trinity Hall
Possessed an octagonal ball
    The cube of whose weight
    Plus penis, plus eight
Was four-fifths of nine-tenths of fuck all.

A YOUNG GIRL OF PEORIA

There was a young girl of Peoria
Who was raped by Sir Gerald du Maurier;
    Next, by three men,
    Sir Gerald again,
And the chef at the Waldorf Astoria.

– and possibly the most celebrated of all Gogarty's (alleged) writings:

THE YOUNG MAN FROM ST JOHN'S

There was a young man from St John's
Who wanted to roger the swans.
    'Oh no!' said the porter,
    'Oblige with my daughter,
But the birds are reserved for the dons.'

Thomas Shalvey

In DJ O'Donoghue's 1894 anthology, The Humour of Ireland, *Shalvey is described as a Dublin market-gardener who wrote songs for James Kearney to sing at 'several music-halls and inferior concert-rooms' in the city. This one dates from about 1850.*

In the first verse a 'shough' is a puff on somebody's

*'dhudeen', or pipe; in the last verse 'Nabocklish' means,
more or less, 'It doesn't matter'.*

SAINT KEVIN AND KING O'TOOLE

As Saint Kevin once was travelling through a place
    called Glendalough,
He chanced to meet with King O'Toole, and asked
    him for a *shough*;
Said the king, 'You are a stranger, for your face I've
    never seen,
But if you have a taste o' weed, I'll lend you my
    dhudeen.'

While the saint was kindling up the pipe the monarch
    fetched a sigh;
'Is there anything the matter,' says the saint, 'that
    makes you cry?'
Said the king, 'I had a gander, that was left me by my
    mother,
And this morning he cocked up his toes with some
    disease or other.'

'And are you crying for the gander, you unfortunate
    ould goose?
Dhry up your tears, in frettin', sure, there's ne'er a bit
    o' use;
As you think so much about the bird, if I make him
    whole and sound,
Will you give to me the taste o' land the gander will
    fly round?'

'In troth I will, and welcome,' said the king, 'give
    what you ask;'
The saint bid him bring out the bird, and he'd begin
    the task;
The king went into the palace to fetch him out the
    bird,
Though he'd not the least intention of sticking to his
    word.

Saint Kevin took the gander from the arms of the
    king,
He first began to tweak his beak, and then to pull his
    wing,

He hooshed him up into the air – he flew thirty miles
    around;
Said the saint, 'I'll thank your majesty for that little bit
    o' ground.'

The king, to raise a ruction next, he called the saint a
    witch,
And sent in for his six big sons, to heave him in the
    ditch;
'*Nabocklish*,' said Saint Kevin, 'I'll soon settle these
    young urchins,'
So he turned the king and his six sons into the seven
    churches.

Anonymous

*A more prosaic view than FS Mahony's of the celebrated
Cork bell-tower was offered by Frank O'Connor in his no-
nonsense travel book,* Irish Miles *(1947), which quotes this
stray couplet – probably from another version of 'The Boys
of Fairhill' (see page 26).*

'SHANDON STEEPLE'

… Shandon Steeple stands up straight,
Coppinger's Lane is undernate.

George Bernard Shaw

*The author (1856–1950) claimed that his 'Opus No. 1' was
this (clearly very youthful) composition.*

'VERSE FOR USE WHILE PETTING A DOG'

Dumpitydoodledum big bowwow
Dumpitydoodledum dandy.

Today's visitors to Coole Park will notice that the great
house has been torn down; still, as an alternative attraction
they will find these verses engraved in facsimile on a series
of stone slabs there. They are taken from five postcards sent
by Shaw as a 'thank you' to Lady Gregory's granddaughters
in or around the early 1920s.

'APPLES FROM COOLE PARK'

Two ladies of Galway, called Cath'rine and Anna,
Whom some call Acushla and some call Alanna
On finding the gate of the fruit garden undone
Stole Grandmamma's apples and sent them to
    London.

And Grandmamma said that the poor village
    schoolchildren
Were better behaved than the well-brought-up Coole
    children
And threatened them with the most merciless
    whippings
If ever again they laid hands on her pippins.

In vain they explained that the man who was
    battening
On Grandmamma's apples would die without
    fattening
She seized the piano
And threw it at Anna
Then shrieking at Catherine 'Just let me catch you'
She walloped her hard with the drawing-room statue.

'God save us, Herself is gone crazy' cried Marian
'Is this how a lady of title should carry on?'
'If you dare to address me like that,' shouted Granny,
'Goodbye to your wages: you shan't have a penny:
Go back to your pots and your pans and your
    canisters'
With that she threw Marian over the banisters.

'And now' declared granny, 'I feel so much better
That I'll write Mr Shaw a most beautiful letter
And tell him how happy our lives are at Coole
Under Grandmamma Darling's beneficent rule.'

Eugene Sheehy

Eugene Sheehy was born in 1883, the year after James Joyce, who as a young man enjoyed evenings of charades, songs and light verse in the Sheehy household. This hymn to Bovril (as written by Wordsworth in his 'Lucy' mode) is the sort of thing Joyce might have heard there. Sheehy, who later became a Circuit Court judge, died in 1958.

BOVRIL

There dwelt among the untrodden ways,
   Beside the Hill of Slane,
An ox whose duty was to graze
   And then to graze again.

And this Ox with a brother strayed;
   He never had a wife –
It was the only friend he made
   In his poor bovine life.

Alas! the brother had to go
   Unto the Fair of Trim,
And now he's in a jar, and O!
   The difference to him!

Niall Sheridan

Niall Sheridan (1912–1998) was part of the UCD generation that included Brian O'Nolan, Donagh Mac Donagh, Charles Donnelly and Cyril Cusack. He published these verses privately in 1934.

PORTRAIT OF A CHRISTIAN HE-MAN

John Aloysius Herbert Pimp,
Good Christian, yet quite hearty,
A thoroughly delightful imp –
The soul of every party.

In student days our hero had
No leanings towards Divinity,
Although he licked a sneering cad
For libelling the Trinity.

His tolerant eye looks not askance
At gambling, if the stakes are slight;
'Tis quite allowable to dance
With girls who never hold too tight.

He leads no musty Temperance Guild,
No toper can John Pimp upbraid –
In countless taverns he has swilled
Hugh quantities of lemonade.

In short, he shuns the ways of old,
He drops Savonarola's tack,
And brings the erring to the fold
With hearty slaps upon the back.

Richard Brinsley Sheridan

*This comes from the playwright's (1751–1816) only comic
opera,* The Duenna *(1775).*

SONG

Give Isaac the nymph who no beauty can boast;
But health and good humour to make her his toast,
If strait, I don't mind whether slender or fat,
And six feet or four – we'll ne'er quarrel for that.

Whate'er her complexion, I vow I don't care,
If brown it is lasting, more pleasing if fair;
And tho' in her cheeks I no dimples should see,
Let her smile, and each dell is a dimple to me.

Let her locks be the reddest that ever were seen,
And her eyes may be e'en any colour but green,
For in eyes, tho' so various in lustre and hue,
I swear I've no choice, only let her have two.

'Tis true I'd dispense with a throne on her back,
And white teeth I own, are genteeler than black,
A little round chin too's a beauty I've heard,
But I only desire she mayn't have a beard.

James Simmons

This much-missed Ulster poet (1933–2001), was occasionally criticized for his airily honest approach to matters of the flesh: his, he said, was 'not a moral muse'.

CAVALIER LYRIC

I sometimes sleep with other girls
In boudoir or cheap joint,
With energy and tenderness
Trying not to disappoint.
So do not think of helpful whores
As aberrational blots;
I could not love you half so well
Without my practice shots.

Anonymous

Just before Lent each year for well over a century, scurrilous verses known as the Skellig (or 'Sceilig') Lists caused great mirth as they passed from hand to hand through parishes in parts of Kerry and Cork. Intended to shame local bachelors and spinsters into marriage, they often caused offence, and so poets disguised themselves behind deliberate errors in spelling and grammar.

The tradition drew on the folk memory that, since Lenten weddings were not permitted, couples had once sailed away to be married in the island monastery of Skellig Michael, off the Kerry coast, where an anomaly with the calendar meant that Lent came late. Rumour had it that the practice had been stopped after drunken orgies and the like on 'Skellig Night' ...

This example, collected from a lady near Castlegregory, is one of the last of the Lists, and possibly the first to be published in its entirety. Names have been changed to protect the innocent.

A SKELLIG LIST, 1951

The Sceilig ship is on the bay the 'Mad Rover' is its name
And its cargo of Bachelors and old Maidens we'll list on the role of fame

The voyage to the Sceiligs may be calm or may be
    rough
But those who stick it out will be seasoned and tough.

The first to step on board the ship was the lazy
    Michael Lynne
Who will have to wait another year before he can
    begin
Two years ago he made a break but it was all in vain
And when he saw 'Tom Slops' fat lass he said he'd try
    again.

At Ballyglass in Annascaul the night was dark and
    windy
Who should I meet coming up the street but Buckley
    and Minnie shy
The next I met was the jobber Breen looking for his
    coat
I said I saw it on Buckley who was acting like the
    Dingle Puck Goat.

Next is Paddy Connolly the swank from Boherbwee
Only for his opponent Patrick Breen what a happy
    man he'd be
From Dingle side there came a lass her name was
    Doreen Britten
Young Tom came on and took her off and left the
    Paddys sitting.

From year to year I see him here Bill Miles the pip
    Detecter
I am sure there is twenty more for him upon the
    'Hanging Dresser'
One day in search of pulp Lizzie Hanlons he did make
Although he got none he'd lots of fun and devoured a
    Xmas cake.

Our musician Patsy Rea who hails from
    Knockmealmore
The hinges he has torn almost off Jeff Millers cabin
    door
He's badly struck in Dora Fay, he say she is the one
And when he get his way they will wheel around
    the fun.

The Sec. of the Clash G.A.A. his name is Edward Breen
Working for old women he is so awful keen
Two years he has been courting that lass they call
    Noreen
But across the seas in a foreign land for the past few
    weeks she has been.

Ye all know Tim Taylor that lad so full of game
He took a trip across the Irish Sea but there he got no
    dame
And now he is back again and Mick Harvey he has
    done out
About Britten they had an argument and it ended in a
    bout.

The next is C.J. Breen the two pence half-penny
    jobber
In courting Patty Fitz he seems to be getting great
    bother
He has a tidy farm and stocks old ewes and rams
But when he'll wed his Patty he'll have to stock some
    prams.

Now Daniel Breen of Conna he is Paddy Parry's right
    hand man
He is in love with Doreen Kavanagh and they say he is
    dead on
Doreen is a beauty the sweetest of them all
But I am sure there's poor hope for Daniel if Rob
    Goggin cares at all.

Our Captain Jimmy Britten his football days are gone
He's courting Mollie McGarry and he say he'll be the
    man
He's out all night with rabbits and sometimes catches
    one
And when he come around the Cross he boasts of
    what he done.

Next Phil Hanrahan he thinks he is a mechanic
If this does not get the lady for him he'll be in an
    awful panic
He often takes a trip to the village of Annascaul
And if there is anything wrong with his Eileen
    Connolly he's sure to fix it all.

The next upon the list is Ben Fitz's daughter Meg
Her Auntie has a lot of cash and she is sure to be her
   heir
This proud maid is now engaged to Mulligan's delicate
   son
And the day they will be married will be a day for fun.

Christine Hanley is the next who is so small and pale
But oh her courting story is a sad and mournful tale
First Don Hanlon left her down then it was Dicky
   Penn
Now she is sad and lonesome and finished up with
   men.

Our little Maisie Casey she is a pretty dame
She has had a go with all the boys but I do not know
   all the names
In Doran's Pete she was deadly struck and taught
   she'd got some where,
But Nora Browne was too sly and sadly left her there.

Next is Nancy Hanley she thinks she is a Queen
Her singing in the choir is enough to make you screem
She is fond of those dances and attend them every
   night
But Cassidy make so little of her that he go where
   ever he like.

At Castle town the 11th of March a team will take the
   field
But a man just 'Old Legs' this parish cannot yield.
His football boots he has hung up and now its women
   and beer
And if he does not get sensible its the 'County Home'
   I fear.

The last is Minnie Hanrahan who once was of men so
   shy
But now she has change her methods and she is very
   sly,
To find out who she is going with is a job too much
   for me
But when she's down in Maharees tis Drummonds for
   the tea.

I must conclude a finish but I had some more to say
All my friends who are not in this I'll deal with some
    other day
When some of you are married and have a child or
    two
Remember they will be out all night just doing what
    you did do.

Frank Sparrow

*A gently satirical account of artistic pretensions in the pre-
1916 Dublin of George Moore, the Orpens and the Yeats
brothers. Sparrow, an architect by profession, wrote the
verses to celebrate the Club's move to new premises in St
Stephen's Green.*

THE ARTS CLUB CIRCULAR

If you long for things artistic,
If you revel in the nebulous and mystic,
If your hair's too long
And your tie's all wrong
And your speech is symbolistic;
If your tastes are democratic
And your mode of life's essentially erratic;
If you seek success
From no fixed address,
But you sleep in somone's attic,
        Join the Arts Club, join the Arts Club,
        Where the souls do congregate,
        Where observance of convention
        Arouses fierce dissension;
        In the Arts Club, in the Arts Club,
        You may sit and dissertate,
        If your trousers bag and your coat-tails sag,
        You'll probably be hailed as great.

Now although the Club's exclusive,
The hereditary element's elusive,
But the presence at the helm
Of a peer of the realm
To a high tone's found conducive.
There are clever folks who lecture,

There are several who live by architecture,
While the Club is rife
With folk whose life
Is a matter of conjecture.
        In the Arts Club, etc.

If you feel a fool, don't show it,
And don't ever let a single person know it,
But join the Club
And pay your sub,
And you'll find yourself a poet;
Don't be a base secessionist –
If a painter, you are bound to be progressionist;
For though it hurts,
Forswear boiled shirts,
And become a Post-Impressionist:
        Join the Arts Club, etc.

If your talents are not patent,
But your taste for domesticity is latent;
If you think aloud
In the presence of a crowd
And your voice is fairly blatant;
If you're moved to thoughts symbolical
By proximity to liquids alcoholical,
If a pint of beer
Makes you a seer
Of visions apostolical:
        Join the Arts Club, etc.

If for Art you've no utility,
If your mind is somewhat lacking in agility,
You can still have tea,
From half-past three,
In complete respectability;
Don't imagine that you need be boisterous –
There's a regular department for the roisterous –
They pursue their horrid revels,
Down at subterranean levels,
In a dungeon damp and cloisterous,
        In the Arts Club, etc.

Margery Stapleton

Sometimes very young children produce verses that simply cannot be improved upon. Here are two charming examples, written when the poet (b. 1962) was about five years old.

THE ROCK OF CASHEL

The Rock of Cashel,
Old and grey,
Bits crumble down
Every day.

... and ...

LOVELY JESUS

Lovely Jesus,
Kind and gentle,
Loves the weak
And loves the mental.

John Stevenson

The potato-loving author, an Ulsterman who died in 1932, published these verses in a volume called Pat M'Carty: Farmer, of Antrim: His Rhymes with a Setting *(1903).*

ODE TO A PRATIE

Thy name is Murphy. On the Antrim hills
There's cruffles and white-rocks; there's skerries, too,
    and dukes,
And kidneys – which is early; and champions and
    flukes –
Which doesn't help the farmer much to pay his bills:
The sort's not recommended. Then there's early rose,
And forty-folds, and flounders – which is bad;
And magnum bonums: – if good seed's to be had
It is the biggest pratie that the country grows,
And tastes not bad. Some grows best in rigs
And some in drills. There's sorts ye cudn't ate;
There's others dry and floury that's a trate;

And weeshy kinds, that's only fit for pigs.
Some likes a sandy sile and some a turfy,
Others do their best in good stiff clay:
There's new varieties appearin' iv'ry day;
But, as I said, thy fam'ly name is Murphy.

Swate lump, thou art beluv'd. Folks dress'd in silk,
And them in tatthers, too raggit to be seen,
Agree to ate ye. Our own beluvit Queen,
She takes her pratie with a sup o' milk;
She's homely in her ways. On his goolden throne
The Zar o' Rooshia, whin he's freezin' cowld,
Calls for a plateful o' ye – so I'm towld.
And in her wee bit cabin, Peg Malone –
God bless the cratur – she ates praties too;
She takes her fingers, while the Duke o' York
And sich like gintry maybe use a fork.
I don't know much o' what the big folks do,
But all extol thy vartues and exalt
Thy fame. I s'pose I needn't say,
Like many a thing we hear o' iv'ry day,
It's best to take ye with a grain o' salt.

THE WAY WE TELL A STORY

Says I to him, I says, says I,
Says I to him, I says,
The thing, says I, I says to him
Is just, says I, this ways.
I hev', says I, a gret respeck
For you and for your breed,
And onything I cud, I says,
I'd do, I wud indeed.
I don't know any man, I says,
I'd do it for, says I,
As fast, I says, as for yoursel',
That's telling ye no lie.
There's nought, says I, I wudn't do,
To plase your feyther's son,
But this, I says, ye see, says I,
I says, it can't be done.

LAG Strong

An all-round 'man of letters' rather than a mere poet,
Strong (1896–1958) is well on the way to being forgotten,
despite his dozens of biographies, novels and books of verse.
But posterity is a fickle jade:

A MEMORY

When I was as high as that
I saw a poet in his hat.
I think the poet must have smiled
At such a solemn gazing child.

Now wasn't it a funny thing
To get a sight of J. M. Synge,
And notice nothing but his hat?
Yet life is often queer like that.

THE BREWER'S MAN

Have I wife? Bedam I have!
    But we was badly mated:
I hit her a great clout one night,
    And now we're separated.

And mornin's, going to my work,
    I meets her on the quay:
'Good mornin' to ye, ma'am,' says I;
    'To hell with ye,' says she.

Alexander Stuart

In the 1920s Canon Alexander Stuart (1868–1942) was
Church of Ireland Rector of Stradbally, County Laois. He
wrote these verses after a picnic at the Rock of Cashel with
Dean Phair of Ossory and Dean Carmody of Down; Canon
Campbell of Grangegorman was also in attendance.

RIVAL DEANS: A LAY OF CASHEL

Once upon a time two worthy Deans together
A visit paid to Cashel's lofty shrine.
They chose, accommodated by the weather,
Upon the grass hard by the walls to dine.

The very reverend gentleman from Down,
Whose fame in antiquaries' lists is sounded,
Portly might well be termed: from calf to crown
Majestically curved, not to say rounded.

While he of Ossory, who sweetly sways
St Canice's fame, I dare not call him skinnier,
But one might say his figure, minus stays,
Follows a pattern strictly rectilinear.

Behold them here, while groundlings chew and swill,
No bite has passed their lips, nor will it pass;
Each waits upon his brother, and until
Ossory moves Down will not take the grass.

It seems as though, like anchorites of yore,
Both sure will perish rather than give way,
So firm they stand – the Rock itself no more
Rigid, immovably erect than they.

But see! A way is found, a compromise
To reconcile conflicting North and South!
Deus ex machina, see Grangegorman rise
While words of wisdom bubble from his mouth:

'O Deans,' I hear him say, 'watch when I drop
This cloak of mine which now I firmly clutch.
Be that the signal, then together plop –
I trust the impact may not jar you much.'

So it was done. But if you say I lie,
Go you to Cashel and you'll be
    confounded;
For in the rock two dints you will espy,
The one acute, the other softly
    rounded.

TD Sullivan

*Though the name of T D Sullivan (1827–1914) is no longer a
very familiar one, in his heyday his influence as MP, editor
and writer was widespread. Patriotic or satirical as the
occasion demanded, his verses were very popular both at
home and in America. We include here five of his less
serious ones, written in several different moods.*

*The satirical chant below comes from the 1860s. It
accuses the Protestant Missionary Societies of trying to
convert the starving with the help of soup – for a member of
the Church of Ireland to be called a 'souper' was to remain
an unpleasant insult.*

*The published verses were introduced with the direction:
'Intended to be sung at the "April Meetings" in the Rotundo,
and by the chief cooks at various "Missionary Stations"
throughout Ireland.'*

LADLE IT WELL

Sweet is soup, and wondrous good,
    Ladle it well, oh ladle it well!
It heals the soul, it warms the blood,
It cheers the mind once dark as mud,
Oh, soup is a genuine saving flood –
    Ladle it well, oh ladle it well!

Throw the tripe and onions in –
    Ladle it well, oh ladle it well!
Be sure the drink is not too thin –
It takes a strong compound to win
A soul right out from Popish sin –
    Ladle it well, oh ladle it well!

There's long Pat Quin – he's yet uncaught –
    Ladle it well, oh ladle it well!
What checked his grace! – I wondered what
Until I tried the soup he got,
And found no turnips in the pot –
    Ladle it well, oh ladle it well!

Just think of last year's bible class –
    Ladle it well, oh ladle it well!
The soup was poor, alas, alas! –
Too well I knew 'twould come to pass –

The wretches all went back to mass!
 Ladle it well, oh ladle it well!

I often think with sigh and groan –
 Ladle it well, oh ladle it well!
Of Darby and of Kate Malone,
Whose souls another cow's shin bone
Would have secured and made our own –
 Ladle it well, oh ladle it well!

Oh, happy days, it must be said –
 Ladle it well, oh ladle it well!
When out from Romish gloom and dread
The sinful spirit may be led
 To glory, by a fresh sheep's head –
Ladle it well, oh ladle it well.

Oh, Darby, Darby, and your wife –
 Ladle it well, oh ladle it well!
Oh, people all, while grace is rife,
Come forth, come forth from sin and strife,
Come drink the saving soup of life –
 Ladle it well, oh ladle it well!

Next, an engaging example of the sort of abuse that
'soupers' might expect from former co-religionists.

RIGGED OUT

I'm a brand from the burning, a genuine saint,
Newly purged and set free from Papistical taint;
Yea, I'm one of that holy, that sanctified troop
Whose souls have been chastened by flannel and soup.

I'll tell how so blessed a change came about: –
I always was lazy, a slouch, and a lout;
I never was willing to delve or to dig,
But I looked for support to my wife and the pig.

My spirit was never confused or perplexed
By the talk in this world about things in the next;
But I felt I'd be certain of one life of bliss
If some one would feed me for nothing in this.

And so by a ditch near my cabin I lay,
With my front to the sun, on a hot summer day,
When the Reverend Oliver Stiggins came by,
And attracted my gaze by the white of his eye.

He spoke, and he said – 'I perceive by your face,
Wretched man, that you're much unacquainted with
    grace.'
'Very true, sir,' said I, 'sure I scarce know the taste
Of the broth or the flesh of a four-footed baste.'

Then he bade me arise and proceed with him home
Till he'd give me some proofs of the errors of Rome:
I went, and the clinchers that Oliver chose
Were a full and complete suit of second-hand clothes.

I felt at the moment the breeches went on
That half of my ancient religion was gone;
Much was done by a vest buttoned up to the throat,
But the grand hit of all was a rusty black coat.

The hat was convincing, as one might expect,
The necktie itself had a certain effect;
Then to pluck away error right out from the roots,
He covered my croobs with a new pair of boots.

Then he raised up his hands and his eyes, and began
To declare, through his nose, I'd 'put off the Old
    Man;'
And he hoped to my newly found faith I'd hold fast –
Which I said that I would – while his garments would
    last.

Then he bade me go talk unto Biddy, my wife,
About ribbons, and cotton, and Protestant life,
And to ask her, with dear Mrs Stiggins' regards,
What stuff would convert her, and how many yards?

I hurried to Biddy – she shrieked with affright,
She laughed and she cried at the comical sight;
She called me an *assal*, a rogue, and a fool,
And fell combing my head with a three-legged stool.

She pitched me right out, and she bolted the door,
I knocked and I shouted, I cursed and I swore:

But soon I grew meek, and I made up my mind,
I could fare very well leaving Biddy behind.

From town unto town have I travelled since then,
Giving good British scripture to women and men,
And indulging at times in a bit of a freak,
But sure Stiggins himself knows the flesh is but weak.

Well, my clothes are supplied, and secure is my pay,
But my wages are settled at so much per *day*,
And I boldly contend that no man has a right
To heed what a souper may do after night.

*In the late nineteenth-century, well-to-do families often took
their holidays in what is now Dún Laoghaire: this 'letter' is
from 'Miss Bessie Green, residing at Kingstown, to Miss
Lizzie Malone, in the County Tipperary.' Though today the
verses may seem charmingly innocuous, Sullivan's point is
perhaps that these impressionable country girls are falling
under dangerous foreign influences in County Dublin.*

A LETTER

My dear little Liz, here's a letter at last,
    And to make it a long one I mean to try:
We are staying at Kingstown these three weeks past,
    Papa and Mamma, and Charlie, and I.
And oh, it's so lovely, with bands and boats,
    And the ocean grand, and the mantling wave,
With robes *à la Watteau*, and braided coats,
    And naval officers, brown and brave.
        And it's oh-hi-ho, and yo-heave-yo,
            And starboard topsail, and helm-a-lee,
        (You'll note, dearest Liz, I am coming to know
            A lot about ships and the deep blue sea).

For Charlie is coaching me every day:
    He shows me the yachts that have just come in,
And he tells all about them, – but, oh, by the way,
    Do you know who is here? – why, that tall Miss
        Glynn.
I saw her last night near the fort, my dear,
    In a rather fantastic and light costume,

Just as the *Connaught* came round the pier,
　　With her foresail set on her stern jib-boom.
　　　And it's oh-hi-ho for a weatherly craft,
　　　　For a three-reefed shroud and a whispering
　　　　　breeze,
　　　For flowing binnacles fore and aft,
　　　　And a backstay cleaving the foaming seas!

You know the regatta will soon take place,
　　The people are fast filling in for it too,
And the fashion runs all upon muslin and lace,
　　With under-jupes flounced in the style *Frou-Frou*.
In a pale blue silk will I dress for the day,
　　With guipure trimming, and bows behind;
And then from a rock I shall look on the bay
　　While the yachts tack up on a quarterly wind.
　　　And it's yo-heave-yo for the snow-white sail
　　　　While the starboard scuppers are floating free,
　　　While the marlin' spike bends in the fresh'ning
　　　　gale,
　　　And the crosstree groans in the plunging sea!

Come up, dearest Liz, to the pleasant sea air;
　　Papa and Mamma will be glad if you do:
You will see the new styles in dress, bonnets, and hair,
　　See some beauties perhaps, and of frights not a few.
And I, dearest Liz, will be happy indeed
　　To teach you the whole of my nautical lore;
I'll give you my Cooper and Marryatt to read,
　　And Charlie will tell you a hundred times more.
　　　And it's oh-hi-ho, and yo-heave-yo,
　　　　And a life on the ocean wave for me,
　　　As out on the shining deep we go
　　　　With mainyard furled and helm-a-lee!

A satire written in 1899. Sullivan includes this note: 'When this squib was written much was being said in some of our literary papers about the desirability of getting more "Celtic glamour" into Irish literature, and a number of young poets were doing their best to fulfil the requirement by publishing ballads about haunted castles, weird apparitions, and sepulchral voices, giving mysterious hints of undiscovered tragedies. The fashion, doubtless, will come round again.'
'Soulth', in verse 2, is from the Irish samhailt, a ghost, while the 'leech' of verse 5 is of course a doctor.

A GLAMOROUS BALLAD

The green-eyed wolf had a long red nose,
    One red nose, and no more had he;
The yellow mist falls and the blue wind blows
    And a shriek rang up from the angry sea.

The brown pig ran o'er the dusky moor –
    What is that there by the hawthorn tree?
A shirt from the wash? But one cannot be sure;
    A shivering soulth 'tis as like to be.

'Who stole, who stole my little grey mare?'
    (The elfin laughter pealed loud and free)
'And left me a goat all horns and hair –
    And 'tis, oh, the terror and grief to me!'

She heard a squeak and she heard a squall,
    She went to the window to hear and see,
And saw atop of a garden wall
    A black thing vanishing noiselessly!

The warrior lay on his couch of pain,
    The leech he spake to him tenderlee –
'Now, what do you think has troubled your brain?'
    'I'm dying for glamour, good leech,' said he.

'In Erin of old, as perhaps you know,
    There was lots of glamour on land and sea;
Now, where it has gone I am going to go.'
    He turned on his side and he ceased to be.

The poet brought this to the publisher's door,
    And soon to his heart went a thrill of glee,
For the publisher said, 'I'll take twenty yards more;
    This make is the fashion just now,' said he.

... and finally ...

WOMEN'S WAYS

Of Women the ways are peculiar: –
    I make the remark now and then,
When I see how they pare a lead pencil,
    Or try to throw stones at a hen.

Anonymous

*One of the most popular of the many drinking songs of
Victorian Ireland.*

A SUP OF GOOD WHISKEY

A sup of good whiskey will make you glad;
Too much of the creatur' will make you mad;
If you take it in reason, 'twill make you wise;
If you drink to excess, it will close up your eyes:
    Yet father and mother,
    And sister and brother
    They all take a sup in their turn.

Some preachers will tell you that whiskey is bad;
I think so, too – if there's none to be had;
Teetotalers bid you drink none at all;
But, while I can get it, a fig for them all!
    Both layman and brother
    In spite of this pother,
    Will all take a sup in their turn.

Some doctors will tell you, 'twill hurt your health,
The justice will say, 'twill reduce your wealth;
Physicians and lawyers both do agree
When your money's all gone, they can get no fee.
    Yet surgeon and doctor
    And lawyer and proctor,
    Will all take a sup in their turn.

If a soldier is drunk on his duty found,
He to the three-legged-horse is bound,
In the face of his regiment obliged to strip;

But a noggin will soften the nine-tailed whip.
    For sergeant and drummer,
    And likewise, his honour
    Will all take a sup in their turn.

The Turks who arrived from the Porte Sublime,
All told us that drinking was held a great crime,
Yet, after their dinner away they slunk,
And tippled, so sly, till they got quite drunk.
    For Sultan and Crommet
    And even Mahomet
    They all take a sup in their turn.

The Quakers will bid you from drink abstain,
By yea and by nay they will make it plain;
But some of the broad-brims will get the stuff,
And tipple away till they've tippled enough.
    For stiff-back and steady,
    And Solomon's lady,
    Will all take a sup in their turn.

The Germans do say they can drink the most,
The French and Italians also do boast;
Ould Ireland's the country (for all their noise)
For generous drinking and hearty boys.
    There each jovial fellow
    Will drink till he's mellow,
    And take off his glass in his turn.

Jonathan Swift

The best-known verses of Dean Swift (1667–1745), such as his Birthday Poems for Stella and 'Verses on the Death of Dr Swift', are so well known and mainstream that they cannot meaningfully be said to have a place in a book of Ireland's 'Other Poetry'. But we seize the chance to remind ourselves of a few short pieces.

In the 'Description' below, it at first appears that the morning is an agreeably ordinary one, but Swift's camera soon zooms in to reveal that most people are not up to much good, including the peer (or bishop) who has not paid his debts, and the coalman and chimney-sweep who seem to be at war with one other:

A DESCRIPTION OF THE MORNING

Now hardly here and there a Hackney-coach
Appearing, show'd the ruddy morn's approach.
Now Betty from her master's bed had flown,
And softly stole to discompose her own.
The slipshod prentice from his master's door,
Had par'd the dirt, and sprinkled round the floor.
Now Moll had whirl'd her mop with dext'rous airs,
Prepar'd to scrub the entry and the stairs.
The youth with broomy stumps began to trace
The kennel-edge, where wheels had worn the place.
The smallcoal-man was heard with cadence deep,
'Till drown'd in shriller notes of chimney-sweep.
Duns at his Lordship's gate began to meet,
And brickdust Moll had scream'd through half a street.
The turnkey now his flock returning sees,
Duly let out a nights to steal for fees.
The watchful bailiffs take their silent stands,
And school-boys lag with satchels in their hands.

In 1728, the Countess of Meath died, and under a previous agreement (or 'jointure') her money reverted to her family. When her husband followed shortly after, Swift wrote these cynical lines:

AN ELEGY ON DICKY AND DOLLY

Under this stone lies Dicky and Dolly,
Doll, dying first, Dick grew melancholly,
For Dick without Doll thought living a folly.

Dick lost in Doll a wife tender and dear,
But Dick lost by Doll twelve hundred a year,
A loss that Dick thought no mortal could bear.

Dick sighed for his Doll and his mournful arms
    cross'd,
Thought much of his Doll, and the jointure he lost,
The first vex'd him much, but the other vex'd most.

Thus loaded with grief, Dick sigh'd and he cried,
To live without both full three months he tried,
But lik'd neither loss, and so quietly died.

One bed while alive held both Doll and Dick
One coach oft carried them when they were quick,
One grave now contains them both *haec et hic.*

Dick left a pattern few will copy after,
Then Reader pray shed some tears of salt water,
For so sad a tale is no subject of laughter.

Meath smiles for his jointure, though gotten so
    late,
The son laughs that got the hard gotten estate,
And Cuffe grins for getting the Alicant plate.

Here quiet they lie, in hopes to rise one day,
Both solemnly put in this hole on a Sunday,
And here rest, *Sic transit gloria mundi.*

*Swift was sometimes paid by the line, and invented what
was called 'Lilliputian Verse', which halved his labour. Here
is a snatch of it, about his craze for landscape gardening,
which he took up while staying with Sir Arthur and Lady
Acheson, friends of his at Market Hill, near Armagh:*

'THE DEAN AS LANDSCAPE GARDENER'
  from
MY LADY'S LAMENTATION AND COMPLAINT
AGAINST THE DEAN

Now see how he sits
Perplexing his wits
In search of a motto
To fix on his grotto;
How proudly he talks
Of zigzags and walks,
And all the day raves
Of cradles and caves;
And boasts of his feats,
His grottos and seats;
Shows all his gewgaws,
And gapes for applause;
A fine occupation
For one in his station!
A hole where a rabbit

Would scorn to inhabit,
Dug out in an hour;
He calls it a bower.
      But, O! how we laugh,
To see a wild calf
Come, driven by heat,
And foul the green seat;
Or run helter-skelter,
To his arbour for shelter,
Where all goes to ruin
The Dean has been doing:
The girls of the village
Come flocking for pillage,
Pull down the fine briers
And thorns to make fires;
But yet are so kind
To leave something behind:
No more need be said on't,
I smell when I tread on't.

*The country cleric is perhaps exaggerating his duties a little
here: this is said to have been set in the Diocese of Meath, a
region normally almost devoid of 'scorching sand'.*

ON A CURATE'S COMPLAINT OF HARD DUTY

I marched three miles through scorching sand
With zeal in heart and notes in hand;
I rode four more to great St Mary;
Using four legs when two were weary.
To three fair virgins I did tie men
In the close bands of pleasing hymen.
I dipped two babes in holy water
And purified their mothers after.
Within an hour, and eke a half,
I preached three congregations deaf,
Which thundered out with lungs long winded,
I chopped so fast that few were minded.
My emblem, the laborious sun,
Saw all these mighty labours done
Before one race of his was run;
All this performed by Robert Hewitt,
What mortal else could e'er go through it?

On his way to Armagh, the Dean was an occasional visitor
to Castle Leslie, in County Monaghan, where the family say
he wrote this undeniably accurate quatrain.

'CASTLE LESLIE'

Here I am in Castle Leslie
With rows and rows of books upon the shelves
Written by the Leslies
All about themselves.

ON HIMSELF

On rainy days alone I dine
Upon a chick and pint of wine.
On rainy days I dine alone
And pick my chicken to the bone;
But this my servants much enrages,
No scraps remain to save board wages.
In weather fine I nothing spend,
But often sponge upon a friend;
Yet, when he's not so rich as I,
I pay my club, and so good bye.

John Millington Synge

This pungent 'curse' by the playwright (1871–1909) was
directed, as he remarks in a note, at 'a sister of an enemy of
the author's who disapproved of The Playboy.*'*

THE CURSE

Lord, confound this surly sister,
Blight her brow with blotch and blister,
Cramp her larynx, lung and liver,
In her guts a galling give her.

Let her live to earn her dinners
In Mountjoy with seedy sinners:
Lord, this judgment quickly bring,
And I'm your servant, J. M. Synge.

Anonymous

The Ireland that spawned Bram Stoker and Sheridan Le Fanu was a ready audience for spine-chilling magazine stories. This grim yarn comes from Zozimus, *June 1870.*

A TALE OF HORROR

I read a dreadful tale last night –
    The terror will not soon depart,
The sense of awe, the wild affright,
    With which it touched and thrilled my heart.
It told how Julia, young and fair,
    Of both her parents soon bereft,
Unto an aged uncle's care –
    A wicked man, alas! – was left.
His wealth was all spent evil-wise,
    He wanted more for new demands,
And then the monster's greedy eyes
    Were turned upon the orphan's lands.
Ere long, some cruel, dark design
    Within his secret heart he nurst,
He muttered of it in his wine,
    He wiped his brow, he stamped and curst.
Two ruffians from a distant glen
    He sent for, and they came with speed,
He gave them wine, and gold, and then
    He bade them do a horrid deed.

They bore the orphan to a wood,
 And just as night's dark shadows fell,
Beneath the leafy screen they stood
 All ready for their work of hell.
When lo! a deep unearthly sound
 Thrilled those dark hearts that seldom feared,
And then, emerging from the ground
 A white-robed, blood-stained form appeared.
Straight towards the wicked pair it sped,
 And while they looked alarmed, perplexed,
It shook its gory locks, and said: –
 'To be continued in our next.'

Anonymous

A disarmingly amateur broadside song, probably from pre-Victorian times, with an inventive line in euphemisms. In verse 2, 'fusee' was a light musket – whence 'fusilier'. 'Gades' in verse 4 must be a misprint for 'jades', meaning 'minxes' (or should one say the more latinate 'minges'?) As to the title, tentatively: a 'tallywag' was then common slang for the male member, and at the same period 'targing' meant 'thrashing'.

TARGIN TALLYO

I am the king of sporting blades,
In Dublin City used to abide,
For courting the pretty fair maids,
Both far and near;
I have been in Italy and,
I have been in France and Spain,
Sicily and Germany,
And now I am back home again.

First when I did enlist,
A bold recruit about sixteen,
I had a play boy like my wrist,
That made the lasses fond and keen,
The Colonel's Lady fancied me,
Abroad with her to come and go,
When she heard I had the fusee,
They call the Targin Tallyo.

But she fain would know or feel the truth
I pull'd out my rusty blade,
Which my two hands could scarcely spang,
With trembling voice she thus replied,
Ha ha ye'll be my waiting man,
Straight to the colonel she went,
This request to her was granted,
In servants livery I was drest,
Abroad with my Mistress to come and go,
Because she knew I had the long fuze,
They call the Targin Tallyo.
But when the colonel come
Of this sad news to know
He lodg'd a bullet in my groin
Which graz'd my Targin Tallyo.

The pretty maids and widow'd wives
They all flock round me in a row
And filthy gades crying alas!
Alas! poor Tallyo
Six weeks I lay then on my back
Till at length my wound began to mend
And Tallyo he got that stiff
He scarce would bend
I was oblig'd to tye him to my thigh
For fear that he should master grow
He cock'd his head and the tye he broke
And there's an end to my Tallyo.

Anonymous

There was a time when almost every sporting organization in the land had its own amateur recruiting song: here is one from December 1921. It was published in TCD Miscellany *to entice undergraduates to join the Trinity College cross-country club (whose gatherings reputedly involved much less running than drinking.)*

THE TCD HARRIERS

There's a spot in Chapelizod where it straggles o'er
    the Liffey:
'Tis a house in common parlance termed a pub.

You can hop upon a Lucan tram and get there in a jiffy,
Then join the Harriers, pay your sub.
The Harriers, the Harriers –
The squelchin', belchin' Harriers –
Oh! Join and pay your sub.

Or if happy you desire a bath – the Yellow House,
    Rathfarnham,
Has upon its kitchen floor a steaming tub,
And no longer need a fellow go unwashed thro' term
    for darn him!
He can join the Harriers and pay his sub,
The Harriers, the Harriers –
The ruddy, muddy Harriers –
Yes, join the Harriers and pay his sub.

There's a widow too, out Dundrum way, with face
    and form most ample
And a nose of the variety called a snub,
And if tea and cake or buttered crumpets you would
    sample,
Just join the Harriers and pay your sub.
The Harriers, the Harriers –
The ramblin', scramblin' Harriers –
Just join the Harriers and pay your sub.

If you're groggy in the thorax or you're weak in the
    abdomen,
If you're having difficulties with your grub,
Or if you merely wish to flee the encircling toils of
    women,
Just join the Harriers and pay your sub.
The Harriers, the Harriers –
The sprawlin', crawlin' Harriers –
Oh! Join the Harriers and pay your sub.

The sub is only ten white bob – you say you'd never
    miss it
But where are you to get it – there's the rub?
Why not invest your overdraft and mortgage your
    deficit
And join the Harriers and pay your sub?
The Harriers, the Harriers –
The hurryin', scurryin' Harriers –
Oh! Join the Harriers and pay your sub.

William Makepeace Thackeray

In the decade after 1843, when his Irish Sketchbook
*appeared, the English novelist Thackeray (1811-1863)
produced copious verses based on Irish models. We reprint
here some selected extracts from one of these shocking
national libels, first published in* Punch *in 1851. It follows a
poetically-minded Irishman through the World's Fair, a vast
trade exhibition held in the sensational new Crystal Palace
in Hyde Park. (This enormous structure was later moved to
what was intended to be a more permanent home in South
London – where it burned down.)*

from
THE CRYSTAL PALACE,
or, MR MOLONY'S ACCOUNT OF THE CRYSTAL
  PALACE, 1851

With ganial foire
   Thransfuse me loyre,
Ye sacred nymphths of Pindus,
   The whoile I sing
   That wondthrous thing
The Palace made o' windows!

   This Palace tall,
   This Cristial Hall,
Which Imperors might covet,
   Stands in High Park
   Like Noah's Ark
A rainbow bint above it.

   'Tis here that roams,
   As well becomes
Her dignitee and stations,
   Victoria great,
   And houlds in state
The Congress of the Nations.

   Her subjects pours
   From distant shores,
Her Injians and Canajians;
   And also we,
   Her kingdoms three,
Attind with our allagiance.

With conscious proide
I stud insoide
And look'd the World's Great Fair in
Until me sight
Was dazzled quite,
And couldn't see for staring.

There's holy saints
And window paints,
By maydiayval Pugin;
Alhamborough Jones
Did paint the tones
Of yellow and gamboge in.

There's statues bright
Of marble white,
Of silver, and of copper,
And some in zinc,
And some, I think,
That isn't over proper.

There's staym ingynes,
That stand in lines,
Enormous and amazing,
That squeal and snort,
Like whales in sport,
Or elephants a-grazing.

For thim genteels
Who ride on wheels,
There's plenty to indulge 'em;
There's droskys snug
From Paytersbug,
And vayhycles from Bulgium.

There's cabs on stands,
And shandthrydanns;
There's wagons from New York here;
There's Lapland sleighs,
Have cross'd the seas,
And jaunting cyars from Cork here.

Look, here's a fan
From far Japan,
A sabre from Damasco:

There's shawls ye get
From far Thibet,
And cotton prints from Glasgow.

There's granite flints
That's quite imminse,
There's sacks of coals and fuels,
There's swords and guns,
And soap in tuns,
And gingerbread and jewels.

There's taypots there,
And cannons rare;
There's coffins filled with roses;
There's canvas tints,
Teeth insthrumints,
And shuits of clothes by Moses.

There's lashins more
Of things in store,
But thim I don't remimber;
Nor could disclose
Did I compose
From May-time to Novimber!

So let us raise
Victoria's praise,
And Albert's proud condition,
That takes his ayse
As he surveys
This Crystal Exhibition.

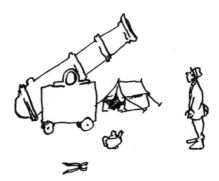

Anonymous

*George Moore's relations with the opposite sex were
shrouded in mystery, and he never married. It was
notoriously said of him that 'he told, but did not kiss.' This
'ballade' appeared in* Secret Springs of Dublin Song, *and
is subtitled 'Inexpressive Nuptial Song'; it has been
suggested that Gogarty had a hand in it – though nobody is
certain which of the following lines are his:*

TO GEORGE MOORE ON THE OCCASION OF HIS
WEDDING

*** *** **** ** **** *****,
****** * ****** ******** ****,
****-****** *** **** ****** ****,
*** **** *** ***** **** *** **,
*** ******* ** ***** *****,
*** ***** ***** *** **** ******
* ***** ******* ******,
**********, ******, ******, ****.

*** ***** ** *** **** **** ***,
*** **** ******* **** *** ******,
*** **** *** ********** ******,
**** ****** ****** ** *******,
**** *** ******, ****** *****
*** ** ** ***, *** **** ** *****
*** **** *** **** **** ****** ******,
**********, ******, ******, ****.

**** *** *** * ** ****
*** ***** **** **** ***** *******' ****,
*** **** ***** **** ** *** **** ***,
****** *** **** *** *** ******,
*** **** ** *** ********,
*** ******* *** **** ******* *****,
***** ****** *** ******* *****—******,
**********, ******, ******, ****.

Envoi
****** ***** *** ****** ** *** ****** —
*** ****** **** ********* ****,
*****—**** **** ******* * ****,
**********, ******, ******, ****.

Anonymous

On the internet, this old favourite is summed up as a 'marvellously silly more or less traditional Irish drinking song.' We have nothing to add, except to say that Ballybay is in County Monaghan.

THE TOWN OF BALLYBAY

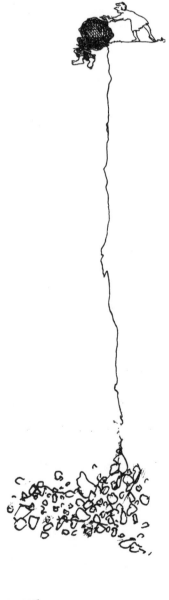

In the town of Ballybay there is a lassie dwelling,
I knew her very well and the story is worth telling:
Her father kept a still and he was a good distiller,
And when she took a drink, well, the devil wouldn't
    fill her.

Chorus:
  With me ring a do a dum, with me ring a do a
    daddio
  With me ring a do a dum, whack fol da daddio

She had a wooden leg that was hollow down the
    middle;
She used to tie a string on it and played it like a fiddle.
She fiddled in the hall, she fiddled in the alleyway,
She didn't give a damn, she had to fiddle anyway.

She said she couldn't dance unless she had her wellies
    on,
But when she had them on she could dance as good as
    anyone.
She wouldn't go to bed unless she had her shimmy
    on –
But when she had it on she would go as quick as
    anyone.

She had lovers by the score, every Tom and Dick and
    Harry,
She was courting night and day, but still she wouldn't
    marry.
And then she fell in love with a fella with a stammer –
When he tried to run away, she hit him with a
    hammer.

She had childer up the stairs, she had childer in the byre,
And another ten or twelve, sat roaring by the fire.

She fed them on potatoes and on soup she made with
    nettles,
Or lumps of hairy bacon that she boiled up in a kettle.

She led a sheltered life eating porridge and black
    pudding;
She terrorised her man until he died right sudden;
And when her husband died, she was feeling very
    sorry –
She rolled him in a bag and she threw him in a quarry.

Anonymous
('Lalec')

*Myles na gCopaleen complained that the Abbey Theatre had
rejected so many of his plays that once, in desperation, he
sent them his hat. Like all his other submissions, it was
returned – with the brim turned down! But if the city's
main theatres were difficult to crack, surely a budding
playwright at Trinity could rely on the College Players?
From a May 1945 issue of* TCD Miscellany.

A TRAGEDY IN THREE ACTS

O, I've got the brain of a Berkeley,
    And the luminous mind of a Burke,
And in handwriting lucid and clerkly
    I wrote out my wonderful work.
        'Twas a vast panorama
        In the form of a drama
From Macbeth to Napoleon the Great;
        But the play,
        Sad to say,
        Was all thrown away,
They turned down my play at the Gate
        – which I hate –
They rejected my play at the Gate!

My wit was not equalled by Congreve,
    And Swift would have praised my technique,
My skill would make even the strong grieve
    And draw howls from the souls of the weak;
        'Twas the epic complete

Pitched in Gardiner Street,
Of the bibulous loves of a cabby;
But the views
Of my Muse
Dublin's destined to lose –
They tore up my play at the Abbey
– so shabby –
They rejected my play at the Abbey!

With the rollicking fun of a Lever,
And the delicate grace of a Moore,
I wrote of a Gay Young Deceiver
And a girl who was clean to the core,
There were cynical guests
And ambiguous jests,
And I laid on the wisecracks in layers;
But then,
Once again,
They dishonoured my pen –
They threw out my play at the Players
– the betrayers –
They rejected my play at the Players!

John Trainor

One of the most beloved of the 'Canal Epics', this appeared on a late ballad-sheet. Its author, a Liverpool Irishman, died in 1910.

THE CRUISE OF THE CALABAR

Come all ye dry-land sailors bold and listen to my song,
There are only forty verses, so I won't detain you long.
'Tis all about the history of a bold young Irish tar,
Who sailed as a man before the mast on board of the
Calabar.

Chorus:
So heave away, my hearties, for we're bound for
lands afar,
As we sail away from James's Street on board of the
Calabar.

The *Calabar* was a clipper flat, stern-fashioned fore and
    aft,
The rudder it stuck away out behind and the wheel
    was a great big shaft.
With half a gale to swell her sail she could make two
    knots an hour;
The smartest craft on the Grand Canal, though only a
    one-horse power.

The skipper was a strapping youth, and his height was
    four-foot-two;
His nose was red and his eyes were black and his hair a
    Prussian blue.
He wore a leather medal that he won in the Crimee
    war,
And his wife was passenger, mate, and cook on board
    of the *Calabar.*

We sailed away with a favouring breeze, the weather it
    was sublime,
But just in the straits of Rialto Bridge, where ye can't
    pass two at a time,
Another craft ran into us, which gave us a serious
    check:
It stove in the starboard paddle-wheel box and
    destroyed the hurricane deck.

While hugging the shore of Inchicore, a very
    dangerous part,
We ran on top of a lump of coal that wasn't marked
    on the chart;
To save ourselves from sinking, and to save each
    precious life,
We hove the main deck overboard, including the
    captain's wife.

Then all became confusion, while the stormy winds
    did blow,
The Bos'un slipped on an orange peel, and fell into the
    hold below.

The Captain cried: ''Tis a pirate's brig, and on us she
    does gain!
When next I sail for Clondalkin, boys, be japers I'll go
    by train!'

So we got our ammunition out to meet the coming foe,
Our cutlasses and boarding pikes and Gatling guns also.
'Put on full steam,' the Captain cried, 'for we are
    sorely pressed';
But the Engineer replied from the bank, 'Sure the
    horse is doing his best!'

O, thick and fast the heroes fell, in torrents the blood
    was spilt;
Great numbers were falling before they were hit, to
    make sure they wouldn't be kilt.
And at last when the pirate surrendered her flag, the
    crew being all on their backs
We found that she was a sister ship, with a cargo of
    cobbler's wax.

The ship is in the marine stores now, the crew in the
    county jail,
And I'm the only survivor left to tell the terrible tale,
But if I could release that ship, I'd sail her off afar,
And Admiral be of the blooming fleet on the fighting
    Calabar.

Anonymous

*In Ireland there was heated support for both sides during
the Boer War. As this very popular song makes clear, things
were no different in South Africa itself.*

'TWAS AN IRISH FIGHT:
HOW THE ENGLISH FOUGHT THE DUTCH
AT THE BATTLE OF DUNDEE

On the mountain side the battle raged, there was no
    stop or stay;
Mackin captured Private Burke and Ensign Michael
    Shea,
Fitzgerald got Fitzpatrick, Brannigan found O'Rourke;

Finnigan took a man named Fay – and a couple of
    lads from Cork.
Sudden they heard McManus shout, 'hands up or I'll
    run you through':
He thought it was a Yorkshire 'Tyke' – 'twas Corporal
    Donaghue!
McGarry took O'Leary, O'Brien got McNamee,
That's how the 'English fought the Dutch' at the
    Battle of Dundee.

Then someone brought in Casey, O'Connor took
    O'Neil;
Riley captured Cavanagh, while trying to make a steal.
Hagan caught McFadden, Carrigan caught McBride,
And Brennan made a handsome touch when Kelly
    tried to slide.
Dicey took a lad named Welsh; Dooley got McGurk;
Gilligan turned in Fahey's boy – for his father he used
    to work.
They had marched to fight the English – but Irish
    were all they could see –
That's how the 'English fought the Dutch' at the
    Battle of Dundee.

Anonymous
('O.M.O.T.M.')

Another verse from TCD *Miscellany, 18 May 1945. After Germany collapses, the Board of Trinity College is urged to take punitive action when loyalist students raise the Union Jack over College Green, Dublin, sparking off a street riot:*

UP THE POLE

Though from war our state's aloof
College shows its cloven hoof;
Peace on earth, but on the roof
Prance the flyboy and the goof
     In Eire's capital.

Pacifists have gone berserk,
Shirkers now no longer shirk,
Lurkers cease for once to lurk,
Workers drop their favourite work –
     Marx's 'Das Kapital.'

Such as grudge not boys their fun,
Such as cry 'The Right has won,'
Fellows who, when day is done,
Itch to fight the prostrate Hun
     Stand shouting 'Capital!'

Lesser breeds without the law,
Ruffians red in tooth and claw,
Yesmen drilled to hail and 'tá,'
Listeners-in to Lord Haw-Haw
     Are making capital.

Thus two factions snarl and fight;
Thus two wrongs don't make a right.
May the Board deplore our plight,
View such crimes in sombre light
     And make 'em capital.

Edward Walsh

*Walsh was a much-travelled army doctor, originally from
Waterford. Between campaigns, he found time to publish his
book of* Bagatelles or Poetical Sketches *(1793), which
contains this light-hearted confession:*

RAPTURE!

The evening spent in Chloe's arms
    Unheeded pass'd away;
No pause we knew from love's alarms,
    'Till rose the dawning day;

Then to the lovely Girl I cry'd,
    'For blissful Joys like these,
No splendid gift shall be deny'd,
    That may the Fancy please;

What brilliant *Gem,* what lust'rous *Pearl*
    Shall deck thy white Ear's tip?
Or grace thy waving auburn Curl?'
    I said, and press'd her lip;

'Nor *Gin* nor *Purl* will I receive,'
    (She answer'd, with a frown)
'You'll surely give what others give?
    Come – give me *Half-a-Crown.*'

Mrs Ward

*We must confess some ignorance as to which Mrs Ward this
may be. The poem comes from a novel entitled* Waves on
the Ocean of Life, a Dalriadan Tale, *which was
published in 1869 and dedicated 'by permission' to Hector's
great-great-grandfather, the ninth earl of Antrim. The
action mostly takes place on the more dramatic crags of the
north Antrim coast, and has a decidedly moral message.
However, sandwiched between two of these dramatic
passages is this less lofty ditty, Mrs Ward's sentiments in
verse on the coastline's most famous antiquity. She clearly
did not think it much worth visiting.*

A SONG OF THE RUINS OF DUNLUCE

And this Dunluce is
Which no other use is,
But for people to look at and walk inside.
And a tower that's round, O,
And quite renowned O;
It's Maeve Roe's room,
All swept by her broom,
And I care not what there is beside.

DA Webb

*David Webb (1912–1994) was that now rare bird, a scientist
with a wide grasp of the humanities. As well as important
botanical works, he wrote a history of Trinity College,
Dublin with RB McDowell (who is mentioned in verse 2
below), and in 1945 he edited an anthology of the best of
TCD Miscellany. Like all sensible editors, he included a
couple of contributions by himself. Here is one of them:*

'MR J.M. HENRY'S ADDRESS TO THE
UNIVERSITY SENATORIAL ELECTORS'

I talk about Hegel, I talk about Freud,
    I talk of the age of the earth;
And if I feel sure that you won't be annoyed,
    I talk of miraculous birth.
I talk about man in the Golden Age,

I talk of Tertullian's views on the stage,
I talk till my listeners go off in a rage
    Or are quite overcome by their mirth.

I talk about Darwin, I talk about Marx;
    I talk about sex by the hour.
I talk of the mother-love instinct in sharks,
    And explain why a lemon is sour.
With a fluency scarcely excelled by McDowell's
I describe how a Manxman pronounces his vowels,
And explain that the muscular tone of the bowels
    Is the root of the Impulse to Power.

I talk of the fire-fighting service in Bray
    And the vitamin content of oats;
I talk of the path of the incident ray,
    And explain how a bicycle floats.
I talk of the Kingdom of God and the Fall,
At a pinch I can talk about nothing at all;
I'm destined, it's plain, for the Senate or Dáil,
    So I hope you will give me your votes.

Anonymous
('Vigil')

In November 1835 The Times *published this extraordinarily
vicious personal attack on Daniel O'Connell. It was soon
being used as ammunition against him in the House of
Commons.*

THE WHIG MISSIONARY OF 1835

Scum condensed of Irish bog!
Ruffian – coward – demagogue!
Boundless liar – base detractor!
Nurse of murders – treason's factor!
Of Pope and priest the crouching slave,
While thy lips of freedom rave;
Of England's fame the vip'rous hater,
Yet wanting courage for a traitor.
Ireland's peasants feed thy purse,
Still thou art her bane and curse.
Tho' thou liv'st an empire's scorn,

Lift on high thy brazen horn –
Every dog shall have his day,
This is thine of brutish sway.
Mounted on a Premier's back,
Lash the Ministerial pack;
At thy nod they hold their places –
Crack their sinews – grind their faces.
Tho' thy hand had stabbed their mother,
They would fawn and call thee brother;
By their leave pursue thy calling,
Rend thy patriot lungs with bawling;
Spout thy filth – effuse thy slime,
Slander is in thee no crime.
Safe from challenge – safe from law –
What can curb thy callous jaw?
Who would sue a convict liar?
On a poltroon who would fire?
Thou may'st walk in open light,
Few will kick thee – none can fight.
Then grant the monster leave to roam,
Let him slaver out his foam,
Only give him length of string,
He'll contrive himself to swing.

Oscar Wilde
(Attrib.)

In 1882 the Denver Times *announced that this verse,
apparently sent to them by one of his former fellow pupils at
Portora, was Oscar Wilde's first poetic utterance. Hmmm.*

'ON CRICKET'

Never more will I play
    With the soaring and gay
But cruel in its fall –
    The mean old cricket ball.

Richard D'Alton Williams

One of the most brilliant and most neglected of the poets who wrote for the Nation until its suppression in 1848, RD Williams (1822–1862) had a unrivalled comic gift – though he received more acclaim for his patriotic poems (written under the uninspired name of 'Shamrock'.) Possibly his only remembered lines are these – the last verse of a poem urging a friend to give up writing poetry:

Hang the bard, and cut the punster,
    Fling all rhyming to the deuce,
Take a business tour through Munster,
    Shoot a landlord – be of use.

Most of his poetry was written when he was still in his twenties – and he had a young man's appreciation of food and drink. In this parody of Thomas Davis's terrible nationalist ballad 'Oh! for a Steed!', 'native' Irish oysters make yet another appearance:

OH! FOR A FEED

Oh! for a feed! A motley feed! A corporation feast
Of hot and cold, of roast and boiled, of fishes, bird
    and beast;
    From cod and snipe
    To leathery tripe,
    Two inches thick at least.

Oh! for a feed! An awful feed! Or else a mighty lunch,
With Niagara cataracts of Irish whiskey punch,
    Port crusty, red,
    And crackling bread,
    Ad libitum to crunch.

Oh! for a feed! A pious feed! With reverend lords to
    dine,
On venison pies of depth profound, and frozen
    Spanish wine;
    With turtle soups,
    And whiskered troops
    Of 'natives,' in their brine.

Oh! for a feed! A bribing feed, at an election spread,
When much is said that's never done, and done that's
    never said,
    And biped swine
    To 'nine times nine'
    Invert their heels and head.

Oh! for a feed! Precarious feed, at boating or pic-nic,
Where 'nobody gets nothink,' and everybody's sick;
    And sudden squalls
    Seize hats and shawls,
    Just borrowed, or on tick.

Oh! for a feed! By hook or crook, from any good soul
    at all,
In rural cot, or pleasure yacht, or festive civic hall,
    Or in poteen still,
    On a Munster hill,
    To stagger, and then to fall.

*Williams practised as a doctor in Dublin and the USA, and
died in Louisiana, aged only forty. His most ambitious work
was* Misadventures of a Medical Student, *a set of long,
cleverly crafted comic poems based on his experiences of
medicine, alcohol, angry creditors, wild parties, bailiffs and
all that goes with being a trainee doctor in Dublin. The
sixth in the series is a* tour de force:

THE DREAM

Thirteen black coffins stood round the hall,
And the skulls grinned down at me, jeeringly all;
And an old maiden's skeleton, gaunt and tall,
In the tattered remains of a mouldering pall,
Clanked her lank shank from a nail in the wall –
My eye! what a swell for a fancy ball!

There were coils of intestine *in tormina* knotted;
Hypertrophied hearts with the arch and carotid;
There were frogs in a basin and toads in a bottle –
A hard liver's liver – an alderman's throttle –
There were noses, from *schirrus*, immense and elastic,
Which pathology designates *heteroplastic* –

If you ask me what that is, more plainly to speak,
I obligingly tell you, at once, it is Greek.

Thirteen black coffins stood round the hall,
And the skulls grinned down at me, horribly all;
And an old maid's skeleton, gaunt and tall,
In the tattered remains of a mouldering pall,
Clanked her lank shank from a nail in the wall.
By Jing! what a swell for a fancy ball!

There were arteries meeting in anastomosis;
Item, caries, callus, superb exostosis;
Hydrocephalic skulls of enormous proportions,
Snakes, fishes, and owls, and all nightmare abortions,
From calves with three heads to tom-cats with three
    tails;
Pigs, poultry, and beetles, bats, badgers, and snails;
But the old maid's skeleton, gaunt and tall,
Was the frightfullest fright in that frightful hall.

Thirteen black coffins stood round the wall,
And the skulls grinned down at me, chattering all;
While the old maid's skeleton, gaunt and tall,
In the tattered remains of a mouldering pall,
Clanked her lank shank, green and yellow with gall.
Old Nick! what a swell for a fancy ball!

Now a strange wild music moaned through that hall,
And a lurid and ghastly glare fell upon all!
The skeletons rattle their yellowish bones,
Pattering, clattering over the stones;
And a murderer's skull, with a grin that made shiver,
Was cracking gall calculi found near a liver.
The three-tailed tabby begins to purr,
And the phantom badger to smoothe his fur.

Thirteen black coffins stand round the hall,
And the skulls grin down at me, mockingly all,
While the old maid's skeleton, gaunt and tall,
In the tattered remains of a mouldering pall,
Clanks her lank shank from a nail in the wall.
Ventrebleu! what a swell at a fancy ball!

Monstrosities bellow and Cerberus howls,
There's a flapping of bats and a hooting of owls;

The stuffed monkeys gibber, the great whales grin,
And the ravenous shark moves his dorsal fin;
The frogs are a-croaking, the toads crawl out,
And the hissing snakes wriggle around and about.

Thirteen black coffins stand round the hall,
And the hollow skulls scowl on me, fearfully all;
But the old maid's skeleton, gaunt and tall,
In the tattered remains of a mouldering pall,
Thin as a ramrod, and yellow with gall,
Clanks her lank shank from a nail in the wall.
Do tell! what a swell! mummy belle! at a ball!

What with coffins and monsters, and death and
      disease,
The devil may smoke a pipe here, if he please,
Though the odour would make the old gentleman
      sneeze,
And the night, too, is awful – at sea in a tub
Ride witches and warlocks and Beelzebub.
There is fear upon earth, there is terror on high,
And the dull glare of tempest is hung in the sky.

Thirteen black coffins move round the hall,
And the pale tenants glare on me, fiendishly all;
And the old maid's skeleton, gaunt and tall,
In the tattered remains of a mouldering pall,
Which she wears with an air, as coquettes do a shawl,
Clanks her lank shank from a nail in the wall,
Kicks up her heels, and sends forth such a squall
As never was heard at bar, bull-bait, or ball.

And still waxes louder the incubus-ball.
The old maid's skeleton, gaunt and tall,
Stalks to an ape from her nail in the wall,
And away they spin in a waltz fantastic;
Thirteen black coffins stump round the hall,
And the foul corses glare at me, hatefully all;
But the old maid's skeleton, rigid and tall,
In the scattered remains of a mouldering pall,
Clanks her lank shank at the incubus ball,
Till her articulations snap, scatter, and fall,
In haste, as if urged by galenicals drastic;
Then an Arctic bear, all shaggy and grim,
Makes love to a porpoise that ogles him,

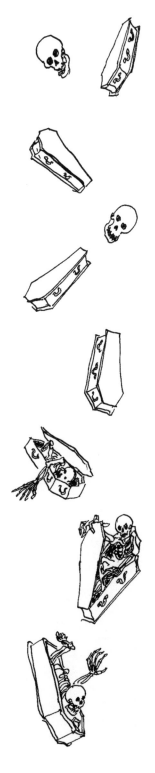

Till away they scramble and climb and swim.
Boas and crocodiles join the revels –
Liars and hypocrites, bigots and devils.

I'd have given more tin than I e'er had the knack to lose
To have shoved from my thorax a grim pterodactylus –
An amphibious monstrosity, half a mile long,
Which geology lately has given to song –
A personified nightmare, ten thousand years lodger
On earth before Adam, that luckless old codger,
'Go it, boots!' and, forgetting my usual urbanity,
I struck out right and left, perhaps uttered profanity,
And danced like a Dervise attacked with insanity,
Till I staggered and fell on a part very tender,
I awoke, and – it seemed I'd 'been out on a bender!'

The following piece of wise advice appeared in the Nation
*over the name 'Milton Byron Scraggs'. It was apparently
dashed off when Williams found a letter in the office from a
suicidal reader who complained that his sweetheart had left
him, attracted by the spurs, sabre and 'shako' (peaked cap)
of a young army colour-sergeant:*

THE JEALOUS STONEYBATTER MAN

Why such a row? What ails you now, desponding
    Stoneybatter man?
You'll jump from off a bridge, indeed! God bless us,
    what's the matter, man?
If she disdain your amorous pain, for military Pat, her
    man,
Because he's very tall and slim, and you're a shorter,
    fatter man,
Speak out the truth, and tell the youth you're quite
    resolved to shatter, man,
To smithereens all rivals, whether parrot, poodle, cat,
    or man –
For love makes all things bellicose – or monkey, dandy,
    rat, or man,
So thrash the sergeant, if you can, then boldly up and
    at her, man,
If you surmise you'll win by sighs, we never met a
    flatter man –

In fact, by dad, you're raving mad, as ever was a
    hatter, man,
Then try a little romping, till her cap and wig you
    tatter, man,
And laud her pa, and praise her ma, especially the
    latter, man,
Soft-sawderize her shape and size, and every feature
    flatter, man,
And oft you'll be asked in to tea, and soft, familiar
    chatter, man,
The barking curs, the jingling spurs, and rattling
    sabre's clatter, man,
Shall sound in vain, tho' sleet and rain upon his shako
    patter, man,
While you within enjoy the din, before a smoking
    platter, man –
That's better tried than suicide, so, courage!
    Stoneybatter man.

John Crawford Wilson

*Wilson, born in County Cork in 1825, spent most of his life
as a literary gent in London. In 1893, these immortal lines,
from a long 'fugitive' poem called 'A New Ode to Saint
Patrick', were extracted by TP O'Connor for the fourth
volume of the* Cabinet of Irish Literature. *In the last
verse, 'skeary' means 'nervous'.*

'HOW CAESAR WAS DRIVEN FROM IRELAND'

When Caesar, by conquests unsated,
    On Erin's soft slopes set his eye,
His troops he debarked, and, elated,
    Strolled forth to a wake, as a spy.
That brawny barbarian, the Briton,
    In Britain he'd beaten anew,
Then furbished fresh fetters to fit on
    The Free-men of Brian Boru.

Disguised in a pair of cord 'britches,'
    Frieze coat, sturdy brogues, and caubeen,
He scrambled through hedges and ditches,
    To where the wake lights could be seen.

He set out quite fearless and hearty,
  Arrived somewhat soon in the night,
And skrewdged himself in ere the party
  Was quite drunk enough for a fight.

He laughed, the big thief, and grew frisky,
  And drank with a mighty good-will
(He'd never afore tasted whisky,
  Or even 'heerd tell' of a 'still').
King Brian Boru sat and eyed him,
  So also did huge Fin-ma-Cool,
And a third, in a cloak, with, beside him,
  A crozier propped up by a stool.

They all seemed to relish the liquor
  (No exciseman near it had been);
The quicker they tippled, the quicker
  They puffed at the fragrant dhudeen.
To Caesar the pipe was extended
  By him with the crozier and cloak,
But Caesar refused, and, offended,
  Said, 'Cities must blaze when I smoke.'

'O cities?' says t'other, quite civil;
  'You'll want a big pipe for that same; –
I know ye.' – 'If so, you're the devil,'
  Says Caesar, 'so tell me my name.'
'Your name and your fame,' says the other,
  'Might both be much safer at home, –
The bogs of green Erin would smother
  Such haythens as Caesar from Rome.'

Then Caesar jumped up in a hurry,
  And turned for to run to the door.
All laughed, for he found, in his flurry,
  His feet fixed like wax to the floor!
'Who are you? what ails me?' he muttered;
  'Why, why should I tremble and faint,
And quake at the words you have uttered!
  I fear neither Satan nor Saint.

What are you? your glances appal me!'
  The other replied with a smile,
'Saint Patrick, my countrymen call me,
  The Guardian of Erin's green Isle.

You've *veni'd,* and *vidi'd, not vici'd* –
    Embark in your fleet, and when there,
I'll send you, if you're not too nice-eyed,
    Such live-stock as Erin can spare.'

Proud Caesar fell down right afore him,
    And grovelled his length as he lay;
Then knelt to the Saint, to adore him,
    But Fin-ma-Cool dragged him away.
He rose, seemed desirous to linger,
    So Brian Boru bade him 'Go!'
Saint Patrick, he lifted his finger,
    And Fin-ma-Cool lifted his toe.

He shot from the spot like a rocket,
    For Fin-ma-Cool kick'd with a will;
His men on the beach felt the shock, it
    Electrified valley and hill,
He fell with a thud on the sod, he
    Was 'telescoped in,' but they rose,
First pulling him out of his body,
    And secondly, out of his clothes.

Away Caesar sailed, sore and weary,
    From Brian Boru and his rule,
From the Saint who had made him feel 'skeary;'
    And the big toe of big Fin-ma-Cool.
Away o'er the billowy Biscay,
    Sea-sickened, soul-saddened, he sped,
Convulsed with a craving for whisky,
    And braved by his bullies for bread.

John Winstanley

*John Winstanley (1676–1750) published his first volume of
witty verses late in life: they were, says Crone's
Biographical Dictionary, 'subscribed to by all the leading
men of his time'. He is now almost entirely forgotten.*

ON MARRIAGE

Cries Celia to a reverend dean,
    'What reason can be given,
Since marriage is a holy thing,
    That there are none in heaven?'

'There are no women,' he reply'd;
    She quick returns the jest;
'Women there are, but I'm afraid
    They cannot find a priest.'

Anonymous

*The source of this spirited ballad is a broadside, very badly
printed, which was issued some time after 1840.*

THE WONDERFUL GREY HORSE

My horse he is white, although at first he was bay,
He took great delight in travelling by night and by day;
His travels were great, if I could the half of them tell,
He was rode in the garden by Adam the day that he
    fell.

When banished from Eden, my horse was losing his
    way,
From all his fatigues, no wonder that now he is grey;
At the time of the flood he was rode by many a spark,
And his courage was good when Noah took him into
    the ark.

On Babylon plains he ran with speed for the plate –
He was hunted next day, it is said, by Nimrod the great;
After that he was hunted again in the chase of a fox,
When Nebuchadnezzar eat grass in the shape of an ox.

He conducted him home straightway into Babylon
    Town,
Where the king was restored once more and solemnly
    crown'd;
He was with King Saul, and all his troubles went
    through,
And was with King David the day that Goliath he slew.

When he saw King David hunted about by King Saul,
My horse took his leave and bid farewell to them all,
He was with King Pharoah in Egypt when fortune did
    smile;
He rode him very stately along the banks of the Nile.

He followed Moses who rode him through the Red Sea,
He then led him out, and he sensibly galloped away;
He was with King Cyrus, whose name is in history
    found,
And he rode on my horse at the taking of Babylon
    Town,

When the Jews remained in chains and mercy
    implored,
King Cyrus proclaimed again to have them restored;
He was in Judea when Judas Maccebus the great
Had rode on my horse, as ancient historians relate.

The poor captive Jews received these news with great
    joy,
My horse got new shoes and pursued his journey to
    Troy.
When the news reached Troy, with my horse he was
    found,
He crossed over the wall, and entered the city I'm told.

The city being in flames, by means of Hector's sad
    fate,
My horse took his leave, and there no longer would
    wait;
I saw him again in Spain, and he in full bloom,
With Hannibal the great, and he crossing the Alps into
    Rome.

My horse being tall, and the top of the Alps very high,
His rider did fall, and Hannibal the great lost an eye;

My horse got no ease although his rider did fall,
He was mounted again by young Scipio who did him
 extol.

On Africa's Plains he conquered that part of the globe.
My horse's fatigues would try the patience of Job;
He was with Brian the Brave when the Munster men
 he did command,
Who in thirty-six battles drove the vile Danes from
 our land.

At the battle of Clontarf he fought on Good Friday all
 day,
And all that remained my horse drove them into the sea;
He was with King James when he reached the Irish
 shore,
But, alas! he got lame, when Boyne's bloody battle
 was o'er.

To tell the truth, for the truth I always like to tell,
He was rode by St Ruth the day that in Aughrim he fell,
And Sarsfield the brave, at the siege of Limerick town,
Rode on my horse and crossed o'er the Shannon I'm
 told.

He was rode by the greatest of men at the famed
 Waterloo,
And Daniel O'Connell long sat on his back it is true,
To shake off the yoke which Erin long patiently bore –
My horse being ill he means to travel no more.

He is landed in Erin, in Kerry he now does remain,
The smith is at work to fit him with new shoes again;
Place Dan on his back he is ready once more for the
 field,
And he never will stop till the Tories he'll make them
 to yield.

Jack B Yeats

We may imagine that we are beginning to understand the paintings of Jack Yeats (1871–1957), until we pick up his fiction. This enigmatic whimsy comes from The Careless Flower *(1947), one of his novels – or rather, as Robert Welsh's most useful* Oxford Companion to Irish Literature *puts it – one of his 'idiosyncratic works of pseudo-autobiography and fantastic narrative':*

'THE RABBITS AND THE HARES'

The rabbits and the hares,
Run together in pairs.
The poker and the tongs
Together belongs.
And the dear little fish
Though they can't think
They can wish.

WB Yeats

Jack's brother, WB (1865–1939), was not a natural writer of comic or curious verses. But could he have been gently guying himself in this poem, taken from The Winding Stair and Other Poems *(1933)? It may or may not be instructive to compare it with the anonymous parody on page 174, which was published fifteen years earlier.*

FOR ANNE GREGORY

'Never shall a young man,
Thrown into despair
By those great honey-coloured
Ramparts at your ear,
Love you for yourself alone
And not your yellow hair.'

'But I can get a hair-dye
And set such colour there,
Brown, or black, or carrot,
That young men in despair
May love me for myself alone
And not my yellow hair.'

'I heard an old religious man
But yesternight declare
That he had found a text to prove
That only God, my dear,
Could love you for yourself alone
And not your yellow hair.'

Anonymous

This popular Dublin song is laden with double meanings.
Its origins are a mystery and, as so often, there are several
versions (none of which quite matches the one here.)

THE ZOOLOGICAL GARDENS

Thunder and lightning is no lark
When Dublin city is in the dark,
So if you've any money go up to the park
And view the Zoological Gardens.

We went out there to see the zoo,
We saw the lion and the kangaroo,
There was he-males and she-males of every hue
Up in the Zoological Gardens.

We went out there by Castleknock
Says she to me, 'Sure we'll court on the lock,'
Then I knew she was one of the rare old stock
From outside the Zoological Gardens.

We went out there on our honeymoon:
Says she to me, 'If you don't come soon,
I'll have to get in with the hairy baboons
Up in the Zoological Gardens.'

Says she to me, 'It's seven o'clock,
And time for me to be changin' me frock,
For I long to see the old cockatoo
Up in the Zoological Gardens.'

Says she to me, 'Me lovely Jack,
I'd love a ride on the elephant's back,
If you don't get up there I'll give you a crack
Up in the Zoological Gardens.'

Oh, thunder and lightning is no lark
When Dublin city is in the dark,
So if you've any money go up to the park,
And view the Zoological Gardens.

Zozimus
(Michael J Moran)

*And so we reach Zozimus. Born Michael Moran in Dublin
in 1796 or so, he was blind from the age of two weeks. Using
a pseudonym borrowed from a bishop of antiquity, he
became celebrated for his verses and songs, which he
normally performed outdoors around the city. He seems to
have died in 1846. The two 'recitations' that follow are his
most famous – though it is doubtful how much of his
original work remains in them: both have passed through
many hands, and almost every singer (or editor) who
touched them has altered the already corrupt texts,
sometimes on purpose, sometimes simply by relying on
memory. The results, however, are excellent:*

SAINT PATRICK WAS A GENTLEMAN

Saint Patrick was a gentleman,
      He came of decent people:
He built a church in Dublin town,
      And on it put a steeple.
His father was a Gallagher,
      His mother was a Brady,
His aunt was an O'Shaughnessy,
      His uncle an O'Grady.

Chorus:
So success attend Saint Patrick's fist,
    For he's a saint so clever;
Oh! he gave the snakes and toads a twist,
    And banish'd them for ever!

The Wicklow Hills are very high,
    And so's the Hill of Howth, sir;
But there's a hill much bigger still,
    Much higher than them both, sir.
'Twas on the top of this high hill
    Saint Patrick preached his sermon,
Which drove the frogs into the bogs,
    And bothered all the vermin.

There's not a mile in Ireland's Isle
    Where dirty vermin musters,
But there he put his dear fore-foot
    And murdered them in clusters;
The toads went pop, the frogs went hop,
    Slap-haste into the water,
And the snakes committed suicide
    To save themselves from slaughter.

Nine hundred thousand reptiles blue
    He charmed with sweet discourses,
And dined on them at Killaloe
    In soups and second courses.
Where blind-worms crawling on the grass
    Disgusted all the nation,
He gave them a rise, which opened their eyes
    To a sense of their situation.

No wonder that our Irish boys
    Should be so free and frisky,
For Saint Patrick taught them first the joys
    Of tippling the whiskey;
No wonder that the Saint himself
    To taste it should be willing,
For his mother kept a sheebeen shop
    In the town of Enniskillen.

Oh! was I but so fortunate
    As to be back in Munster,
'Tis I'd be bound, that from that ground

I never more would once stir.
For there Saint Patrick planted turf,
    And plenty of the praties;
With pigs *galore, ma gra, ma store,*
    And cabbages – and ladies!

Final chorus:
Then my blessing on Saint Patrick's fist,
    For he's the darling Saint, O!
Oh, he gave the snakes and toads a twist –
    He's a beauty without paint, O!

THE FINDING OF MOSES

On Aegypt's banks, contagious to the Nile,
King Pharaoh's daughter went to bathe in style.
She took her dip, and she came unto the land,
And to dry her royal pelt, she ran along the strand.
A bulrush tripped her, whereupon she saw
A smiling baby in a wad of straw;
She took him up and says she in accents mild,
'Oh tar-an-agers, girls, which one of yis owns the child?'

She took him up and she gave a little grin
For she and Moses were standing in their skin,
'Bedad now,' says she, 'it was someone very rude
Left a little baby by the river in his nude.'
She took him to her oul lad sitting on the throne,
'Da,' says she, 'will you give the boy a home?'
'Bedad now,' says he, 'sure I've often brought in worse.
Go, my darling daughter, and get the child a nurse.'

An oul blackamore woman among the crew
Cried out, 'You royal savage, what's that to do with you?
Your royal ladies is too meek and mild
To beget dishonestly this darling little child.'
'Ah then,' says the Pharaoh, 'I'll search every nook
From the Phoenix Park down to Donnybrook,
And when I catch a hoult of the bastard's father
I will kick him from the Nile down to the Dodder.'

Well they sent a bellman to the Market Square
To see if he could find a slavey there,
But the only one now that he could find
Was the little young one that left the child behind.
She came up to the Pharaoh, a stranger, mareyah,
Never lettin' on that she was the baby's ma.
And so little Moses got his mammy back
Which shows that co-in-ci-dence is a nut to crack.

*A much longer rendition of 'Moses' was published in 1871 in
a little book called* Memoir of The Great Original
ZOZIMUS *by 'Gulielmus Dubliniensis Humoriensis'. Could
this version possibly be the work of the real Zozimus,
stripped of its later accretions? It starts pretty well, but the
lines soon lengthen and take on what WB Yeats, referring to
Zozimus, called 'the intolerable cadence of the eighteenth
century'. It begins:*

THE FINDING OF MOSES IN THE NILE

On Egypt's plains, where flows the ancient Nile,
Where Ibix stalks, and swims the crockadile,
Where burning suns for ever shed their glare,
And rainless countries dry the parchèd air,
'Tis here the pyramids ascend on high,
And lofty temples tell of times gone by,
When mighty monarchs made their people slaves,
And with their victims filled ten thousand graves.
The Israelite, oppressed for full four hundred years,
In anguish cried aloud, and shed the captive's tears …

*And so it goes on, until 36 lines later, Moses has been
rescued at last. The poems ends in patriotic vein:*

…They little thought that boy in time would wield a
    rod,
Which rescued from their bondage the Israel of God.
A conquered nation, though down-trod, it still is never
    crushed,
A Liberator always comes when Freedom's voice is
    hushed;
And so our own dear land, in time we all shall see
The Saxon rulers gone – Old Ireland shall be free!

Though the words above are resounding enough, if they are the unretouched work of that enigmatic figure in Turkish costume glimpsed by James Kearney at the Ball of Dandyorum, then the 'great original' Zozimus would surely never have made it into Dublin's mythology. No, just as the balladeers took his Moses story in one direction, a bad 'Proper Poet' has evidently taken it in another. So have any authentic remnants of his work survived at all? Perhaps so: in the seventeen lines below, also found in the Gulielmus Memoir, we may at last be hearing a snatch the 'Other Poetry' of the real Zozimus:

THE SONG OF ZOZIMUS

Gather round me boys, will yez
Gather round me?
And hear what I have to say,
Before ould Sally brings me
My bread and jug of tay.
I live in Faddle Alley,
Off Blackpits near the Comb;
With my poor wife called Sally,
In a narrow, dirty room.
Gather round me, and stop yer noise,
Gather round me till my tale is told;
Gather round me, ye girls and ye boys,
Till I tell yez stories of the days of old;
Gather round me, all ye ladies fair,
And ye gentlemen of renown;
Listen, listen, and to me repair,
Whilst I sing of beauteous Dublin town.

As far as we know, Zozimus never composed a song about the Garden of Eden. For the present editors, this is a pity: it would have brought the book neatly round again to A and Fergus Allen and old Adam and Eve in that Genesis Brewery. But no matter; by now a little crowd has formed at the corner of the street and the man in the long coat has started singing again. Let us quietly tiptoe away.

Acknowledgments and Thanks

The Editors and Publisher offer warm thanks to the following for permission to reproduce copyright material in this book, and for their generosity. Every effort has been made to trace copyright holders, but despite strenuous researches in a few cases this has proved impossible. The publishers would be interested to hear from any copyright holders not here acknowledged.

Fergus Allen: 'The Fall' from his *The Brown Parrots of Providencia* (published Faber and Faber, 1993) and 'Après La Danse' (published *TCD Miscellany*, May 1945), to the author and Faber and Faber.

Dominic Behan: 'The Sea Around Us' (© words by Dominic Behan, Coda Music Ltd/Bucks Music Group Ltd), and 'McAlpine's Fusiliers' (© words by Dominic Behan, Harmony Music Ltd/Bucks Music Group Ltd), to Bucks Music Group Ltd.

John Betjeman: 'The Small Towns of Ireland', from his *High and Low* (published John Murray, 1968) and 'The Arrest of Oscar Wilde at the Cadogan Hotel', from *John Betjeman's Collected Poems* (published John Murray, 1958), reproduced by permission of John Murray (Publishers) Ltd; 'The Dingle Peninsula' reproduced by kind permission of Mrs R Lycett-Green.

Ned Buckley: 'Our Army Jumping Team', from *The Bard of Knocknagree, Ned Buckley* (edited by Jerry O'Leary, 2004), to Jerry O'Leary.

Michael Courtenay Burke: 'The Summons', from *The Summons* (by The Rev. Michael C. Burke, published Talbot Press 1936), to Frank Fahy, Educational Company of Ireland.

Hubert Butler: 'The Saints Leave Ireland – A Poem', from his *Ten Thousand Saints* (published Wellbrook Press, 1972), to Lilliput Press.

Michael Coady: 'The Carrick Nine' from his *One Another* (published Gallery Press, 2003), to the author and Gallery Press.

Brian Coffey: 'Kallikles', from *Ireland Today*, Feb. 1937, to John Coffey.

Maurice James Craig: 'Ballad to a Traditional Refrain' and 'Thoughts on Causality', to the author.

Anthony Cronin: "'Fairway's' Faraway', from his *New and Selected Poems* (published by Carcanet/Raven, 1982), to the author.

Jimmy Crowley: 'Clonakilty Blackpudding', to Freestate Publishers and Jimmy Crowley (author and composer).

JP Donleavy: 'Mary Maloney' and 'Did your Mother' from his *The Ginger Man* (published Neville Spearman 1956), to the author.

Morgan Dockrell: 'Prize Tips', 'They Have Their Exits', and 'Jacuzzi Fantasy', to the author.

Charles Donnelly: 'Mr Sheridan's Morning Prayer' from *Charles Donnelly: The Life & Poems* (by Joseph Donnelly, published Dedalus Press, 1987), to Joseph Donnelly.

Paul Durcan: 'Ashplant, New Year's Eve, 1996' from his *Greetings to Our Friends in Brazil* (published Harvill, 1999), to the author.

Robert Farren: 'The Pets' from his *This Man Was Ireland* (published Sheed & Ward, 1943), to Ronan Farren.

Gabriel Fitzmaurice: 'What's a Tourist?' from his *Dear Grandad* (published Poolbeg Press, 2001), to the author.

WP Fogarty: 'Private Judgment' from his *Magic Camels* (published Shakespeare Head Press, 1939), to Blackwell Publishing Ltd.

Oliver St John Gogarty: 'Ringsend', 'Molly', 'Suppose', 'Brian O'Lynn', 'On a Fallen Electrician', 'Sing a Song of Sexpence', 'Goosey Goosey Gander Censored "to Ridicule the Irish Censors"', 'The Young Maid Of Madras', 'A Professor Of Trinity Hall', 'A Young Girl Of Peoria', 'The Young Man From St John's' from *The Poems & Plays of Oliver St John Gogarty* (edited by AN Jeffares, published Colin Smythe Ltd, 2001), to Colin Smythe Ltd on behalf of Veronica J O'Mara.

Anne Le Marquand Hartigan: 'Heirloom' from her *Long Tongue* (published Beaver Row Press, 1982), to the author.

Michael Hartnett: 'If I were King of England' from his *A Book of Strays* (edited by Peter Fallon, published Gallery Press, 2002), to Gallery Press.

Seamus Heaney: 'A Keen for the Coins' from *Something Beginning with P* (edited by Seamus Cashman, published O'Brien Press, 2004), copyright Seamus Heaney, to the author.

Rudi Holzapfel: 'Churchgate Collection' from his *An Cheapach* (published Sunburst Press, 1993), to Ulla Holzapfel.

Crawford Howard: 'The Arab Orange Lodge', to the author.

Douglas Hyde: 'Making Punch', from *Douglas Hyde: A Maker of Modern Ireland* (by JE and GE Dunleavy, published University of California Press, 1991), by kind permission of Douglas Sealy.

'Paul Jones' and all other extracts from *Dublin Opinion*: with gratitude to the estate of the late CE Kelly.

Patrick Kavanagh: 'Who Killed James Joyce' from his *Collected Poems* (published Martin Brian & O'Keeffe, 1972) and 'Justifiable Homicide' from *Sacred Keeper* (by Peter Kavanagh, published Goldsmith Press, 1970). Reprinted from *Collected Poems*, ed. Antionette Quinn (Allen Lane, 2004) by kind permission if the Trustees of the Estate of the late Katherine B. Kavanagh, through the Jonathan Williams Literary Agency.

Richie Kavanagh: 'Chicken Talk', from his album of the same name, to the author.

Peadar Kearney: 'Fish and Chips' (words & music by Peader Kearney; copyright Waltons Music), to Niall Walton.

James Kelly: 'Down the Street where Jimmy Lives' and 'The Ol' Black Can', to James Kelly on behalf of the estate of his grandfather.

Brendan Kennelly: 'Under the Table' from his *Familiar Strangers: New & Selected Poems 1960–2004* (published Bloodaxe Books, 2004 – www.bloodaxebooks.com), 'Your Wan's Answer' from his *The Little Book of Judas* (Bloodaxe Books, 2002) and 'To No One' from his *Poetry My Arse* (Bloodaxe Books, 1995), to the author and publisher.

Osbert Lancaster: 'Eireann Afternoon' from his *Façades and Faces* (published John Murray, 1950), by kind permission of Lady Lancaster.

CS Lewis: 'March for Strings, Kettledrums, and Sixty-three Dwarfs' (poem from 'The Narnian Suite' by CS Lewis) from his *Poems* (edited by Walter Hooper, published G Bles, 1969), copyright © 1964 CS Lewis Pte Ltd. Reprinted by permission.

Fergus Linehan: 'The Blackbird' and 'The Shaving Ghost', to the author.

Alec McAllister: 'The Breaking of Maggie', to Mrs McAllister of Larne.

Donagh Mac Donagh: 'Juvenile Delinquency' from his *The Hungry Grass* (published Faber and Faber, 1957), to Faber and Faber.

Patrick MacDonogh: 'No Mean City' from his *Poems* (edited by Derek Mahon, published Gallery Press, 2001), to Gallery Press.

Patrick MacGill: 'Fair Ladies' from his *Songs of Donegal* (published Herbert Jenkins 1921) to Caliban Books.

Iggy McGovern: 'Pomes Indigest', to the author; 'Time Up' from his *The King of Suburbia* (published Dedalus Press, 2005), to Pat Boran, Dedalus Press and the author.

Shane MacGowan: 'The Sick Bed of Cuchullain' from the Pogues' album, *Rum, Sodomy, and the Lash* (Stiff, 1985), to the publisher, Perfect Songs Ltd.

MJ MacManus: 'The O'Flanagan-Brownes', 'A Ballade of Portadown' and 'The Author's Lament' from his *Dublin Diversions* (published Talbot Press, 1928) and 'Pocket-Book Wisdom' from his *Rackrent Hall and other Poems* (published Talbot Press, 1941), to the estate of M J MacManus.

Louis MacNeice: 'Night Club', 'Death of an Actress' and 'Bagpipe Music' from *The Collected Poems of Louis MacNeice* (published Faber and Faber, 1966), to David Higham Associates.

Derek Mahon: 'Anglo-Irish Clerihews' from his *The Hudson Letter* (published Gallery Press, 1995), to Gallery Press.

Tommy Makem: 'Lord Nelson' (© Tinwhistle Music/Bucks Music Group Ltd, London), to the author.

Hugh Maxton: 'To a Dublin Host' and 'Faxes to the Critic: III' from his *Gubu Roi* (published Lagan Press, 2000), to the author.

Spike Milligan: 'You Must Never Bath in an Irish Stew' and 'It would be Obscene', (copyright © *A Children's Treasury of Milligan 2001*, Virgin Books Ltd), to Virgin Books Ltd.

Ewart Milne: 'Long Live the King' from the *Beau*, No 2, 1982/3, to Maurice Scully.

James Montgomery: The Canal Boat' from *The Dublin Book of Recitations* (edited by Mrs Cruise O'Brien, M.A., published Talbot Press, 1915), to the Montgomery family, with thanks to Christine O'Neill.

Christy Moore: 'Joxer Goes To Stuttgart', 'St Brendan's Voyage', and 'The Rose of Tralee (Me and the Rose)' to the author.

Mary Myler: 'Putting My Foot in it' from her *'Yours' in Verse* (published Arklow, 2003) to Thomas Myler and the Myler family.

Flann O'Brien: 'Strange but True' and 'We wouldn't Say it unless we Knew' from his *Myles Before Myles* (edited by John Wyse Jackson, published Grafton, 1988), 'The Workman's Friend' and 'A Workin' Man' from his *At Swim-Two-Birds* (published Longmans, 1939) and 'After Horace' from his *Further Cuttings from Cruiskeen Lawn* (edited by Kevin O'Nolan, published Hart-Davis, MacGibbon, 1976), to Stephen P Maher of Daniel C Maher, Solicitors, Dublin.

O'Dearest Limericks: to Geraldine Cannon.

George Bernard Shaw: 'Verse for Use while Petting a Dog' from *Bernard Shaw: Collected Letters 1926-1950* (edited by Dan H Laurence, published Max Reinhardt, 1988) and 'Apples from Coole Park' (from *Me and Nu* by Anne Gregory, published Colin Smythe Ltd, 1978), to the Society of Authors, on behalf of the Estate of Bernard Shaw.

Eugene Sheehy: 'Bovril' from *The Dublin Book of Recitations* (edited by Mrs Cruise O'Brien, M.A., published Talbot Press, 1915), to Mrs Helen Sheehy.

James Simmons: 'Cavalier Lyric' from *The Selected James Simmons* (edited by Edna Longley, published Blackstaff Press, 1978), to Gallery Press.

Alexander Stuart: 'The Rival Deans: A Lay of Cashel' to Martin Anderson.

Jack B Yeats: 'The Rabbits and the Hares' from his *The Careless Flower* (published Pilot Press, 1947) to AP Watt Ltd on behalf of Gráinne Yeats, Executrix of the Estate of Michael Butler Yeats.

WB Yeats: 'For Anne Gregory' from *The Collected Poems of WB Yeats* (published MacMillan, 1971), as above.

Our further thanks are due to many kind people. In addition to the debt we owe to those writers and publishers mentioned above, for quite separate help and encouragement of all sorts we are grateful to many, including Fergus Allen, Martin Anderson, Stan Banks, Elizabethanne Boran, John Brannigan, Andrew Carpenter, Rachel Churchill, Anthony Cronin, Jeremy Crow, Terry Cunningham, Morgan and Susi Dockrell, JP Donleavy, Joseph and Kay Donnelly, Frank Fahy, Ninian Falkiner, Brian J Goggin, Roger Goodwillie, Selina Guinness, Des Hanafin, Samantha Holman of the ICLA, Cara Lancaster, Melosina Lenox-Conyngham, Jerry Lidwill, Fergus Linehan, Bill McCormack, Billy Mills, Juno Moore, John R Murray, Jerry O'Leary, Micheál O Nualláin, Rosie and Colin Polden, Sam Powell-Tuck, Peter Razzell, David Rose, Andrew Russell, Maurice Scully, Douglas Sealy, Micheline Sheehy Skeffington, Colin Smythe, Mary Whelan, Peter Thompson, Peter van de Kamp, Roy Waters, Peter White, all at the Central Catholic Library, including Peter Costello (Hon. Librarian), Ken MacGowan and Teresa, the staffs of the National Library, the Department of Irish Folklore at University College, Dublin, the National Library of Scotland's wonderful website (www.nls.uk), MCPS (Ireland), Tralee Public Library, Arklow Public Library, North Wexford Mobile Library, the Representative Church Body Library, and the Library & Manuscripts Department of Trinity College, Dublin.

JWJ: More personally, for their manifold generosities I would like to raise a glass to my own extended family, including Ruth, Peter, Patrick, Michael, Margery, Thomas, Eoghan, Daniel, Conor, and Adam, and especially to my mother Lois, whose mind is richly stocked with story, verse and song. All of these gentle souls now know more about Zozimus and Co. than they ever wished to.

HMcD adds: I too have been much helped in my researches by many kind people and would like in particular to thank Felix McKillop, Maeve McKeown and Robert Morrow, who tracked down the families of several deceased county Antrim poets, and found several more splendid poems I had not known about, Nelson and Clover Bell and Lucy Freeman for their many useful ideas, as well as their elucidation of several peculiar words, and I would also like to thank my many friends and my three children, who have all bravely tolerated my attempts at amusing them over the years by indulging in Irish humorous recitations. If it had not been for their tact, occasional encouragement and forbearance I would never have got involved in this poetic adventure in the first place.

Index of Titles and First Lines

First lines are given in italics.

Abdulla Bulbul Ameer 101
'Adam's First Poem' 326
'After Horace' 304
'After the Fall' 356
After the legshows and the brandies 248
Ah Ma, give us a penny 47
Alas! how dismal is my tale, 317
'All over the world,' the traveller said, 23
All you that are here attend, I pray, 198
Although I am an author 247
Amo, amas, 317
The Anatomy of the Oyster 99
And they lookede aboute for a rudelie manne, 214
And this Dunluce is 405
Andrew Magrath's Reply to John O'Tuomy 352
Anglo-Irish Clerihews 253
'An Antrim Limerick' 357
'Apples from Coole Park' 363
Après La Dance 3
The Arab Orange Lodge 169
Are Ye Right There, Michael? 105
Arrah, murther, but times is hard, 294
The Arrest 126
The Arrest of Oscar Wilde at the Cadogan
    Hotel 19
Arthur McBride 4
The Arts Club Circular 370
As down by Anna Liffey, 200
As down the glen came McAlpine's men 16
*As I rode out through Galway Town to seek for
    recreation* 121
'As if a brick had fallen on my head 54
*As Saint Kevin once was travelling through a place
    called Glendalough,* 361
Ashplant, New Year's Eve, 1996 86
At half-past three, distinctly haggard, 3
At my rising up I pray 77
At six-to-four and five-to-two 66
*At the dead of the night, when by whiskey
    inspired,* 194
'At the Lake' 358
At the Sign of the Bell on the road to Clonmel 321
The Athlone Landlady 5

Augustus Eusebius Locke 140
Auld Granny Gray 47
The Author's Lament 247

Bacon and Greens 300
'Bacon is Bacon' 163
Bad Luck to this Marching 211
The Bag of Nails 7
Bagpipe Music 250
Ball o' Yarn 8
The Ball of Dandyorum 198
A Ballad 306
A Ballad of Christmas Days 271
A Ballad of Master McGrath 9
The Ballad of William Bloat 42
Ballad to a Traditional Refrain 65
A Ballade of Portadown 246
Ballade of Vanished Beauty 192
Ballinamona 11
A Band of Cupids th' other Day 276
The Bank of Ireland 345
Barney Hughes's bread, 46
The Battle on the Stair 12
Battle Song of the Irish Christian Front: 232
'Battle's a Cod' 192
Beauing, belling, dancing, drinking, 341
*The beef and the beer of the Saxon may build up
    good, strong, hefty men;* 300
Before I came across the sea 295
Behind the house I bought was spread a field: 192
Behold my happiness, 326
Bellewstown Hill 60
The Bells of Shandon 255
Beneath me hear in stinking clumps, 347
Beneath these poppies buried deep, 289
Biddy Mulligan 20
The Birth of Saint Patrick 227
The Blackbird 217
A boat sailed out of Brandon in the year of 501 282
Bon ton decrees that it is vile 184
The Bonfire on the Border 316
Bovril 364
The Boys from Ballysodare 25

The Boys of Fairhill 26
The Breaking of Maggie 233
The Brewer's Man 374
Brian O'Linn 27
Brian O'Linn was a gentleman born, 27
Brian O'Lynn 134
Brian O'Lynn had the pox and the gleet, 134
A bright-born day in merry, merry May, 143
Bright is the day, and as the morning fair, 141
The British Army 28
Brother Bill and Jamima Brown 30
The Buttermilk Lasses 40
'But, Locke,' she said 210

The Canal Boat 277
The Canon says: 'Yes,' 99
The Carrick Nine 48
Carrots from Clonown 43
'Castle Leslie' 387
Cavalier Lyric 366
The Chant of the Coal Quay 45
The Charladies' Ball 307
Charlie Chaplin went to France 46
The chemist makes experiments 111
Chicken Talk 196
'Children, what's a tourist? 98
Churchgate Collection 166
'A Civilized Man' 358
Clonakilty Blackpudding 67
The Cobbler 52
Cockles and Mussels 269
The Cod Liver Oil 53
The College's Saturday Night 55
Colm had a cat, 95
Come all ye bould Free Staters now and listen to my lay, 69
Come all ye dry-land sailors bold and listen to my song, 398
Come all ye lads and lassies prime 303
Come all ye loyal Irishmen, 90
Come all you fellow travelling men of every rank and station 87
Come all you young fellows, whoever you be, 40
Come, get the black, the mourning pall, 258
Come hither, Terence Mulligan, and sit upon the floor, 126
Come pay attention for a while, my good friends one and all, 339
A Complete Account of the Various Colonizations of Ireland 57
The Coughing Old Man 62
'Country Life' 213

The Cow Ate the Piper 63
Cries Celia to a reverend dean, 416
The Cruise of the Calabar 398
The Crystal Palace 392
The Curse 387
The Curse of Doneraile 317
The Cycles Of Time 103

The day that came after the snow, was fixed for the Meet at the Hatchet; 161
De Groves ov de Pool 268
'De Valera had a Cat' 71
'The Dean as Landscape Gardener' 385
Death of an Actress 249
Delaney's Donkey 157
'The Delights of Dublin' 71
Description of an Author's Bed-Chamber 135
Description of Dublin 73
A Description of the Morning 384
'Did your Mother ...' 77
Did your mother come from Jesus 77
'The Dingle Peninsula' 20
The distant Seychelles are not so remote 210
Ditty 74
Do you remember what I used to call you 264
Doran's Ass 78
Down the Street where Jimmy Lives 201
A dreadful dream I fain would tell 25
The Dream 409
'Dublin City' 214
The Dublin Fusiliers 83
Dumpitydoodledum big bowwow 362

Each female so pretty in country and city, 62
The Earthquake 87
Eighteen sixty nine being the date of the year, 9
Eireann Afternoon 210
An Elegy on Dicky and Dolly 384
An Elegy on the Death of a Mad Dog 136
Encounter with an Eileen 189
The Enniskillen Horse 90
Episode 188
Epitaph on Edward Purdon 137
Epitaph on Largebones – The Lawyer 347
Epitaph on Robert Southey 289
Erin aboo! though the desolate ocean 127
The evening spent in Chloe's arms 404
The extraordinary thing about cows is 302

Fair Ladies 239
'Fairway's' Faraway 66
The Fall 1

Fame 93
A Fat Man's Tragedy 186
Faxes to the Critic: III 264
A fig for Saint Denis of France – 251
A fig for the mad-heads who prate Nationality, 313
The Finding of Moses 424
The Finding of Moses in the Nile 425
Finnegan's Wake 96
*The First Day of Christmas and the family's raving
    mad,* 271
'*First for the Bible, then the printing-press,* 164
First Paddy struck the ball, John stopt its course, 58
*First time I heard a naughty word, was when I was
    a child.* 196
Fish and Chips 200
For Anne Gregory 420
The fountains drink caves subterren, 98
The Four Farrellys 109
'*From Great Londonderry*' 118
From great Londonderry to London so merry, 118
From the Trenches 314

The Galbally Farmer 119
The Galway Races 120
The Garden of Eden (described in the Bible) 1
Gather round me boys, will yez 426
The Gay Old Hag 124
'*George Berkeley and God: An Exchange*' 355
George Moore Becomes the Priest of
    Aphrodite 275
George Moore Eats a Grey Mullet 274
The Giants' Causeway 31
The Giants' Causeway, I used to hear them say, 31
Give Isaac the nymph who no beauty can boast; 365
A Glamorous Ballad 381
*The glare on Kilmashogue awoke the Burghers of
    Dundrum,* 55
The Glendalough Saint 125
God grant I may be present 115
Good evening, all me jolly lads, 167
Good people all, of every sort, 136
Good reader! if you e'er have seen, 290
Goosey Goosey Gander 134
Goosey Goosey Gander Censored 134
GPO Door 140
The Grand International Show 313
Green Little Island 116
The green-eyed wolf had a long red nose, 381
The Groves of Blarney 265
Guinness and Company's Drayman 150

The Hatchet 161

Have I wife? Bedam I have! 374
He sipped at a weak hock and seltzer 19
'*He was an Irish Landlord*' 22
Heirloom 159
Hence let wise Farmers understand, 80
Her husband passed on the street outside. 204
Here he stands in the open air, 166
Here I am in Castle Leslie 387
Here I sit, so sad and lonely, 221
Here lies poor Ned Purdon, from misery freed, 137
Here's a health to you, my darlin' 228
Here's my tribute to 'lectrician Joe, 134
Here's up them all says the boys of Fairhill. 26
The Hero of Ballinacrazy 354
Hints Originally Intended for the Small
    Farmers of the County of Wexford 80
His vices have made, and still make him so poor, 209
Ho, Citizen of The Third Rock! 242
Holy Mary Mother of God 47
Holy Moses! Have a look! 346
Hot Asphalt 167
'*How Caesar was Driven from Ireland*' 413
'*How can we stop men sinning?*' *wailed the
    monks.* 35
The Humours of Donnybrook Fair (I) 171
The Humours of Donnybrook Fair (II) 309

I always laughed when father sang. 191
I am so – drunk – that I ca – ca – I cannot 260
I am the king of sporting blades, 389
I feel the gaunt woods straining 185
I had a first cousin called Arthur McBride, 4
'*I killed a verse speaker,*' *said the Playboy* 196
I love – oh! more than words can tell 153
I love to see the 'Cork Exam' 32
I marched three miles through scorching sand 386
I met a friend the other day 293
I put an ant in a Spider's web; 239
I read a dreadful tale last night – 388
I remember 155
I remember, I remember a night of long ago – 343
I sailed away from France, alas! 274
I saw, in Dresden, on a windy day, 163
I see from the paper that Florrie Forde is dead – 249
I sell the best brandy and sherry, 352
I sent McCann out 47
I sometimes sleep with other girls 366
I talk about Hegel, I talk about Freud, 405
I took her to dine 248
I was at a railway station, upon the Dublin line, 30
I was watching the needleboats at San Sabba 242
I will arise and go now, and go to Innisfree, 315

I will live in Ringsend 134
I will not give to Fianna Fáil. 166
Ideal Poems: Y...s 174
If Bishops could 205
If I live to be very old 93
If I were King of England ... 160
If my own botheration don't alter my plan, 329
If respite you'd borrow from turmoil or sorrow, 60
If those old poets of Maigue 357
If you long for things artistic, 370
I'm a brand from the burning, a genuine saint, 377
I'm a buxom fine widow, I live in a spot, 20
I'm a poet, God help me, and I must cry! 74
I'm a rattling boy from Dublin town, 240
I'm a young married man, 53
I'm Trooper Robin Rape, a sojer from the Cape 149
In a mean abode on the Shankill Road 42
In a small hotel in London I was sitting down to dine, 109
In Glendalough lived an old saint, 125
In good Victoria's humdrum days 275
In Praise of the City of Mullingar 175
In the county Tyrone, near the town of Dungannon, 327
In the Jacuzzi pool I sit 76
'In the juvescence of the year' 269
In the merry month of June 8
In the steamy, stuffy Midlands, 'neath an English summer sky, 130
In the sweet County Limerick one cold winter's night, 11
In the town of Athy one Jeremy Lanigan 122
In the town of Ballybay there is a lassie dwelling, 396
In the year ninety-eight, when our troubles were great, 63
In the year of our Lord, eighteen hundred and six 182
'An Incident near Macroom' 177
'Ireland's Struggle' 14
Irish Castles in the Air 178
The Irish Colonel 79
The Irish Guards 207
The Irish Jubilee 179
An Irish lad 330
The Irish Rover 182
The Isle of Innisfree 315
It was a night in dark November 333
It was at the pantomime 59
It was in the year of '88, in the merry month of June, 280
It was Sammy McNello that done it 236
It would be Obscene 265

It's Little for Glory I Care 212
It's no go the merrygoround, it's no go the rick shaw, 250
I've been soft in a small way 141
I've dreamed a while on Tara's hill, 246

Jacuzzi Fantasy 76
James was born in 1882 358
The Jealous Stoneybatter Man 412
Jingle 317
John Aloysius Herbert Pimp, 364
Johnny Kenchinow 258
Johnny McEldoo 190
Jolly Phoebus his car to the coach-house had driven, 335
Joxer Goes To Stuttgart 280
Joyce went out one day 358
Joyce's Voices 358
Just now with the advent of Spring 356
Justifiable Homicide 196
Juvenile Delinquency 235

K for Kennedy's 203
Kallikles 54
Katty Flannigan 194
A Keen for the Coins 163
'Kennedy's Bread' 203
Kerry Places 82
The Kerry Recruit 205
Killaloe 261
The King was in his countinghouse 133
'The Knight of Glin' 209
Knockanure both mane and poor, 82

La Femme Savante 210
Ladle it Well 376
A landlord from Maigueside, Ó Tuomy, 356
Lanigan's Ball 122
The Last of the Leprechauns 228
The Lay of Oliver Gogarty 69
Lazy Mary will you get up, 48
Let others betake them to Western Plains 104
Let school-masters puzzle their brain, 137
A Letter 379
The Limb of the Law 312
Listen for a while 284
Little Emily of Dee 220
The Lonely Man 221
Long Live the King 274
A Longford Legend 223
Lord Nelson 257

Lord Nelson stood in pompous state upon his pillar high 257
Lord Tomnoddy 224
Lord, confound this surly sister, 387
The Louse House of Kilkenny 225
Love *Versus* the Bottle 231
Lovely Jesus 372
A loyal band of Orangemen from Ulster's lovely land, 169
Lucinda 146

The Maigue Poets 357
'Making Punch' 172
March for Strings, Kettledrums, and Sixty-three Dwarfs 215
The March of Intellect 138
'Martin Luther was a Friar' 262
The Martyr III
'Mary Maloney' 77
Mary Maloney's beautiful arse 77
Mass-houses, churches, mixt together, 73
McAlpine's Fusiliers 16
McCormack and Richard Tauber 243
Memory 264
A Memory 374
Men of Erin! Men of Erin! 33
Mickey Free's Ancestry 214
Molly 132
Molly through the garden 132
Monto 164
The Moore Statue 291
Moral Positions: A Dream 288
Moryah 262
Motor Bus 131
'Mr J M Henry's Address to the University Senatorial Electors' 405
Mr Sheridan's Morning Prayer 77
Mrs Matilda O'Flanagan-Browne 245
Mrs McGrath 292
My back it is deal, 344
My dear little Liz, here's a letter at last, 379
My Father said, 159
My horse he is white, although at first he was bay, 416
My Lord Tomnoddy's the son of an earl, 224
My name is O'Kelly, I've heard the Revelly 206
My name is Owen O'Duffy, 232
My name it is Nell, quite candid I tell, 297
'Myles Na Gopaleen' 356

Napoleon is the Boy for Kicking up a Row 294
The Native Irishman 295
Near St James's Gate on Thomas-street side, 150

'Neath the horse's prick 14
Nell Flaherty's Drake 297
Never more will I play 407
'Never shall a young man, 420
A New Ode to Saint Patrick 338
Night Club 248
The Night-Cap 335
1940 115
No Irish Need Apply 299
No Mean City 239
Nonsense 290
Now de war, dearest Nancy, is ended, 268
Now Delaney had a donkey that everyone admired, 157
Now hardly here and there a Hackney-coach 384
Now see how he sits 385
Now this is a tale that the turf men tell, in the glow of the fo'c'sle light, 277
Now will I try a most Hercule- An 260

O henny penny! O horsed half-crown! 163
O Jimmie Joyce you are my darling 214
O, I've got the brain of a Berkeley, 397
O, Tuomy! you boast yourself handy 352
Och, Dublin city, there is no doubtin', 214
Ochone, ochone! Just hear our wails 75
Ode to a Pratie 372
Of all the conchiferous shell-fish, 99
Of an old King in a story 45
Of course you're right 264
Of Drinking 98
Of gay women the gayest 302
Of Women the ways are peculiar: – 382
The O'Flanagan-Brownes 245
Oh alas what can I do 202
Oh! For A Feed 408
Oh! for a feed! A motley feed! A corporation feast 408
Oh, I met with Napper Tandy and he took me by the hand, 342
Oh! Learning's a very fine thing, 138
Oh! lovely Lucy Lanigan, my distant twinkling star! 146
Oh, Lucy, my aesthetic darling, 343
'Oh, Mary Brady' 214
Oh, Mary Brady, you are my darlin, 214
Oh, me name is Dick Darby, I'm a cobbler; 52
Oh! once we were illigint people, 214
Oh the Bansha Peelers went out one night 347
Oh, the first of me downfall, I set out the door; 225
Oh there was an old woman from Wexford and in Wexford she did dwell; 323
Oh! 'Tis of a bold major a tale I'll relate, 223

Oh! 'twas Dermott O'Nowlan M'Figg 309
Oh what a happy place it is 201
Oh widow McGrath lived in Kilrush, 292
The Ol' Black Can 202
The Old Alarm Clock 320
'Old King Cole' 45
The Old Leather Breeches 321
The Old Woman from Wexford 323
Omniscient omnipotent Myles 356
On a Curate's Complaint of Hard Duty 386
On a Fallen Electrician 134
'On a Windy Day' 163
On Aegypt's banks, contagious to the Nile, 424
'On Cricket' 407
On Deborah Perkins 325
On Egypt's plains, where flows the ancient Nile, 425
On Himself 387
On Marriage 416
On ODEAREST a patient named Paul 356
On rainy days alone I dine 387
On Sorrel Hill the Druid sat 333
On the eighteenth day of November, 177
On the eighth day of March it was, some people say, 227
On the mountain side the battle raged, there was no stop or stay; 400
On Visiting Westminster Abbey 346
Once upon a time two worthy Deans together 375
One day as I went down the road to town, 217
One evening of late as I happened to stray, 119
One morning in March I was digging the land, 205
One Paddy Doyle lived near Killarney 78
One pleasant morning in this new millennium 48
Open, ye bogs, and swallow down 215
The Orangeman's Hell 236
The Origin of the Limerick 356
The other day in mood sublime 332
T'other night, after hearing Lord Dudley's oration 288
O'Tuomy's Drinking Song 352
The Ould Orange Flute 327
Our Army Jumping Team 32

Paddy MacShane's Seven Ages 329
Paddy's Burial 330
Paddy's Pastoral Rhapsody 228
Paneful 332
The Paradise of Lecturers 129
'Patrick Kavanagh' 356
The Peeler and the Goat 347
The Pets 95
Phases Of The Celtic Revival 127

The Picture of Dorian Gray 253
The Pig 333
Pindaric Ode Written on a Winter Evening not Far from Sorrel Hill 333
The Piper who Played before Moses 156
'A Plea' 215
Please give me, Lord, it's all I ask, 304
Pocket-Book Wisdom 248
Pomes Indigest 242
The Pope and the Sultan 334
The Pope sits in St Peter's chair, 334
Portrait of a Christian He-Man 364
Private Judgment 99
Prize Tips … 74
A Professor of Trinity Hall 360
Putting my Foot in it 293

'The Rabbits and the Hares' 419
The Ragman's Ball 339
A Railway of Rhyme 260
The Rakes of Mallow 341
Rapture! 404
The Rattling Boy from Dublin 240
The Rearing of the Green 342
Red brick in the suburbs, white horse on the wall, 65
Repentant Son 191
Retrospect 343
A Rhyme of Llanfair P.G. 359
A Riddle 344
Rigged Out 377
Ringsend 134
Rival Deans: A Lay of Cashel 375
The Rock of Cashel 372
A Rope, a Rope, to hang the Pope 47
The Rose of Kenmare 141
The Rose of Tralee (Me and the Rose) 284
Run over by an ambulance? 66

Sacrifice 113
Said the King to the Colonel: 79
'A Sailor Courted a Farmer's Daughter' 350
Saint Brendan's Voyage 282
Saint Kevin and King O'Toole 361
Saint Patrick of Ireland, My Dear! 251
Saint Patrick was a Gentleman 422
The Saints Leave Ireland – A Poem 35
Sambo's Right to be Kilt 152
Says I to him, I says, says I, 373
Says Mrs Doyle to Mrs Grant, 12
The Sceilig ship is on the bay the 'Mad Rover' is its name 366
Scum condensed of Irish bog! 406

The Sea Around Us 15
'Shandon Steeple' 362
The Shaving Ghost 218
She rode a stranger's donkey 103
She was one of the Early Birds 59
She was tall thin an' thirty, wi' glossy black hair 233
Shillelagh Conn Mulligan Bryan O'Toole 228
Shillin' a Day 206
Shlathery's Mounted Fut 107
A short time ago an Irishman named Docherty 179
Should any enquire about Eirinn, 57
The Sick Bed of Cuchulainn 243
Sing a Song of Sexpence 133
Sit down and I'll tell you the tale 188
A Skellig List, 1951 366
Slaughter, Slaughter, Holy Water 47
The Small Towns of Ireland 17
The small towns of Ireland by bards are neglected, 17
Smoking, sleeping, poteen drinking, 213
A Social Problem 184
Some critics think the test of every verse 185
Some sing ye of Venus the goddess, 325
Some tell us 'tis a burnin' shame 152
Song [from *She Stoops to Conquer*] 137
Song [from *The Duenna*] 365
The Song of the British 'Ero 149
A Song of the Ruins of Dunluce 405
'A Song of Trifles' 94
Song of William, Inspector of Drains 104
The Song of Zozimus 426
The sons of the prophet were hardy and bold, 101
The Spanish love their onions, 43
Stammering or Tipsy Ghazzel 260
'The Sting' 359
Strange but True 302
Striking a Light at Night 164
'A Suitable Appointment' 214
The Summons 33
A Sup of Good Whiskey 382
A sup of good whiskey will make you glad; 382
Suppose 133
Suppose the Pope had G.P.I. 133
Sweet Chloe advised me, in accents divine, 231
Sweet God on high the Shaving Ghost, 218
Sweet is soup, and wondrous good, 376
Switzerland 130

'A Tackle on Terence' 58
A Tale 276
A Tale of Horror 388
Targin Tallyo 389
The TCD Harriers 390

There dwelt among the untrodden ways, 364
There once was a man who said, 'God 355
There was a bomb-scare at the Last Supper. 204
There was a King in Hesperland 306
There was a wee fellow frae Clough 357
There was a young girl of Peoria 360
There was a young maid of Madras 360
There was a young man from St John's 360
There was a young man of Tralee 359
'There was a Young Thing on a Ship' 84
There was an old man of Dunluce 355
There was an old piper, old and hoary, 156
There was Johnny McEldoo and McGee and me 190
There was nobody purer than Joyce 358
There's a spot in Chapelizod where it straggles o'er the Liffey: 390
There's not in this wide world a statue less neat 291
They have their Exits 75
They say that the lakes of Killarney are fair, 15
Thirteen black coffins stood round the hall, 409
The Thirteenth Lock 143
This is the tale of Joshua Parr 186
This pearl-pale poem that I have pondered o'er, 174
This world is all a bubble, no matter where we go, 178
Though from war our state's aloof 402
Though naughty flesh will multiply 239
Thoughts on Causality 66
Thunder and lightning is no lark 421
Thy name is Murphy. On the Antrim hills 372
Tim Finnegan lived in Walkin Street, 96
Time Up 242
Tipp'rary breeds a hardy lot, 71
To a Dublin Host 263
To Chloe 141
To Donnybrook steer all you sons of Parnassus – 171
To George Moore on the Occasion of his Wedding 395
To My First Love 155
To No One 204
To write PRIZE POETRY these days 74
Tottie De Vere 230
The Town of Ballybay 396
The Town of Passage 336
Tra oz Montes 185
The traditional poets of Maigue 357
A Tragedy in Three Acts 397
The tragedy of poor Molly Bloom 358
A trifling song you shall hear, 94
Truth in Parenthesis 153
'Twas an Irish Fight: How the English Fought the Dutch at the Battle of Dundee 400
'Twas in the sweet town of Athlone 5

'Twas on July the twenty-eighth 316
Two ladies of Galway, called Cath'rine and Anna 363
The Two Travellers 23

Ulysses by James Joyce 358
Uncle took a Beecham's Pill 188
Under the river Ouse at Bedford 274
Under the Table 204
Under this stone lies Dicky and Dolly 384
Up and down the Peninsula 20
Up the Pole 402

'Valentine from Eileen Vance' 214
Valuable Recipe for the Emerald Isle 147
'Verse for Use while Petting a Dog' 362
'Verses for the Unveiling of a Statue' 166
Very Blank Verse 185
Very well unknown across my city, 263

Wanted, a maid to scrape and scour, 299
Was I drunk upon that dance-floor? 189
Way down in Clonakilty in the year of '89 67
The Way we Tell a Story 373
We all know that Judas was led to betray 345
We were out picking blackberries 314
We wouldn't Say it unless we Knew 302
We're not so old in the Army List, 207
We're the boys that make the noise 116
Well everyone was very nice, and, speaking as a
   Czech, 113
Well if you've got a wing O! take her up to
   Ring O! 164
Well, you've heard about the indians with their
   tommyhawks and spears 83
Were I sublimer than the Grecian rhymer, 45
What a happy chap 326
'What an Illigant Life' 213
What an illigant life a friar leads, 213
What drink is so nice 172
What is this that roareth thus? 131
What's a Tourist? 98
When a boy straight up from Clare heard his mother
   called a mère 261
When Caesar, by conquests unsated, 413
When first I came to London 320
When I Consider 271
When I consider how the hair of your chest 271
When I lived in sweet Ballinacrazy, dear, 354
When I was as high as that 374
When I was young I had a twist 28
'When Judas Iscariot' 159

When Judas Iscariot rode off in his chariot 159
When little M L E of D 220
When the soldiers passed through Llanfairpwll-
   gwyngyllgogerychwyrndrobwllllantysilio-
   gogogoch 359
When things go wrong and will not come right 302
When you might be a name for the world to acclaim,
   and when
Opulence dawns on the view, 129
Where the Red Lion, staring o'er the way, 135
The Whig Missionary of 1835 406
Who Killed James Joyce? 195
Who threw the stone that brought the window
   down 235
Who wants to be a Milliner? 188
Why such a row? What ails you now, desponding
   Stoneybatter man? 412
Wilde Oscar Wilde 343
Will you come a boating, my gay old hag, 124
With deep affection 255
With ganial foire 392
With plucking pizzicato and the prattle of the
   kettledrum 215
Women's Ways 382
The Wonderful Grey Horse 416
A Workin' Man 303
The Workman's Friend 302
'Would You?' 15
Would you be deemed a man of wit 147
Would you live on women's earnings? 15
Would you talk a little less about O'Connell? 262

Ye may strain your muscles 175
Year in year out, I tramp Sandymount Strand 86
Yes, we must parted be 230
You can tell by my feet I'm a limb of the law 312
You may talk of Columbus's sailing 105
You may talk of your outings, your picnics and
   parties 307
You Must Never Bath in an Irish Stew 264
You very merry people all I pray you list a minute 7
You've heard o' Julius Caesar, an' the great
   Napoleon, too 107
A Young Girl of Peoria 360
'A Young Lady Reporter from Youghal' 351
The Young Maid of Madras 360
The Young Man from St John's 360
Your Wan's Answer 205

The Zoological Gardens 421
* * * * * * * * * , * * * * * * * * * * , 395